D0386091

Price Measurements
and Their Uses

Studies in Income and Wealth
Volume 57

National Bureau of Economic Research
Conference on Research in Income and Wealth

Price Measurements and Their Uses

Edited by **Murray F. Foss,
Marilyn E. Manser,
and Allan H. Young**

The University of Chicago Press

Chicago and London

MURRAY F. FOSS is a visiting scholar at the American Enterprise Institute for Public Policy Research. MARILYN E. MANSER is assistant commissioner for economic research, Bureau of Labor Statistics, U.S. Department of Labor. ALLAN H. YOUNG is chief statistician, Bureau of Economic Analysis, U.S. Department of Commerce.

The University of Chicago Press, Chicago 60637
The University of Chicago Press, Ltd., London
© 1993 by the National Bureau of Economic Research
All rights reserved. Published 1993
Printed in the United States of America

02 01 00 99 98 97 96 95 94 93   1 2 3 4 5

ISBN: 0-226-25730-4 (cloth)

Copyright is not claimed for chap. 1 by Stephen D. Oliner, "Comment" on chaps. 3, 4, and 5 by Jack E. Triplett, chap. 6 by Paul R. Liegey, Jr., chap. 7 by Marshall Reinsdorf, chap. 8 by Thomas Betsock and Irwin B. Gerduk, and chap. 10 by Richard C. Ziemer and Pamela A. Kelly.

Library of Congress Cataloging-in-Publication Data

Price measurements and their uses / edited by Murray F. Foss, Marilyn E. Manser, Allan H. Young.
   p. cm.—(Studies in income and wealth; v. 57)
   "This volume contains part of the papers, discussion, and roundtable remarks presented at the Workshop on Price Measurements and Their Uses in Washington, D.C., on March 22–23, 1990"—Prefatory note.
   Includes bibliographical references and index.
   1. Price indexes—Congresses. 2. Computers—Prices—Congresses. 3. Semiconductors—Prices—Congresses. 4. Consumer prices indexes—Congresses. I. Foss, Murray F. II. Manser, Marilyn E. III. Young, Allan H. IV. Series
HC106.3.C714 vol. 57
[HB231]
338.5'28—dc20
                                         93-6874
                                         CIP

⊗ The paper used in this publication meets the minimum requirements of the American National Standard for Information Sciences—Permanence of Paper for Printed Library Materials, ANSI Z39.48-1984.

National Bureau of Economic Research

Officers

George T. Conklin, Jr., *chairman*
Paul W. McCracken, *vice-chairman*
Martin Feldstein, *president and chief executive officer*

Geoffrey Carliner, *executive director*
Charles A. Walworth, *treasurer*
Sam Parker, *director of finance and administration*

Directors at Large

John H. Biggs
Andrew Brimmer
Carl F. Christ
George T. Conklin, Jr.
Don R. Conlan
Kathleen B. Cooper
Jean A. Crockett
George C. Eads

Martin Feldstein
George Hatsopoulos
Lawrence R. Klein
Franklin A. Lindsay
Paul W. McCracken
Leo Melamed
Robert T. Parry

Peter G. Peterson
Douglas D. Purvis
Robert V. Roosa
Richard N. Rosett
Bert Seidman
Eli Shapiro
Donald S. Wasserman

Directors by University Appointment

Jagdish Bhagwati, *Columbia*
William C. Brainard, *Yale*
Glen G. Cain, *Wisconsin*
Franklin Fisher, *Massachusetts Institute of Technology*
Saul H. Hymans, *Michigan*
Marjorie B. McElroy, *Duke*

James L. Pierce, *California, Berkeley*
Andrew Postlewaite, *Pennsylvania*
Nathan Rosenberg, *Stanford*
Harold T. Shapiro, *Princeton*
Craig Swan, *Minnesota*
Michael Yoshino, *Harvard*
Arnold Zellner, *Chicago*

Directors by Appointment of Other Organizations

Marcel Boyer, *Canadian Economics Association*
Reuben C. Buse, *American Agricultural Economics Association*
Richard A. Easterlin, *Economic History Association*
Gail Fosler, *The Conference Board*
A. Ronald Gallant, *American Statistical Association*
Robert S. Hamada, *American Finance Association*

Charles Lave, *American Economic Association*
Rudolph A. Oswald, *American Federation of Labor and Congress of Industrial Organizations*
Dean P. Phypers, *Committee for Economic Development*
James F. Smith, *National Association of Business Economists*
Charles A. Walworth, *American Institute of Certified Public Accountants*

Directors Emeriti

Moses Abramovitz
Emilio G. Collado
Thomas D. Flynn

Gottfried Haberler
Geoffrey H. Moore
James J. O'Leary

George B. Roberts
William S. Vickrey

Since this volume is a record of conference proceedings, it has been exempted from the rules governing critical review of manuscripts by the Board of Directors of the National Bureau (resolution adopted 8 June 1948, as revised 21 November 1949 and 20 April 1968).

Contents

Prefatory Note

This volume contains part of the papers, discussion, and roundtable remarks presented at the Workshop on Price Measurements and Their Uses in Washington, D.C., on March 22–23, 1990.

Funds for the Conference on Research in Income and Wealth are provided to the National Bureau of Economic Research by the Bureau of the Census, the Bureau of Economic Analysis, the Bureau of Labor Statistics, the Internal Revenue Service, Statistics Canada, the Department of Energy, and the National Science Foundation; we are indebted to them for their support. We also thank Murray F. Foss, Marilyn E. Manser, and Allan H. Young, who served as workshop organizers and editors of this volume.

Executive Committee, March 1990

Charles R. Hulten, chair	Stanley Lebergott
Ernst R. Berndt	Robert E. Lipsey
Geoffrey Carliner	Marilyn E. Manser
Christopher K. Clague	Robert P. Parker
Frank de Leeuw	Sherwin Rosen
W. Erwin Diewert	Charles A. Waite
Zvi Griliches	

Volume Editors' Acknowledgments

We are very much indebted to Kirsten Foss Davis for arranging the conference on which this volume is based. We would also like to thank two anonymous referees for their helpful comments. Special thanks are due also to Teresa A. Price of the Bureau of Economic Analysis, Randa Murphy of the

American Enterprise Institute, and Patricia A. O'Neal of the Bureau of Labor Statistics for assistance in preparing the manuscript.

We note with sadness and a deep sense of loss the death of Edward F. Denison on October 23, 1992. Best known for his pioneering work in growth accounting, Edward Denison made important contributions to the Conference on Research in Income and Wealth from the 1940s through the present volume.

Introduction

Murray F. Foss, Marilyn E. Manser, and Allan H. Young

This volume contains papers, comments on papers, and a panel discussion that were presented at the Workshop on Price Measurements and Their Uses, held by the Conference on Research in Income and Wealth in Washington, D.C., on March 22–23, 1990. The purpose of the workshop was to review current research, to consider how the research could be applied to the programs of the federal statistical agencies—particularly the Bureau of Labor Statistics (BLS) and the Bureau of Economic Analysis (BEA)—and to identify potential avenues of new research. The workshop brought together persons actively engaged in price measurement research with economists and statisticians in government agencies who collect prices, construct the official price indexes, and use those price indexes in preparing the national economic accounts and in economic analysis.[1]

The subject matter of the conference, price indexes and how they are used to deflate the GNP and other broad aggregates, has not been of great concern to economists of late, although there have been a few notable exceptions.[2] Yet no one doubts that the practical construction of price indexes bears directly on

Murray F. Foss is a visiting scholar at the American Enterprise Institute for Public Policy Research. Marilyn E. Manser is assistant commissioner for economic research, Bureau of Labor Statistics, U.S. Department of Labor. Allan H. Young is chief statistician, Bureau of Economic Analysis, U.S. Department of Commerce.

Views expressed are those of the authors and do not represent official positions of the American Enterprise Institute, the Bureau of Labor Statistics, or the Bureau of Economic Analysis.

1. The workshop did not attempt to provide an overview of the various types of price indexes that are produced and all the methodological issues relating to them. For that purpose, see U.S. Department of Labor (1988). For information on the preparation of constant-dollar GDP in the national economic accounts by BEA, see BEA (1987a, 1987b, 1988, 1990). In addition, Cartwright (1986), Cartwright and Smith (1988), Cole et al. (1986), and Sinclair and Catron (1990) describe the computer price indexes prepared by the two agencies.

2. In empirical work, these include Robert J. Gordon, Zvi Griliches, and Jack Triplett.

how we perceive many of the most fundamental attributes of the economy, such as how much living standards and productivity have grown over the long run, how real wages in this country compare with those abroad, and, at a time of large budget deficits, how much the nation's capital stock has increased.

The measurement of price change for high-tech products was the main focus of the workshop. Computers are now so important in the economy and their prices have fallen so much that careful measurement of their long-run price behavior is essential for the proper measurement of trends in real GNP or GDP, its investment components, and the capital stock. For example, when BEA introduced a new price index for computers in 1985, the growth rate of real GNP for the period 1982–88 was revised from 3.8 percent per year to 4.1 percent.

High-tech items were the subject of about half the workshop papers. The papers on personal computers and semiconductors break new ground with estimates of price change that differ from those from official government sources. Making use of the hedonic approach to price change—in the spirit of the 1985 IBM-BEA undertaking for the price of mainframe computers—the paper on personal computers arrives at a price decline that is much greater than the change shown by BEA for personal computers. In addition, an apparent anomaly is cleared up. It had been puzzling that, at the same time as official indexes of computer prices were showing dramatic decreases, the price index for semiconductors published by BLS was essentially flat. Any bias in the measured price of an intermediate good like semiconductors does not affect productivity growth for the entire private economy, but it does affect the allocation of productivity change among industries.

It should come as no surprise that there is still debate over the use of the hedonic approach to quality adjustment in price indexes. The issues were joined in the panel discussion that came in the closing session of the workshop, in which panelists were asked to discuss the implications of the treatment of prices of high-tech goods for the measurement of productivity change. The discussion among some of the major protagonists of a long-running controversy was enlightening, although it is doubtful that a meeting of minds between the two main camps emerged.

The papers other than those concerned with high-tech products covered a variety of topics that have been dealt with before but remain in the category of unfinished business. Two have important implications for possible biases in the measurement of consumer prices. One reports on the recent introduction of hedonic techniques to adjust for quality change in apparel. The other takes up the shift of consumer purchases away from higher-price independent food stores to lower-price chain supermarkets, a substitution that the consumer price index (CPI) has never treated as a price decline. This is not just a question concerning the 1980s, the time period that was the focus of the paper. The boom in supermarkets dates from the early post–World War II period; indeed, food chains were already prominent in the 1920s. Readers should find BEA's treatment of military aircraft prices of interest in light of the discussion of computer prices. The paper on steel prices lends support to those who claim that price rigidity under conditions of weak demand is mainly a statistical illusion. Another paper presents the hypothesis that the Robinson-Patman Act, a law dating from 1936 that prohibits price discrimination, plays an important role in this apparent rigidity.

High-Tech Products

BLS and BEA Approaches

The papers on prices of high-tech products and the panel discussion reflect and build on recent developments in the federal statistical agencies. Because of the difficult conceptual and practical problems, BLS did not develop price indexes for computer equipment as part of the major PPI (producer price index) revision that was begun in the late 1970s and was essentially completed by 1986. In contrast to the indexes for computers, BLS has for some time produced PPIs for semiconductors using the conventional approach to quality-change adjustment described below, but outside researchers have been critical of the indexes.

BEA was aware of the rapid price declines for computers but did not have a satisfactory procedure for handling them. Until 1985, BEA used an assumption of no price change for computers in the calculation of constant-dollar GNP. This assumption became increasingly untenable as purchases of computers by business and other sectors grew rapidly and as prices of computers continued to plummet.

In 1985, following a cooperative research effort with IBM, BEA introduced a price index for computers in the U.S. national economic accounts. This development was a milestone in national economic accounting in that the use of the hedonic approach represented a distinct departure from the conventional approach to handling quality change in price measurement that had been employed by BLS and other statistical agencies in the United States and abroad.[3] Among the price indexes for capital goods in the national income and product accounts, the index for computers and peripheral equipment is unique in its very rapid and prolonged decline. In the period 1972–84 covered by the IBM-BEA study, the index declined 83 percent, or about 14 percent per year.

Under the conventional PPI approach to quality change, once BLS has determined that a specification change has occurred in an item being priced for

---

3. The computer price index is not the first price index in the U.S. national accounts to be based on hedonic techniques. The first was probably that for single-family houses, which was developed at the Census Bureau and introduced into the accounts in 1974.

the PPI, it follows one of several procedures. If it has no data to make a specific quality adjustment—the typical situation—two possibilities are open. If it decides that a specification change is "small"—using well-defined criteria for smallness—it ignores the change and treats any price difference from the previous month as pure price change. If the specification change is "large," and if the new model has a higher price than the old model, BLS employs a linking procedure that treats all the observed price change as an improvement in quality. If the new model has a lower price, a zero quality change is assumed, and the difference in price is counted as a price decline.[4] In those instances where specifications change and BLS obtains data from the respondent on the cost of that specification change, however, it uses cost as a measure of the quality adjustment. Cost is the appropriate theoretical measure of quality adjustment in an output price index like the PPI and the method that BLS prefers.

The hedonic approach uses a regression equation—the hedonic function—to relate the prices of individual models of a product to an array of major price-determining "characteristics" of the product. It can overcome those shortcomings of the conventional approach that assign all the observed difference in price between new and old models either to price or to quality.

In the IBM-BEA effort, the data on list prices and characteristics used were taken from publicly available sources and covered certain producers for the period 1972–84. For mainframe computer processors, the selected price-determining characteristics were main memory capacity and a summary measure of the speed with which instructions are executed. In addition, the hedonic functions were modified in order to allow for the failure of the prices of existing models to adjust promptly to the prices of new models. This was accomplished by allowing for the coexistence of two (or more) sets of prices—one for products based on an old technology (or technologies) and the other for products based on a new technology. Procedures similar to those for processors were used for disk drives, printers, and general purpose displays.

The IBM-BEA effort of 1985 did not include a price index for microcomputers (PCs), but BEA introduced such an index two years later. This index, unlike that for mainframes, was not based on hedonic techniques; it was instead a "matched-model" index. In a matched-model index, the price change associated with a new model is assumed to be the same as the price change of the continuing, that is, matched, models. The use of a matched-model index reflected partly the availability of data and partly BEA's judgment that such an index would adequately capture the full price decline in the PC market.

---

4. In the CPI, in contrast, when it is determined that a "large" specification change has occurred but no information is available to make a specific quality adjustment, the price change for that price quote is assumed to be the same as the price change of comparable goods. For additional detail on quality-adjustment procedures, see U.S. Department of Labor (1988).

In January 1991, BLS introduced a price index for computers within the PPI framework, following experimental presentation of the index in 1989 and 1990. Given its relatively recent origin, it was not surprising that the index received only limited attention at the workshop.[5] The BLS index differs from that prepared by BEA in that it is based on transactions prices collected from a probability sample of producers and does not rely exclusively on the hedonic approach for quality adjustments. The quality-adjustment methodology used in the BLS index is a composite of the conventional PPI approach, the hedonic approach, and the use of price change of matched models approach. Although the BLS and BEA indexes differ in implementation, the agencies view them as reflecting the same conceptual approach to price measurement, that is, the resource-cost approach.[6]

Research Issues

The workshop devoted much attention to several questions that arise in the measurement of prices of high-tech goods. One such question concerned the nature of markets for computers. Apparently, prices of old models do not promptly fall to match the performance-adjusted price of the new models. Why should this be so, and how is the phenomenon to be modeled? A second question concerned the extent to which other high-tech products display very rapid price declines. Two such products, both closely related to the mainframe computers included in the IBM-BEA study, were considered at the workshop: microcomputers (PCs) and semiconductors, an important input in the manufacture of computers. Another question was whether list prices for mainframe computers (which were used in the IBM-BEA work on computers) are suitable proxies for transactions prices. A fourth question, already alluded to, was of a different nature: Is the approach to price measurement represented by the BEA (and BLS) computer price index appropriate? Consideration of this question raises fundamental issues concerning the definition of output and capital and the purpose of productivity measurement.

Computer Prices

Stephen D. Oliner explored a relatively untapped data set on computers, namely, the asking prices for used IBM mainframe computers as compiled in the trade publication *Computer Price Guide*. He found that list prices serve as

5. A paper on how the inclusion of electronic computing equipment price indexes would affect the capital equipment component of the PPI was presented at the workshop but is not included in this volume.

6. In 1990, BEA began to use quarterly values of a weighted average of the BLS subindexes for thirty-two-bit and greater than thirty-two-bit word size computers to interpolate between annual estimates of its index for mainframe processors. BEA also began using the subindexes for sixteen-bit and thirty-two-bit word size computers in place of its matched-model index for PCs. In 1991, in the comprehensive revision of the national economic accounts, BEA introduced separate price indexes for imports and exports of computers and peripheral equipment.

reasonable proxies for transaction prices in this market. He also found that prices of old models do not promptly adjust to reflect the price declines occasioned by the introduction of new models. Oliner's results lend support to the rate of price decline for mainframe computers in the IBM-BEA study. Oliner also used the same data set to estimate the rate at which used IBM mainframe computers depreciate and analyzed data on the installed stock of IBM mainframes to derive the implied distribution of retirements.

Ernst R. Berndt and Zvi Griliches report on a hedonic study of PC prices that uses detailed data from the so-called list and discount U.S. markets for personal computers. The *list market* refers to the list prices as advertised by brand name manufacturers; the *discount market,* to prices as advertised by discount stores. An important aspect of the study is the authors' consideration of how to treat time, age, and vintage variables econometrically within a hedonic equation. This issue arises because there is an identity between the year in which the model is observed and the sum of the year in which the model was first introduced and its age in years.

Berndt and Griliches's results, which the authors characterize as preliminary, suggest a rate of price decline of about 25 percent per year from 1982 to 1988, substantially more than the 16 percent per year rate in the matched-model index for PCs used by BEA.[7] Separate regressions for the list and discount markets provide little evidence that the rate at which PC prices decline differs in the two markets. Separate regressions for new, continuing, and exiting models suggest that the price decline for continuing models may be larger than the price declines associated with the introduction of new models—the opposite experience from that observed for mainframe computers.

Semiconductors

Papers in this session addressed the question of whether it is reasonable that the PPI for semiconductors has not shown declines similar to the BEA computer price series. Papers by Ellen R. Dulberger, on the one hand, and by John R. Norsworthy and Show-Ling Jang, on the other, using different data and methodologies, conclude that semiconductor prices fell far more during the 1970s and the first part of the 1980s than did the PPI series. Using trade data (Dataquest) on memory chips and various index formulas, Dulberger constructs price series for so-called MOS memory chips. Her alternative chain price index series differ somewhat from one another, but all show considerably greater price declines than does a series she constructs to approximate the PPI fixed-based Laspeyres weighting procedures. Further, this fixed-based approximation itself falls far more rapidly than the official PPI series. Dulberger offers the hypothesis that delays in introducing new products into the PPI may be a major source of this difference. For example, she demonstrates that

---

7. These rates of price decline are expressed as actual rates in order to be consistent with other studies; in their paper, Berndt and Griliches present PC prices relative to the consumer price index.

the point at which dynamic random access memory (DRAM) chips (a type of MOS memory chip) are first introduced into a price index does indeed have a major effect on the price declines subsequently recorded in such an index. Finally, although lack of suitable data prevents her undertaking a careful examination of the question, Dulberger argues that, in view of the quality improvements that have occurred in chips and the complex electronic components into which they are assembled, their prices should show declines like those in the BEA deflator for computer processors.

In contrast to Dulberger's direct price index construction approach, Norsworthy and Jang investigate the extent of quality change in semiconductors by estimating a cost function and derived input demand functions for industries that use semiconductors. Their model is estimated separately using U.S. time-series data for 1968–86 for three four-digit industries: computers, telephone and telegraph apparatus, and other telecommunications equipment. Unmeasured quality change in semiconductor input for each industry is specified to be related to a quality adjustment index that is assumed to depend on two characteristics of semiconductor industry output—density of DRAM chips and bit width of microprocessor chips. The coefficients of the two included characteristics variables are found to vary by using industry. However, the authors conclude that, for all three industries, the hypothesis of no characteristics-related quality change is strongly rejected. Norsworthy and Jang's resulting quality-adjusted semiconductor prices fell even more rapidly than did the BEA computer price index.

Kenneth Flamm produces price indexes for DRAMs. He focuses on a relatively short recent period, citing evidence that, for the first time in the history of the semiconductor industry, substantial and sustained increases in the quality-adjusted price of memory chips occurred in 1987 and 1988. He uses data on actual sales contracts for DRAMs in 1985–89 to estimate an econometric model of forward pricing in DRAMs. Contract length is found to have a generally small and insignificant role as a determinant of contract pricing. Overall, his results show much smaller price differentials between American and European purchasers of DRAMs than had been indicated in published Dataquest series. He constructs quality-adjusted price indexes by weighting together chips of a given density that differ in speed and "organization." Flamm estimates that prices of 256K and 1M DRAM chips increased about 68 percent and 44 percent, respectively, from 1986 to 1988.

In his comment on the three semiconductor papers, Jack E. Triplett concludes that they all indicate that the PPI sampling mechanism has not worked for this industry. Much discussion about the problem of improving price indexes for industries experiencing rapid technological change has focused on the need to introduce new samples into the PPI more frequently. This is a problem that BLS has recognized for many years. Dulberger's finding of a significant effect of "introduction delays" on an index for DRAMs, if also true for semiconductors in general, would imply that extremely rapid introduction of new samples is needed. Triplett suggests an alternative, not for producing indexes on a current monthly basis, but rather for producing indexes for analytic purposes. Using this approach (which is similar to a proposal by the French statistical agency), hedonic methods would be used on available industry data on list prices and characteristics of all the products produced by the industries, and the PPI sampling methodology would be reoriented to collect discounts by product class that would be used to correct the hedonic indexes.

Panel Discussion: Implications of BEA's Treatment of Computer Prices and Productivity Measurement

The panel discussion was organized for the purpose of exploring issues raised by Edward F. Denison in his 1989 book *Estimates of Productivity Change by Industry,* which was highly critical of the computer price index introduced by BEA at the end of 1985.

Denison is concerned about the size of the declines in computer prices and the effect of these declines on the measurement of real GNP for the business sector, real business investment and capital stocks, and national income, depreciation, and profits expressed in current year prices. The first part of Denison's discussion essentially reiterates his view as presented in his 1989 book. Denison prefers that capital be measured in terms of consumption forgone, advocating an approach to the measurement of capital and productivity change similar to that set forth some years ago by Thomas K. Rymes, another member of the panel. Denison did not address in detail the consumption-forgone aspect, but it was taken up more fully by Charles R. Hulten as well as by Rymes.

If capital goods are always changing in quality, how is it possible to maintain a continuous time series of capital goods prices? Aside from his fundamental preference for the consumption-forgone approach, Denison notes the availability of other options. One method is to equate different products at a common date according to their costs. Another possibility, which Denison would prefer, is to equate different products according to value to the user, that is, by the value of their marginal products. However, information of this kind is ordinarily not known, and the method is rejected on practical grounds. Denison concludes that the new method that BEA has adopted for computers is neither of these approaches. BEA compares different computers according to the main characteristics that users are interested in, namely, memory and speed. In Denison's view, this exaggerates the extent of the price decline by focusing solely on computer performance and ignoring the labor and other costs that the user must incur.

Bringing in an argument made by Triplett (1991), BEA maintains that it has not changed its method of treating quality change because, in equilibrium, marginal costs and marginal revenues are equal. In response to this issue,

Denison says that Triplett's point is not as useful as it seems. One is still faced with the problem of comparing a new model with an older one that may no longer be on the market and for which an imputation must be made. Imputations may differ according to the method used.

Denison also raises a timing issue, claiming that new products are introduced prematurely so that the price drop is accentuated. That is, BEA links the new item at too early a stage on the learning curve. Finally, Denison notes that, by using fixed price weights, BEA exaggerates the contribution of computer output to the growth of real GNP, thereby overstating GNP growth.

Griliches believes that linking computers by performance characteristics in hedonic equations is indeed the proper approach because these are the characteristics that buyers are mainly interested in. He also takes issue with Denison about the appropriate date for introducing new models. If new models have few purchasers at their very high introductory prices, that is simply a fact of the market. It means that the weight is very small, but the price drop as the new product gains acceptance and production costs fall is no less real.

Although in advocating the use of consumption forgone to measure capital Denison gives up on ever being able to deflate specific capital goods by specific goods deflators, Griliches maintains that such a lack of comparability exists as much at the consumer level as at the level of capital goods. He concedes, however, that, at the aggregate level, deflating capital by a consumer price index might be useful for welfare measurement.

Rymes, like Denison, is concerned with the proper identification of the sources of output growth. When the price of a new capital good is linked to the price of an existing capital good at a common date according to resource cost (or price)—the conventional approach—some of the technological improvement embodied in the new capital good is assigned to capital. This approach to quality adjustment keeps capital goods prices relatively low and, as a consequence, the volume of real investment and the capital stock relatively high. In Rymes's view, this is an overweighting of input quantity and results in an underweighting of productivity increase. As he sees it, such distortion can be observed as one moves from, say, final demands to intermediate industries: semiconductor inputs will be overweighted and productivity underweighted in the computer industry; likewise, ceramic inputs may be overweighted in the semiconductor industry. Rymes argues that quality-adjusted price indexes, like BEA's new computer price index, exacerbate a problem that existed before the computer revolution; indeed, they make it difficult, if not impossible, to derive a useful measure of productivity change as a component of output growth either in the aggregate or by industry.

Rymes wants to exclude from the capital stock the technological component that has traditionally kept capital goods prices relatively low and, in the case of BEA's mainframe computer index, is keeping them even lower. In his view, all that should be reflected in the capital stock is what is needed to sustain the level of output. Rymes advocates use of an approach attributable to Roy Harrod (and implemented by Laurence Read) where distinctions between capital and technological change are more clearly maintained.

Although Hulten was not the last speaker, his remarks provide a clarification of the Rymes-Denison consumption-forgone approach versus the conventional (capital goods deflation) approach. The conventional way of measuring capital stock is as the sum of past investment adjusted for the using up of capital. In Rymes's view, since with the passage of time technological change makes it possible to lessen the amount of resources needed to reproduce a given stock of capital, factor input should be limited to the amount of saving (consumption forgone) required to reproduce such a stock.

Hulten's analysis concludes that, whereas the controversy had previously been viewed as a debate over the appropriate definitions of output and capital for growth analysis, it really boils down to a difference in objectives for productivity analysis. In the Rymes-Denison view, the conventional measure of capital includes a component that is more properly classified as technical change. Their preferred measure of total factor productivity would exclude this component from capital. In Hulten's opinion, both approaches are correct for answering different questions. The approach that uses the conventional definition of capital and total factor productivity answers the question of how much the production function has shifted relative to a given capital-labor ratio. The Denison-Rymes approach answers the question of how much more output growth there is because of technical change, that is, the initial rise in output associated with the improved technology and, in addition, all subsequent increases in output that follow in its wake.

In the discussion that followed, most of the panelists expressed agreement with Hulten's proposition that there are two approaches to productivity measurement and that they answer different questions. Griliches, in particular, prefers to measure productivity change in terms of observed prices and quantities in an industry and to be able to relate it to such factors as research and development in the "industry." He would prefer to deal with the effect of the additional capital that is induced by technological change in a subsequent stage of analysis. Rymes disagreed with Griliches with respect to which approach is most relevant in considering the effects of technical progress.

Thus, much of the discussion focused on the first of Denison's two points (the consumption-forgone standard). To the extent that Denison's second point was discussed, none of the other panelists agreed with him that the BEA computer price is inappropriate, although the measurement of prices of computers and other high-tech goods is not a closed matter. There was general agreement on the distorting effect of the interaction of the computer price index and BEA's use of fixed price weights in calculating real GNP. This particular problem has been recognized by BEA; in early 1992, the Bureau introduced alternative measures of GDP in which the weights are changed at more or less frequent intervals.

Quality-Change Issues in Consumer Prices

The papers in this section deal with two aspects of the treatment of quality change that may lead to bias in consumer price measures if not taken into account. The first is the widely discussed problem that arises when products disappear and are replaced with new versions. The second concerns changes in quality that may be associated with shifts among types of retail outlets. Presently, all price-level differences between outlets are implicitly assumed in the CPI to correspond to quality differences, but, to the extent that that is not the case, there will be an upward bias in the index.

Paul R. Liegey, Jr., reported on research to adjust apparel commodities in the CPI for quality change. Many apparel commodities are marketed on a seasonal basis, with one or more markdowns from the introductory price during the course of the season. For these commodities, price increases by and large occur only at the time of introduction. Standard CPI linking procedures would not work if applied to this market, and there was concern that the special procedures used by BLS might have led to an understatement of price changes.

Liegey reports on the experimental use of hedonic techniques for introducing replacement items for two types of apparel—women's coats and jackets and women's suits. For women's coats and jackets, the use of the hedonic technique gives an annual price change from October 1988 to October 1989 almost 4 percentage points larger than that in the published CPI, suggesting a downward bias in the index. For women's suits, the hedonic technique results in an annual change over half a percentage point less than the published index. Liegey suggests that this difference in outcome for women's suits may reflect a differential rate of success among the apparel components in excluding quality change from the published price change. Liegey also reports that BLS began to use hedonic techniques in the CPI in January 1991 for about twenty types of apparel.

Marshall Reinsdorf considers whether the CPI accurately reflects the shift of purchases away from full-price and high-price stores to chains and other lower-price retail outlets. Although Denison raised this issue some thirty years ago as a potential source of upward bias in retail price measures, it is only very recently that economists have begun to pay attention to it again. The theoretical problem is in some ways analogous to the bias in a cost-of-living index with fixed weights when consumers shift their purchases as relative prices change. Comparing prices at outlets linked into the CPI with those at the outlets they replaced, Reinsdorf finds a potential for an upward bias in the food-at-home component of the CPI (about 0.25 percent per year, assuming that everything else is comparable). In another part of the paper, he presents some comparisons of food items as carried in the CPI, on the one hand, and as shown by BLS in the "average price" series for specific food items paid by urban consumers. From January 1980 to January 1990, with few exceptions, the prices of the food items in the CPI went up about 2 percent per year more than the corresponding items in the "average price" series. In Reinsdorf's view, this may reflect a lower quality of services offered by the lower-price outlets, but the differences are sufficiently striking to warrant continued investigation.

Transactions Prices

The PPI is designed to measure changes in transactions prices of producers; the official definition is "changes in net revenues received by producers." Thomas Betsock and Irwin B. Gerduk of BLS describe the difficulties that the Bureau experienced in obtaining transactions prices from steel producers, who had typically reported list prices for the PPI. In 1985, actual market prices for sheet steel were far below list prices. For BLS, reporting difficulties reached crisis proportions in the fall of that year, when producers finally reduced list prices to reflect actual market prices more accurately but at the same time curtailed buyers' discounts and thus raised their actual realized prices over immediately preceding market levels. For PPI purposes, BLS chose to take the level correction at the cost of missing a month-to-month price rise. Although major producers continued to report list prices through the 1980s, there is reason to believe that the steel industry had a change of heart in 1990 and is now showing much more genuine cooperation with BLS. Since the end of 1989, one cannot help but be impressed by the differences in the paths traced by transactions prices for sheet steel, on the one hand, and list prices, on the other.

Murray F. Foss's paper deals with the same problem of obtaining accurate transactions prices from business for the PPI. He hypothesizes that the existence of the Robinson-Patman Act, which makes price discrimination illegal except under certain conditions, inhibits many businessmen from reporting transactions prices because they may be making price concessions that either are or might be viewed as being in violation of the law. In the fieldwork for their 1970 study of industrial prices, Stigler and Kindahl found that businessmen were reticent about reporting selling prices because of the Robinson-Patman Act. Although government enforcement of Robinson-Patman over the last several years has been greatly reduced, the threat of private suits remains. Foss believes that BLS might be able to enlist better reporting by business for the PPI if it encouraged producers to report averages (of several transactions) to a greater extent, such as is now being done with steel producers.

Price Indexes for Defense

Richard C. Ziemer and Pamela A. Kelly give a very detailed description of the complex procedures used by BEA to deflate defense purchases in the GNP. As an aid in exposition, they set up a numerical "model" involving hypothetical aircraft that describes how improvements in various types of aircraft are treated. Quality is said to change if there is a physical change in an aircraft type that permits the aircraft to fulfill its mission better in the opinion of the Defense Department. Adjustments are made on the basis of costs; that is, the value of a quality improvement is measured by the cost of the improvement. The authors also describe how BEA deals with the "learning-curve" phenomenon, that is, the decline in costs as production of a new defense item increases.

Arthur J. Alexander criticizes the use of cost as a measure of quality change for defense goods because improved products can be made at costs that are lower than those of older products. This has been a commonly voiced criticism of BLS's and BEA's treatment of quality change of capital goods. Drawing on his own research, Alexander cites examples of improved aircraft engines that were introduced at lower costs than the costs of the engines that were replaced. The improvements, which took the form of greater reliability and reduced maintenance costs, were the result of increased experience on the part of the engine manufacturer and substantial expenditures of research and development funds supplied by the Department of Defense.

Directions for Future Research

What was presented and commented on at the workshop suggests the importance of additional research on these topics. This is especially true of the high-tech field, where the development of price indexes of high-tech products that adequately account for quality change moves ahead at a slow pace while such products are proliferating. Continued investigation of quality adjustment procedures for items where technical change is rapid is extremely important. In addition, research is needed on alternative practical methods for data collection in these cases, such as suggested by Triplett.

If the proper measurement of prices of computer products is a contemporary concern, it is fair to ask how important high-tech products were treated in official price indexes in the past. Erwin Diewert raised this point in his paper at the fiftieth anniversary conference in 1988 (see Diewert 1990). Automobiles were not introduced into the CPI until 1935, when total passenger car registrations in the United States exceeded 22 million. The nature of the price index was doubtless a major consideration because the CPI of its day covered only urban wage earners and clerical workers, who typically did not purchase new passenger cars. Checking the historical record in this regard could have important implications for measuring the growth of real output and productivity in the early part of the twentieth century.

The workshop raised questions about the proper treatment of military goods such as aircraft. The present BEA procedure apparently ignores maintenance aspects of quality that must be important to the military. In addition, Robert Gordon has recently published price indexes for commercial aircraft that behave quite differently from the BEA prices for military aircraft (see Gordon 1990).

Several areas apart from high-tech products merit further investigation. The experience with steel sheet prices is probably not unique, and the reporting of list prices is probably not uncommon. There is a large body of price data on purchases of common civilian items by the U.S. General Services Administration that could be used to compare with revised PPI data since the late 1970s, especially during recessions. Research by Reinsdorf has shown the possibility of a large seller substitution bias for food at home and for gasoline; further work, using hedonic methods, is needed to develop point estimates. In addition, studies of seller substitution bias for other goods would be important.

Research on a broad range of price measurement issues and development of new or improved price series would benefit from both increased availability of data from private-sector sources and increased use of micro data within the statistical agencies. Studies of particular industries are needed, such as that being carried out by Berndt, Griliches, and Rosett (1992) for pharmaceuticals using data provided by several firms within the industry. More cooperative undertakings, such as that employed in the IBM-BEA computer project, might be a helpful approach. For increased use of government-collected micro data to be possible, improved support for longitudinal micro data files is needed.

Some issues in the price measurement field that were not addressed at the workshop are of major importance for future research. Development of consumer price measures for the flow of services from durable goods is one example. Another is the choice of alternative functional forms for price indexes, the practical importance of which has been clearly demonstrated, especially for investment goods (Young 1992; Triplett 1992). Theoretical work on defining the output of service-sector industries is a necessary first step in development of price indexes or in improvement of existing indexes for services; this topic was the focus of a separate National Bureau of Economic Research/Conference on Research in Income and Wealth conference also held in 1990 (see Griliches 1992). The appropriate treatment in price indexes of government-mandated pollution and safety equipment is still debated. For some purposes, measures of well-being more general than real personal consumption or real gross domestic product may be of interest, and these would require development of corresponding price measures. It should be obvious that price research is a field where much remains to be done.

References

Berndt, Ernst R., Zvi Griliches, and Joshua Rosett. 1992. Auditing the producer price index: Micro evidence from prescription pharmaceutical preparations. NBER Working Paper no. 4009. Cambridge, Mass.: National Bureau of Economic Research, March.

Bureau of Economic Analysis (BEA). U.S. Department of Commerce. 1987a. *Foreign transactions*. Methodology Paper Series MP-3. Washington, D.C., May.

————. 1987b. *GNP: An overview of source data and estimating methods*. Methodology Paper Series MP-4. Washington, D.C., September.

————. 1988. *Government transactions*. Methodology Paper Series MP-5. Washington, D.C., November.

————. 1990. *Personal consumption expenditures*. Methodology Paper Series MP-6. Washington, D.C., June.

Cartwright, David W. 1986. Improved deflation of purchases of computers. *Survey of Current Business* 66 (March); 7–10.

Cartwright, David, and Scott Smith. 1988. Deflators for purchases of computers in GNP: Revised and extended estimates, 1983–88. *Survey of Current Business* 68 (November); 22–23.

Cole, Rosanne, Y. C. Chen, Joan A. Barquin-Stolleman, Ellen Dulberger, Nurhan Helvacian, and James H. Hodge. 1986. Quality-adjusted price indexes for computer processors and selected peripheral equipment. *Survey of Current Business* 66 (January): 41–50.

Denison, Edward F. 1989. *Estimates of productivity change by industry*. Washington, D.C.: Brookings.

Diewert, W. Erwin. 1990. Comment [on Triplett]. In *Fifty years of economic measurement,* ed. Ernst R. Berndt and Jack E. Triplett. Studies in Income and Wealth, vol. 54. Chicago: University of Chicago Press (for the National Bureau of Economic Research).

Gordon, Robert J. 1990. *The measurement of durable goods prices*. Chicago: University of Chicago Press (for the National Bureau of Economic Research).

Griliches, Zvi, ed. 1992. *Output measurement in the service sector*. Studies in Income and Wealth, vol. 56. Chicago: University of Chicago Press (for the National Bureau of Economic Research).

Sinclair, James, and Brian Catron. 1990. An experimental price index for the computer industry. *Monthly Labor Review* 113 (October): 16–24.

Stigler, George, and James Kindahl. 1970. *The behavior of industrial prices*. New York: Columbia University Press (for the National Bureau of Economic Research).

Triplett, Jack E. 1991. Two views on computer prices and productivity. Discussion Paper no. 45. Washington, D.C.: Bureau of Economic Analysis, U.S. Department of Commerce.

————. 1992. Economic theory and BEA's alternative quantity and price indexes. *Survey of Current Business* 72 (April): 49–52.

U.S. Department of Labor. 1988. Bureau of Labor Statistics. *BLS handbook of methods*. Bulletin no. 2285. Washington, D.C., April.

Young, Allan H. 1992. Alternative measures of change in real output and prices. *Survey of Current Business* 72 (April): 32–48.

I   High-Tech Products: Computers

1 Constant-Quality Price Change, Depreciation, and Retirement of Mainframe Computers

Stephen D. Oliner

Over the past two decades, business equipment spending has shifted away from heavy machinery and motor vehicles toward "information-processing" equipment, particularly computers. Indeed, between 1970 and 1990, the Bureau of Economic Analysis (BEA) estimates that constant-dollar investment in office and computing equipment grew at an annual rate of 18.1 percent, far above the 3.3 percent growth averaged for the remaining categories of producers' durable equipment. Given the increasing use of computers by U.S. businesses, estimates of price change for these goods are of substantial importance.

Two distinct facets of price change for computers can be studied. First, how rapidly have the prices of computing equipment fallen over time? Any meaningful answer to this question must adjust for the enormous improvements in the power of computers. Such estimates of constant-quality computer prices are needed not only to deflate investment outlays for computing equipment but also to calculate output in the computer industry and to construct broad indexes of inflation. In recent years, considerable work has been done to estimate constant-quality prices for computing equipment (for a comprehensive review of this literature, see Triplett 1989). Moreover, as described in Cartwright (1986), the results of this work have been used to construct price measures in the national income and product accounts. Nonetheless, this literature is still in its early stages, and much further work is needed to sharpen the

Stephen D. Oliner is a senior economist at the Board of Governors of the Federal Reserve System.

The author wishes to thank Melynda Dovel, William Nelson, and Eric Wiland for providing excellent research assistance and to acknowledge helpful comments from Ellen Dulberger, Spencer Krane, Marilyn Manser, John Musgrave, David Wilcox, Allan Young, and especially Rosanne Cole. Any opinions expressed herein are his own and do not necessarily represent those of the Board of Governors or the staff of the Federal Reserve System.

Copyright is not claimed for this paper.

results obtained to date. In particular, all the recent studies reviewed in Triplett (1989) employ manufacturers' list prices, leaving open the possibility that the resulting estimates do not adequately characterize the behavior of actual transaction prices.

A second aspect of price change for computers concerns the rate at which the value of this equipment declines with age—that is, the rate of depreciation. For a cohort of computers installed at a given time, depreciation of the cohort reflects both the price decline for the equipment remaining in service as the cohort ages and the increase in the proportion of units retired from service, for which price is assumed to be zero. Such estimates of cohort depreciation are a vital input for calculating capital stocks. In contrast to the substantial effort undertaken to estimate constant-quality prices for computers, the literature on depreciation and retirement of these goods is surprisingly sparse. There appears to be no systematic study of retirement patterns. And the most commonly cited estimate of economic depreciation for office and computing equipment, that of Hulten and Wykoff (1981b), is based solely on prices for typewriters (see Hulten and Wykoff 1979, 87), for lack of price data on computers.

This paper provides new estimates of the rate of economic depreciation and the rate of constant-quality price change for a large sample of IBM mainframe computers. These estimates are derived from a rich and virtually untapped source of data, the *Computer Price Guide,* a quarterly bluebook that lists asking prices in the secondhand market for commonly traded models of IBM computer equipment. The paper also analyzes separate data on the installed stock of various IBM mainframe models to derive the implied retirement pattern for these computers and to construct estimates of cohort depreciation. The value of the paper is in bringing new data to the analysis of long-standing and important pricing questions.

The paper is organized as follows. Section 1.1 identifies the primary determinants of price for IBM mainframe computers in the secondhand market. On the basis of this discussion, section 1.2 specifies the "hedonic" price equations used to estimate constant-quality price change and depreciation for my sample of IBM mainframes. Section 1.3 describes the price data in more detail and discusses the construction of other variables used in the econometric work. Section 1.4 estimates constant-quality price change for my sample, using both IBM list prices and the corresponding asking prices in the secondhand market. This section examines whether the results obtained in previous studies with list prices are altered when the analysis is redone with secondhand prices, which should reflect any discounting from list by IBM. Section 1.5 presents the empirical results concerning depreciation and retirement, and section 1.6 uses these results to assess potential biases in BEA's published gross and net capital stocks for office and computing equipment. Section 1.7 summarizes the findings of the paper.

1.1   A Pricing Model for IBM Mainframe Computers

This section lays out a model for the price of IBM mainframe computers. The goal is to motivate the econometric equations used below to estimate price change for these assets. I pay particular attention to the concept of age that belongs in the econometric equations.

Perhaps the most distinctive feature of the secondhand market for IBM mainframes—in fact, for all IBM computing equipment—is that the age of the particular unit for sale is irrelevant to market participants. Indeed, in the *Computer Price Guide,* age is never listed as part of the description of the computer. Thus, two IBM model 360/30 mainframes, one shipped from IBM in 1965 and the other in 1967, are perfect substitutes in the market. This lack of concern for age results directly from IBM's unique policy for maintaining its equipment. Subject to certain conditions, IBM will provide maintenance service for a monthly fee that may vary across models but does not vary a-cross different units of a given model.[1] Effectively, IBM supplies insurance against the purchase of a lemon. The buyer of any IBM mainframe computer can expect it to perform like new by paying a fee that is unrelated to the age of a particular unit. As a result, the market does not care about such age differences.

Although all units of a given model will sell at the same price, a second concept of age is relevant for pricing. Define *model age* as the time that has elapsed since the first shipment of a model. The IBM 360/30 was first shipped in 1965; thus, all 360/30 units had a model age of ten years in 1975. Similarly, all units of the 370/145 model, first shipped in 1971, had a model age of four years in 1975. The 370/145, the younger model, would be expected to command a higher price than the 360/30 at any given time for two reasons. First, the 370/145 is the more powerful computer, thereby generating higher rental income in each period of use. Second, the 370/145 likely has more periods of profitable use remaining before obsolescence causes retirement to occur.

To obtain a mathematical expression that relates IBM mainframe prices to model age and other factors, I begin by assuming that the market for these assets is in equilibrium; the assumption of equilibrium is relaxed later in the section. Let $\mathbf{z}(v)$ denote the vector of characteristics embodied in a mainframe model first shipped in period $v,$ and let $\tau = t - v$ denote the age of this model at time $t;$ $\mathbf{z}(v)$ can thus be written as $\mathbf{z}(t - \tau)$. Next, let $R[\mathbf{z}(t - \tau), t, \tau]$ denote the net rental income generated in period t by a mainframe of model age τ that embodies the vector of characteristics $\mathbf{z}$. $R(\cdot, \cdot, \cdot)$ depends (1) on

---

1. IBM will offer this contract to any purchaser of IBM computing equipment that is "in good working condition [at the time of sale] and was covered under an IBM maintenance agreement in the previous location" (*Computer Price Guide,* January 1986, 43). Given the adverse effect on resale value of failing to meet these rather mild conditions, almost all IBM equipment qualifies for the maintenance agreement at resale.

$z(t - \tau)$, because these performance features determine the real services provided by the mainframe; (2) on time, because price changes affect the nominal value of these services; and (3) on a separate argument in τ, as a way of capturing the influence of factors, others than **z,** that may be correlated with model age.

One factor included in (3) would be differences in IBM maintenance fees across models; for a model nearing obsolescence, the cost of IBM maintenance effectively becomes infinite at the time IBM terminates service contracts for the model. Another age-related factor would be the expense of keeping personnel trained to operate older models that may be used only on an infrequent basis.[2] Finally, as an empirical matter, **z** likely omits certain performance characteristics that contribute to value. If these omitted characteristics are correlated with model age, τ will act as their proxy. For all these reasons, a general formulation of net rental income should include a separate argument in model age.

Given this specification of net rental income for IBM mainframes, the purchase price can be expressed as the present value of future net income flows. This price will depend on all the factors that influence rental income and can thus be written $P[z(t - \tau), t, \tau]$. $P(\cdot, \cdot, \cdot)$ is a general expression for the price of a new or used IBM mainframe computer and can be regarded as a "hedonic" function that relates price to its basic determinants (for an introduction to hedonic functions, see Triplett 1986). $P(\cdot, \cdot, \cdot)$ differs from the hedonic function for other durable goods only in the way that age has been defined. Typically, the measure of age that enters $P(\cdot, \cdot, \cdot)$ is the span of time over which a particular *unit* has been in use. This specification makes sense for goods that deteriorate with use (such as automobiles). However, as argued earlier, this concept of age is irrelevant in the market for IBM computing equipment. Age becomes important for pricing only when used at the level of distinct models, which have different embodied characteristics and input requirements.

Thus far, I have assumed that the market for IBM mainframes is in equilibrium, in that all models lie on a single pricing surface $P[z(t - \tau), t, \tau]$. That is, after controlling for the effects on price of the characteristics **z,** time, and model age, there are no price differences across models. Fisher, McGowan, and Greenwood (1983) argued that such an equilibrium seldom prevails for computers, as the prices of existing models are not immediately marked down to compete with the lower constant-quality price of a new model. Dulberger (1989) found empirical support for slow repricing on the basis of list prices

---

2. Note that I have specified net rental income to be a function of labor costs. Implicitly, I have a "putty-clay" model of computer operations in mind: firms can choose from a range of computers with different labor requirements, but these requirements are fixed once a particular computer has been installed. With fixed proportions ex post, net rental income equals gross income minus required labor costs.

for a sample of IBM and plug-compatible mainframes. Her data suggest that two distinct price regimes tend to exist in that market just after the introduction of a new technology: one regime for models embodying best-practice technology and a higher-priced regime for the set of nonbest models. Eventually, the nonbest models either get repriced down to compete with the best-practice models or leave the market. Although Dulberger's findings suggest that each occurrence of disequilibrium is temporary, nonbest models will, on average, carry a price premium because they spend some time in the higher-priced regime. (Similar evidence of disequilibrium in the market for disk drives is presented in Cole et al. 1986.)

The hedonic function $P(\cdot, \cdot, \cdot)$ can be modified to allow for multiple regimes by introducing an argument that shifts the surface. Let $B(v, t)$ equal one if the vintage v model embodies best technology at time t, and let $B(v, t)$ be greater than one if the model has nonbest technology at time t. Noting that $B(v, t) = B(t - \tau, t)$, the hedonic function that incorporates disequilibrium is

$$(1) \qquad P[\mathbf{z}(t - \tau), t, \tau; B(t - \tau, t)],$$

with $\partial P/\partial B > 0$. Expression (1) captures the idea that nonbest models tend to lie on a higher hedonic surface than best-technology models.

The types of price change studied in this paper can be written as derivatives of the natural log of expression (1). The first is the rate of constant-quality price change over time, $\partial \ln(P)/\partial t$. This partial derivative measures the rate of price change over time conditional on a fixed set of embodied characteristics, a fixed value of model age, and a single hedonic surface. It is a pure measure of inflation that abstracts from changes over time in the mix of mainframes being priced.

The second dimension of price change is the rate of depreciation—the change in asset price with age, holding time fixed. Typically, the rate of depreciation is defined to include all age-related effects on price and would thus be measured in expression (1) as the total derivative

$$(2) \qquad \left. \frac{d \ln(P)}{d\tau} \right| t \text{ fixed} = \frac{\partial \ln(P)}{\partial \mathbf{z}} \cdot \frac{\partial \mathbf{z}}{\partial \tau} + \frac{\partial \ln(P)}{\partial \tau} + \frac{\partial \ln(P)}{\partial B} \cdot \frac{\partial B}{\partial \tau}.$$

Narrower measures of the age-related change in price can also be defined. One such measure is the rate of depreciation that controls for differences across models in the embodied characteristics $\mathbf{z}$. This measure equals the sum of the second and third terms on the right-hand side of equation (2). An even narrower concept of age-related price change is simply the partial derivative of price with respect to τ, the second term on the right-hand side of the equation. Section 1.6 below explores the appropriate choice among these alternative measures.

1.2 The Econometric Model

The previous section identified the variables that affect the price of IBM mainframe computers. These variables include performance characteristics, time, model age, and an index that distinguishes models with best-practice technology from all others. Theory alone, however, cannot determine the form of the estimating equation. Following the tradition in the hedonic literature on computer prices (see Triplett 1989, table 4.2), I adopt the double-log form for the relation between price and the characteristics **z** in the econometric equation. For a single hedonic surface, the double-log assumption yields an estimating equation of the general form

$$(3) \qquad \ln P = \alpha + \sum_i \beta_i \ln(z_i) + f(t) + h(\tau),$$

where $f(t)$ and $h(\tau)$ are functions of time and model age, respectively. The usual specification of $f(t)$ in hedonic equations uses a dummy variable for each time period. Because my data set has relatively few observations per period, I economize on degrees of freedom by specifying both $f(t)$ and $h(\tau)$ to be fifth-order polynomials. These polynomials are of high enough order to capture a wide range of time- and age-related price movements. Equation (3) then becomes

$$(4) \qquad \ln P = \alpha + \sum_i \beta_i \ln(z_i) + \sum_{j=1}^{5} \gamma_j t^j + \sum_{j=1}^{5} \delta_j \tau^j.$$

For mainframe computers, the consensus view is that two characteristics largely determine the quality of a given model: speed of computation and main memory capacity (again, see Triplett 1989). Although the measurement of memory capacity is straightforward, there is no universally accepted index of speed, in large part because the speed of a processor depends on its mix of tasks. A crude measure of overall speed—which has been adopted in most of the recent empirical studies in this area—is millions of instructions processed per second, the MIPS rating. I specify **z** to consist of the model's MIPS rating and its main memory capacity.

To allow for multiple price regimes, I generalized equation (4) to have different constant terms for best and nonbest models. Moreover, I let the polynomial function in t differ across these two sets of models to accommodate possible shifts over time in the gap between the two price surfaces. Given this generalization, a rule is needed to distinguish models with best-practice technology from all other models. Dulberger (1989) defined best-practice models at time t as those having main memory chips with the greatest density then available. She argued that advances in semiconductor technology, which historically have driven the improvements in performance of computer processors, are highly correlated with increases in chip density. Thus, chip density acts as a proxy for the level of embodied technology.

Following Dulberger's argument, I assigned each model to a technology class on the basis of the density of its memory chip. For example, all models with 64KB (kilobit) chips were placed in a single class, those with 288KB chips were put in a second class, and so on. Given these class assignments, I defined a dummy variable BEST, which took the value of one for models in the class with the densest chip available at the time of the price observation and zero for other models. Now, the generalized version of equation (4) can be written

(5) $\ln P = \alpha_1 + \alpha_2 \text{BEST} + \beta_1 \ln(\text{MIPS}) + \beta_2 \ln(\text{Memory})$

$$+ \sum_{j=1}^{5} (\gamma_j + \pi_j \text{BEST}) t^j + \sum_{j=1}^{5} \delta_j \tau^j.$$

In the previous section, I argued that prices of mainframe computers likely depend on model age (but not the age of individual units of that model). Price might also be related to a second concept of age, one based on the model's technology class. To illustrate the distinction between these two measures of age, note that IBM began shipping mainframes with 64KB memory chips in 1979. However, the first shipment of its model 3081-K, which also used the 64KB chip, was not until 1982. The age of the 3081-K in 1982 would be zero when defined in terms of the model itself but three years when defined in terms of the technology class. A priori, it is not clear which of these concepts of age is more closely correlated with obsolescence of IBM mainframes, and I use both age measures in the empirical work below.

Finally, I added a dummy variable to equation (5), denoted NEW, that equals one if the price observation refers to a new unit and zero if not. New IBM mainframes often trade in the secondhand market, as dealers place orders with IBM for equipment in short supply and then resell the equipment to firms wanting immediate delivery. From the viewpoint of performance, new and used units are identical. However, tax considerations are likely to make the new unit sell for a higher price in the secondhand market than the same unit used. During most of my sample period, new computing equipment was eligible for an investment tax credit—which ranged up to 10 percent of the unit's purchase price—while the credit was highly restricted for used equipment.[3] Adding the NEW dummy variable to the estimating equation yields

(6) $\ln P = \alpha_1 + \alpha_2 \text{BEST} + \beta_1 \ln(\text{MIPS}) + \beta_2 \ln(\text{Memory})$

$$+ \sum_{j=1}^{5} (\gamma_j + \pi_j \text{BEST}) t^j + \sum_{j=1}^{5} \delta_j \tau^j + \rho^* \text{NEW},$$

---

3. The investment tax credit was eliminated in 1986. As an indication that the credit had created a wedge between the prices of new and used units, the *Computer Price Guide* noted in late 1986 that "the difference in value between new and used [units] is going to narrow. . . . From now on, used equipment is going to be a more attractive alternative, at prices closer to list price" (*Computer Price Guide Readers Report,* October 1986, 1).

where τ is defined either by the age of a particular model or by the age of that model's technology class. Equation (6) is the basic equation estimated in the empirical part of the paper.

1.3   Data for Estimating Constant-Quality Price Change and Depreciation

The primary data source for this paper was the *Computer Price Guide,* a bluebook for computing equipment published quarterly since late 1970 by Computer Merchants Inc., a dealer in the secondhand market for this equipment. Each issue of the *Guide* contains price quotes for commonly traded mainframe computers, minicomputers, personal computers, and various types of peripheral equipment. Because the secondhand market for non-IBM equipment is so thin, the *Guide* has listed only IBM equipment since 1978. The data set that I created from the *Guide* includes fifty-two models of IBM mainframe computers, spanning the period from the fourth quarter of 1970 to the fourth quarter of 1986. The IBM 360, 370, 4300, and 30XX families are well represented in the sample.[4]

For each entry in the *Guide,* two prices are shown. The first is the average asking price in the secondhand market during the month or two prior to publication of the *Guide;* this price is a composite of quotes to retail customers seeking immediate delivery. It is not the actual sale price for any particular transaction. The second price provided for each entry is IBM's list price prevailing a few weeks before publication of the *Guide.* Somewhat misleadingly, the *Guide* continues to show a list price for a model even after IBM has ceased production; presumably, the list price shown is the final one at which IBM sold the model. To avoid the use of contaminated data, my empirical work employs the list prices in the *Guide* only for periods before the year of IBM's final shipment. (For the year of final IBM shipment for each model in my sample, see app. table 1A.1.)

Each issue of the *Guide* typically priced different configurations of a particular mainframe model, many of which included peripheral equipment or other attachments to the basic processing unit. To keep the sample as homogeneous as possible, I attempted to price only the model's "minimum configuration," which consists of the central processing unit (CPU), the main memory, and other required components (such as cooling units). As a result, I omitted all entries with peripheral equipment and included entries that had optional attachments to the CPU only when the minimum configuration was not listed.

Besides information on prices, the estimation of equation (6) requires data for age, the BEST dummy, MIPS, and memory size. Memory size, measured

---

4. Prices from the *Guide* were previously used by Archibald and Reece (1979) to estimate constant-quality price change for large IBM mainframe systems over the period 1970–75. Their study, however, did not attempt to estimate depreciation.

in kilobytes, was taken directly from the *Guide,* which includes this information for every entry. MIPS ratings were obtained from a variety of sources, principally Lias (1980) and issues of *Computerworld*'s "Annual Hardware Roundup." Appendix table 1A.1 lists the MIPS rating for each model in the sample and the source of the rating. Table 1A.1 also lists the date of initial shipment for each model, from which I calculated the model age for each price observation (in quarters). The data needed to calculate the value of BEST and the age of the technology class for each price observation are contained in tables 1A.1 and 1A.2; table 1A.1 shows the technology class for each model, adopting the class codes in Dulberger (1989), while table 1A.2 provides the date of first shipment for each class.[5] Using these tables, I calculated the age of the technology class for each price observation as the pricing date minus the date of first shipment from the model's technology class, in quarters. Table 1A.2 also shows the period over which each technology class represented the best technology, from which I calculated the value of the BEST dummy variable for each observation.[6]

1.4   Constant-Quality Price Change

This section estimates constant-quality prices for IBM mainframe computers, focusing on whether the results are sensitive to the use of list prices in place of actual transaction prices. Ideally, one would assess the bias imparted by list prices by directly comparing the results based on list prices to those based on transaction prices. Unfortunately, transaction prices are proprietary information, so this approach cannot be implemented. Instead, I draw inferences about the behavior of IBM's transaction prices by examining prices in the secondhand market. This procedure implicitly assumes that IBM's transaction prices move closely with secondhand prices, reflecting the ability of firms to buy equipment in either market.

1.4.1   IBM's Discounts on Mainframe Computers

The data in the *Guide* can be used to infer the extent of IBM's price discounts. Let LP(IBM) and TP(IBM) denote, respectively, IBM's list price and

---

5. There was some ambiguity in defining the date of first shipment for the technology class with magnetic core memory (class 1), the precursor to semiconductor memory. Magnetic core memory was used for the 360 family, but also for earlier models not included in my sample. I set the first shipment date of this technology class equal to the first shipment of the 360s in my sample—April 1965—rather than the first shipment of any processor with core memory.

6. A few models in the 370 family were introduced with relatively low-density chips but were subsequently upgraded to use denser chips. Because the *Guide* does not indicate which version of such models is being priced, I cannot determine the appropriate technology class for price observations after the date of the upgrade. To solve this problem, I assumed that price observations in the *Guide* before the upgrade refer to the lower-density version of the model while prices after the upgrade pertain to the enhanced version. This rule assigns a unique technology class to each price observation.

transaction price for a particular mainframe model. Further, let AP(SHM) and TP(SHM) denote, respectively, the asking price and the transaction price for the same model in the secondhand market. I assume that AP(SHM) = TP(SHM).

For the typical case in which the secondhand market price refers to a used unit while IBM's price refers to a new unit, the latter will include a premium, denoted TAX, equal to the value of the investment tax credit. IBM may be able to extract an additional premium, denoted SVC, equal to the value of the service it provides at the time of sale. A third premium, denoted MAINT, may result from IBM's offer of a year of free maintenance for new units (the *Computer Price Guide Readers Report,* July 1975, 139, documents this IBM practice). Accounting for these premiums, IBM's transaction price will be related to the secondhand asking price as follows:

$$TP(IBM) = AP(SHM) + TAX + SVC + MAINT.$$

Dividing each side by IBM's list price and subtracting one from each side yields

$$(7) \quad \frac{TP(IBM)}{LP(IBM)} - 1 = \frac{AP(SHM)}{LP(IBM)} + \frac{TAX + SVC + MAINT}{LP(IBM)} - 1.$$

The left-hand side of the equation gives IBM's rate of discount, while the first term on the right-hand side equals the ratio of the secondhand market asking price to IBM's list price, which is provided in the *Guide.* Data for the TAX, SVC, and MAINT premiums are not known for individual models. However, the *Guide* states that, before the elimination of the investment tax credit in 1986, "it was difficult to interest users in a used piece of gear, unless the price was at least 12% to 15% below IBM's list price" (*Computer Price Guide Readers Report,* October 1986, 1). Using this information, I specified the total premium, TAX + SVC + MAINT, to be 15 percent of list price, implying that

$$(8) \quad \frac{TP(IBM)}{LP(IBM)} - 1 = \frac{AP(SHM)}{LP(IBM)} + \frac{.15 * LP(IBM)}{LP(IBM)} - 1$$
$$= \frac{AP(SHM)}{LP(IBM)} - .85.$$

Consequently, I inferred that IBM was discounting from list price whenever the ratio of the *Guide's* asking price for used units to IBM's list price was below 0.85.

Table 1.1 displays this ratio for mainframe models estimated still to be in production at the pricing date (recall that only these models have valid list prices in the *Guide*). Column 1 covers the entire sample period, 1970–86. The first entry in the column represents the average price ratio for models first shipped less than four quarters earlier; the second entry represents the average

Table 1.1   **Average Ratio of *Computer Price Guide* Asking Price to IBM List Price, for Used Units, by Age of Model (standard errors in parentheses)**

Age in Quarters	All Models in Production at Pricing Date		All Models in Production at Pricing Date with Ratio ≥ 0.6	
	1970–86 (1)	1972–84 (2)	1970–86 (3)	1972–84 (4)
0–3	.850	.847	.850	.847
	(.018)	(.023)	(.018)	(.023)
4–7	.787	.795	.813	.817
	(.015)	(.016)	(.013)	(.015)
8–11	.743	.802	.802	.802
	(.026)	(.016)	(.016)	(.016)
12–15	.729	.729	.822	.822
	(.034)	(.034)	(.028)	(.028)
16–19	.453	.453	.621[a]	.621[a]
	(.032)	(.032)		
Average ratio	.758	.766	.816	.813
Sample size	146	116	119	97

[a]Based on a single observation. Standard error is not meaningful.

for models first shipped four to seven quarters earlier, and so on down the column. For models less than four quarters old, the ratio of the secondhand market price to IBM's list price averaged 0.85, indicating that IBM was not discounting from list. However, for older models, the ratio drops steadily and is more than two standard errors below 0.85 in each age group. Column 1, therefore, points to widespread discounting after a model has been available for about one year. Column 2 restricts the sample to 1972–84, the period covered by Dulberger (1989), with little change in the results.

In both columns, the calculated price ratio becomes so small for models aged sixteen to nineteen quarters as to raise questions about the quality of the data. One possible explanation is that the ratios are distorted by the inadvertent use of list prices from the *Guide* for models no longer in production, owing to difficulties in determining exactly when IBM stopped shipping a given model on the basis of publicly available data. In columns 3 and 4, I recalculated the average ratios for each age group after omitting any observation for which the price ratio was below 0.6—that is, for which the discount from list was greater than 25 percent ($0.6 - 0.85$). All the observations removed by this filter occurred in the four quarters just prior to my estimated ending date of IBM shipments, and two-thirds were within two quarters of this date. The concentration of the low ratios close to the end of IBM's estimated production period supports the view that columns 1 and 2 included list prices for models actually out of production. If the low ratios had been due, instead, to random errors in the data, these ratios would have been spread evenly throughout IBM's production period.

Columns 3 and 4 indicate that, after filtering, the price ratio remains above 0.8 for all but the oldest age group. The ratio for this group is based on a single observation and merits little attention. Focusing on the other age groups, the average ratios for the models aged zero to three quarters and those aged twelve to fifteen quarters are within one standard error of 0.85 and thus provide no significant evidence of IBM discounting. Although the average ratios for the models aged four to seven quarters and those aged eight to eleven quarters are more than two standard errors below 0.85, the point estimates imply IBM discounts from list of less than 5 percent. On balance, these results suggest that IBM's list prices for mainframe computers proxied reasonably well for actual transaction prices, at least until 1986.

1.4.2   Estimates of the Hedonic Pricing Equation

As the next step in the analysis, I compared the estimates of equation (6) based on IBM list prices with those based on prices in the secondhand market. To avoid the use of invalid list prices, I restricted the sample for these regressions to models still in production at the pricing date. In addition, I required that the ratio of asking price to IBM list price be at least 0.6, as in columns 3 and 4 of table 1.1. These two requirements yielded a sample of 145 observations, to which I applied ordinary least squares.[7]

Table 1.2 presents selected estimation results using IBM's list price as the dependent variable. The first column is meant to approximate the hedonic regressions run by Dulberger (1989) and other researchers, who omitted measures of age from the set of regressors. The explanatory variables in column 1 include all those shown in equation (6) except for the fifth-order polynomial in τ. Column 2 adds the polynomial function of model age to the regression, while column 3 instead adds the polynomial with age measured by the model's technology class.

The results in all three columns indicate that MIPS and memory size have positive, highly significant effects on price. The coefficients show that processing speed is a more important determinant of price than is memory capacity, consistent with the findings in Dulberger (1989) and Cartwright (1986). In addition, the terms in BEST and $\Sigma(\text{BEST}*t^j)$ are jointly significant in each regression. This result can be seen in the bottom row of the table, which reports the F-statistic for the null hypothesis that the coefficients on these terms are all zero. In each column, the value of the F-statistic is well above its 1 percent critical value of about 2.95. Thus, along with Dulberger, I find evidence of different list-price regimes for mainframes embodying best and non-best technology. Moreover, including age as an explanatory variable does not alter this result.

---

7. This sample of 145 observations is slightly larger than the sample used in col. 3 of table 1.1 because I have included price observations for new equipment.

Table 1.2 **OLS Estimates of the Hedonic Price Equation with IBM List Price as Dependent Variable (*t*-statistics in parentheses)**

| | Age Variable in Regression | | |
| | None | Model | Tech. Class |
Regressor	(1)	(2)	(3)
ln(MIPS)	0.758	0.777	0.727
	(23.6)	(23.3)	(41.3)
ln(Memory)	0.203	0.188	0.203
	(6.1)	(5.4)	(11.1)
R^2	0.984	0.985	0.996
F-statistic for insignificance of all terms in BEST	4.52	4.09	8.17

Note: Each regression was based on a sample of 145 observations considered to have valid list prices; see the text for specific selection criteria. In addition to ln(MIPS) and ln(Memory), the explanatory variables for each regression included a constant, BEST, NEW, and fifth-order polynomials in Time and BEST*Time. The regressions reported in cols. 2 and 3 also included a fifth-order polynomial in the age variable shown.

Table 1.3 **OLS Estimates of the Hedonic Price Equation with Secondhand Market Asking Price as Dependent Variable (*t*-statistics in parentheses)**

| | Age Variable in Regression | | |
| | None | Model | Tech. Class |
Regressor	(1)	(2)	(3)
ln(MIPS)	0.806	0.821	0.794
	(33.4)	(32.3)	(37.7)
ln(Memory)	0.234	0.220	0.232
	(9.4)	(8.3)	(10.6)
R^2	0.992	0.992	0.994
F-statistic for insignificance of all terms in BEST	10.31	10.11	1.81

Note: Each regression was based on a sample of 145 observations considered to have valid list prices; see the text for specific selection criteria. In addition to ln(MIPS) and ln(Memory), the explanatory variables for each regression included a constant, BEST, NEW, and fifth-order polynomials in Time and BEST*Time. The regressions reported in cols. 2 and 3 also included a fifth-order polynomial in the age variable shown.

Table 1.3 reports the same set of regression estimates as in table 1.2, with the dependent variable now equal to the secondhand market price. On the whole, the estimates are similar to those derived from list prices. There is no material change in the estimated coefficients on MIPS and memory size. Further, we continue to find evidence of multiple price regimes. The null hypothesis that the coefficients on BEST and $\Sigma(\text{BEST}*t^j)$ are jointly zero is rejected at any reasonable significance level in columns 1 and 2 and at about the 10 percent level in column 3. Overall, the results in table 1.3 suggest that the finding of disequilibrium is not generated by the use of list prices.

1.4.3   A Further Look at Disequilibrium

In tables 1.2 and 1.3, multiple price regimes appeared to characterize equation (6). I now take a closer look at the prices for models with best technology (BEST = 1) relative to those with nonbest technology (BEST = 0). To isolate the effect of disequilibrium, the comparison should be between best and nonbest models that are otherwise identical. Imposing this requirement, equation (6) implies that

$$P_b/P_{nb} = \exp[\ln(P_b) - \ln(P_{nb})] = \exp\left(\alpha_2 + \sum_{j=1}^{5}\pi_j t^j\right),$$

where b and nb denote, respectively, best-technology models and nonbest models. Values of P_b/P_{nb} different than unity provide evidence of disequilibrium. This ratio will vary over time, and table 1.4 presents the average value of the ratios computed during each quarter of the period 1973:1–1981:4.[8]

The price ratio shown in the first row of column 1 was generated by the list-price regression without any age variables. That regression is essentially the one run by Dulberger to discern disequilibrium in her sample of mainframe processors. Consistent with her results, I find that models incorporating best technology have list prices 7.7 percent (1 − 0.923) below those for otherwise identical models with nonbest technology. Column 1 also shows that using secondhand market prices in place of IBM list prices does not materially change this result, as best-technology models sell for about 11 percent less than nonbest models. As shown in column 2, these results are largely unaffected by the inclusion of model age in the set of regressors. Best-technology models still appear to be at least 5 percent cheaper than nonbest models.[9] However, the results change markedly when the regression includes age terms based on technology class, as shown in column 3. The average ratio computed with list prices jumps to 1.167, indicating that best-technology models carry a sizable price *premium* over nonbest models. When secondhand market prices are used in the regression, the ratio is about unity.

The results in column 3 are at odds with Dulberger's characterization of disequilibrium and need to be examined more closely. As noted above, setting

8. Even though my full sample covers 1970–86, I computed the average price ratio only for 1973–81. The subsample of 145 valid list prices had no observations for nonbest models outside 1973–81, and I did not want to extrapolate the results out of sample.

9. Although table 1.4 does not present standard errors for the price ratios, it is unlikely that the ratios displayed in cols. 1 and 2 actually equal one. For these ratios to equal one at all times, α_2 and π_j ($j = 1, \ldots, 5$) must be jointly zero. However, the F-tests reported in tables 1.2 and 1.3 rejected this hypothesis at any reasonable confidence level for the sets of α_2 and π_j coefficients used to compute the ratios in the first two columns of table 1.4.

Table 1.4   **Price of Models with Best Technology Relative to Models with Nonbest Technology (average, 1973:1–1981:4)**

	Age Variable in Regression		
Price Measure	None (1)	Model (2)	Tech. Class (3)
IBM list	0.923	0.946	1.167
Secondhand market	0.889	0.903	1.020

Note: These ratios are based on the regressions reported in tables 1.2 and 1.3

$P_b/P_{nb} = \exp(\alpha_2 + \Sigma \pi_j t^j)$ forces all regressors apart from BEST to be equal across best and nonbest models. In column 3, that means we have forced the age of the technology class to be the same across these two groups. This constraint makes little sense in that, by definition, the best-technology models are those with new technology while the nonbest models are those with old technology. That is, the value of BEST and the age of the technology class jointly distinguish best-technology models from nonbest models. This reasoning suggests that the comparison in column 3 should allow for differences in both BEST and the age of the technology class. (Note that cols. 1 and 2 implicitly allow the age of the technology class to differ across best and nonbest models because that variable is excluded from the set of regressors.) With this broader approach,

$$P_b/P_{nb} = \exp\left[\alpha_2 + \sum_{j=1}^{5} \pi_j t^j + \sum_{j=1}^{5} \delta_j(\tau_b^j - \tau_{nb}^j)\right].$$

To calculate this adjusted measure of the price ratio, I used the estimates of δ_j from the regressions reported in the third column of tables 1.2 and 1.3. I also set τ_b and τ_{nb} to the average age of the technology class for best and nonbest models, respectively. The resulting value of P_b/P_{nb} is 0.852 when using IBM list prices and 0.745 when using secondhand market prices. Now, the results based on regressions that include the age of the technology class are qualitatively similar to the others in table 1.4. Best-technology models sell at a discount relative to nonbest models, supporting Dulberger's result. This discount does not appear to be an artifact of using IBM list prices. If anything, substituting prices in the secondhand market for IBM list prices slightly increases the amount of discount. Both sets of prices suggest that existing models of IBM mainframes are not repriced down immediately at the introduction of models embodying superior technology.[10]

10. Berndt and Griliches (1990) offer several possible explanations for the relatively high prices of older models. First, users may be willing to pay a premium for older models because of the large base of existing software and because they understand how to use these models; conversely, the prices of new models may be held down by uncertainty about their performance and by the limited amount of available software. Second, computer manufacturers may set the prices of new

1.4.4   Constant-Quality Price Change

Table 1.5 presents the rates of constant-quality price change implied by the regressions reported in tables 1.2 and 1.3. The main issue that I examine is whether the rate of price decline based on IBM list prices is different than that based on prices in the secondhand market for the same models. Each entry in table 1.5 represents the average annual rate of constant-quality price change over either 1973–81 or 1973–86, calculated as

$$(9) \qquad \{[P(t_1)/P(t_0)]^{1/(t_1 - t_0)} - 1\} * 100,$$

where $t_0 = 1973$ and $t_1 = 1981$ or 1986.[11] These estimates of price change begin in 1973 because the subsample of valid list prices has no observations before that year. For models with nonbest technology, the price observations end in 1981, dictating the period 1973–81 shown in the table. For best-technology models, observations are available through 1986, and the table presents the average rate of constant-quality price change over both 1973–81 and 1973–86; the estimates for the latter period are shown in parentheses.

Virtually all the estimates in the table show constant-quality prices declining at average annual rates of around 20 percent. In particular, substituting secondhand market prices for IBM list prices has—with one exception—only a small effect on the estimated rate of price decline. The outlier in the table is the 8 percent decline shown at the bottom of column 3. This entry is heavily influenced by a single year, 1981, when prices are estimated to have more than doubled. There are few sample observations for nonbest models in that year. Excluding 1981, the average rate of price decline for this entry becomes 23.5 percent, similar to the other estimates in the table. Overall, the close match between the results based on list prices and those based on secondhand market prices suggests that the use of list prices in recent studies has not given a misleading impression of constant-quality price change for mainframe computers.

To complete this section, table 1.6 compares the constant-quality price

---

models relatively low to encourage purchases of an unfamiliar technology—i.e., to use low prices as a form of advertising. Third, the price premium for older models may simply reflect the higher quality of unobserved characteristics of models that have survived in the marketplace. The first two hypotheses imply a temporary premium for nonbest models, while the third hypothesis implies a long-term premium. Dulberger's finding that the premium for nonbest models was temporary argues against unobserved characteristics as the source of multiple prices for mainframe processors.

11. To see how the price ratio $P(t_1)/P(t_0)$ is calculated, note that eq. (6) can be written as

$$\ln P(t) = A + \sum_{j=1}^{5} (\gamma_j + \pi_j \text{BEST}) t^j,$$

where A represents all terms in the equation that are not explicit functions of time. Thus,

$$P(t_1)/P(t_0) = \exp[\ln P(t_1) - \ln P(t_0)] = \exp\left[\sum_{j=1}^{5} (\gamma_j + \pi_j \text{BEST}) (t_1^j - t_0^j)\right].$$

Table 1.5   **Average Annual Rate of Constant-Quality Price Change, 1973–81**

	Age Variable in Regression		
	None (1)	Model (2)	Tech. Class (3)
Best-technology models:			
IBM list price	− 19.9	− 19.7	− 23.9
	(− 20.2)	(− 19.8)	(− 19.9)
Secondhand market price	− 22.0	− 21.8	− 23.7
	(− 22.2)	(− 22.0)	(− 22.0)
Nonbest models:			
IBM list price	− 18.6	− 18.8	− 22.1
Secondhand market price	− 22.0	− 21.8	− 8.0

Note: These ratios are based on the regressions reported in tables 1.2 and 1.3. Figures in parentheses refer to 1973–86.

Table 1.6   **Alternative Measures of Constant-Quality Price Change Based on List Prices (percentage change in average price from previous year to year shown)**

	Oliner		Dulberger (3)	Cartwright (4)	Gordon (5)
Year	Best Tech. (1)	Nonbest Tech. (2)			
1973	NA	NA	5.9	21.3	NA
1974	27.2	− 2.9	− 22.3	11.5	NA
1975	0.1	− 0.6	− 2.7	− 30.1	NA
1976	− 17.1	− 5.5	− 1.9	− 8.8	NA
1977	− 27.3	− 14.4	− 35.8	− 31.6	NA
1978	− 32.4	− 23.8	− 47.5	− 28.3	− 12.1
1979	− 33.6	− 31.0	− 7.4	− 35.7	− 21.4
1980	− 31.8	− 33.7	− 27.0	− 12.5	− 19.6
1981	− 27.6	− 29.3	− 36.0	− 19.3	− 29.1
1982	− 22.1	NA	− 11.7	− 15.1	− 21.0
1983	− 17.0	NA	− 9.4	− 16.0	− 9.1
1984	− 14.9	NA	− 15.0	NA	− 28.6
1985	− 18.7	NA	NA	NA	NA
1986	− 30.3	NA	NA	NA	NA
Averages:					
1973–83	− 19.8	NA	− 21.7	− 19.6	NA
1973–81	− 19.9	− 18.6	− 24.3	− 20.6	NA
1977–84	− 26.0	NA	− 23.4	NA	− 20.4

Sources: Columns 1 and 2: From regression estimates reported in table 1.2, col. 1 above. Column 3: Dulberger (1989, table 2.6, column labeled "Regression" index, p. 58). Column 4: Cartwright, from Triplett (1989, table 4.9, col. 3, p. 186). Column 5: Gordon (1989, table 3.7, col. 6, pp. 104–5).

Note: "NA" indicates not available.

indexes computed in this paper with those calculated by Dulberger (1989), Gordon (1989), and Cartwright (whose results, although unpublished, are cited in Triplett 1989, table 4.9). All the indexes in table 1.6 are similar in that they (1) are based on list prices for IBM mainframes or other "plug-compatible" makes and (2) are derived from the coefficients on time variables in hedonic regressions that omit measures of age. Moreover, in all cases, I calculated the rates of price change from equation (9). Despite these common features, the alternative indexes can differ because of variations in data sources, in the composition of the sample, and in the sample period used for estimation.

The bottom part of the table presents the average annual rate of price change for each index over several time periods. On the whole, the estimates are remarkably similar across columns. All the studies find that price declines averaged between 18.5 and 26 percent per year for the periods indicated. Moreover, as shown by the individual year entries in the table, all the indexes available back to the early 1970s indicate that the most rapid price declines were concentrated during the late 1970s and early 1980s. Even with the differences for particular years, the various studies all convey the same basic impression of constant-quality price changes for mainframe computers.

1.5 Depreciation and Retirement Patterns

This section shifts the focus away from price change over time to price change associated with age. As a mainframe model ages, its price will tend to fall because obsolescence draws ever closer. In addition, with advancing age, an increasing fraction of the installed units of that model will have been removed from service. Thus, to measure depreciation for a cohort of mainframes, one needs information on the rate of depreciation for units that remain in service and on the rate of retirement. Implicitly, the units no longer in service carry a zero price, and this zero price needs to be averaged with the prices observed in the secondhand market to obtain an uncensored estimate of depreciation (for further discussion, see Hulten and Wykoff 1981a). In equation form, the effect of age on price, corrected for censoring, can be written

$$\bar{P}(\tau) = [1 - F(\tau)] * P(\tau) + F(\tau) * 0 = [1 - F(\tau)] * P(\tau) = S(\tau) * P(\tau),$$

where $P(\tau)$ is the price observed in the secondhand market at age τ, $F(\tau)$ is the probability that a given unit will have been retired by age τ, and $S(\tau) \equiv 1 - F(\tau)$ is the probability of survival to age τ. The correction for censoring scales the observed price by the survival probability for a unit at that age. Both $P(\tau)$ and $\bar{P}(\tau)$ can be regarded as having been normalized to unity at age 0; thus, these series represent the percentage of initial value remaining at age τ.[12]

---

12. To express $\bar{P}(\tau)$ as $S(\tau) * P(\tau)$, I have assumed that units removed from service have a market price of zero. This assumption will be violated if the assets retired by U.S. companies are

The first part of this section estimates $F(\tau)$ for IBM mainframe computers, the second part estimates $P(\tau)$, and the third part brings the two pieces together to estimate $\tilde{P}(\tau)$.

1.5.1 Estimates of the Retirement Distribution

I estimated the retirement distribution for mainframe computers using data on the installed stocks of various IBM models compiled by the International Data Corporation (IDC). My data from the IDC run from the end of 1970 to the end of 1986. For several IBM 360 models, I extended the series back to 1965 on the basis of IDC data shown in Phister (1974).[13] Retirement distributions were calculated for fourteen IBM mainframe models: models 20, 30, 40, and 65 in the 360 family; models 135, 138, 145, 148, 155, and 165 in the 370 family; and models 3031, 3032, 3033N, and 3033S in the 30XX family.[14]

The IDC data provide a time series of installed stocks for each model but no information on shipments from IBM or on retirements. My method for inferring the pattern of retirements can be illustrated with the following example:

	1975	1976	1977	1978	1979	1980	1981	1982	1983
Installed stock	0	100	400	500	450	400	250	100	0
Shipments (inferred)	0	100	300	100	0	0	0	0	0
Retirements (inferred)	0	0	0	0	50	50	150	150	100

In this example, the installed stock rises through 1978 and then declines through 1983. I assumed that shipments ceased in 1978, the peak year for the installed stock, and that retirements began the following year, when the stock began to decline. Starting in 1979, I take the change in the stock from the previous year to be the estimate of retirements. This method implies that 50 units were retired in 1979 and 1980, 150 units in 1981 and 1982, and 100

---

not scrapped but rather sold to U.S. consumers or for use abroad. To refine $\tilde{P}(\tau)$, it would be useful to have information on the value and destination of computing equipment exiting the U.S. business sector.

13. Over the years 1970–74, the IDC data on installed stocks shown in Phister (1974, 333) often differed from the IDC data I obtained in 1987, reflecting revisions to the data in the intervening years. To splice together the two IDC series for a given model, I level-adjusted the series in Phister for 1965–70 by the ratio of the 1970 value of my IDC series to the 1970 value of the Phister series.

14. The models in the 360 and 370 families were almost fully retired by the end of my IDC data in 1986; only 4 percent of the 360 units and 5 percent of the 370 units remained in service in that year. However, the retirement of the four 30XX models was less complete by 1986, with 30 percent of these units still in service. To fill in the tail of the 30XX distribution, I assumed that one-third of the remaining units of each model were retired in each year after 1986. These assumed retirements continued until only 5 percent of the total installed units for each model remained in the stock.

units in 1983. It seemed reasonable to assume that retirements do not begin until IBM stops shipping a model; to assume otherwise would mean that firms are scrapping units that could be sold in the secondhand market for a substantial fraction of IBM's list price.

The next task was to determine the age of the units retired in any year. As discussed earlier, age can be defined either for specific models or for an entire technology class. A retirement distribution can be constructed for each of these definitions of age. The distribution based on model age relates retirements to the time elapsed since the first unit of a model was shipped. In contrast, the distribution based on the age of a model's technology class relates retirements to the first shipment of any model from that technology class, thus providing information on the economic life of an embodied technology, rather than that of a model.

These two distributions correspond to the concepts of age used so far in the paper. However, neither distribution is appropriate for constructing capital stocks from data on investment outlays, as in the perpetual inventory method. In that method, the units purchased in a given year represent the inflow to the stock, and one must determine how long *these particular units* remain in service. Accordingly, I used the IDC data to construct a distribution of retirements based on the age of individual units, employing two alternative assumptions to identify their date of installation.[15]

One assumption is that the oldest units are the first retired, the analogue to first-in first-out (FIFO) accounting for inventories. This assumption would be appropriate if all firms tended to keep a computer for a fixed number of years, regardless of when the computer was acquired. Under this FIFO retirement pattern, all fifty units retired in 1979 in the above example are assumed to have been produced in 1976 and are thus three years old at retirement. The alternative assumption is that all vintages are represented proportionately among the units retired in each year. Returning again to the example, the fifty units retired in 1979 represent 10 percent of the peak stock. Under this alternative assumption, 10 percent of the units shipped in 1976, 1977, and 1978 are assumed to be retired in 1979, thus implying a mixture of one-, two-, and three-year-old units leaving the stock. This second assumption would be appropriate if firms tended to retire their computers whenever improved models become available, regardless of the number of years of service already obtained from the existing units.

Because it is not obvious which of these assumptions is more realistic a

---

15. As discussed earlier, the age of individual units has no bearing on prices in the secondhand market; model 360/30 units shipped by IBM in different years all sell at the same price at a given date. However, even if all firms scrapped their 360/30s at the same date (when their market price fell below scrap value), there would be a nondegenerate distribution of (unit) ages at retirement because the units were shipped by IBM at different times. In practice, the 360/30s were not all retired simultaneously, and a somewhat different—but again nondegenerate—distribution of unit ages at retirement would result.

priori, I calculated the retirement distribution for each of the fourteen models in both ways. I then produced an aggregate distribution for the 360 models, the 370 models, the 30XX models, and all fourteen models under both the FIFO method and the proportional method. These aggregates were constructed as a weighted average of the retirement distribution for each model in the aggregate, with the weights based on total shipments of each model in constant dollars.[16]

The results of this exercise are displayed in figures 1.1–1.4. The bars in figures 1.1 and 1.2 show the retirement distribution for the weighted aggregate of all fourteen models, with figure 1.1 displaying the FIFO retirement pattern and figure 1.2 the proportional retirement pattern. Both versions of the aggregate distribution have a mean retirement age of about 6.5 years and are strongly asymmetric, with a long right-hand tail. The proportional version in figure 1.2 is less tightly concentrated around the mean than the FIFO version; this spreading occurs because units of every vintage are assumed to be retired in each year.

The asymmetry that characterizes both versions of the distribution may have a simple economic interpretation. For mainframe computers, retirement occurs primarily because the model becomes obsolete, not because of wear and tear or accidental damage. As a result, few units will be retired until a superior model becomes available. When an improved model is introduced, firms that want cutting-edge technology will retire their existing units, producing the burst of retirements evident in figure 1.1 at five to six years of age. At the same time, other firms whose needs continue to be well served by older technology will retain their existing models until the cost advantage of replacement becomes apparent. These firms are responsible for the long tail in the retirement distributions. Thus, an asymmetric retirement pattern may be the rule for goods such as mainframe computers for which obsolescence rather than decay causes retirement.

For the purpose of comparison, the solid line in figures 1.1 and 1.2 shows the "Winfrey S-3" retirement distribution used by BEA for calculating stocks of office and computing equipment, while the dashed line represents the

---

16. My method of weighting involved the following steps. First, I inferred the number of units shipped annually for each model using the IDC data on installed stocks. Next, I determined the nominal value of these shipments by multiplying the units shipped by a measure of average price. For the models in the 370 and 30XX families, this price measure was the average of IBM's list price for units with maximum memory size and units with minimum memory size, as shown in Dulberger's (1989) data base. For the 360 models, I obtained the same information from Phister (1974, 342–47). Phister shows only one set of IBM prices for each model, which pertains to a period about two years after the first installation. I applied this single set of prices to each year of shipments. Finally, I converted the nominal shipments in each year to constant dollars by deflating with BEA's implicit price deflator for investment in office and computing equipment. The result was a vector of annual constant-dollar shipments for each model, which I summed to get total shipments for the model. The weight applied to each model's retirement distribution was this constant-dollar estimate of total shipments divided by the constant-dollar total summed across all models in the aggregate.

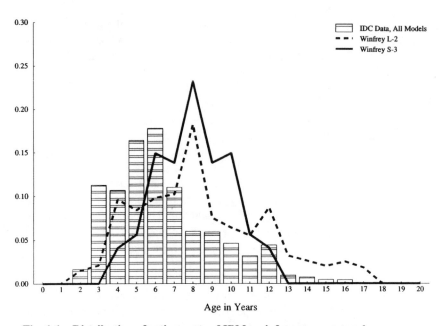

Fig. 1.1   Distribution of retirements of IBM mainframe computers by age based on FIFO retirement pattern

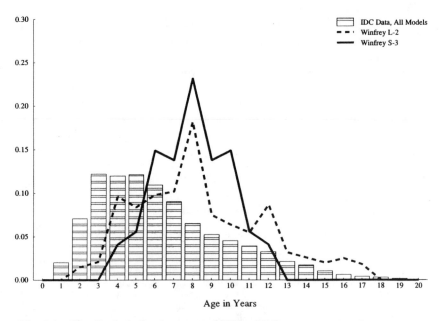

Fig. 1.2   Distribution of retirements of IBM mainframe computers by age based on proportional retirement pattern

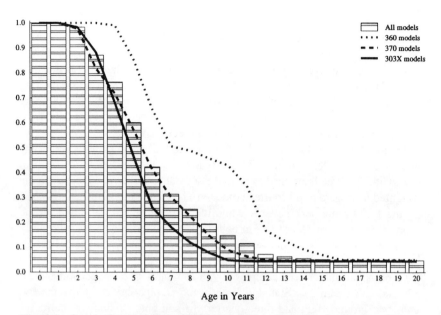

Fig. 1.3 **Survival probability of IBM mainframe computers by age based on FIFO retirement pattern**

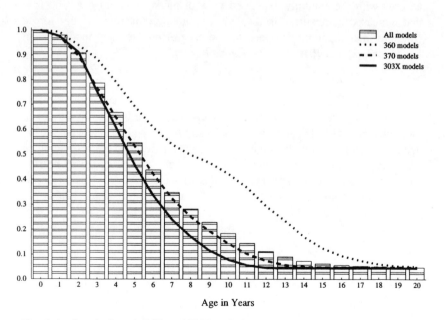

Fig. 1.4 **Survival probability of IBM mainframe computers by age based on proportional retirement pattern**

"Winfrey L-2" distribution, an asymmetric retirement distribution applied by BEA to consumer durable goods. Both Winfrey distributions are plotted with an average retirement age of eight years.[17] The symmetric Winfrey S-3 is clearly a poor approximation to either distribution calculated with the IDC data. The Winfrey L-2 provides a somewhat better fit by virtue of its long right-hand tail. Moreover, if asymmetry is a general trait of the retirement distributions of "high-technology" equipment, as suggested above, the Winfrey L-2 would dominate the S-3 for a broad set of assets.

Figures 1.3 and 1.4 explore the differences in retirement patterns across the 360, 370, and 30XX families. These figures plot the probability of survival $S(\tau)$, with the three lines pertaining to the separate families and the bars to the weighted aggregate of all fourteen models. The results in figure 1.3 are based on the FIFO retirement pattern, while those in figure 1.4 are based on the proportional pattern. As shown in both figures, the models in the 360 family had longer service lives, on average, than the 370 and 30XX models. Indeed, after ten years of use, more than 40 percent of the 360 units are estimated to have remained in service, compared with estimates of 5–15 percent for the 370 and 30XX families. Stated differently, the average service life for the 360 units was around eight and three-quarter years in both versions of the retirement distribution, well above the six-year average for the 370s and the five-and-a-half-year average for the 30XXs. Accordingly, it appears that average service lives for IBM mainframes have become shorter over time. This finding accords with a commonly expressed view of market participants, who note that increased competition in the industry, among other factors, has forced computer manufacturers to speed up the pace of product introductions (see, e.g., the *Computer Price Guide Readers Report,* April 1979, 1).

1.5.2   Estimates of Depreciation

As discussed in section 1.1 above, the age of a mainframe computer model can affect its price through several channels. Referring back to equation (1), these channels include age-related changes in the embodied characteristics **z,** age-related jumps across hedonic surfaces, and any residual effect of aging on price. Typically, empirical studies of depreciation—including the pioneering work of Hulten and Wykoff (1981a, 1981b)—measure depreciation as the combination of all these effects. This summary measure, which I label *full* depreciation, is the total derivative

$$\frac{d \ln(P)}{d\tau}\bigg|_{t \text{ fixed}}.$$

---

17. Until recently, BEA had assumed an eight-year average lifetime for all cohorts of office and computing equipment. However, in the revision of the national income and product accounts released in December 1991, BEA shortened this mean life to seven years for all post-1977 cohorts while retaining the eight-year mean life for all earlier cohorts. This revision was due, in part, to evidence (discussed below) of a shift toward shorter service lives for mainframe computers.

A simple way to estimate this total derivative is to omit the characteristics **z** and the terms proxying for disequilibrium from the regression equation. By doing so, the coefficient on age picks up all age-related influences in price. I estimated such an equation by removing ln(MIPS), ln(Memory), and all terms in BEST from the set of regressors. Moreover, as a first step, I also imposed the restriction that depreciation be geometric, producing the following stripped-down version of equation (6):

$$(6')\qquad \ln P = \alpha_1 + \sum_{j=1}^{5} \gamma_j t^j + \delta * \tau + \rho * \text{NEW},$$

in which δ measures the geometric rate of depreciation.

Columns 1 and 4 of table 1.7 present the resulting OLS estimates of δ from the entire sample of 1,905 observations. As shown by the first entry in column 1, each additional *quarter* of model age is estimated to reduce price 8.7 percent. Thus, over a full year, an IBM mainframe model depreciates about 29.4 percent.[18] This rate is slightly faster than the 27.3 percent depreciation rate estimated by Hulten and Wykoff (1979) for Royal typewriters, which they applied to the entire class of office and computing equipment. The two figures, however, are not comparable because Hulten and Wykoff's estimate has been adjusted for retirement (i.e., it measures $\tilde{P}[\tau]$, not $P[\tau]$). If my depreciation estimate were adjusted for retirement, it would become more rapid, moving further away from Hulten and Wykoff's estimate.[19]

As shown in column 4, the full depreciation rate for a mainframe technology class is estimated to be 5.76 percent per quarter, about 20.6 percent for each year of age. This rate is considerably slower than that for individual models, implying that an embodied technology has a longer economic life than any single model in that technology class. IBM extends the economic life of a technology class by introducing new models from the class over the course of several years, with each model filling a particular market niche. As an example of this practice, IBM first shipped mainframes with 64KB memory chips in early 1979 (the model 4331–1); four years later, IBM introduced the model 4341–12, also built around the 64KB chip.

The depreciation rates shown in columns 1 and 4 capture, as noted above, all age-related effects on prices. This total effect can be decomposed into the

---

18. The 29.4 percent estimate is derived as

$$100 * \{[P(\tau + 1)/P(\tau)]^4 - 1\} = 100 * \{[\exp(\delta)]^4 - 1\}.$$

19. To see that adjusting $P(\tau)$ for retirement raises the rate of depreciation, recall that $\tilde{P}(\tau) = P(\tau)S(\tau)$. Then,

$$d[\ln \tilde{P}(\tau)]/d\tau = d[\ln P(\tau)]/d\tau + d[\ln S(\tau)]/d\tau,$$

so that the depreciation rate adjusted for retirement equals the unadjusted rate plus the percentage change in the probability of survival. Because the probability of survival falls with age, this percentage change is negative, which makes the adjusted depreciation rate more negative than the unadjusted rate.

Table 1.7   **OLS Estimates of Geometric Depreciation (*t*-statistics in parentheses)**

	Age of Model			Age of Technology Class		
	Full	Partial	Residual	Full	Partial	Residual
Regressor	(1)	(2)	(3)	(4)	(5)	(6)
τ	−.0870	−.0439	−.0433	−.0576	−.0397	−.0395
	(37.2)	(36.6)	(32.9)	(22.3)	(39.7)	(34.9)
Inclusion of:						
ln(MIPS)	No	Yes	Yes	No	Yes	Yes
ln(Memory)	No	Yes	Yes	No	Yes	Yes
BEST	No	No	Yes	No	No	Yes
BEST*Time	No	No	Yes	No	No	Yes
R^2	.441	.882	.892	.234	.890	.897

Note: Each regression used the full sample of 1,905 observations. The dependent variable was the secondhand market price from the *Computer Price Guide*. Each regression included a constant, the NEW dummy variable, and a fifth-order polynomial in Time, in addition to the terms shown in each column. When included, BEST*Time entered as a fifth-order polynomial.

separate parts identified in equation (2). The remaining columns of table 1.7 present this decomposition for the geometric pattern of depreciation. Columns 2 and 5 add terms in ln(MIPS) and ln(Memory) to equation (6'), thus controlling for the effects of the characteristics **z** on depreciation. This partial depreciation rate is about 4.4 percent per quarter in column 2 and 4.0 percent per quarter in column 5, roughly 16 percent per year of aging. Thus, even controlling for differences in MIPS and memory size, IBM mainframe models and technology classes depreciate at a fairly rapid pace, reflecting the influence of all factors other than **z** that are correlated with age. Columns 3 and 6 add BEST and the fifth-order polynomial in BEST*Time to the set of regressors, which then controls for disequilibrium as well as the characteristics **z**. The estimates of δ in these two columns show the residual effect of aging on price, $\partial \ln(P)/\partial \tau$. The similarity of the depreciation estimates in columns 2 and 3 and in columns 5 and 6 indicates that disequilibrium has little effect on the estimated rate of geometric depreciation.

Thus far, the pattern of depreciation has been forced to be geometric. Table 1.8 reports depreciation estimates that remove this restriction by replacing the δ*τ term in equation (6') with

$$\sum_{j=1}^{5} \delta_j \tau^j + \Theta * \text{Time} * \tau.$$

The latter term allows the rate of depreciation to change over time, a generalization suggested by the finding that service lives for IBM mainframe models appear to have become shorter since the demise of the 360 family.

The structure of table 1.8 is the same as that of table 1.7, the only difference

Table 1.8   **OLS Estimates of General Depreciation (*t*-statistics in parentheses)**

Regressor	Age of Model			Age of Technology Class		
	Full (1)	Partial (2)	Residual (3)	Full (4)	Partial (5)	Residual (6)
τ	0.0288	0.0778	0.1033	−0.3441	−0.0837	−0.1680
	(.4)	(2.3)	(2.9)	(3.3)	(2.4)	(4.2)
τ^2	0.0015	−0.0013	−0.0041	0.0383	0.0228	0.0293
	(.2)	(.4)	(1.3)	(4.1)	(7.6)	(8.5)
τ^3	−1.1E-4	3.8E-5	1.6E-4	−0.0018	−0.0012	−0.0014
	(.4)	(.3)	(1.3)	(5.0)	(10.7)	(11.2)
τ^4	1.1E-6	−1.6E-6	−4.0E-6	3.3E-5	2.4E-5	2.6E-5
	(.2)	(.8)	(1.9)	(5.5)	(12.3)	(12.5)
τ^5	4.3E-9	2.1E-8	3.7E-8	−2.1E-7	−1.5E-7	−1.7E-7
	(.1)	(1.5)	(2.7)	(5.7)	(13.0)	(13.0)
Time*τ	−0.0021	−0.0022	−0.0020	2.3E-4	−0.0012	−0.0012
	(7.9)	(19.3)	(16.8)	(1.0)	(16.1)	(11.9)
Inclusion of:						
ln(MIPS)	No	Yes	Yes	No	Yes	Yes
ln(Memory)	No	Yes	Yes	No	Yes	Yes
BEST	No	No	Yes	No	No	Yes
BEST*Time	No	No	Yes	No	No	Yes
R^2	0.462	0.903	0.909	0.253	0.922	0.923
F-statistic for constant geometric depreciation	14.8	84.3	70.7	9.7	157.3	131.8

Note: Each regression used the full sample of 1,905 observations. The dependent variable was the second-hand market price from the *Computer Price Guide*. Each regression included a constant, the NEW dummy variable, and a fifth-order polynomial in Time, in addition to the terms shown in each column. When included, BEST*Time entered as a fifth-order polynomial.

being the expanded set of age coefficients reported for each regression. The results in table 1.8 indicate that depreciation for IBM mainframes has not occurred at a constant geometric rate. The *F*-statistic for the null hypothesis of constant geometric depreciation ($\delta_2 = \delta_3 = \delta_4 = \delta_5 = \Theta = 0$), shown at the bottom of the table, is significant in every column at the 1 percent level. For the regressions that measure depreciation based on model age, the chief violation of the null hypothesis is the significance of Θ, the coefficient on Time*τ. Thus, although the depreciation pattern may be close to geometric at any given time, the best-fitting geometric rate has become more rapid over time. For the regressions that measure depreciation of a technology class, the geometric form is not appropriate at any point in time, as indicated by the uniformly significant coefficients on the higher-order terms in τ. In addition, the estimated coefficient on Time*τ in columns 5 and 6 points to a speedup in the depreciation rate over time.

Figures 1.5 and 1.6 plot the depreciation patterns implied by the estimates in table 1.8; figure 1.5 portrays the patterns based on model age and figure 1.6 those based on the age of the technology class. Because these depreciation schedules vary over time, the figures show the schedules at the mean pricing date in the sample, 1979:2. In both figures, the solid line represents the full measure of depreciation, computed from the regressions that exclude MIPS, memory size, and the terms in BEST. The dotted line depicts the partial measure, which controls for the effects of MIPS and memory size on depreciation but not for the effect of disequilibrium. The dashed line shows the residual measure, which controls for the effects of MIPS, memory size, and disequilibrium. For comparison, the bars in each figure represent the geometric pattern of full depreciation estimated in table 1.7.

In both figures, the schedule of full depreciation shows a considerably faster loss of value than the partial and residual measures, as would be expected. Further, as seen in figure 1.5, increases in model age imply essentially monotonic declines in value, although the depreciation schedules are not sufficiently convex to be geometric. The depreciation schedules shown in figure 1.6, however, do not even decline monotonically, displaying a local maximum at age 4. This pattern can be explained as follows. When age is defined by technology class, the models introduced late in a product cycle have an age at inception of three or four years. Because these models are differentiated from their predecessors within the technology class and may be in short supply, they tend to sell initially at relatively high prices, producing the sharp deviation from the geometric form shown in figure 1.6. This premium, however, quickly erodes, as these models with aging technology are soon forced to compete with models that embody the next generation of technology.

As revealed by figures 1.5 and 1.6, the depreciation schedules based on model age are quite different from those based on the age of the technology class. Each set of schedules is useful in answering a particular question. The depreciation patterns in figure 1.6 provide information on age-related losses of value for each new wave of semiconductor technology, taking account of IBM's efforts to extract full value from the technology by embedding it in a large number of different models. In contrast, the depreciation patterns in figure 1.5 summarize the age-related loss of value for a single model from its date of introduction.

For the purpose of constructing stocks of computing equipment from data on investment flows, these latter estimates of depreciation are the more appropriate ones. In particular, IBM can sustain—and, for a while, increase—the value of a technology class by introducing differentiated models, even though the value of each model falls steadily with age. The rise in value for a technology class will not characterize the depreciation pattern for an investment cohort, which moves ever closer to obsolescence with each year of age. For this reason, I focus on the depreciation estimates based on model age for the rest of the paper.

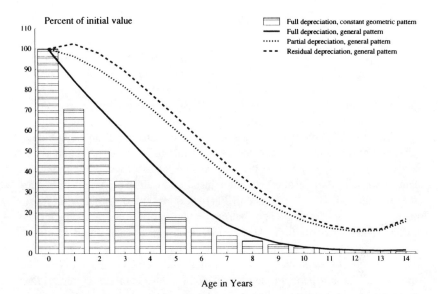

Fig. 1.5   Depreciation of IBM mainframe computers based on model age

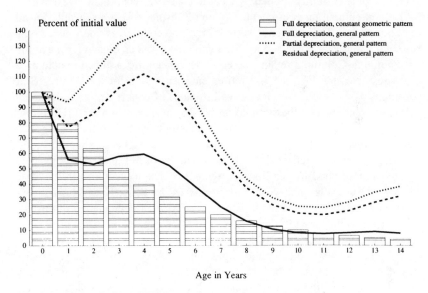

Fig. 1.6   Depreciation of IBM mainframe computers based on age of technology class

1.5.3   The Combined Effect of Depreciation and Retirement

Given an estimated retirement distribution from the IDC data and an estimated depreciation schedule from the *Guide* data, one can calculate depreciation for an entire cohort of IBM mainframes, $\bar{P}(\tau)$. As outlined above, $\bar{P}(\tau) = S(\tau)P(\tau)$, the proportion of units still in service at age τ multiplied by the percentage of initial value retained by these units at that age.

BEA also calculates an estimate of $\bar{P}(\tau)$, although it applies to the broad aggregate of office and computing equipment, not just mainframe computers. BEA assumes that depreciation occurs in a straight-line pattern over an asset's service life. Thus, given a ten-year service life, an asset would retain 90 percent of its initial value one year after installation and 80 percent two years after installation. BEA's estimate of $\bar{P}(\tau)$ takes account of the fact that retirements occur, not at a single age, but over a number of years, as characterized by the Winfrey distribution. As a result, BEA breaks each dollar of investment into the share with a one-year life, the share with a two-year life, and so on. Each cohort is depreciated by the straight-line method over its service life, and the results are then summed across cohorts to obtain the aggregate $\bar{P}(\tau)$ for that asset.

Table 1.9 presents six alternative estimates of $\bar{P}(\tau)$. Column 1 shows the $\bar{P}(\tau)$ schedule currently applied by BEA to post-1977 cohorts of investment in office and computing equipment. Column 2 displays BEA's schedule for all earlier cohorts. The difference between the two columns is due solely to the use of a seven-year mean service life in column 1 and an eight-year mean life in column 2. Column 3 retains the eight-year mean life assumed in column 2 but substitutes the Winfrey L-2 retirement distribution for the Winfrey S-3. Columns 4–6 present my alternative estimates of cohort depreciation. Each of these columns uses the survival probability $S(\tau)$ based on the FIFO retirement pattern for the aggregate of all models (shown by the bars in fig. 1.3 above). However, the depreciation schedule $P(\tau)$ differs across the three columns; columns 4–6 reflect, in turn, the schedules of full, partial, and residual depreciation plotted by the lines in figure 1.5. All six columns in the table employ the so-called half-year convention used by BEA. Under this convention, new goods are assumed to suffer a half year of depreciation during the year in which they are installed. This convention explains why the age 0 entry in each column differs from 100.

All three BEA schedules imply rapid cohort depreciation. Three years after installation, roughly half the cohort's initial value has been lost; at age 5, only 20–30 percent of initial value remains. Naturally, the loss of value is most rapid in column 1, owing to the use of a shorter mean service life. Given a common mean life, the Winfrey S-3 and L-2 distributions (cols. 2 and 3) produce nearly identical results between ages 0 and 5. Because almost three-quarters of initial value has been depreciated by age 5, the two distributions produce similar estimates of net capital stocks, as seen in the next section. My alternative estimates of cohort depreciation span a wider range. The schedule

Table 1.9   **Cohort Depreciation Schedules (percentage of initial value of investment remaining at each age)**

| | BEA | | | Oliner, by Measure of Depreciation | | |
| | Winfrey S-3 | | Winfrey L-2 | | | |
Age in Years	7-Yr. Life (1)	8-Yr. Life (2)	8-Yr. Life (3)	Full (4)	Partial (5)	Residual (6)
0	92.4	93.3	92.8	91.4	99.2	104.3
1	77.2	79.9	78.4	77.5	95.1	105.5
2	62.0	66.6	64.3	64.1	86.9	98.4
3	46.9	53.2	51.0	46.1	69.5	79.0
4	32.8	40.3	39.2	31.1	53.2	60.9
5	20.5	28.5	29.5	17.5	35.1	40.6
6	11.1	18.6	21.4	8.3	20.0	23.4
7	5.0	10.8	14.9	3.9	11.5	13.6
8	1.7	5.5	10.2	1.9	7.0	8.4
9	0.4	2.4	7.1	0.9	3.9	4.7
10	0.1	0.8	4.8	0.4	2.3	2.7
11	0.0	0.2	3.0	0.2	1.4	1.6
12	0.0	0.0	1.8	0.1	0.8	0.9
13	0.0	0.0	1.1	0.1	0.7	0.8
14	0.0	0.0	0.6	0.1	0.9	1.0
15	0.0	0.0	0.2	0.0	0.0	0.0

Note: Columns 1–3 are from printouts provided by John Musgrave of BEA. Columns 4–6 are constructed from the FIFO retirement distribution aggregated over all models and the depreciation schedules shown by the solid, dotted, and dashed lines in fig. 1.5.

in column 4, based on full depreciation, virtually matches the BEA schedule in column 1. In contrast, the partial and residual measures of depreciation in columns 5 and 6 imply markedly slower losses of value than any of the BEA schedules.

On the basis of the different estimates of cohort depreciation in columns 4–6, one can argue that BEA depreciates investment in office and computing equipment at about the right rate or much too quickly. The next section resolves this ambiguity. There, I show that the estimate in column 5 is the most appropriate one for constructing net capital stocks from investment spending when both are expressed in constant dollars. This result suggests that BEA's constant-dollar net stock of office and computing equipment is constructed with a schedule of overly rapid depreciation.

1.6   Alternative Estimates of Capital Stock

Do my estimates of depreciation and retirement patterns imply substantial revisions to BEA's published stocks of office and computing equipment for the private nonresidential business sector? I consider this question first for

BEA's gross capital stock and then for its net capital stock. For an in-depth description of BEA's methodology, see U.S. Department of Commerce (1987).

1.6.1   Gross Capital Stock

BEA's gross capital stock represents the initial purchase value of all previous investment still in service. No adjustment is made for depreciation. In equation form, the gross capital stock can be written

$$(10) \qquad\qquad GS(t) = \sum_{\tau=0}^{T} I(t - \tau)S(\tau),$$

where $I(t - \tau)$ is investment spending at time $t - \tau$, and $S(\tau)$ is the proportion of this investment expected to survive τ years after installation. T is the maximum lifetime of the capital good, assumed to be constant across vintages. For a "one-hoss shay" asset—which provides a fixed level of service until retirement—the gross stock can be regarded as an indicator of that service flow. Thus, the gross stock is useful in analyses of output and productivity involving one-hoss shay assets, such as IBM computing equipment.[20]

To assess potential biases in BEA's gross stock of office and computing equipment, I calculated equation (10) with four alternative survival patterns $S(\tau)$, denoted $S_1(\tau), \ldots, S_4(\tau)$. $S_1(\tau)$ is the survival pattern used by BEA before the revisions introduced in December 1991; this prerevision $S(\tau)$ comes from the Winfrey S-3 retirement distribution with an eight-year mean service life. $S_2(\tau)$, the survival pattern currently used by BEA, is the same as $S_1(\tau)$ for pre-1978 cohorts; however, for later cohorts, $S_2(\tau)$ uses the shorter seven-year mean life. $S_3(\tau)$ substitutes the Winfrey L-2 retirement distribution for the S-3 but retains BEA's current assumptions regarding mean service lives. Finally, $S_4(\tau)$ incorporates my estimates of the FIFO survival patterns for the IBM 360, 370, and 30XX families, which were shown in figure 1.3 above.[21] Specifically, $S_4(\tau)$ varies across investment cohorts as follows:

$$S_4(\tau) = \begin{cases} 360 \text{ survival pattern for pre-1970 cohorts;} \\ 370 \text{ survival pattern for 1970–79 cohorts;} \\ 30XX \text{ survival pattern for post-1979 cohorts.} \end{cases}$$

By applying the survival functions $S_1(\tau), \ldots, S_4(\tau)$ to BEA's constant-dollar series on investment in office and computing equipment, I obtained the gross capital stocks denoted $GS_1(t), \ldots, GS_4(t)$.

Table 1.10 displays the BEA gross stocks $GS_1(t)$ through $GS_3(t)$, each di-

---

20. Note that the one-hoss shay assumption is a very strong one. In addition to requiring that the flow of output from the good remain constant with age, it requires that there be no increase in maintenance and repair costs to achieve that constant output flow.

21. The survival patterns based on the proportional retirement distributions yield results similar to those reported in table 1.10 below and are omitted for brevity.

Table 1.10   **Constant-Dollar Gross Stock of Office and Computing Equipment (ratio of alternative BEA Stocks to GS₄)**

	BEA Gross Stock in Numerator of Ratio		
Year	Prerevision (GS_1)	Current (GS_2)	Winfrey L-2 (GS_3)
1965	0.908	0.908	0.931
1970	0.882	0.882	0.923
1975	1.003	1.003	1.019
1980	1.130	1.130	1.115
1985	1.119	1.090	1.076
1990	1.214	1.149	1.127

Note: See the text for definitions of GS_1 through GS_4.

vided by $GS_4(t)$. A value of 1.0 indicates that the particular BEA gross stock equals the gross stock based on my estimate of survivals. As shown in the first column, BEA's prerevision gross stock trended up from 90.8 percent of GS_4 in 1965 to 121.4 percent in 1990. This upward trend reflects BEA's use, before the recent revision, of a constant service life for office and computing equipment. Until 1970, GS_1/GS_4 was less than one because the eight-year mean service life assumed by BEA was shorter than the mean life that I found for the 360 models. By 1975, the difference between GS_1 and GS_4 had disappeared, as many of the 360 models had been retired and replaced by shorter-lived 370 models. However, with the continued substitution of the 370 and 30XX models for 360 models, BEA's prerevision stock moved substantially above my estimate of the gross stock. Thus, by failing to capture the shift toward shorter service lives, BEA had overstated considerably the growth of the constant-dollar gross stock of office and computing equipment.

BEA attempted to correct this bias by introducing a one-year reduction in the mean service life of post-1977 investment cohorts. The second column of table 1.10 indicates that this change was only partly successful. Given the lag between investment and the beginning of retirements, BEA's revision did not affect its estimate of the gross stock until after 1980. As a result, BEA's estimate of the gross stock of office and computing equipment continues to grow too rapidly until that year. Still, BEA's revision does appear to have eliminated the excessive growth in the gross stock during the 1980s.

As a final point, note that the ratios shown in the second and third columns are quite similar. This similarity implies that BEA's estimate of the gross stock would not change much if the Winfrey L-2 retirement distribution were substituted for the S-3, given a fixed mean service life. Thus, BEA's use of a symmetric distribution when a skewed distribution may be more appropriate does not, by itself, introduce much bias into the gross stock. The more serious problem is that BEA likely has not yet built a sufficient downward trend into its assumed mean service life of office and computing equipment. This conclusion is bolstered by the preliminary results in Oliner (1992), which showed a substantial reduction over time in the average service lives of computer peripheral equipment, another important class of assets within the aggregate of office and computing equipment.

1.6.2   Net Capital Stock

BEA's net capital stock represents the value of all previous investment outlays after subtracting depreciation. In equation form, the net capital stock can be written as

$$(11) \qquad \mathrm{NS}(t) = \sum_{\tau=0}^{T} I(t - \tau) \, \tilde{P}(\tau),$$

where, as above, $\tilde{P}(\tau)$ is the proportion of the initial value of an investment cohort still remaining τ years after installation.

Table 1.9 above reported three measures of $\tilde{P}(\tau)$ based on model age, each incorporating a different measure of depreciation. Which is the appropriate one for use in equation (11)? I now show that, when constructing a constant-dollar net stock from BEA's constant-dollar investment series, $\tilde{P}(\tau)$ should not be based on the full measure of depreciation.

To explore this issue, assume that the market for computing equipment is always in equilibrium and that the market price can be written as

$$(12) \qquad P(t, \tau) = f(t)g[\mathbf{z}(t - \tau)]h(\tau),$$

where $f(t)$ represents the influence of time on price, holding age and characteristics fixed; $g[\mathbf{z}(t - \tau)]$ represents the influence of embodied characteristics on price; and $h(\tau)$ is the residual effect of age on price. Equation (12) restricts these three effects to be multiplicative. Now, the question at hand can be stated as follows: if the constant-dollar net stock is calculated as a weighted sum of past constant-dollar investment outlays (as in eq. [11]), how should the weights be constructed in terms of the functions on the right-hand side of equation (12)?

To begin, let $\mathrm{IU}(t, \tau)$ represent the number of units of age τ computing equipment still in service at time t. Then, in current dollars, the net stock can be written

$$(13) \qquad \mathrm{NSCURR}(t) = \sum_{\tau=0}^{T} \mathrm{IU}(t, \tau)P(t, \tau),$$

which is the number of units of each investment cohort still in service at time t multiplied by the period t price of each such unit, summed over cohorts. The constant-dollar counterpart to equation (13) simply deflates the current-dollar value to the prices of some base year. Denoting the deflator by $\mathrm{PD}(t)$, the constant-dollar net stock is

(14) $$\text{NS}(t) = \sum_{\tau=0}^{T} \text{IU}(t, \tau)P(t, \tau)/\text{PD}(t).$$

Now, $\text{IU}(t, \tau)$ can be written as $\phi(\tau)\text{IU}(t - \tau, 0)$, where $\text{IU}(t - \tau, 0)$ is the number of new units installed at time $t - \tau$, and $\phi(\tau)$ is the proportion of these units still in service at age τ. Further, $\text{IU}(t - \tau, 0)P(t - \tau, 0)$ equals $I(t - \tau)\text{PD}(t - \tau)$ because both represent current-dollar investment at time $t - \tau$. Thus

$$\text{IU}(t, \tau) = \phi(\tau)\text{IU}(t - \tau, 0) = \phi(\tau)I(t - \tau)\text{PD}(t - \tau)/P(t - \tau, 0).$$

Substituting this expression for $\text{IU}(t, \tau)$ into equation (14) yields

(15)
$$\text{NS}(t) = \sum_{\tau=0}^{T} I(t - \tau) *$$
$$\{\phi(\tau)[\text{PD}(t - \tau)/\text{PD}(t)][P(t, \tau)/P(t - \tau, 0)]\}.$$

The term in braces is the expression for $\bar{P}(\tau)$ that we are seeking.

To complete the derivation, we must relate this bracketed expression to the functions in equation (12). First, as constructed by BEA, the deflator for office and computing equipment is a constant-quality price measure; thus

$$\text{PD}(t - \tau)/\text{PD}(t) = f(t - \tau)/f(t).$$

Second, using equation (12),

$$P(t, \tau)/P(t - \tau, 0) = \{f(t)g[z(t - \tau)]h(\tau)\}/\{f(t - \tau)g[z(t - \tau)] h(0)\}$$
$$= [f(t)h(\tau)]/[f(t - \tau)h(0)].$$

Substituting these expressions for the price ratios into equation (15) and canceling terms yields

(16) $$\bar{P}(\tau) = \phi(\tau)[h(\tau)/h(0)]$$

as the weight on $I(t - \tau)$. This weight is simply the proportion of units surviving to age τ multiplied by the percentage of initial value remaining at age τ for these units. The crucial point is that $h(\tau)/h(0)$ represents the schedule of *partial* depreciation; it measures the effects of aging on price after controlling for the influence of z. As indicated at the outset, $\bar{P}(\tau)$ should not be based on an estimate of full depreciation, $P(t, \tau)/P(t, 0)$.

The intuition for the use of a partial depreciation measure is simple. The weight on $I(t - \tau)$ indicates that one constant dollar of vintage $t - \tau$ investment is worth $\phi(\tau)[h(\tau)/h(0)]$ constant dollars of vintage t investment. Because BEA deflates current-dollar outlays with constant-quality prices, one constant dollar of investment has the same embodied quality for all vintages. Thus, one constant dollar of vintage $t - \tau$ investment that remains in service will be worth less than a full constant dollar of vintage t investment only because of price differences due to factors other than the embodied characteristics. These price differences are captured in what I have called the partial measure of depreciation.

For assets subject to slower technological change than computers, the distinction between full and partial depreciation is less important. In the extreme case of no embodied improvement, $\mathbf{z}(t - \tau) = \mathbf{z}(t)$ for all τ and

$$P(t, \tau)/P(t, 0) = \{f(t)g[\mathbf{z}(t - \tau)]h(\tau)\}/\{f(t)g[\mathbf{z}(t)]h(0)\}$$
$$= h(\tau)/h(0),$$

indicating that the full and partial measures coincide. However, for assets undergoing rapid technological change, such as computers, the distinction between the two measures is crucial for constructing constant-dollar net capital stocks.

The only theoretical point left to explore is the effect of disequilibrium on the weights in equation (11). To examine this question, the expression for $P(t, \tau)$ in equation (12) must be augmented to include a term for multiple price regimes:

$$P(t, \tau) = f(t)g[\mathbf{z}(t - \tau)]h(\tau)B(t - \tau, t).$$

As in section 1.1 above, $B(t - \tau, t)$ indexes the hedonic price regime for a vintage $t - \tau$ asset at time t, with $B(\cdot, \cdot) = 1$ for models embodying best technology and $B(\cdot, \cdot) > 1$ for nonbest models.

Now, the steps that led from equation (12) to equation (16) can be repeated to yield the new weight. The result, it turns out, hinges on the properties of $PD(t)$, BEA's price deflator for computing equipment. On the basis of the discussion in Cartwright (1986), BEA's computer deflator incorporates prices for a broad set of models sold in each year, some proportion of which embody best technology. $PD(t)$ therefore depends on $B(t - \tau, t)$ for all vintages $t - \tau$ in BEA's sample at year t. Letting $B'(t)$ denote the weighted average value of $B(t - \tau, t)$ across these vintages, the deflator $PD(t)$ can be written as $f(t)B'(t)$. Then, the ratio of the deflator at times $t - \tau$ and t is

$$PD(t - \tau)/PD(t) = [f(t - \tau)B'(t - \tau)]/[f(t)B'(t)].$$

With this specification for $PD(t - \tau)/PD(t)$, it can be shown that

$$(17) \quad \tilde{P}(\tau) = \phi(\tau)\frac{h(\tau)}{h(0)}\frac{B(t - \tau, t)}{B(t - \tau, t - \tau)}\frac{B'(t - \tau)}{B'(t)} \equiv \phi(\tau)\frac{h(\tau)}{h(0)}\bar{B}.$$

$\tilde{P}(\tau)$ now depends on the product of ratios involving the indexes B and B'. To help interpret (17), assume that the deflator reflects only the prices of best-technology models and that all vintages embody best technology when new; given these assumptions, $B'(t) = B'(t - \tau) = B(t - \tau, t - \tau) = 1$, so that $\bar{B} = B(t - \tau, t)$. Then, $\tilde{P}(\tau)$ will be greater than $\phi(\tau)[h(\tau)/h(0)]$ whenever $B(t - \tau, t)$ exceeds unity—that is, whenever the vintage $t - \tau$ cohort moves to a higher price surface as it ages. When this happens, the vintage

$t - \tau$ cohort has, in effect, appreciated relative to the new cohort, and the weight on $I(t - \tau)$ should be raised accordingly.

As a practical matter, we know too little about the properties of BEA's computer deflator to specify $\tilde{B}$. However, some headway can be made under the assumption that the period t deflator is constructed only from the prices of vintage t models (which may or may not embody best technology). In this case, $B'(t) = B(t, t)$, $B'(t - \tau) = B(t - \tau, t - \tau)$, and (17) reduces to

$$(17') \qquad \tilde{P}(\tau) = \phi(\tau)\frac{h(\tau)}{h(0)}\frac{B(t - \tau, t)}{B(t, t)}.$$

The measure of depreciation in $(17')$ is $[h(\tau)B(t - \tau, t)]/[h(0)B(t, t)]$. This ratio controls for differences in the characteristics z across vintages but includes any price differences stemming from disequilibrium. This measure of depreciation is what I have called the partial measure. Thus, in the presence of disequilibrium, the partial depreciation schedule—not the narrower residual schedule—is the theoretically appropriate one for use with BEA's constant-dollar investment series.

Using equation (11), I calculated the constant-dollar net stock for office and computing equipment for four specifications of the cohort depreciation schedule $\tilde{P}(\tau)$, denoted $\tilde{P}_1(\tau), \ldots, \tilde{P}_4(\tau)$. Parallel to the survival patterns defined in connection with table 1.10 above, $\tilde{P}_1(\tau)$ is the cohort depreciation schedule used by BEA prior to the December 1991 revision, $\tilde{P}_2(\tau)$ is the schedule currently used by BEA, $\tilde{P}_3(\tau)$ is the hypothetical schedule based on the Winfrey L-2 distribution, and $\tilde{P}_4(\tau)$ is the schedule calculated from my time-varying survival function $S_4(\tau)$ combined with the partial depreciation schedule shown by the dotted line in figure 1.5 above. These four cohort depreciation functions yield a set of net capital stocks denoted $NS_1(t), \ldots, NS_4(t)$.

Table 1.11 displays the ratios NS_1/NS_4, NS_2/NS_4, and NS_3/NS_4. All the ratios in the table are less than one, indicating that each version of BEA's net

Table 1.11   **Constant-Dollar Net Stock of Office and Computing Equipment (ratio of alternative BEA Stocks to NS$_4$)**

	BEA Net Stock in Numerator of Ratio		
Year	Prerevision (NS$_1$)	Current (NS$_2$)	Winfrey L-2 (NS$_3$)
1965	0.708	0.708	0.741
1970	0.716	0.716	0.747
1975	0.819	0.819	0.829
1980	0.860	0.841	0.842
1985	0.866	0.813	0.814
1990	0.866	0.791	0.796

Note: See the text for definitions of NS$_1$ through NS$_4$.

stock is smaller than the net stock implied by my estimate of $\tilde{P}(\tau)$. That is, BEA depreciates each cohort of office and computing equipment more rapidly than my estimates of retirement and *partial* depreciation suggest is appropriate. The key to this result is the use of partial rather than full depreciation. BEA effectively uses a full measure of depreciation by writing off the entire value of an asset prior to retirement. To eliminate the downward bias in the level of its net stock, BEA must shift to a partial depreciation schedule.

In addition to this bias concerning levels, BEA's prerevision estimate overstated the growth rate of the net stock by failing to account for the trend toward shorter service lives. As shown in the first column, BEA's prerevision net stock grew from 70.8 percent of my estimated net stock to 86.6 percent between 1965 and 1990. In addition, this comparison almost surely understates the excessive growth of BEA's prerevision net stock because NS_4 was based on a fixed schedule of partial depreciation rather than on one that becomes more rapid over time. In the 1991 revision, BEA partially corrected the upward bias to the growth rate of its published net stock, as can be seen by comparing the first and second columns. However, this revision did not fix the overstatement of the growth rate before the late 1970s. To do so would require adding some downward tilt to the mean service life prior to 1978.

1.7   Conclusion

This paper used data from the *Computer Price Guide,* an industry bluebook, to estimate the rate of constant-quality price decline for IBM mainframe computers and their rate of depreciation. The paper also estimated the retirement distribution for IBM mainframes from separate data on the installed stocks of various models. The estimates of depreciation and retirement patterns were then used to assess BEA's published capital stocks for office and computing equipment.

In previous studies, estimates of constant-quality prices for mainframe computers have been based on manufacturers' list prices, owing to the absence of actual transaction prices. This paper examined whether the use of list prices substantially biased the results of those studies. On the whole, the answer was no. Using price quotes in the secondhand market, I inferred IBM's actual transaction prices for a number of mainframe models and found little evidence of discounting from list price over the period 1970–86. Moreover, these secondhand prices yielded estimates of constant-quality price change similar to those obtained with IBM list prices. In particular, both sets of prices indicated that constant-quality price declines for IBM mainframes averaged about 20 percent at an annual rate between the early 1970s and the mid-1980s. My results also support Dulberger's (1989) finding of disequilibrium in the mainframe market, a result that had been open to question because it was based on list prices. Whether using list prices or secondhand market prices, I found that older models were not marked down immediately to compete with newer, best-technology models.

The retirement pattern for IBM mainframes was calculated from fourteen models representing the 360, 370, and 30XX families. The distribution for the full set of models had a mean retirement age of 6.5 years. Although most retirements were estimated to occur within six years of installation, the distribution had a long right-hand tail. A key feature of the distribution was that service lives appear to have become shorter over time, with the mean life for the 360 models at about eight and three-quarter years and that for the 370 and 30XX models at six years or less.

Several measures of depreciation were estimated in the paper. The broadest one captured all age-related effects on price, the usual measure estimated in studies of depreciation. According to this measure, IBM mainframe models lose value fairly rapidly after introduction; in the geometric approximation to this schedule, prices declined nearly 30 percent with each year of age. I also estimated a less inclusive measure of depreciation, called partial depreciation, that controls for differences in embodied characteristics across models. Although this is not the standard notion of depreciation, section 1.6 proved that this measure is the appropriate one for constructing net capital stocks from past investment outlays when both are expressed in constant dollars. The geometric approximation to this partial measure showed mainframe prices declining about 16 percent with each year of model age.

As a complement to the depreciation measures for individual mainframe models, one can measure depreciation of the underlying technology. All the models with the same level of technology—defined by the density of their main memory chip—form a technology class. The depreciation schedules for a technology class did not display steady declines in value; rather, price increased between the first and the fourth years of age. This pattern likely reflects IBM's practice of introducing models late in a product cycle to fill a market niche; these models sell at relatively high prices even though they embody old technology. IBM apparently has been able to preserve the value of a technology despite relentless depreciation of the individual models in which the technology is embodied.

Whether measuring depreciation of a model or of a technology class, statistical tests always rejected the hypothesis of a constant geometric depreciation schedule. The schedules based on model age were not sufficiently convex, while those based on age of the technology class did not even decline monotonically, as noted above. Moreover, virtually all the schedules indicated that depreciation has become more rapid over time, consistent with a trend toward shorter service lives.

My estimates of depreciation and retirement suggest certain biases in BEA's constant-dollar gross and net stocks of office and computing equipment. Before the revisions introduced in December 1991, BEA set the mean service life for office and computing equipment at a constant eight years. By failing to account for the apparent trend toward shorter service lives, BEA likely overstated the trend growth of both the gross and the net stocks. Although BEA's 1991 revision shortened the mean service life for all post-1977 cohorts of office and computing equipment to seven years, this change does not appear to have fully eliminated the overstatement of trend growth rates. A second problem afflicts BEA's constant-dollar net stock of office and computing equipment. This stock is computed using a cohort depreciation schedule that declines more rapidly than the theoretically appropriate schedule based on partial depreciation. As a result, BEA consistently has understated the level of the net stock. The 1991 revision did not address this problem.

Although this appraisal of BEA's capital stocks was based solely on results for IBM mainframe computers, Oliner's (1992) analysis of depreciation and retirement patterns for computer peripheral equipment generally backs up the results found here. In particular, the shift toward shorter service lives and the speedup in the pace of depreciation appear to characterize peripheral equipment as well as mainframes. One hopes that BEA will reexamine its published capital stocks for office and computing equipment in light of emerging research findings in this area.

Data Appendix

For each IBM mainframe model in my sample, table 1A.1 below lists the dates of initial and final shipment from IBM, the MIPS rating, and the technology class for the model, as well as the sources for this information. Table 1A.2 provides further information on each technology class, including the first date a model in my sample was shipped from the class and the period for which each class represented best technology.

Table 1A.1   **Shipment Dates, MIPS Rating, and Technology Class**

Model	First Shipment from IBM		Final Shipment from IBM		MIPS		Technology Class	
	Date	Source[a]	Date	Source[a]	Value	Source[a]	Value	Source[a]
360 family								
20	12/65	15	1970	16	0.038	20	1	17
30	6/65	14	1969	16	0.036	13	1	17
40	4/65	14	1970	16	0.07	13	1	17
50	8/65	14	≤1970	12	0.158	13	1	17
65	11/65	14	≤1970	12	0.568	13	1	17
370 family								
115	3/74	14	1976	4	0.055	13	5	2
115-2	4/76	14	1978	19	0.077	13	5	25
125	4/73	14	1976	4	0.08	13	4,5	2
125-2	2/76	14	1978	19	0.099	13	5	25
135	4/72	14	1974	4	0.161	13	2,3	3
138	11/76	14	1979	4	0.214	13	4	3
145	6/71	14	1974	4	0.3	13	2,3	3
145-2	6/71	24	1974	18	0.3	24	2,3	18
148	1/77	14	1978	4	0.425	13	4	3
155	1/71	14	1972	4	0.55	13	1	2
155-2	1/71	24	1972	18	0.55	24	1	18
158	4/73	14	1977	4	0.829	13	4,5	2
158-3	9/76	14	1978	19	0.9	13	5	25
165	4/71	14	1972	4	1.9	13	1	2
168	5/73	14	1977	4	2.3	13	4,5	2
168-3	6/76	14	1978	19	2.5	13	5	25
30XX family								
3031	3/78	14	1980	4	1.045	13	5	2
3032	3/78	14	1979	4	2.5	13	5	2
3033-N	1/80	14	1981	4	4.0	13	5	2
3033-S	1/81	11	1981	4	2.3	6	5	2
3033-U	3/78	14	1983	4	5.9	13	5	2
3081-D	Q3/81	5	1982	22	10.0	7	8	25
3081-G	Q3/82	5	1983	21	11.4	8	8	2
3081-GX	Q1/84	5	1985	22	12.5	9	8	2
3081-K	Q2/82	5	1983	21	15.4	2	8	2
3081-KX	Q1/84	5	1985	22	16.3	9	8	2
3083-B	Q4/82	5	1983	22	5.7	8	8	2
3083-BX	Q1/84	5	1985	22	6.0	9	8	2
3083-E	Q1/83	5	1983	22	3.1	8	8	2
3083-EX	Q1/84	5	1985	22	3.3	9	8	2
3083-J	Q4/82	8	1983	22	7.9	8	8	2
3083-JX	Q1/84	8	1985	22	8.4	9	8	25
3084-QX	Q2/84	8	1985	22	29.1	9	8	25
4300 family								
4331-1	3/79	14	1983	12	0.2	6	8	25
4331-2	8/80	14	1983	18	0.4	6	8	25
4341-1	11/79	14	1983	4	0.7	6	8	2

(*continued*)

Table 1A.1   (continued)

Model	First Shipment from IBM Date	First Shipment from IBM Source[a]	Final Shipment from IBM Date	Final Shipment from IBM Source[a]	MIPS Value	MIPS Source[a]	Technology Class Value	Technology Class Source[a]
4341-2	Q2/81	1	1983	4	1.2	6	8	2
4341-10	Q1/82	1	1983	4	0.58	9	8	2
4341-11	Q1/82	1	1983	4	0.88	9	8	2
4341-12	Q1/83	1	1983	4	1.2	9	8	2
4361-5	Q2/84	1	1987	21	1.14	9	9	25
4381-1	Q1/84	23	1986	22	2.1	9	9	25
4381-2	Q2/84	23	1986	22	2.7	9	9	25
4381-3	Q1/85	23	1986	22	4.8	10	9	25
4381-12	Q1/86	5	1988	21	2.7	5	10	25
4381-13	Q1/86	5	1988	21	3.7	5	10	25
4381-14	Q1/86	5	1988	21	6.5	5	10	25

[a]Key: 1 = Computer Information Resources, *Computer Price Watch* (January 1986). 2 = Printout of data base from Dulberger (1989). 3 = Printout of data base from Dulberger (1989), cross-checked with her table 2.2. 4 = Final year in sample from Dulberger (1989). 5 = Gartner Group, *IBM Large Computer Market* (Midyear 1986): 8. 6 = Tom Henkel, "Annual Hardware Roundup," *Computerworld,* 13 July 1981, 12. 7 = Tom Henkel, "Annual Hardware Roundup," *Computerworld,* 2 August 1982, 24. 8 = Tom Henkel, "Annual Hardware Roundup," *Computerworld,* 8 August 1983, 30. 9 = Tom Henkel, "Annual Hardware Roundup," *Computerworld,* 20 August 1984, 24. 10 = Tom Henkel, "Annual Hardware Roundup," *Computerworld,* 19 August 1985, 24. 11 = International Data Corp., *EDP Industry Report,* 30 September 1983, 19. 12 = International Data Corp., IBM PIC file, Installed Base—U.S. (final year in which number of installed units rises). 13 = Lias (1980). 14 = Padegs (1981). 15 = Phister (1974, 344). 16 = Phister (1974, 333) (final year in which number of installed units rises). 17 = Phister (1974, table II.2.11.1, line 69, pp. 343 and 345). 18 = Assumed same as model 1. 19 = Assumed two-year production period. 20 = Assumed equal to average of MIPS for 360/22 and 360/25, for which MIPS ratings found in Lias (1980). 21 = Lloyd Cohn (International Data Corp.), telephone conversation, 25 January 1990. 22 = Rosanne Cole, telephone conversation, 20 March 1990. 23 = Rosanne Cole, telephone conversation, 25 July 1990. 24 = Ellen Dulberger, telephone conversation, 29 April 1986. 25 = Ellen Dulberger, telephone conversation, 6 February 1990.

Table 1A.2   **Further Information on Technology Classes**

Class	Chip Density	First Shipment of IBM Model from the Class	Period as Best Technology
1	0.0025KB	4/65	4/65–5/71
2	0.125KB	6/71	6/71–3/73
3	1KB (Bipolar chip)	4/73	Never
4	1KB (FET chip)	4/73	4/73–2/74
5	2KB	3/74	3/74–2/79
8	64KB	3/79	3/79–12/83
9	288KB	1/84	1/84–12/85
10	1MB	1/86	1/86–

Note: KB = kilobits, MB = megabits. Models in classes 6 and 7, which have 4KB and 16KB memory chips, respectively, were not represented in my sample.

References

Archibald, Robert B., and William S. Reece. 1979. Partial subindexes of input prices: The case of computer services. *Southern Economic Journal* 46 (October): 528–40.

Berndt, Ernst R., and Zvi Griliches. 1990. Price indexes for microcomputers. An exploratory study. NBER Working Paper no. 3378. Cambridge, Mass.: National Bureau of Economic Research.

Cartwright, David W. 1986. Improved deflation of purchases of computers. *Survey of Current Business* 66 (March): 7–10.

Cole, Rosanne, Y. C. Chen, Joan A. Barquin-Stolleman, Ellen Dulberger, Nurhan Helvacian, and James H. Hodge. 1986. Quality-adjusted price indexes for computer processors and selected peripheral equipment. *Survey of Current Business* 66 (January): 41–50.

Computer Price Guide (Chappaqua, N.Y.: Computer Merchants Inc). Various issues.

Dulberger, Ellen R. 1989. The application of a hedonic model to a quality-adjusted price index for computer processors. In *Technology and capital formation*, ed. Dale W. Jorgenson and Ralph Landau. Cambridge, Mass.: MIT Press.

Fisher, Franklin M., John J. McGowan, and Joen E. Greenwood. 1983. *Folded, spindled, and mutilated: Economic analysis and U.S. v. IBM*. Cambridge, Mass.: MIT Press.

Gordon, Robert J. 1989. The postwar evolution of computer prices. In *Technology and capital formation*, ed. Dale W. Jorgenson and Ralph Landau. Cambridge, Mass.: MIT Press.

Hulten, Charles R., and Frank C. Wykoff. 1979. Tax and economic depreciation of machinery and equipment. Phase II of *Economic depreciation of the U.S. capital stock: A first step*. Submitted to U.S. Treasury Department, Office of Tax Analysis, Washington, D.C.

———. 1981a. The estimation of economic depreciation using vintage asset prices. *Journal of Econometrics* 15:367–396.

———. 1981b. The measurement of economic depreciation. In *Depreciation, inflation, and the taxation of income from capital*, ed. Charles R. Hulten. Washington, D.C.: Urban Institute Press.

Lias, Edward J. 1980. Tracking those elusive KOPS. *Datamation* 26 (November): 99–105.

Oliner, Stephen D. 1992. Estimates of depreciation and retirement for computer peripheral equipment. Typescript.

Padegs, A. 1981. System/360 and beyond. *IBM Journal of Research and Development* 25 (September): 377–90.

Phister, Montgomery, Jr. 1974. *Data processing technology and economics*. Santa Monica, Calif.: Santa Monica Publishing Co.

Triplett, Jack E. 1986. The economic interpretation of hedonic methods. *Survey of Current Business* 66 (January): 36–40.

———. 1989. Price and technological change in a capital good: A survey of research on computers. In *Technology and capital formation*, ed. Dale W. Jorgenson and Ralph Landau. Cambridge, Mass.: MIT Press.

U.S. Department of Commerce. Bureau of Economic Analysis. 1987. *Fixed reproducible tangible wealth in the United States, 1925–85*. Washington, D.C.: U.S. Government Printing Office.

2 Price Indexes for Microcomputers: An Exploratory Study

Ernst R. Berndt and Zvi Griliches

In recent years, a considerable amount of research has focused on the construction and interpretation of price indexes for computers.[1] The computer market is a fascinating one, for technological change has been rapid, there has been a great deal of entry and exit of firms and models, and, particularly in the microcomputer market, models have been simultaneously sold at different prices by standard retail and discount vendors.

Because of the rapid technological change and turnover of models and firms, Fisher, McGowan, and Greenwood (1983) have characterized the mainframe computer market as typically being in "disequilibrium." One consequence of this is that price indexes have been used for two rather different purposes, one to deflate expenditures or purchases into constant dollars, and the other to trace out movements in a technological frontier, such as a price-performance ratio.

If quality-adjusted prices reacted instantaneously and fully to the introduction of new technology, then an index that traced out the technological frontier

Ernst R. Berndt is professor of applied economics at the Massachusetts Institute of Technology, Sloan School of Management, and is a research associate at the National Bureau of Economic Research. Zvi Griliches is the Paul M. Warburg Professor of Economics at Harvard University and program director of productivity and technical change studies at the National Bureau of Economic Research.

The authors gratefully acknowledge the financial support of the Alfred P. Sloan Foundation and the National Science Foundation to the National Bureau of Economic Research and the helpful comments of Rosanne Cole and Allan H. Young. They have benefited from the able research assistance of Joanna Stavins and by having access to earlier research on this topic by Jeremy Cohen and Amy Kim. Proprietary data on microcomputer shipments and installations by PC model were kindly provided to them by Bruce A. Stephen and Lloyd Cohen of the International Data Corp.

1. See, e.g., the classic study by Chow (1967) as well as more recent ones by Archibald and Reece (1978), Gordon (1989, 1990), Michaels (1979), Oliner (1986), and Triplett (1989a).

would be identical to one that covered all models sold in the marketplace. In periods of disequilibrium, however, the two quality-adjusted price indexes might differ, with consumers tolerating transactions at more than one quality-adjusted price. One reason for such multiple price transactions would be if the supply of some new models is initially limited and, in spite of this excess demand, manufacturers offered new models at lower prices to facilitate dissemination of information about the new low-price technology. Another reason would be if surviving models were of higher quality in some unobserved characteristics or benefited from the accumulation of specialized software and know-how. The extent of such price disequilibrium is of course an empirical issue; some recent evidence on this issue for the mainframe computer market is presented by Dulberger (1989).

Although the mainframe computer market has received considerable attention, to the best of our knowledge there has been little empirical work on the microcomputer (PC) market.[2] In this paper, we focus attention on the interpretation of implicit price indexes and coefficients from hedonic price equations using detailed data from the list and discount U.S. microcomputer markets.[3] We define a *discount price* as that advertised for a particular model sold by a vendor other than the manufacturer and a *list price* as that advertised by the brand-name manufacturer; for example, we classify the advertised price of an IBM personal computer sold by 47th St. Photo as being a discount price, while we categorize the price advertised by IBM for the same model as being a list price. Much of the discount market is mail order. Presumably, transactions in discount markets take place at advertised prices, whereas considerably fewer transactions occur at list prices. Unfortunately, data by transactions prices are not available to us.

Our work builds on the research of two of our students, Cohen (1988) and Kim (1989). Cohen originally gathered and assembled price and characteristics data covering the time period 1976–87; the data, which he updated to include 1988, were then examined further by Kim. On the basis of hedonic regression equations with pooled data, both Cohen and Kim generated implicit PC price indexes for list and discount markets. Before doing estimation, both Cohen and Kim divided nominal prices for each model by the consumer price index (hereafter we call this CPI-adjusted price index a *relative* price index). Representative findings from Cohen and Kim are presented in table 2.1, as are the PC price index computed by Gordon (1990) and the BEA "official" PC price index. Both Gordon's and BEA's price indexes employ

---

2. A very brief discussion of PCs is presented in Gordon (1989, 1990). See also Catron (1989) and Sinclair and Catron (1990).

3. Hedonic regression methods and their interpretation are discussed in, among others, Griliches (1961, 1971, 1988), Triplett (1986), and Berndt (1991). Theoretical foundations for interpreting hedonic price equations are found in, among others, Rosen (1974) and Epple (1987). For a historical discussion of the incorporation of hedonic regression methods into official price indexes, see Triplett (1990).

Table 2.1 **Relative Price Indexes for Microcomputers Based on Hedonic Regressions and Matched-Model Procedures**

| | Hedonic Regressions | | | | Matched-Model Procedure | | |
| | Cohen | | Kim | | | | |
Year	List Prices	Discount Prices	List Prices	Discount Prices	Gordon	BEA	CPI
1976	4.7709						0.5828
1977	2.7347						0.6262
1978	2.0878	1.4558					0.6727
1979	1.8015	1.3638					0.7471
1980	1.6923	1.4726					0.8535
1981	1.4189	1.2700			1.3441		0.9345
1982	1.0000	1.0000	1.0000	1.000	1.0000	1.000	1.0000
1983	0.7118	0.4613	0.687	0.464	0.7459	0.777	1.0306
1984	0.5926	0.6225	0.617	0.920	0.5576	0.568	1.0651
1985	0.3898	0.3798	0.409	0.595	0.3871	0.511	1.1076
1986	0.2581	0.2494	0.268	0.393	0.2916	0.369	1.1291
1987	0.1913	0.1680	0.194	0.259	0.2201	0.321	1.1715
1988			0.123	0.200			1.2176
Average annual growth rates (AAGRs), (%) 1982–87	− 28.16	− 30.01	− 27.96	− 23.68	− 26.12	− 20.33	3.22
Entire period covered by the study (%)	− 25.36	− 21.33	− 29.48	− 23.53	− 26.03		

Note: All the computer price indexes are relative to the CPI: i.e., the nominal computer prices have been divided by the consumer price index. Data are taken from Cohen (1988, app. D, p. 70), renormalized to 1982 = 1.000; from Kim (1989, app. 22); and from Gordon (1990, table 6.13, p. 237), renormalized and divided by the CPI. The BEA index is from the November 1988 issue of the *Survey of Current Business*, table 1, p. 22 (divided by the CPI). For further discussion of the Gordon and BEA indexes, see n. 4 below.

"matched-model" procedures.[4] To facilitate comparison of indexes, in the bottom row of table 2.1 we present AAGRs (average annual growth rates) for all the price indexes over the same time interval, 1982–87.

As is seen in table 2.1, all relative price indexes suggest rapid declines in the quality-adjusted price of microcomputers.[5] Cohen reports an AAGR of − 25.36 percent in relative price of PCs over the time frame 1976–87 for list prices and a slightly lower − 21.33 percent for discount prices. Kim finds an AAGR of − 29.48 percent for list prices for 1976–88 and − 23.53 percent for discount prices. Gordon's calculations suggest an AAGR of − 26.12 per-

4. Gordon's index is based on data covering twenty-one PC model years for 1981–87, taken from advertisements in *Business Week* and *PC Magazine*. Precisely how the BEA PC price index is constructed is not clear. According to Cartwright and Smith (1988, 22), "For personal computers (PC's), a matched model index was introduced in 1987. It is now constructed using price changes of IBM PC's, judgmentally adjusted by BEA to reflect price changes for other models, for 1983 and price changes of models sold by IBM and three additional manufacturers for 1984–87."

cent for the shorter period 1982–87 (a mix of list and discount prices), while the BEA relative price index falls at a smaller AAGR of − 20.33 percent for the same period.

The research results we report in this paper extend the work of Cohen, Kim, and Gordon in a number of related ways. First, we focus attention on the more general interpretive implications of the fact that the PC market is a changing one during the period 1982–88, involving shake outs of some models, successful innovations for others, and dramatic changes in product characteristics. The data sample that we observe is opportunistic in the sense that it represents new (not secondhand) models only and within that set only those that survived for one year or more. We examine whether surviving vintages are priced at a premium and how prices of surviving vintages adjust when new models are introduced incorporating technological advances.

Second, we examine several econometric implications of the fact that, owing to differential survival rates in the marketplace, our data are in the form of an unbalanced panel. In particular, we explore implications for estimation of how one implements empirically the identity that the year in which the model is observed is the sum of the year in which the model was first introduced and its age in years since introduction. A diagnostic test is discussed and implemented for checking our hedonic specification. Issues of sample selectivity are also addressed.

Finally, we construct and comment on a variety of price indexes that can potentially serve as deflators for microcomputer investment series or as measures that trace out a technological frontier in the PC market.

2.1 The Data

The data set available for this study includes price and technical attribute measures for new (not used) personal computers sold in the United States from 1976 to 1988. The 1976–87 data were originally collected and analyzed by Cohen (1988); these data have been updated by Cohen to 1988, have been employed by Kim (1989) in further analysis, and have undergone additional revisions by us. The primary source of technical data was the *Byte* magazine comprehensive technical reviews. Since both list and discount prices often varied within each calendar year, the June issues of *Byte, PC Magazine,* and *PC World* were employed for list price data, while ads in the "Science and Technology" and "Business" sections of a Sunday *New York Times* issue in early June of each year were employed to obtain discount prices.[6] Additional data sources included the *Dataquest Personal Computer Guide* and IBM pricing and technical data.

---

5. To convert the relative price indexes into nominal price indexes and thereby make entries in table 2.1 consistent with published numbers, simply multiply the relative price index by the appropriate CPI (given in the last column of table 2.1).

6. The first PC advertising appeared in the *New York Times* in 1981.

Characteristic and performance data collected by Cohen include RAM (the amount of random access memory standard on each PC model, measured in kilobytes [KB]), MHZ (the clock speed, measured in megahertz, or millions of cycles per second), HRDDSK (the amount of storage on the hard disk, if one exists, measured in megabytes [MB]), NUMFLP (the number of floppy disk drives standard on each model), SLOTS (the total number of eight-, sixteen-, and thirty-two-bit slots available for expansion boards), and AGE (the number of years the model has been sold on the market, where the model has an age of zero in its initial year).

As we noted earlier, an important feature of the PC market is that it is changing very rapidly. A model introduced in year 0 may survive with unchanged characteristics into year 1, year 2, or even longer, or, as is often the case, it may survive with differing characteristics into other years (we call this a changed *version* of the model). Other models may exit after being in the market only one year. Hence, the stock of models sold in any given year consists of new and incumbent models and, among the incumbent models, new and old versions.

To highlight the evolution of the PC market, in table 2.2 we present arithmetic means of characteristics for models newly introduced from 1982 through 1988. As is seen there, the mean nominal price decreased slightly, about 3 percent, from $3,617.61 in 1982 to $3,508.47 in 1988, while mean RAM increased more than tenfold from 94.92 to 1,069.39KB, MHZ clock speed jumped more than three times from 4.4046 to 14.8201, and the mean hard disk storage rose from 0 to 43.638MB.

In table 2.3, we summarize the mixed nature of the PC market from 1982 to 1988, including new and up to age 3 models, separately for the total, list, and discount markets. For the total market, 58 percent (722 of 1,265) are new models, 29 percent (372) are models that survived one year (perhaps with changed characteristics and reduced prices to meet the market competition

Table 2.2		Mean Values of Characteristics for New Models, 1982–88					
Year	N	RAM	MHZ	HRDDSK	NUMFLP	SLOTS	Nominal Price
1982	13	94.92	4.4046	0.000	1.154	3.308	3,617.61
1983	59	122.78	4.6807	2.161	1.237	3.322	3,017.66
1984	80	204.00	5.1998	3.012	1.338	3.325	3,026.96
1985	61	326.69	5.9974	4.607	1.295	4.000	2,991.15
1986	123	539.25	7.6016	11.220	1.195	5.081	2,955.60
1987	245	773.09	10.1033	22.355	1.098	5.016	3,251.40
1988	141	1,069.39	14.8201	43.638	1.014	5.993	3,508.47

Note: N is the number of new models by year; RAM is kilobytes of random access memory standard on each model; MHZ is clock speed in megahertz; HRDDSK is the amount of storage on the hard disk, if one exists, in megabytes; NUMFLP is the number of floppy disk drives standard on each model; SLOTS is the total number of eight-, sixteen-, and thirty-two-bit slots available for expansion boards; and nominal price is the price in current (nominal) dollars.

Table 2.3   **Vintage Composition of Microcomputer Market, 1982–88**

| Year | No. of Price Observations | | | | |
	AGE = 0	AGE = 1	AGE = 2	AGE = 3	Total
1982:					
Total	13	7	12	9	41
List	10	5	4	5	24
Discount	3	2	8	4	17
1983:					
Total	59	9	5	6	79
List	53	5	3	1	62
Discount	6	4	2	5	17
1984:					
Total	80	44	3	0	127
List	63	25	2	0	90
Discount	17	19	1	0	37
1985:					
Total	61	39	12	2	114
List	59	18	5	0	82
Discount	2	21	7	2	32
1986:					
Total	123	35	23	6	187
List	106	26	13	2	147
Discount	17	9	10	4	40
1987:					
Total	245	92	42	11	390
List	217	63	30	9	319
Discount	28	29	12	2	71
1988:					
Total	141	146	32	8	327
List	129	59	5	0	193
Discount	12	87	27	8	134
Grand total	722	372	129	42	1,265
List total	637	201	62	17	917
Discount total	85	171	67	25	348

from frontier models), 10 percent (129) survived two years, and 3 percent (42) remained in the marketplace for three years.

Altogether, about 72 percent of our model observations are taken from the list market, while 28 percent represent discount quotations. However, as is also seen in table 2.3, the age composition of models varies considerably between the list and the discount markets. Specifically, discount markets tend to have a much smaller proportion of new models and much larger proportions of one-, two-, and three-year-old models. Finally, it is worth noting that, in our data set, some models are sold in both the list and the discount markets (e.g., IBM and Compaq) and are therefore "observed" twice, while others are only in the list market (e.g., PC Limited); however, no model is observed only in the discount market.

To focus attention on issues involved in interpreting coefficients with unbalanced panels, in this paper we adopt in essence the regressors and functional form employed by Cohen and Kim, in which the logarithm of the real price (LRPRICE) is regressed on the logarithm of several characteristics, including LRAM, LMHZ, LHRDDSK (log[HRDDSK] + 1]), LNUMFLP (log[NUMFLP + 1]), LSLOTS (log[SLOTS] + 1]), and a number of dummy variables.

The dummy variables for characteristics include PROC16 (= 1 if model has a sixteen-bit processor chip, otherwise 0), PROC32 = 1 if model has a thirty-two-bit processor chip), DBW (= 1 if system comes with a monochrome monitor), DCOLOR (= 1 if system comes with a color monitor), DPORT (= 1 if model is portable or convertible), DEXTRA (= 1 if model has a significant piece of additional hardware included, otherwise 0; examples of such extra hardware include modems, printers, or an extra monitor), and DDISC (= 1 if system price is discounted by the vendor).

The dummy variables for manufacturers are DIBM (= 1 if system is made by IBM), DAPPLE (Apple), DCOMMO (Commodore), DCMPQ (Compaq), DNEC (NEC), DRDIOSH (Radio Shack), DPCLIM (PC Limited), and DOTHER (made or sold by any other company than those noted above).

Finally, a number of time and vintage effect dummy variables are employed. For time effects, the dummy variables T82, T83, . . . , T88, take on the value of 1 if the PC model was sold in that year and otherwise equal 0. For vintage effects, the dummy variables V79, V80, . . . , V88 take on the value 1 if the model was originally introduced in that year and otherwise equal 0.

The above variables, as well as several other measures, were included as regressors in a number of specifications examined by Cohen and by Kim using data beginning in 1976. Since the PC market was very small from 1976 until the entry of IBM in late 1981 (only 156 models were introduced before 1982), in this paper we confine our attention to the period 1982–88 and the 1979–88 vintages, restricting our sample to PC models whose age is three years or less, and dividing the AGE variable into three dummy variables, AGE1, AGE2, and AGE3, with a new model having an implicit age of 0. The data used in our regression analysis are summarized in table 2.4, where we present sample means as well as minimum and maximum values of the various variables.

2.2 Econometric Issues

Our data set comes in the form of an unbalanced panel, in that the number of observations by age, and by vintage, varies by year. Let the vintage of model i (the year in which it was first introduced) be V, where $V = 79, 80, . . . , 88$; let the year (time period) in which the model is observed be T, where $T = 82, 83, . . . , 88$; and let the age of the model of vintage V observed in time period T, in years, be A, where A is either 0, 1, 2, or 3. This yields the identity that, for any model observation,

Table 2.4   **Summary of Microcomputer Data, 1982–88**

Variable	Mean	Minimum Value	Maximum Value
PRICE	2,846.96	40.00	13,995.00
RAM	560.73	1.00	4,096.00
MHZ	8.3474	1.00	25.00
HRDDSK	17.199	0.00	314.00
NUMFLP	1.1526	0.00	2.00
SLOTS	4.5644	0.00	21.00
AGE	0.5976	0.00	3.00
PROC16	0.5510	0.00	1.00
PROC32	0.1344	0.00	1.00
DBW	0.4213	0.00	1.00
DCOLOR	0.0285	0.00	1.00
DPORT	0.1747	0.00	1.00
DEXTRA	0.0206	0.00	1.00
DDISC	0.2751	0.00	1.00
DIBM	0.0988	0.00	1.00
DAPPLE	0.0427	0.00	1.00
DCMDRE	0.0285	0.00	1.00
DCMPQ	0.0648	0.00	1.00
DNEC	0.0427	0.00	1.00
DRDIOSH	0.0490	0.00	1.00
DPCLIM	0.0166	0.00	1.00
DOTHER	0.6569	0.00	1.00
T82	0.0324	0.00	1.00
T83	0.0635	0.00	1.00
T84	0.1004	0.00	1.00
T85	0.0901	0.00	1.00
T86	0.1478	0.00	1.00
T87	0.3083	0.00	1.00
T88	0.2585	0.00	1.00

$$N = 1,265$$

(1) $$T \equiv V + A.$$

If T, V, and A were treated as continuous variables, one could not simultaneously introduce all three as regressors in a linear equation to be estimated by least squares, for exact collinearity would result. To avoid such collinearity, only two of the three could be included directly, and estimates for the third could be computed indirectly using (1). Alternatively, as has been discussed by Fienberg and Mason (1985), one could specify instead a model with nonlinear transformations of all three variables, such as their squared values.[7]

---

7. However, one cannot identify parameters in a full quadratic expansion of the three variables owing to the identity in (1). For discussions in the context of age, period, and cohort models, see Fienberg and Mason (1985) and Wilmoth (1989).

To begin with, suppose that one specified the regression equation

(2) $$\ln P_{ivat} = \delta + \delta_v V + \delta_a A + X'\delta_x + \varepsilon_{ivat},$$

where V and A are continuous variables, and X is a vector of model i–specific characteristics variables. This regression equation is equivalent to one with the $A = T - V$ identity from (1) substituted into (2); that is, it is equivalent to a regression equation with V, T, and X as regressors rather than V, A, and X:

(3) $$\begin{aligned}
\ln P_{ivat} &= \delta + \delta_v V + \delta_a(T - V) + X'\delta_x + \varepsilon_{ivat}\\
&= \delta + (\delta_v - \delta_a)V + \delta_a T + X'\delta_x + \varepsilon_{ivat}\\
&= \delta + \delta_v' V + \delta_a A + X'\delta_x + \varepsilon_{ivat}
\end{aligned}$$

where $\delta_v' \equiv \delta_v - \delta_a$. In particular, direct and implicit least squares estimates of the δ, δ_v, δ_a, and δ_x coefficients in (2) and (3) are numerically equivalent, as are the equation R^2 values. Similarly, one could substitute $V \equiv T - A$ from the identity in (1) into (2) and obtain a regression equation with T, A, and X as regressors rather than V, T, and X as in (2) or V, A, and X as in (3):

(4) $$\begin{aligned}
\ln P_{ivat} &= \delta + \delta_v(T - A) + \delta_a A + X'\delta_x + \varepsilon_{ivat}\\
&= \delta + \delta_v T + (\delta_a - \delta_v) A + X'\delta_x + \varepsilon_{ivat}\\
&= \delta + \delta_v T + \delta_a' A + X'\delta_x + \varepsilon_{ivat}
\end{aligned}$$

where $\delta_a' \equiv \delta_a - \delta_v$. Given the algebra of least squares, direct and implicit estimates of the δ, δ_v, δ_a, and δ_x parameters in (2), (3), and (4) are identical, as are the equation R^2 measures.

However, as we show below, when T, V, and A are discrete dummy variables rather than continuous, and if the coefficients of these variables are to be held constant over time and/or vintage, then by construction the simple adding-up conditions implied by (1) no longer hold, and least squares direct and implicit estimates of the parameters depend on the equation fitted. This raises a number of issues involving the interpretation of dummy variable coefficients and the maximal parameterization possible that avoids exact collinearity.[8]

In terms of interpretation, consider the following equation, analogous to (4), where T and A are vectors of dummy variables with T82 and A0 deleted, and the vintage dummy variables in V are all deleted:

(5) $$\ln P_{ivat} = \alpha + T'\alpha_t + A'\alpha_a + X'\beta + u_{ivat}.$$

In this case, one might interpret estimates of the α_t as changes in the quality-adjusted price index relative to 1982, holding age fixed. Similarly, estimates of the α_a can be interpreted as the effects of age (relative to a new model of age 0) on price, holding time fixed. Intuitively, the α_t parameters in this T-A specification represent the general movement in average PC prices, given the average rate at which selectivity occurs in the sample.

---

8. A related discussion of this issue in the context of age, period, and cohort effects in earnings equations is presented by Heckman and Robb (1985).

While cumulated evidence from the mainframe market suggests that the α_t should decline with time (see, e.g., Cartwright 1986; Cole et al. 1986; Gordon 1989; and Triplett 1989a), it is not clear what one should expect for signs of the estimated α_a, which represent the effects of quality differentials on models of different ages sold contemporaneously, holding time fixed. According to one line of thinking, new models of superior quality should command a premium price, and, if market competition forced the valuations of all characteristics of incumbent models to obsolescence at the same rate, prices of surviving vintages would decline appropriately. Thus, since the time dummy captures the full price effect, one might expect estimates of α_1, α_2, and α_3 to be approximately zero. On the other hand, selectivity in the marketplace reveals survival of the fittest, and, if there are unmeasured characteristics (e.g., compatible software or hardware, differential service policies and warranties), then the age coefficients may to some extent be providing an estimate of the unobserved positive quality differentials among the survivors as vintages progress. To unscramble the obsolescence and selectivity components of the estimated age coefficients, one would need to assume that all the quality differences among vintages were already captured in the changing computer characteristics and their associated coefficients, assuring thereby that age coefficients reflected selectivity alone.

Alternatively, one might specify a regression equation using the vintage V and age A dummy variables rather than the T and A as in (5):

(6) $$\ln P_{ivat} = \alpha + V'\alpha_v + A'\alpha_a + X'\beta + u_{ivat},$$

where, say, the V82 vintage dummy variable was omitted. In terms of interpretation, note that, if the technical characteristics variables captured virtually all the quality changes embodied in models, then the vintage coefficients would essentially be capturing the decline in prices by vintage (i.e., by date of introduction), which in turn is some average of the difference between A and the implicit T over ages. Similarly, given that the specification (6) conditions on vintages, one can interpret the α_a age coefficients as representing the average price decline of surviving models over the sample years, reflecting the identity (1), $A \equiv T - V$ for all vintages. In a sense, it is another measure of the average rate of improvement in the quality of new computers, which forces the price of incumbent models to decline.

In spite of its apparent similarity with (5) given the identity (1), the specification in (6) is in fact quite different, except for the special case when models of only one age are considered (e.g., only AGE $= 0$ models). There are at least two reasons for this. First, the number of dummy variable coefficients is greater in (6) than in (5), for in (5) there are six time (T83–T88) and three age (A1–A3) coefficients, while in (6) there are nine vintage (V79–V88, V82 omitted) and three age (A1–A3) parameters. Thus, in general, one should not expect least squares estimates of α_a and β to be to same in the two specifications.

Second, while the age coefficients condition on time in (5), in (6) the conditioning is on vintage. In particular, in (6) the α_a age coefficients are interpreted as the effect on price of age (relative to a new model), holding vintage V (not time T) fixed. Since the conditioning changes, least squares estimates should also be expected to differ in (5) and (6).

To understand this better, consider a V-A specification such as (6). An implicit time coefficient such as that for, say, T88 could be computed in four different ways:

(7)
$$\alpha_{t,88} = \alpha_{v,88} + \alpha_{a,0}, \quad \alpha_{t,88} = \alpha_{v,87} + \alpha_{a,1},$$
$$\alpha_{t,88} = \alpha_{v,86} + \alpha_{a,2}, \quad \text{and/or } \alpha_{t,88} = \alpha_{v,85} + \alpha_{a,3}.$$

Similarly, with T-A specifications as in (5), the implicit vintage coefficient for, say, V85 could be computed alternatively as

(8)
$$\alpha_{v,85} = \alpha_{t,85} - \alpha_{a,0}, \quad \alpha_{v,85} = \alpha_{t,86} - \alpha_{a,1},$$
$$\alpha_{v,85} = \alpha_{t,87} - \alpha_{a,2}, \quad \text{and/or } \alpha_{v,85} = \alpha_{t,88} - \alpha_{a,3}.$$

Least squares estimation of the V-A and T-A specification implicitly weight and average over these four possibilities in different ways, and thus there is no reason to expect implicit and direct estimates of the α_v, α_a, and/or α_t coefficients to be numerically equivalent in the T-A and V-A models, unless the rates of vintage improvement, time inflation, and age depreciation are all constant functions of elapsed time. In this special case, identity (1) also holds for all the relevant dummy variable coefficients.

But, if the V-A and T-A specifications yield varying estimates because of their distinct conditioning and use of differing information, how is one to choose among them? For purposes of computing quality-adjusted price indexes, the directly estimated time coefficients based on (5) have a clear interpretation, and, for that reason, specification (5) has formed the basis of almost all hedonic price index studies. But is it necessary to delete the V variables completely? Can one not employ a specification that efficiently uses information simultaneously from the T, A, *and* V dummy variables yet avoids exact collinearity?

This issue has been addressed by Hall (1971), whose context involved use of a balanced panel data set for secondhand trucks. In our context, the maximal parameterization consistent with avoiding exact collinearity among the T, V, and A dummy variables turns out to be one in which eight of the original ten vintage dummy variables are added to the T-A specification (5); that is, two (not one) of the vintage dummies are deleted from the original set of ten (V79–V88) (see especially Hall 1971, 248).[9] We can write such a specification as

9. There is intuitive appeal to this additional normalization. Hall defined the price index as the product of vintage effects (embodied technical progress), depreciation, and time (disembodied technical progress). Thus, the logarithm of the price index is the sum of these three effects, each

(9) $$\ln P_{ivat} = \alpha + T'\alpha_t + A'\alpha_a + V'\alpha_v + X'\beta + u_{ivat},$$

where the vector of dummy variables in V consists of eight elements. As Hall noted, coefficients on the α_v should be interpreted as *differences* from the average rate of growth of technical progress embodied but unobserved in pairwise comparisons of vintages. For example, if one omitted the V82 and V83 dummy variables, the α_v coefficient estimates should then be interpreted as a contrast; for example, the coefficient on the V88 dummy variable should then be interpreted as the *difference* between the average 1988 vintage effect and the mean of the average vintage effects for 1982 and 1983. Alternatively, one can think of these as contrasts, deleting the middle vintages and interpreting the remaining coefficients as measuring period (acceleration) from the average rate of technological change. We suggest that a necessary condition for a hedonic price equation to be satisfactory is that the portion of quality change not captured by the characteristics variables should be unrelated to vintages; that is, in a desirable specification, the α_v should be approximately zero.[10]

It follows that, since the α_v coefficients represent contrasts in average rates of growth due to unobserved quality change, one can interpret a test that the $\alpha_v = 0$ as corresponding to a test that changes in characteristics among models and over time adequately capture quality changes between vintages and that average unobserved vintage effects are not systematically different in pairwise comparisons across vintages. Further, if it were found that the α_v are simultaneously different from zero, then one might interpret that result as suggesting model misspecification, reflecting either the effect of omitted characteristic variables or invalid stability constraints on the characteristics parameters over time. Hence, as noted above, a desirable specification would yield nonrejection of the null hypothesis that the α_v simultaneously equal zero, in which case (5) would be empirically supported as a special case of (9).[11]

Hypotheses concerning parameter restrictions can of course be tested using the standard F-test methodology. As has been emphasized by, among others, Arrow (1960) and Ohta and Griliches (1976), when samples are large and

---

in rates of growth. To normalize the level of the price index, one normalizes levels of each of the three effects; i.e., one deletes one variable from each of the T, V, and A dummy variable sets and normalizes relative to that variable. But, in addition, one must normalize at least one of the growth rates since the product of the three effects implies that components are unidentified. This additional normalization is accomplished by deleting an additional vintage variable, thereby yielding a contrast in levels of the logarithmic regression, which is equivalent to a normalization in growth rates of one of the three components. For additional discussion, see Hall (1971).

10. Implicit in this test is the assumption that the different characteristics contained in the various vintages appreciate (owing to inflation) and depreciate (owing to technological change) at the same rate.

11. It is worth noting here that the choice of which two dummy variables to delete from the V vector is arbitrary in the sense that goodness of fit and numerical values of least squares estimates of α and the β's will be unaffected. However, the interpretation and numerical values of the least squares estimates of the α_t, α_a, and α_v will depend on this choice.

standard test procedures are employed, one is likely to reject most simplifying parameter restrictions on purely statistical grounds, even though they may still serve as adequate approximations for the purpose at hand. There are several ways one can deal with this problem.

First, to accommodate the larger sample size, we can compensate by choosing very tight significance levels for the standard F-tests. In this paper, we do that by choosing .01 significance levels. Second, one could adopt the more agnostic and conservative criterion that the null hypothesis holds only approximately rather than exactly in the sample. In such a case, as Leamer (1978) has shown, one could employ a Bayes procedure that, in essence, decreases the significance level as the sample size n increases. Although we investigated use of the Leamer-Bayes procedure, we do not report results based on it here in detail since, for every hypothesis we tested, the test statistic was less than the critical value and thus in each case the null hypothesis was not rejected.[12]

Finally, since in our hedonic regressions the dependent variable is LRPRICE, the root mean squared errors (RMSE) measure the unexplained variation in prices in, roughly, percentage units. A reasonable criterion is to use the difference in the RMSE of the constrained and unconstrained regressions as a relevant measure of the price-explanatory power of a particular model. As our alternative test criterion, we will therefore reject the null hypothesis when the RMSE under the alternative results in a reduction of more than 5 percent in the RMSE (the standard deviation of the unexplained variation in log prices). With an average RMSE of around 0.40, this RMSE criterion implies that we are looking for a movement of at least about 0.02, say, from 0.40 to 0.38, before we will "give up" on the more parsimonious parameterization implied by the null hypothesis.

2.3 Initial Results

We begin with results from a T-A model in which the time and age dummy variables are included but the vintage dummies omitted, as in (5). Results are presented in table 2.5 for three regressions—a pooled sample, list price observations, and discount price observations. In each case, the dependent variable is the logarithm of the real price (LRPRICE), and the variables are essentially those as in Cohen and Kim. Recall that, in many cases, a particular model appears in both the list and the discount markets. Given the specification of dummy variables, in each regression the estimated intercept term cor-

---

12. Specifically, we computed the Bayes factor asymptotic approximation developed by Leamer (1978, 108–14), translated from the condition that it exceeds one into an F-value expression that Leamer has shown to be equal to $(n - k) \cdot (n^{q/n} - 1)/q$, where n is sample size, k is the number of free parameters estimated in the unconstrained regression, and q is the number of parameter restrictions. For an application of Leamer's adjustment to the standard F-test procedure in the context of large samples, see Ohta and Griliches (1976).

Table 2.5   **Parameter Estimates for Specifications with Time and Age Dummy Variables Included—Pooled, List, and Discount Samples for 1982–88**

Variable	Pooled Sample		List Price Sample		Discount Price Sample	
	Estimated Parameter	t-Statistic	Estimated Parameter	t-Statistic	Estimated Parameter	t-Statistic
Intercept	4.8101	41.934	4.7316	33.152	4.4924	23.823
LRAM	0.3140	14.804	0.3313	12.746	.2721	7.875
LMHZ	0.3157	7.668	0.2197	4.409	.5482	7.620
LHRDDSK	0.1688	19.876	0.1716	17.710	.1543	9.005
LNUMFLP	0.4304	8.588	0.4753	7.869	.2913	3.365
LSLOTS	0.1721	8.483	0.1502	5.921	.2396	7.211
AGE1	0.1193	3.911	0.1296	3.531	.0414	0.735
AGE2	0.1542	3.448	0.2352	3.984	.0192	0.268
AGE3	0.2984	4.034	0.5333	4.748	.1469	1.454
PROC16	0.2087	5.817	0.2501	5.894	.1319	2.037
PROC32	0.5193	8.101	0.6560	8.829	.1926	1.500
DBW	0.0261	0.844	0.0222	0.633	−.0511	−0.944
DCOLOR	0.0315	0.423	0.0463	0.491	−.0129	−0.110
DPORT	0.3565	8.943	0.3400	6.763	.4703	7.273
DEXTRA	0.2756	3.242	0.2698	2.733	.4609	2.706
DDISC	−0.2903	−9.460				
DAPPLE	0.2729	3.627	0.1982	1.999	.4470	3.938
DCMDRE	−0.3291	−3.776	−0.3763	−3.089	−.1226	−0.981
DCMPQ	0.2678	4.176	0.3598	4.045	0.2266	2.394
DNEC	0.1114	1.548	0.2369	2.399	−0.0265	−0.251
DRDIOSH	0.0618	0.891	0.0162	0.205	0.4644	3.127
DPCLIM	−0.5047	−4.927	−0.4707	−4.402		
DOTHER	0.0062	0.141	0.0430	0.823	0.0027	0.034
T83	−0.3974	−4.768	−0.2193	−2.081	−0.8034	−5.889
T84	−0.4085	−5.017	−0.3494	−3.350	−0.2933	−2.298
T85	−0.8567	−10.110	−0.7645	−7.039	−0.7820	−5.845
T86	−1.2755	−14.937	−1.1804	−10.770	−1.2660	−9.402
T87	−1.6121	−18.728	−1.5201	−13.805	−1.6758	−12.368
T88	−2.0331	−22.412	−1.9813	−16.876	−1.9611	−14.177
R^2		0.7416		0.7003		0.8220
N		1,265		917		348
Root MSE		0.4166		0.4181		0.3796

responds to that for a model of age 0 in 1982 that has an eight-bit processor, no monitor, and no extras, is not portable, is not in the discount market, and is made by IBM.

A number of results are worth noting. First, the coefficient on LMHZ is positive and significant in all three regressions but is largest in the discount market; coefficients on the LSLOTS variable follow a similar pattern. Coefficients on LRAM and LNUMFLP are also positive and significant but, in contrast, are larger in the list than in the discount market.

Second, in all three regressions, the coefficients on the age variables are positive, holding time fixed, suggesting that the age effects of selectivity are substantial. Interestingly, the effect of age is largest in the list market, where the age premium is statistically significant and increases with age, implying that list prices of surviving computers do not drop "fast enough." In the discount market, however, the age coefficients are statistically insignificant and follow no pattern. This suggests that some type of selectivity is occurring in the transition from list to discount markets and that, conditional on having entered the discount market, there is little age selectivity remaining.

Third, in terms of other dummy variable coefficients, estimates of PROC16 and PROC32 are positive, statistically significant, and larger in the list than discount market, and the positive DPORT parameter estimate is larger in the discount market. Although the general patterns of the time coefficient estimates are similar in the list and discount markets—revealing declines in quality-adjusted prices since 1982—in the discount market the pattern of estimates between T83, T84, and T85 is not monotonic, suggesting that the discount market is more volatile or that the discount sample is too small in these years to generate reliable parameter estimates.

Fourth, notice also that the DDISC coefficient in the pooled regression is negative ($-.2903$) and significant, as expected. We tested the null hypothesis that, aside from a parallel shift due to being in the discount market, all coefficients are identical in the list and discount markets. The F-test statistic corresponding to this null hypothesis is 2.77, while the .01 critical value is 1.73. Hence, on the basis of the F-test criterion, the null hypothesis of parameter equality in discount and list markets is rejected.[13] However, in terms of RMSE, the improvement under the alternative hypothesis is only 1.94 percent. Overall, we interpret these results as suggesting modest support for the null hypothesis of parameter equality in the two markets (aside from a parallel shift).

We also applied two other Chow-type tests to check for parameter equality over different subsets of the data. First, we ran separate regressions for the age equals zero-, one-, two-, and three-years-old subsamples and compared the residual sums of squares with those from the pooled model reported in column 1 of table 2.5. The calculated F-test statistic is 2.66, while the .01 traditional critical value is 1.44; however, the improvement in RMSE under the alternative hypothesis is 4.52 percent. Hence, although a tight criterion suggests rejection of the null, the RMSE approach lends marginal support in favor of the null hypothesis.[14]

Second, we ran seven yearly regressions, one for each year from 1982 to 1988, and then compared the residual sums of squares from these regressions

---

13. The Bayes-Leamer critical value is 7.39, considerably greater than the computed F-statistic of 2.77.

14. This F-test statistic value of 2.66 is also much smaller than the Bayes-Leamer large sample–adjusted critical value of 8.11.

with those from the pooled model reported in column 1 of table 2.5. With this test, we found more support for the notion of parameter instability. In particular, the F-test statistic for the null hypothesis of parameter equality is 5.18, much larger than the .01 critical value of 1.32.[15] Moreover, the improvement in RMSE under the alternative hypothesis is substantial—15.76 percent. Thus, parameters do not appear to be stable. We will return to a discussion of parameter instability over time later in this paper.

2.4   Further Results

To this point, our analysis has involved use of a traditional hedonic equation with time and age dummies. As discussed earlier, however, an alternative specification involves including vintage and age dummies—see equation (6)—instead of the time and age dummies as in (5). Recall that regression results (including R^2, parameter estimates, and standard errors) will vary somewhat when using the V-A specification rather than the T-A representation and that this should not be surprising, for, in (5), the total number of T-A dummy variable coefficients estimated directly is nine, while in (6) it is twelve. The R^2 and RMSE values given at the bottom of table 2.6 illustrate such variation among the various T-A and V-A specifications.[16]

One result of particular interest concerns the age coefficients. As is seen in table 2.6, with the V-A specification the age coefficients are negative and statistically significant and increase in absolute value with age. We interpret these age coefficients, conditioning on vintage, as capturing the average decline in prices of surviving computer models given steady improvements in new computers entering the market, that is, as the average difference between the time and the vintage effects. In a somewhat vague sense, therefore, these age coefficients capture the average effect of technical progress–induced obsolescence in our sample.

Since the interpretations and results from the T-A and V-A specifications differ considerably, and although our purpose of computing price indexes lends a priori support to use of the T-A model specification in table 2.5, one might still question whether using information from vintages in addition to that contained in the T-A model significantly improves model fit. In the previous section, we noted that a fuller T-A-V specification is possible, provided that two variables are deleted from the V vector. Moreover, in our context, a test for the null hypothesis that the α_v coefficients are simultaneously equal to zero can be interpreted as a specification test, providing information on

---

15. The corresponding Bayes-Leamer critical value is larger at 9.03.

16. While not reported here for reasons of space, it is worth noting that the slope coefficient estimates differ between the T-A and the V-A specifications, although in many cases the differences are not large.

Table 2.6   **Selected Parameter Estimates with Time and Age and Vintage and Age Dummy Variable Specifications for Pooled, List, and Discount Samples, 1982–88 (absolute values of *t*-statistics in parentheses)**

AGE1	0.1193	0.1296	0.0414	−0.2535	−0.2523	−0.2513
	(3.911)	(3.531)	(0.74)	(8.450)	(7.008)	(4.409)
AGE2	0.1542	0.2352	0.0192	−0.5846	−0.5026	−0.6707
	(3.448)	(3.984)	(0.27)	(12.44)	(7.978)	(8.943)
AGE3	0.2984	0.5333	0.1469	−0.8577	−0.5666	−1.0561
	(4.034)	(4.748)	(1.454)	(10.72)	(4.427)	(9.429)
T83	−0.3974	−0.2193	−0.8034			
	(4.768)	(2.081)	(5.889)			
T84	−0.4085	−0.3494	−0.2933			
	(5.017)	(3.350)	(2.298)			
T85	−0.8567	−0.7645	−0.7820			
	(10.11)	(7.039)	(5.845)			
T86	−1.2755	−1.1804	−1.2660			
	(14.94)	(10.77)	(9.402)			
T87	−1.6121	−1.5201	−1.6758			
	(18.73)	(13.80)	(12.37)			
T88	−2.0331	−1.9813	−1.9611			
	(22.41)	(16.88)	(14.18)			
V79				1.5830	1.2007	1.9415
				(8.650)	(4.727)	(7.164)
V80				1.0504	0.9474	1.1670
				(7.450)	(4.174)	(5.693)
V81				0.4454	0.5003	0.3439
				(3.095)	(2.690)	(1.415)
V83				0.1646	0.0942	0.3536
				(1.770)	(0.819)	(2.267)
V84				−0.1888	−0.2287	−0.0707
				(2.030)	(1.972)	(0.450)
V85				−0.5502	−0.5869	−0.4144
				(5.731)	(4.890)	(2.527)
V86				−0.9763	−1.0051	−0.8583
				(10.06)	(8.172)	(5.298)
V87				−1.2928	−1.3289	−1.2157
				(13.19)	(10.72)	(7.551)
V88				−1.8130	−1.8808	−1.3605
				(16.94)	(14.36)	(6.637)
R^2	0.7416	0.7003	0.8220	0.7455	0.7059	0.8112
N	1,265	917	348	1,265	917	348
Root MSE	0.4166	0.4181	0.3796	0.4140	0.4149	0.3927

whether the effects of unobserved and omitted characteristic variables are systematic among vintage comparisons and/or whether equality constraints on characteristics parameters are invalid over vintages.

We therefore ran an additional regression in which eight vintage dummy variables were added to the model reported in column 1 of table 2.5 and V82 and V83 were deleted. The F-test statistic for the null hypothesis that $\alpha_v = 0$ is 5.94, the traditional .01 F-critical value is 2.51, and the improvement in RMSE is almost up to our 5 percent threshold.[17] Hence, although the evidence is not clear cut, we interpret these results as providing some support for the alternative hypothesis, suggesting a reassessment of the T-A specification in column 1 of table 2.5, looking in particular for the parameter restrictions that might be contributing to the rejection of the null hypothesis.

This led us to reexamine our earlier year-by-year regressions and to look for patterns of parameter inequality over time. Inspection revealed that, although coefficients on a number of variables trended over time, the most marked trends were for coefficients on the LRAM, LMHZ, LHRDDSK, and DOTHER variables. We then specified and estimated two additional models using pooled data, one with overlapping samples in which three separate regressions were run for the overlapping periods 1982–84, 1984–86, and 1986–88, and the other for the entire period 1982–88 with several time-interaction variables added, LRAM * TC, LMHZ * TC, LHRDDSK * TC, and DOTHER * TC, where TC is a time counter increasing annually from zero in 1982 to six in 1988. Results from these *overlapping* and *time-interaction* regressions are presented in table 2.7.

The results presented in table 2.7 represent an improvement in the model specification, accounting somewhat for the considerable variation among parameter estimates over time. For example, in the 1982–84, 1984–86, and 1986–88 regressions, coefficient estimates on LRAM, LHRDDSK, LNUMFLP, and DOTHER fall continuously, while that on LMHZ increases. Trends are also apparent in several other coefficients. Moreover, when the pooled 1982–88 regression model with time interactions is estimated, negative and statistically significant estimates are obtained for LRAM * TC, LHRDDSK * TC, and DOTHER * TC, while that on LHMZ * TC is positive and significant. Hence, both these more general specifications appear to provide improved estimates.

To check further on the validity of these two specifications, we added to each regression the set of eight dummy vintage variables and then tested the null hypothesis that $\alpha_v = 0$. Our results are more satisfying and lend qualified support for the models reported in table 2.7. In particular, as shown in table 2.8, for 1982–84 and 1984–86 the calculated F-statistics are less than the .01 critical values, for 1986–88 the calculated F-statistic is larger, but in all three cases the improvement in RMSE with vintage variables included is less than 1.5 percent.[18] Hence, for all three overlapping models, whatever the effects of omitted and unobserved characteristics, they do not appear to be systematic among vintage comparisons.

17. The corresponding Bayes-Leamer criterion value is 7.09, only slightly larger than the calculated F-statistic of 5.94.

18. The corresponding Bayes-Leamer test criteria for the three overlapping models are 5.23, 6.20, and 6.72, respectively, each of which is larger than the calculated F-statistic.

Table 2.7   Parameter Estimates for Pooled Overlapping Samples and for Pooled Sample for 1982–88 with Time Interactions

| | Overlapping Pooled Samples | | | | | | Pooled Sample 1982–88 with Time Interactions | |
| | 1982–84 | | 1984–86 | | 1986–88 | | | |
Variable	Estimate	t-Stat.	Estimate	t-Stat.	Estimate	t-Stat.	Estimate	t-Stat.
Intercept	4.1805	19.447	4.6522	22.881	4.5653	29.790	3.7782	25.066
LRAM	0.4622	9.872	0.1925	4.768	0.1652	6.883	0.6297	15.857
LRAM * TC							−0.0855	−9.416
LMHZ	0.0818	1.047	0.4041	6.521	0.4580	9.427	0.1968	2.846
LMHZ * TC							0.0370	2.228
LHRDDSK	0.2405	7.591	0.2090	12.190	0.1603	20.061	0.2302	7.612
LHRDDSK * TC							−0.0137	−2.301
LNUMFLP	0.6089	5.880	0.3916	4.976	0.1625	2.753	0.3271	6.644
LSLOTS	0.2429	5.453	0.2613	8.136	0.1134	4.930	0.1556	7.965
AGE1	0.1527	2.030	0.1321	2.725	0.1593	5.134	0.1410	4.835
AGE2	0.0217	0.172	0.0793	0.983	0.1701	3.841	0.1593	3.733
AGE3	0.3827	2.644	0.1758	1.070	0.1907	2.342	0.2496	3.525
PROC16	0.1429	1.751	0.1255	2.302	0.2824	7.338	0.2170	6.315
PROC32			0.2736	1.097	0.6040	9.392	0.6152	9.573
DBW	0.1538	2.163	0.0644	1.387	−0.1190	−3.771	0.0013	0.046
DCOLOR	0.3498	1.547	−0.0070	−0.042	−0.0249	−0.340	0.0590	0.831
DPORT	0.0770	0.890	0.4723	7.067	0.5019	11.217	0.3967	10.365
DEXTRA	0.0283	0.166	0.2670	2.201	0.3137	3.092	0.2132	2.615
DDISC	−0.3445	−5.196	−0.2430	−4.778	−0.3053	−9.508	−0.2946	−10.061

(continued)

Table 2.7 (continued)

Variable	Overlapping Pooled Samples						Pooled Sample 1982–88 with Time Interactions	
	1982–84		1984–86		1986–88			
	Estimate	t-Stat.	Estimate	t-Stat.	Estimate	t-Stat.	Estimate	t-Stat.
DAPPLE	0.2993	1.925	0.4641	4.158	0.2439	2.911	0.2199	3.047
DCMDRE	−0.4662	−2.331	−0.3954	−2.681	−0.3076	−3.292	−0.3672	−4.409
DCMPQ	0.4631	2.535	0.2757	2.756	0.0913	1.395	0.1929	3.109
DNEC	0.2916	1.686	−0.0582	−0.482	0.0580	−0.770	0.0399	0.578
DRDIOSH	0.4379	3.113	−0.0387	−0.335	−0.3162	−3.964	0.0704	1.056
DPCLIM			−0.3583	−1.988	−0.5025	−5.331	−0.5136	−5.247
DOTHER	0.2680	2.408	0.1467	1.996	−0.1316	−2.878	0.2607	3.498
DOTHER * TC							−0.0648	−4.405
T83	−0.5203	−5.631					−0.2552	−3.144
T84	−0.6203	−6.173					0.0029	0.034
T85			−0.4015	−7.196			−0.0787	−0.710
T86			−0.7694	−12.584			−0.0319	−0.218
T87					−.3365	−9.915	0.1372	0.722
T88					−.7561	−18.667	0.2680	1.110
R^2	0.8310		0.7336		0.7810		0.7668	
N	247		428		904		1,265	
Root MSE	0.4183		0.3889		0.3595		0.3965	

Note: Coefficients on the time dummy variables across estimated models are not comparable since different base years are implicit.

Table 2.8   **Test Results for Null Hypothesis That Vintage Effects Are Zero in the Pooled Overlapping Samples and in the Pooled Sample for 1982–88 Model with Time Interactions**

Pooled Samples	Calculated F-Statistic	.01 Critical F-Value	% Change in RMSE
Overlapping 1982–84	2.72	3.32	1.45
Overlapping 1984–86	3.30	3.78	0.84
Overlapping 1986–88	5.85	3.32	1.08
1982–88 with time interactions	3.55	2.51	0.82

With the pooled 1982–88 time-interaction model, results are roughly similar to those from the overlapping models. The calculated F-statistic is larger than the .01 critical value, and the improvement in the RMSE when vintage variables are added is less than 1 percent.[19] Thus, there is little basis to choose among these two specifications. However, we expect that the constant change in parameters implied by the interactive time counter would become increasingly inappropriate as additional time observations were added. On this criterion, therefore, we have a mild preference for the specification involving three overlapping regressions.

Although further experimentation with other combinations of characteristics variables would most likely be useful, we now move on to using several of the most promising specifications to construct quality-adjusted price indexes for PCs.

2.5 Price Indexes

On the basis of the results of these various hedonic price equations, we can construct price indexes in a variety of ways. Although possibilities are limited when quantity sales data on the various models are unavailable, numerous procedures can be implemented given enough available data. In this section, we construct and comment on several price indexes, all based on our hedonic regression equations but varying in their interpretation and in their use of parameter estimates and quantity weights.

We begin with price indexes based on direct transformations of estimated hedonic price coefficients, interpreted as price indexes holding quality constant over time. In the first three rows of table 2.9, we present implicit PC price indexes computed directly from the three T-A regression equations reported in table 2.5, constructed simply as the exponentiated estimated coefficients on the time dummy variables, with T82 set to zero. The values in parentheses are percentage changes from the previous year, computed as

19. The Bayes-Leamer criterion in this case is 7.07, about twice the size of the calculated F-statistic.

Table 2.9   Alternative Implicit Quality-Adjusted Relative Price Indexes for Microcomputers Based on Direct Hedonic Regression Estimates

Procedure	1979	1980	1981	1982	1983	1984	1985	1986	1987	1988	AAGR 1982–88
T-A pooled				1.000	0.672	0.665	0.425	0.279	0.200	0.131	−28.7
					(−33)	(−1)	(−36)	(−34)	(−28)	(−35)	
T-A list				1.000	0.803	0.705	0.466	0.307	0.219	0.138	−28.1
					(−20)	(−12)	(−34)	(−34)	(−29)	(−37)	
T-A discount				1.000	0.448	0.746	0.458	0.282	0.187	0.141	−27.9
					(−55)	(−67)	(−39)	(−38)	(−34)	(25)	
V-A pooled	4.869	2.859	1.561	1.000	1.179	0.828	0.577	0.377	0.274	0.163	−26.1
		(−41)	(−45)	(−36)	(18)	(−30)	(−30)	(−35)	(−27)	(−41)	
V-A list	3.322	2.579	1.649	1.000	1.099	0.796	0.556	0.366	0.265	0.152	−26.9
		(−29)	(−36)	(−39)	(10)	(−28)	(−43)	(−34)	(−28)	(−43)	
V-A discount	6.969	3.212	1.410	1.000	1.424	0.932	0.661	0.424	0.269	0.256	−20.3
		(−54)	(−56)	(−29)	(42)	(−35)	(−29)	(−36)	(−43)	(−14)	
New models only				1.000	0.716	0.620	0.420	0.266	0.195	0.116	−30.2
					(−28)	(−13)	(−32)	(−37)	(−27)	(−41)	
Overlapping				1.000	0.594	0.538	0.360	0.249	0.178	0.117	−30.1
					(−41)	(−9)	(−33)	(−31)	(−29)	(−34)	
Time interactions				1.000	0.560	0.494	0.296	0.182	0.129	0.086	−33.6
					(−44)	(−12)	(−40)	(−39)	(−29)	(−33)	

Note: The price indexes are relative to the CPI. Values in parentheses are percentage changes form the previous year, computed as $100 * (PI_t - PI_{t-1})/PI_{t-1}$, where PI is the relative price index.

$100 * (PI_t - PI_{t-1})/PI_{t-1}$, where PI is the price index. Note that the price indexes in the T-A model are the estimated time effects from regressions holding age and other characteristics constant. Overall, we see that average annual growth rates (AAGRs) are similar for the pooled, list, and discount equations (about -28 percent per year), although the estimated indexes for discounted models tend to be somewhat unstable from 1983 to 1985.

In the second set of three rows in table 2.9, implicit price indexes are presented that are based on direct exponentiation of the estimated vintage coefficients from the V-A specifications in table 2.6. The interpretation of these price indexes is slightly different—they are time effects reflecting the year of introduction and hence the average pace of technological change. As is seen in table 2.9, these price indexes suggest slightly slower declines in quality-adjusted prices than those based on T-A regressions (especially for discount models) and also reveal greater instability, particularly between 1982 and 1985.

One might think of these V-A price indexes as tracing out quality-adjusted price indexes for various vintages having AGE = 0 (since price indexes for 1979–88 are computed directly from the V79–V88 vintage coefficients, assuming AGE = 0), but estimation of the underlying coefficients is based on a sample including models of all ages. An alternative procedure for constructing a price index for new models only—an index that might be construed as tracing out the technological "frontier"—is to estimate parameters from a data sample restricted to new models, that is, to models with AGE = 0. Implicit price indexes computed from such a regression are reported in the row "new models only" in table 2.9.[20] There it is seen that a "new model only" price index declines more rapidly than those based on full-sample T-A and V-A specifications; in particular, the AAGR from 1982 to 1988 is -30.2 percent.

The two final implicit price indexes computed directly from hedonic regression equations without use of quantity sales weights are given in table 2.9 in the last two rows—"overlapping" and "time interactions." The overlapping price indexes are based on the three overlapping regressions reported in table 2.7. They are computed by directly exponentiating the coefficient estimates on the time dummy variables, linked so that, for example, the implicit 1985 and 1986 price indexes are the products of the exponentiated coefficients for 1984 and 1985 and for 1984 and 1986, respectively. Notice that, with an overlapping index procedure, the quality weights are constant only for subperiods and that coefficient estimates reflect varying sample means among subperiods. Interestingly, the overlapping price indexes fall at almost the same AAGR as that based on a "new models only" regression, although the overlapping price indexes fall more rapidly in the earlier years.

---

20. The underlying regression equation is of the same form as in table 2.5, except that age variables are deleted. Price indexes are computed directly by exponentiating the estimated coefficients on the time dummy variables.

The computation of price indexes based on the time-interaction model requires use of sample characteristics data, not just values of estimated coefficients. For example, using parameter estimates on the time interaction terms reported in table 2.7 for the log change in quality-adjusted prices between year t and year $t - 1$, we first compute

$$
\ln \tilde{p}_t - \ln \tilde{p}_{t-1} = (\alpha_t - \alpha_{t-1}) - .0855 * \text{LRAM}'_t
$$
(10)
$$
+ .0370 * \text{LMHZ}'_t - .0137 * \text{LHRDDSK}'_t
$$
$$
- .0648 * \text{TC}_t * \text{DOTHER}'_t,
$$

where the $'_t$ on LRAM, LMHZ, LHRDDSK, and DOTHER refer to the sample mean of these variables between year t and year $t - 1$. To calculate the price index, we simply cumulate the values in (10) over 1982–88 (letting $\alpha_{1982} = 0$) and then exponentiate them. This price index moves more rapidly—a decline of 33.6 percent per year—than that based on either new models or overlapping regressions. This large decline reflects the fact that sample means of the variables are all increasing with time, and these means are multiplied by the relatively large negative coefficients in (10).

One important problem with each of the above price indexes is that they fail to reflect changes over time in the mix of models. Recall that the direct hedonic regression coefficients in the T-A models can be interpreted as holding quality constant either by fixing the base of characteristic values over time or by fixing their valuation (parameter estimates). In a world with rapidly evolving new technologies, the notion of a fixed characteristic base as portraying representative transactions becomes increasingly inappropriate. What would be preferable is an index number procedure that accounts for compositional changes in models over time.[21] Such a computation requires, of course, quantity and revenue sales data by model year. As our final index number computations, we now consider a Divisia index that weights quality-adjusted prices of models by their revenue shares.

Specifically, our calculation of a (Tornqvist approximation to the) Divisia index proceeds as follows. First consider a model j observed in both period 0 and period 1. Let

$$
(11a) \qquad \ln P_{1,j} = Z'_{1,j}\hat{\beta} + \hat{\alpha}_1 + \varepsilon_{1j},
$$

$$
(11b) \qquad \ln P_{0,j} = Z'_{0,j}\hat{\beta} + \hat{\alpha}_0 + \varepsilon_{0j},
$$

where $Z_{1,j}$ and $Z_{0,j}$ are vectors of all regression variables except for the time dummy variables in year 1 and 0, the $\hat{\alpha}$'s are estimated coefficients on the time dummy variables, and the ε's are least squares residuals. This implies that

$$
\ln P_{1,j} - \ln P_{0,j} = (Z'_{1,j} - Z'_{0,j})\hat{\beta} + (\hat{\alpha}_1 - \hat{\alpha}_0) + (\varepsilon_{1j} - \varepsilon_{0j}),
$$

---

21. For a recent discussion of weighting issues in the context of compositional changes, see Triplett (1989b) and the references cited therein.

which can be rearranged to yield the expression

$$(12) \quad \ln P_{1,j} - \ln P_{0,j} - (Z'_{1,j} - Z'_{0,j})\hat{\beta} = (\hat{\alpha}_1 - \hat{\alpha}_0) + (\hat{\varepsilon}_{1j} - \hat{\varepsilon}_{0j}).$$

The left-hand side of (12) states that the log change in the quality-adjusted price of model j from 0 to 1 equals the change in observed prices minus the change in quality, where quality is evaluated using least squares regression coefficients and values of the characteristics. Alternatively, the right-hand side of (12) states that an equivalent way of computing the log change in the quality-adjusted price of model j is simply to sum the difference in estimated time dummy coefficients (which, implicitly, hold quality characteristics constant) plus the difference in the computed residuals (which reflects changes in the unmeasured attributes of the model). The choice of which of these two methods to employ in computer quality-adjusted prices can be based on relative computational convenience.

Several other features of (12) are worth noting. First, if there is no change in the characteristics of model j between 0 and 1 (i.e., the model has not become a new version in period 1), then $(Z'_{1,j} - Z'_{0,j}) = 0$ in (12), and, in essence, the quality-adjusted log price change is computed using the traditional matched-model procedure. Second, if the least squares residual is the same in the two time periods (i.e., if $\varepsilon_{1j} - \varepsilon_{0j} = 0$), then the log change in quality-adjusted prices is simply equal to the change in the time dummy coefficients. Note that residuals have a useful interpretation in the hedonic price equation, for they provide evidence on whether, relative to the overall market, a particular model is over- or underpriced.[22] An interesting issue concerns the relation between these residuals and the revenue shares garnered by each model. Since for each year the sum of residuals is zero, we would expect that, if shares are uncorrelated with residuals, it would also be the case that $\Sigma s_j \varepsilon_j \approx 0$.

Once (12) is computed for every model j in years 0 and 1, the log change in quality-adjusted prices over all models is calculated as the revenue share–weighted sum of the individual model j log changes in quality-adjusted prices,

$$(13) \quad \ln \tilde{P}_1 - \ln \tilde{P}_0 = \sum_{j=1}^{J} \bar{s}_j (\ln \tilde{P}_{1,j} - \ln \tilde{P}_{0,j})$$
$$= \sum_{j=1}^{J} \bar{s}_j (\varepsilon_{1j} - \varepsilon_{0j}) + \hat{\alpha}_1 - \hat{\alpha}_0,$$

where the $\tilde{}$, superscript is the quality-adjusted price (computed for individual j models using either side of eq. [12]), $\bar{s}_j$ is the arithmetic mean of $s_{j,1}$ and $s_{j,0}$, and s_j is the share of model j's value of shipments in the total value of shipments over all models in the appropriate time period.

---

22. This under- or overpricing might also of course reflect the effects of unobserved omitted variables or of differential market power in differing segments of the PC market.

The calculation in (12) is feasible only when model j is part of a surviving cohort of models. In fact, however, some models exit the market each year, while others enter. To account for these entering and exiting models, several adjustments must be made to (12) and (13).

Consider the case of a model that enters the market in time period 1. Obviously, its price cannot be observed in period 0, and thus use of (12) to compute a quality-adjusted price index is not feasible. One can, however, use the estimated hedonic regression equation to predict such missing prices. Specifically, we substitute the right-hand side of (11b) into (12), set $Z_{1j} = Z_{0j}$ and $\varepsilon_0 = 0$, and then rearrange. This yields an expression for quality-adjusted log-price changes for entering models in period 1, computed in two alternative but equivalent ways as

$$(14) \qquad \ln P_{1,j} - Z'_{1,j}\hat{\beta} - \hat{\alpha}_0 = \hat{\alpha}_1 - \hat{\alpha}_0 + \varepsilon_{1j}.$$

Similarly, for exiting models that were observed in period 0 but not in period 1, we employ hedonic regression procedures to predict the price of that model would it have survived to period 1. Specifically, we substitute (11a) into (12), set $Z_{1j} = Z_{0j}$ and $\varepsilon_1 = 0$, and then rearrange. This yields the appropriate log change in the quality-adjusted prices for existing models as

$$(15) \qquad Z'_{0,j}\hat{\beta} + \hat{\alpha}_1 - \ln P_{0,j} = \hat{\alpha}_1 - \hat{\alpha}_0 = \varepsilon_{0j}.$$

Once these log changes in quality-adjusted prices are computed for all incumbent, entering, and exiting models, we calculate revenue shares (setting $s_{0,j}$ to zero for entering models and $s_{1,j}$ to zero for exiting models, thereby effectively using half the last or first observed share weight) and then compute an aggregate log change in quality-adjusted prices over all models using (13).

Several other points are worth noting. First, an interesting feature of (12), (14), and (15) is that they employ as information the values of the least squares residuals. Hence, the Divisia quality-adjusted index number procedure takes into account whether those models that exited (or entered) had prices above or below the average quality-adjusted prices. Note, however, that the weight given these exiting and entering models is likely to be minor since their average revenue share in periods 0 and 1 is in most cases rather small.

Second, empirical implementation of this Divisia index number procedure requires data on value of shipments by model. Proprietary data on shipments, installations, and value of shipments by model and year for about 950 of the 1,265 models in our estimation sample were kindly provided by the International Data Corporation (IDC). These data formed the basis of the share weights used in (13).

Restricting our sample to models covered by the IDC data set and computing revenue values by model year as the product of the IDC estimates of average price paid and number of models shipped, we computed Divisia quality-adjusted price indexes separately for incumbent, entering, and exiting models and for selected aggregates.[23] Our results, using parameter estimates from the *T-A* pooled and *T-A* overlapping regressions, are presented in table 2.10. A number of results are worth noting.

We begin with results from the *T-A* pooled regressions. First, inspection of the top row of table 2.10 reveals that the quality-adjusted Divisia relative price index for all PC models declined at an AAGR of −28.2 percent from 1982 to 1988, virtually identical to the AAGR of −28.7 percent for the direct hedonic *T-A* pooled price index.

Second, although the AAGRs over the entire period are nearly equal for these indexes, the Divisia index reveals a much smoother decline over time, with year-to-year declines ranging between 20 and 37 percent, whereas year-to-year declines for the direct *T-A* pooled index vary from 1 to 36 percent.

Third, changes in the price indexes for the incumbent models are quite different from those models entering and exiting between 1982 and 1988. As shown in the next three rows in table 2.10, the price declines of the incumbent models were on average larger (−30.6 percent) than those for the entering (−24.9 percent) and exiting (−20.0 percent) models. Note that these results can be reconciled with the econometric findings reported earlier for the *T-A* specification, for which estimated coefficients on the age variables were positive, provided one interprets the latter result as reflecting selectivity due, perhaps, to unobserved positive quality differentials among the survivors as vintages progress.

Fourth, the pricing strategies employed for entering and exiting models are quite different. Over the period 1982–88, the price declines for entering models (−24.9 percent) were on average larger than those for exiting models (−20.0 percent). However, while for exiting models prices were on average flat between 1982 and 1985, these models exhibited very large price declines from 1985 to 1988.

In the bottom panel of table 2.10, we present Divisia relative price indexes using parameter estimates from the overlapping regressions. The most interesting result is that, in spite of using a rather different set of regressions, the AAGR from 1982 to 1988 is hardly affected. Specifically, the AAGRs for the pooled and overlapping regressions for all computer models are −28.2 and −28.0 percent, respectively; for incumbent models, −30.6 and −30.5 percent; for entering models, −24.9 and −22.4 percent; and for exiting models, −20.0 and −23.7 percent. Although there are year-to-year variations between the Divisia pooled and overlapping regression price indexes, the AAGRs for 1982–88 are reasonably robust.

23. We divided revenues among list and discount listings of the same model in proportion to the relative number of listings. It is also worth noting that mean values of the revenue shares of continuing, entering, and exiting models from 1982 to 1988 are 54, 26, and 20 percent, respectively. There is considerable variation in these shares over our sample time period, however.

Table 2.10   **Alternative Divisia Quality-Adjusted Relative Price Indexes for Microcomputers Based on *T-A* Pooled and *T-A* Overlapping Regression Estimates**

Regression and Sample	1982	1983	1984	1985	1986	1987	1988	AAGR 1982–88 (%)
T-A pooled estimation:								
All computer models	1.000	0.638	0.510	0.385	0.283	0.188	0.136	−28.2
		(−36)	(−20)	(−25)	(−26)	(−34)	(−28)	
Incumbent models only	1.000	0.580	0.438	0.330	0.247	0.160	0.112	−30.6
		(−42)	(−24)	(−25)	(−25)	(−35)	(−30)	
Entering models only	1.000	0.716	0.562	0.379	0.270	0.201	0.179	−24.9
		(−28)	(−22)	(−33)	(−29)	(−26)	(−11)	
Exiting models only	1.000	0.804	1.188	1.005	0.682	0.410	0.263	−20.0
		(−20)	(48)	(−15)	(−32)	(−40)	(−36)	
T-A overlapping estimation:								
All computer models	1.000	0.576	0.465	0.359	0.282	0.193	0.140	−28.0
		(−42)	(−19)	(−23)	(−21)	(−32)	(−27)	
Incumbent models only	1.000	0.542	0.422	0.317	0.250	0.160	0.113	−30.5
		(−46)	(−22)	(−25)	(−21)	(−36)	(−29)	
Entering models only	1.000	0.756	0.586	0.453	0.355	0.261	0.218	−22.4
		(−24)	(−22)	(−23)	(−22)	(−26)	(−16)	
Exiting models only	1.000	0.591	0.780	0.638	0.440	0.299	0.197	−23.7
		(−41)	(32)	(−18)	(−31)	(−32)	(−34)	

Note: The price indexes are relative to the CPI. Values in parentheses are percentage changes from the previous year, computed as $100 * (PI_t - PI_{t-1})/PI_{t-1}$, where PI is the relative price index.

2.6 Summary

The simultaneous existence of incumbent, entering, and exiting models raises issues of product heterogeneity in the microcomputer market and of the nature of price and quality competition and creates ambiguity in how one constructs and interprets price indexes. These are the issues on which we have focused attention in this paper.

Specifically, we have reported results from a variety of hedonic regression equations using an unbalanced panel data set for 1,265 model years from 1982 to 1988 and have developed and implemented empirically a specification test for selecting preferable hedonic price equations. We have discussed in detail the alternative interpretation of dummy variable coefficients in models having time and age, vintage and age, and all the time, age, and vintage dummy variables as regressors. On the basis of these estimated hedonic price equations, we then computed quality-adjusted price indexes using a variety of procedures. This provided us with indexes having varying interpretations—constant average quality price indexes, price indexes for new models only, and quality-adjusted price indexes portraying representative transactions that take into account the changing model composition in our sample over time. Not surprisingly, average annual growth rates for these varying price indexes also differed, although all showed a substantial decline in quality-adjusted prices over the period 1982–88.

Our research is preliminary, and much remains to be done. One item high on our research agenda involves obtaining model-specific performance measures for specific numerical tasks, such as the number of instructions executed per unit of time, and then redoing the hedonic regressions with such performance measures added as regressors. Moreover, issues of parameter instability and choice of variables to include in the set of characteristics are also potentially important and need further examination. Finally, given that the least squares residuals either provide economic information on over- or underpricing of models relative to the market as a whole or reflect the effects of omitted variables or differential market power in different PC market segments, an interesting extension would involve examining in greater detail the relations among residuals for entering, incumbent, and exiting models and realized market shares.

References

Archibald, Robert B., and William S. Reece. 1978. Partial subindexes of input prices: The case of computer services. *Southern Economic Journal* 46 (October): 528–40.

Arrow, Kenneth J. 1960. Decision theory and the choice of a level of significance for the *t*-test. In *Contributions to probability and statistics,* ed. I. Olkin, W. Hoeffding, S. G. Gurye, W. G. Madow, and H. B. Mann. Stanford, Calif.: Stanford University Press.

Berndt, Ernst R. 1991. The measurement of quality change: Constructing an hedonic price index for computers using multiple regression methods. In *The practice of econometrics: Classic and contemporary.* Reading, Mass.: Addison-Wesley.

Cartwright, David W. 1986. Improved deflation of purchases of computers. *Survey of Current Business* 66 (March): 7–9.

Cartwright, David W., and Scott D. Smith. 1988. Deflators for purchases of computers in GNP: Revised and extended estimates, 1983–1988. *Survey of Current Business* 68 (November): 22–23.

Catron, Brian. 1989. Price measurement for computer hardware: A demonstration of quality adjustment techniques. Working paper. Washington, D.C.: U.S. Department of Labor, Bureau of Labor Statistics, Office of Prices and Living Conditions, 14 April.

Chow, Gregory C. 1967. Technological change and the demand for computers. *American Economic Review* 57 (December): 1117–30.

Cohen, Jeremy M. 1988. Rapid change in the personal computer market: A quality-adjusted hedonic price index, 1976–1987. S.M. thesis, Massachusetts Institute of Technology, Alfred P. Sloan School of Management, May.

Cole, Rosanne, Y. C. Chen, Joan A. Barquin-Stolleman, Ellen Dulberger, Nurhan Helvacian, and James H. Hodge. 1986. Quality-adjusted price indexes for computer processors and selected peripheral equipment. *Survey of Current Business* 66 (January): 41–50.

Dulberger, Ellen R. 1989. The application of an hedonic model to a quality-adjusted price index for computer processors. In *Technology and capital formation,* ed. Dale W. Jorgenson and Ralph Landau. Cambridge, Mass.: MIT Press.

Epple, Dennis. 1987. Hedonic prices and implicit markets: Estimating demand and supply functions for differentiated products. *Journal of Political Economy* 95 (January): 59–80.

Fienberg, Stephen E., and William M. Mason. 1985. Specification and implementation of age, period and cohort models. In *Cohort analysis in social research,* ed. William M. Mason and Stephen E. Fienberg. New York: Springer-Verlag.

Fisher, Franklin M., John J. McGowan, and Joen E. Greenwood. 1983. *Folded, spindled and mutilated: Economic analysis and U.S. v. IBM.* Cambridge, Mass.: MIT Press.

Gordon, Robert J. 1989. The postwar evolution of computer prices. In *Technology and capital formation,* ed. Dale W. Jorgenson and Ralph Landau. Cambridge, Mass.: MIT Press.

———. 1990. *The measurement of durable goods prices.* Chicago: University of Chicago Press (for the National Bureau of Economic Research).

Griliches, Zvi. 1961. Hedonic price indexes for automobiles: An econometric analysis of quality change. In *The price statistics of the federal government.* General Series no. 73. New York: Columbia University Press (for the National Bureau of Economic Research). (Reprinted in Griliches 1971.)

———. 1971. Introduction: Hedonic prices revisited. In *Price indexes and quality change: Studies in the new methods of measurement,* ed. Zvi Griliches. Cambridge, Mass.: Harvard University Press.

———. 1988. Postscript on hedonics. In *Technology, education, and productivity.* New York: Blackwell.

Hall, Robert E. 1971. The measurement of quality change from vintage price data. In *Price indexes and quality change: Studies in new methods of measurement,* ed. Zvi Griliches. Cambridge, Mass.: Harvard University Press.

Heckman, James J., and Richard Robb. 1985. Using longitudinal data to model age, period and cohort effects in earnings equations. In *Cohort analysis in social research,* ed. William M. Mason and Stephen E. Fienberg. New York: Springer-Verlag.

Kim, Amy Y. 1989. Hedonic price indices and an examination of the personal computer market. Honors undergraduate thesis, Harvard College, Department of Economics, March.

Leamer, Edward E. 1978. *Specification searches: Ad hoc inference with nonexperimental data.* New York: Wiley.

Michaels, Robert. 1979. Hedonic prices and the structure of the digital computer industry. *Journal of Industrial Economics* 27 (March): 263–75.

Ohta, Makoto, and Zvi Griliches. 1976. Automobile prices revisited: Extensions of the hedonic hypothesis. In *Household production and consumption,* ed. Nestor E. Terleckyj. Studies in Income and Wealth, vol. 40. New York: Columbia University Press (for the National Bureau of Economic Research).

Oliner, Stephen D. 1986. Depreciation and deflation of IBM mainframe computers: 1980–1985. Washington, D.C.: Federal Reserve Board, June. Typescript.

Rosen, Sherwin. 1974. Hedonic prices and implicit markets: Product differentiation in pure competition. *Journal of Political Economy* 82 (January/February): 34–55.

Sinclair, James, and Brian Catron. 1990. An experimental price index for the computer industry. *Monthly Labor Review* 113 (October): 16–24.

Triplett, Jack E. 1986. The economic interpretation of hedonic methods. *Survey of Current Business* 86 (January): 36–40.

———. 1989a. Price and technological change in a capital good: A survey of research on computers. In *Technology and capital formation,* ed. Dale W. Jorgenson and Ralph Landau. Cambridge, Mass.: MIT Press.

————. 1989b. Superlative and quasi-superlative indexes of price and output for investment goods: Office, computing and accounting machinery. Discussion Paper no. 40. Washington, D.C.: U.S. Department of Commerce, Bureau of Economic Analysis, July (rev.).

————. 1990. Hedonic methods in statistical agency environments: An intellectual biopsy. In *Fifty years of economic measurement,* ed. Ernst R. Berndt and Jack E. Triplett. Chicago: University of Chicago Press (for the National Bureau of Economic Research).

Wilmoth, John. 1989. Variation in vital rates of age, period, and cohort. Research Report no. 89-141. Ann Arbor: University of Michigan, Population Studies Center, April.

Comment   Rosanne Cole

These papers deal with the main outstanding empirical issues associated with the construction and interpretation of hedonic-based price indexes in general and computer price indexes in particular. In addition, the Oliner paper contains estimates of the rate of depreciation and of the retirement distribution for a set of computers and an assessment of the possible bias in BEA estimates of real gross and net stocks of this class of assets.

The contribution of the Berndt-Griliches paper is primarily methodological. The authors employ a sample of microcomputer list and discount prices to illustrate and deal with the econometric issues involved in estimating hedonic regressions from data in the form of an unbalanced panel. Of specific concern is the interpretation of the various time-related coefficients, given that one never really knows whether the included set of characteristics is the "correct" one. They develop and implement empirically a test for detecting inadequacy in the specification of hedonic equations—inadequacy of the set of included characteristics and/or invalid stability constraints on the characteristics' coefficients over time. Finally, they construct a variety of price indexes: constant average quality price indexes; price indexes reflecting changes over time in model mix or changing average quality; and price indexes for new, continuing, and exiting models only.

Berndt and Griliches regard their results for microcomputers as preliminary. Obtaining improved measures of characteristics (I return to this topic later) ranks high on their agenda for further work on these products. But their main contribution is the provision of a diagnostic tool whose use, when coupled with technical knowledge of the products under study, should benefit and improve the credibility of future hedonic studies.

Rosanne Cole, now a consultant, was formerly director of economic research and forecasting at the IBM Corp.

Computers have received considerable attention largely because of the difficulties these products pose for price measurement. They provide an example of products subject to rapid technological improvement in a rapidly changing marketplace. There is relatively frequent entry and exit of firms and a steady stream of models introduced and of models discontinued. Indeed, the market for computers has been characterized as in "disequilibrium" caused by technological change.

Multiple Prices

Previous work, especially Dulberger's (1989) study of intermediate and large-size computer processors (so-called mainframe computers), has emphasized one aspect of disequilibrium: the existence for a time of multiple quality-adjusted prices when models embodying new technology are introduced into the marketplace.

Oliner employs a largely untapped body of data, secondary market asking prices for IBM mainframe computers, to ask how these prices compare with list prices and whether Dulberger's finding of multiple prices was merely an artifact. His analysis confirms Dulberger's finding. The secondary market data show price premiums on old models comparable to those found in the list price data.[1]

The question has important practical implications. If the quality-adjusted prices of existing products adjust instantaneously and fully to the introduction of new models, then a price index covering only the most technologically advanced models would be the same as the price index covering all models that are sold. Moreover, these price indexes would be the same as a price index based on matched-models procedures so it might not even be necessary to turn to hedonic methods.

There are some suggestions of multiple prices for microcomputers reported by Berndt and Griliches in their table 2.10, but they are of a perverse nature. There, the quality-adjusted price indexes for entering models are persistently higher than those for continuing models. These price differentials are not of the Dulberger variety, which arise when models embodying new technology come into the marketplace, persist for a short time, and then vanish. The period of time that the differentials persist depends partly on the time it takes for new "families" of models to be brought into full production.

The rapid increase in production of new families of microcomputers and their short delivery schedules during 1982–88 (the period covered by the price

---

1. This result is a fairly strong one because it takes some time for models to appear in the *Price Guide*. For example, ten of the thirty-three models produced during the period studied by Dulberger, 1972–84, were not quoted in the *Price Guide* until they were out of production. Of the twenty-three models in current production and also quoted in the *Price Guide,* seven were first quoted at age 1, ten at age 2, five at age 3, and one at age 4. The majority (twenty-three of thirty-four) of models produced during 1985–88 were not quoted in this secondary market data until they were out of production. Moreover, it should be noted that Dulberger's sample was not limited to IBM models.

indexes in table 2.10) suggest that there was much less imbalance between the demand for and supply of these products than was typical historically for mainframes. One would therefore expect prices to adjust quickly and fully to the introduction of new models, but not to "overadjust." The price differentials in table 2.10 are, in my judgment, more of the ordinary garden variety, which arise when prices have not been adequately adjusted for quality differences among the products to which they refer.

Characteristics Measures

One of the problems encountered in implementing hedonic techniques to correct prices for quality differences is obtaining appropriate measures of characteristics. In the case of computers, the problem is especially severe for measures of speed. There is always a trade-off between measures that are adequate for the purpose at hand and measures that are also comparable across the range of products under consideration.

There is a second type of problem that is a level-of-aggregation issue. Computer processors are one component of a computing system (or network of system components); auxiliary storage devices (disk drives, tape drives) are another. Measures of speed that are adequate at a single component level are generally inadequate at a higher level of aggregation. Thus, for example, equivalent MIPS (millions of instructions processed per second) is an adequate measure of processor speed, but it is an inadequate measure of speed for small computers that house both the processor and the auxiliary storage devices under one cover ("box").

The speed measure employed for microcomputers in the Berndt-Griliches paper is at the lowest level, clock rate (logic cycles per second). Logic cycle time is the highest speed at which a microprocessor could theoretically operate (neglecting a memory speed constraint). Even though this measure is roughly comparable across the range of the *microprocessors* contained in the products that they consider, it is not an adequate measure of the speed of the *microcomputers* that they price. Preferable measures of speed are equivalent MIPS (which takes account of memory cycle time) at the processor level or a benchmark performance measure (which in addition takes account of the speed of the embedded auxiliary storage device) at the computer level.

A comparison of clock rate with other publicly available speed measures for a set of IBM PCs is given in table C.1: equivalent MIPS, at the processor level, and benchmark measures, at the computer level. Two types of benchmark measures are shown: the Whetstone, a widely used performance benchmark for scientific applications, and NSTL performance benchmarks.[2] The

---

2. The performance benchmark tests were conducted by National Software Testing Laboratories, Inc. (NSTL), Plymouth Meeting, PA (215-941-9600) and reported in the *PC Digest* "Ratings Report" (see the April 1987 issue).

Table C.1   Comparisons of Speed Measures, Selected IBM PCs

| | | Processor Speed (expressed relative to PC/XT) | | |
	Model	Clock Rate (MHz)		Vax Equivalent MIPS
	PC/XT	4.77	1.0	1.0
	PC/AT	6	1.3	2.96
	PC/AT	8	1.7	4.14
	PS/2:			
	Model 30	8	1.7	
	Model 50	10	2.1	5.17
	Model 60	10	2.1	
	Model 80	16	3.4	

| | Computer Speed: Benchmarks (expressed relative to PC/XT) | | | |
| | | NSTL Performance Benchmarks | | |
	Whetstone	Simple Average	Spreadsheet	World Processing	General Ledger
PC/XT	1.0	1.0	1.0	1.0	1.0
PC/AT (6MHz)	3.14	2.7	2.9	2.6	2.5
PC/AT (8MHz)	4.38	3.5	4.0	3.3	3.2
PS/2:					
Model 30		2.1	2.3	2.1	2.0
Model 50	5.47	4.4	4.9	4.2	4.0
Model 60		4.6	4.9	4.3	4.2
Model 80		7.6	9.0	7.2	6.6

Sources: VAX MIPS and Whetstone measures are constructed from a table sourced as Power Meter v. 1.2, The Database Group (testing performed by *PC Week* and reported in *PC Week,* (8 September 1987, 1). NSTL performance benchmark measures are constructed from results of performance benchmarks tests reported in the "Ratings Report" in *PC Digest,* April 1987, 16, 20, 23–28, and used with permission of NSTL, a Division of Datapro Research Group, Plymouth Meeting, Pa. 19462.

NSTL benchmark tests are unusual because they are conducted for a fairly wide range of applications (spreadsheet, word processing, relational data base, etc.) and performance of each application is tested under more than one application software package. Although the entries in table C.1 draw only on results for IBM PCs for three popular applications, results for other applications and for other brand-name PCs that rely on Intel microprocessors (Compac, Tandy, etc.) were also published in the same report.

The comparisons in table C.1 show that, on the basis of clock rate, the PS/2 model 30 has the same speed as one model of the PC/AT; all the NSTL measures show its speed to be slower. The speed of the PS/2 model 50 is twice that of the PC/XT based on the clock rate measure; all the alternatives show it to be four to five times as fast. The PS/2 model 80 is nearly three and a half times as fast as the PX/XT when measured by clock rate but six to nine times as fast on the basis of the NSTL measures of speed.[3]

This same measurement problem exists for the other brand-name micro-computers included in the data set studied by Berndt and Griliches. The error introduced is such that prices of higher-speed models are persistently under-corrected for quality change.[4] I suspect that this is the main reason for the perverse price differentials between entering and continuing models in the quality-adjusted price indexes shown in table 2.10 of Berndt and Griliches's paper.

Given my view that the Berndt-Griliches study has produced questionable correction for quality change, I remain unconvinced that hedonic techniques are preferable to matched-models procedures for purposes of constructing quality-adjusted price indexes for microcomputers. This preference, however, is conditioned on the assumption that the sample of models priced is refreshed with sufficient frequency as to remain representative of models sold.[5]

Depreciation, Obsolescence, and the Concept of Age

Oliner's hedonic regressions can be regarded as treating the decline in market value of a computer as it ages as consisting of two components: the part attributable to the rate of technological obsolescence and the part attributable to the rate of change in the market value of the computer's characteristics. There are two concepts of age for purposes of estimating the obsolescence component of depreciation: one based on model age and one based on age of the technology embodied in the model. Judging by the regression results (reported in Oliner's tables 1.7 and 1.8), the preferred concept would be the one based on age of the technology embodied in the model, not the one based on model age. On an annual basis, the rates compound to 14.7 percent (table 1.7, col. 5) and 16.1 percent (table 1.7, col. 2), respectively.[6] Thus, it appears that the choice between the two concepts matters more for purposes of interpreting than for estimating a geometric rate of obsolescence of these products from hedonic regressions.

3. As a general rule, numerically intensive applications require a relatively small amount of data movement, or "disk accesses." Consequently, a spreadsheet or the Whetstone benchmark will show relative speed measures close to the measures of processor speed. In contrast, word processing or general ledger are applications that require considerable disk activity. Benchmarks based on this type of application will show relative speed measures for the computer that are slower than the processor speed measures. A summary measure of computer speed can be obtained by striking a simple or weighted average of the benchmark results.

4. The hedonic work underlying the Bureau of Labor Statistics (BLS) experimental price indexes for microcomputers employed the clock rate measure of speed and is subject to the same criticism.

5. But see Triplett's Comment (in this volume). One problem threading through the workshop sessions on computer price indexes and semiconductor price indexes was the difficulty of fitting these products into the producer price index (PPI) sampling methodology.

6. The estimated rates of depreciation are altered only slightly by allowing for disequilibrium: the 14.7 percent becomes 14.6 percent, and the 16.1 percent becomes 15.9 percent.

The two concepts of age produce very different patterns of depreciation, however, as a comparison of Oliner's figures 1.5 and 1.6 illustrates. Oliner has an interesting interpretation of the two. My own would be somewhat different. Since I would expect the depreciation pattern of these products to be dominated by technological obsolescence, I conclude that the results show that a new model embodying new technology declines in price as it ages far less rapidly than a new model embodying a three- or four-year-old technology. In summary, the model age–price profile is dominated by the age of the technology that the model contains.

Processors do not wear out with use, as do products with moving parts, nor do they suffer from metal fatigue. They become obsolete, not when repairs can no longer be justified, but when other complementary resouces are unjustifiably large compared with those required to operate models embodying the most advanced technology. The time pattern of the lines in fig. 1.6 suggests that it takes two generations of new technology to make the old fully obsolete; this seems consistent with the long tail on the retirement distribution that Oliner estimates.

Retirement, Depreciation, and "Real" Capital Stock Estimates

A major contribution of the Oliner paper is the evidence presented on the pattern of the distribution of retirements of this set of products. The Winfrey S-3 is clearly shown to be a poor approximation of reality. As one might guess from Oliner's results, it is probably also a poor approximation of the retirement distribution of other types of office and computing equipment.

Rather than having to rely on Winfrey approximations, it would of course be preferable to develop estimates of retirement distributions and average service lives from a historical set of data on maintenance contracts covering this (or any) class of assets. Such a data set is not publicly available, at least to my knowledge. Despite their "second-best" aspect, data on stocks are available (although not from a single or costless source) for other types of computing equipment. I endorse Oliner's recommendation for a further research effort along the lines that he describes.

Oliner's evidence on retirements and the decline in average service lives convinces me that the BEA estimates of real gross stocks of processors, relying as they do on a Winfrey S-3 distribution with a constant eight-year average service life, would overstate the growth of these stocks. I am glad he now agrees that an overly rapid rate of depreciation has historically been employed to obtain estimates of the net stocks from the gross stocks.[7] Only the obsolescence component, or partial depreciation, as Oliner calls it, should be applied.

Two factors account for the decline in average service lives and the increase in the depreciation rates that Oliner observes, and both can change direction

---

7. The first version of the paper did not distinguish partial depreciation for purposes of estimating real net stocks from real gross stocks.

over time. One is the pickup in the pace of introducing new technology. The second is an increase in the average age of the technology contained in the new models in his sample. On the basis of the data in Oliner's appendix tables 1.A.1 and 1.A.2, the 360 models embodied new technology, the new 370 models had an average technology age of two years, and the new 303X models had an average technology age of five years. These two factors together produced the earlier obsolescence and shorter service lives that Oliner notes (his fig. 1.3). An answer to the question of whether these findings would hold for other types of computers and computing equipment—and, for that matter, for other types of high-tech equipment—awaits further research. Certainly, Oliner's work is an important first step.

Reference

Dulberger, Ellen R. 1989. The application of a hedonic model to a quality-adjusted price index for computer processors. In *Technology and capital formation,* ed. Dale W. Jorgenson and Ralph Landau. Cambridge, Mass.: MIT Press.

II High-Tech Products: Semiconductors

3 Sources of Price Decline in Computer Processors: Selected Electronic Components

Ellen R. Dulberger

Technological change in electronic components has been largely responsible for the increased capabilities of products to process and store information. The rapid pace of technological change embodied in chips and the packages in which they are connected makes their lives short. This creates difficult problems in measuring the output and prices of these products and hence value-added in industries consuming them. These measurement problems may be responsible for large errors in components of the producer price index (PPI) resulting in price declines far smaller than actual and hence inconsistent with larger declines in the implicit deflator for computing equipment in the national income and product accounts (NIPA).

This paper focuses on those electronic products used in the manufacture of computer processors. Evidence is presented that supports the view that prices of these products decline much more rapidly than measured by the PPI for these products and, as should be the case, even more rapidly than prices for computer processors. Provided first is a description of the electronic products used in computer processors. Next the (un)reasonableness of price changes in components of the PPI as compared with those in newly developed measures is explored. Alternative price indexes for selected electronic products constructed here are examined for differences arising from choice of formula, and an explicit assessment of the effect of delayed introduction of new products is provided. Finally, the alternative indexes are assessed for consistency with the NIPA deflator for computer equipment purchases. Section 3.1 contains descriptions and discussions of electronic components used in the manufacture

Ellen R. Dulberger is program manager, economics, at IBM Corp.

The author gratefully acknowledges support from and discussions with Rosanne Cole of IBM and is indebted to Tom Orzell of IBM for his programming expertise. In addition, she thanks Marilyn Manser of the Bureau of Labor Statistics and Jack Triplett of the Bureau of Economic Analysis for their excellent comments and suggestions.

of computer processors and the technological change that these products have undergone. Section 3.2 presents the data, describes the alternative price indexes constructed, and examines their credibility.

3.1 Products

Electronic packages contain many electrical circuit components that become circuits when interconnected. The lowest-level semiconductor device that contains circuits or circuit components is the chip. The complexity and cost of an electronic package increase with the number of chips interconnected and the number of interconnections in the package.[1] The first-level package provides the support and protection for the small, fragile chip terminals. Cards on which chips are mounted are the most common second-level package. These simple packages are used in the manufacture of many consumer products such as compact disc players and hand calculators where the total chip count is likely to be less than ten. When used in higher-level packages, cards (sometimes called daughter boards) are plugged into third-level packages (sometimes called mother boards). These third-level packages are the guts of personal computers (such as the IBM PS/2 and the Apple PC) today. The total number of chips in these third-level packages is usually in the tens.

The microelectronic packages described thus far are simple and inexpensive compared with those in high-performance computer processors. These packages consist of relatively few chips, and the amount of heat that they generate does not require additional chip cooling within the electronic package.

The logic of large general purpose computers today is made of complex electronic component packages of thousands of chips. To achieve the speeds at which they process instructions, the packages and chips interconnected therein are very different from the products described earlier in design, materials, and production processes used.[2] Examples of the logic packages produced by two manufacturers of large general purpose processors illustrate two different ways of achieving high levels of integration. In the case of the Hitachi 680, the chips are mounted in multichip modules (MCMs), which are then connected to polyimid-glass (P-G) cards. These P-G cards are in turn cable connected to P-G boards, which are air cooled (see Tummala and Rymaszewski 1989, table 1-2, p. 26). A very different logic package is used in an IBM 3090 processor. It contains chips mounted on multilayer ceramic substrates in water-cooled thermal conduction modules (TCMs). The TCMs are connected using a pin-through hole process onto epoxy-glass boards, which are cable connected and water cooled.[3]

1. For a discussion of the complexity and cost of interconnections, see Noyce (1977).
2. For a discussion of complex high-level ceramic packages, see Black (1986).
3. For an analogous discussion of electronic packaging hierarchy as it pertains to communication equipment, see Mayo (1986).

3.1.1   Technological Change

Major improvements in the performance of these products, that is, in the speed at which instructions are executed and in the capacity to store information in main memory, have come from increased density at the chip level (more circuits and bits on the chip) and denser interconnections on the package. Technological advances in density result when finer lines can be drawn closer together, shortening the distance the electrons travel yet not generating so much heat that the circuits melt.

Main Memory

The first product to be manufactured once a new level of density has been achieved is the memory chip. The reason for this is based on the differences in function between memory and logic. Memory elements are infrequently actively used in an operation, and they are much simpler physically than are logic circuits (most often called gates), so a memory cell occupies less area on a silicon chip than does a logic circuit and will require fewer chip-to-chip connections, making it easier to manufacture. Therefore, for a given technology, defined in terms of chip density and materials and process, such as complementary metal-oxide semiconductor, CMOS, the first product manufactured will be memory chips. The relation between density, application, and interconnections is reproduced in figure 3.1.

In general, main memory in processors of all sizes is composed of the same MOS (metal oxide on silicon) dynamic random access memory (DRAM) chips, although the final memory package will differ with the memory size in the final product. The same is not true for logic. Logic packages in high-performance and low-end processors differ all the way down to the chips themselves. In low-end processors, the logic chips are often made using the same manufacturing process and, indeed, are manufactured on the same production lines as the memory chips. As is the case for CMOS chips, improvements in logic parallel improvements in memory, as illustrated in figure 3.2. Quality-adjusted price declines in CMOS logic chips will be at least as steep as those in memory, but they will be steeper when design changes permit more work to be accomplished in a cycle.

In 1974, DRAMs stored 4k (kilobits) of data. 64k DRAMs were in use in 1979, and by 1985 1 Mb DRAMs were widely used. The Dataquest history of prices and quantities of DRAMs is provided in the upper panel of table 3.1. For each density, it is observed that quantities shipped have increased at a rapid pace for at least four years after introduction and that, during that time, prices decline rapidly as well. The lower panel of table 3.1 presents the value shares of shipments by density through time. Indeed, in three of the four cases shown, the market share of chips embodying new technology exceeds 20 percent just one year after introduction.

Transformations of the entries in table 3.1 to refer to kilobits rather than

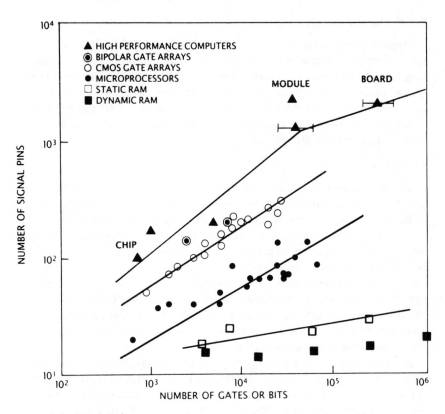

Fig. 3.1   Rent's rule

Note: Rent's rule describes the relation between the number of logic circuits on a chip and the number of pins (leads) needed to connect the chip to the rest of the system. The rule is empirical, worked out in the 1960s as experience with chips was accumulated. Rent's rule forms part of an overall model linking the properties of materials, devices, and circuits with those of the system in which they work.

Source: Meindl (1988).

chips are presented in table 3.2. Although new, denser chips are introduced at higher prices per kilobit than the prevailing prices of those against which they compete, it usually takes less than two years for the new chip to offer the lowest price per kilobit. It should be noted that computers need not have used each of these chips in each year they were available. Indeed, indicated in table 3.2 by parentheses are observations that are not relevant to the main memories in computer processors according to Dulberger's (1989) sample, which was used in the Bureau of Economic Analysis (BEA) price deflator for computing equipment.[4] If this sample is representative of the use of DRAMs by the universe of computer processor manufacturers, then prices in parentheses would

---

4. This sample is composed of large and intermediate IBM and plug-compatible processors.

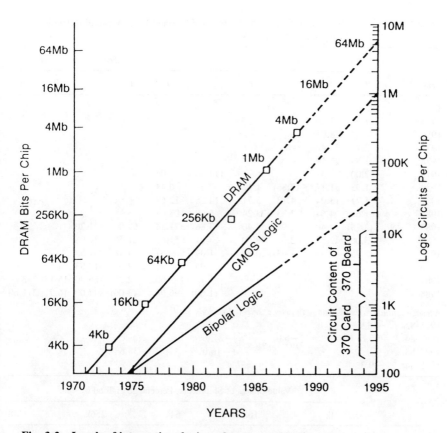

Fig. 3.2   Levels of integration: logic and memory chips
Note: Progress in level of integration. By 1980, circuits per single random logic chip matched the circuit content of an IBM 370 card, introduced ten years earlier. In another five to ten years, the circuits per single chip reached those of an IBM 370 board.
Source: Tummala and Rymaszewski (1989).

not enter a price index of inputs to processors. Indeed, the big price increases at the end of the 4k chip's life would not enter the price index.

The success of the new chips introduced at a higher than prevailing price per kilobit is in need of explanation. Common sense suggests that something is missing; only products offering lower quality-adjusted prices should drive existing products out of production. Although the important attribute of these chips is the amount of data they store, their use in higher-level packages may justify their higher price. By reducing amounts of other resources that manufacturers will consume in making the final product, final memory package cost may be lowered.

For example, to achieve the same maximum memory capacity with new chips that are four times as dense as the previous generation requires one-

Table 3.1   DRAMs Used in Main Memories of Selected Large General Purpose Processors, Merchant Market

	4k		16k		64k		256k		1Mb	
Year	P	Q	P	Q	P	Q	P	Q	P	Q
1974	(23.00)	.62								
1975	7.25	5.29								
1976	4.44	28.01								
1977	2.75	57.42								
1978	1.83	77.19								
1979	2.00	70.01			117.50	0.04				
1980	1.93	31.17	(7.88)	1.12	62.50	0.44				
1981	1.71	13.04	4.13	5.71	14.38	12.63				
1982	1.68	4.64	2.33	23.24	5.69	103.97				
1983	(2.75)	2.40	1.96	57.40	3.86	371.34	69.00	1.70		
1984	(3.00)	2.25	2.06	40.60	3.21	851.60	21.50	37.98		
1985	(3.75)	2.35	(1.63)	20.91	1.09	509.67	4.98	201.58		
1986					1.03	404.91	2.31	618.53	34.50	5.66
1987					(1.10)	152.60	2.35	766.30	15.13	42.60
1988					(1.60)	96.90	(3.06)	947.00	16.71	211.60

Average annual rates of change in prices, selected periods

1975–82	− 18.9				
1982–84	(33.6)		(− 6.0)	− 24.9	
1984–88				(− 16.0)	− 38.6
1975–84	− 9.3				

	Value Shares of Shipments, Percentage of Total by Year				
	4k	16k	64k	256k	1Mb
1974–78	100.0				
1979	97.1		2.9		
1980	62.3	9.1	28.6		
1981	9.8	10.4	79.8		
1982	1.2	8.3	90.5		
1983	0.4	6.7	85.8	7.0	
1984	0.2	2.3	75.1	22.4	
1985	0.6	2.1	34.6	62.7	
1986			20.3	70.1	9.6
1987			6.4	68.9	24.7
1988			2.3	44.0	53.6

Note: Parentheses indicate values available from Dataquest that would not enter an input price index for computer processors according to Dulberger's sample. P = dollars/chip. Q = thousands of units.

Source: Dataquest, *Semiconductor Industry Service.*

Table 3.2   **DRAMs Used in Main Memories of Selected Large General Purpose Processors, Merchant Market Prices (dollars/kilobit)**

Year	4k	16k	64k	256k	1Mb (1,024k)
1974	(5.750)				
1975	1.813				
1976	1.109				
1977	0.688				
1978	0.456				
1979	0.500		1.836		
1980	0.481	(0.492)	0.977		
1981	0.428	0.258	0.225		
1982	0.419	0.145	0.089		
1983	(0.688)	0.123	0.060	0.270	
1984	(0.750)	0.129	0.050	0.084	
1985	(0.938)	(0.102)	0.017	0.019	
1986			0.016	0.009	0.034
1987			(0.017)	0.009	0.015
1988			(0.025)	(0.012)	0.016

Average annual percentage change in lowest price/kilobit, selected periods, chips used in processors

1975–82	−35.0	(4k in 1975 compared with 64k in 1982)
1982–84	−25.0	(64k in both periods)
1984–87	−43.5	(64k in 1984 compared with 256k in 1987)
1987–88	77.8	(256k in 1987 compared with 1Mb in 1988)
1975–84	−32.9	
1975–87	−35.7	

Note: Entries are computed by dividing Dataquest prices in table 3.1 by the number of kilobits per chip. Parentheses indicate values available from Dataquest that would not enter an input price index for computer processors according to Dulberger's sample.

fourth the number of chips. Packaging fewer chips requires fewer interconnections, less complex packages, and sometimes fewer levels of packaging. In this way, the previous maximum size of main memory costs less per unit of capacity (commonly measured in megabytes) to manufacture, thus enabling producers to pass along these lower costs to their customers.

By the time the new chips have come down in price to where they offer the lowest price per kilobit, their use is widespread in smaller processors and other products with smaller packaging requirements. This widespread use hastens the disappearance of previous generations. A price index constructed on the basis of kilobits as the only attribute may be biased in the direction of understating the quality-adjusted price declines in these products.

If quality-adjusted prices of higher levels of packaging kept pace with those of the chips, we would see similar price declines in the price per megabyte of main memory. Some evidence is provided by Cole et al. (1986), who found that the change in the price per megabyte of main memory was −23.6 percent per year for the period 1975–84. This suggests that the declines in the quality-adjusted prices of higher levels of packaging were close but did not quite keep pace with those of chips.[5]

It is important to recognize that packaging is often as important as the chip in producing lower quality-adjusted prices. Examples of some packages are useful in understanding the complexity of packages that resulted in capacities shown in table 3.3.[6] In 1975, one main memory package was composed of 32,000 2k chips packaged on four-chip modules packaged on thirty-two-module cards, eight of which plugged into each of four boards that were cable connected. By the mid-1980s, a card, 250 × 170 millimeters, could hold 160 chips. This meant card capacities of 4MB with 256k DRAMs and 16MB with 1Mb chips. Half a gigabyte was achieved by connecting 16MB on both sides of sixteen cards at the board level (4,000 1Mb chips) (Tummala and Rymaszewski, 1989, 57).

Logic

Comparisons of performance in logic chips and packages in high-end processors are not easily made. Improvements at the chip level reduce the inter-level connections. Improving packaging achieves a reduction in wiring length, thus shortening the distance traveled. This is key to improving CPU (central processing unit) cycle time, a major determinant of processor speed. Table 3.4 provides CPU cycle time and processor speed measured in 370 equivalent MIPS for selected large general purpose processors.[7] In addition, for three processors, the contributions to CPU cycle time of the chips and the packages are shown. A comparison of performance characteristics of selected processors and embodied chips and packages is shown in table 3.4.[8]

Table 3.4 shows that the relation between CPU cycle time and processor speed may be different across manufacturers. In addition, improvements in chips may occur at a different rate than improvements in the package. The Amdahl 470 processor was 50 percent faster in terms of 370 equivalent MIPS

5. The price indexes produced by Cole et al. (1986) were used by BEA in deflating purchase of computing equipment in the NIPAs, 1972–84.

6. For a detailed description of the main memory of the IBM 370/168, see Rajchman (1977, 1225).

7. MIPS, millions of instructions per second, is a widely used measure of processor speed in which each instruction is weighted by its frequency of use in a specific job mix. For more discussion of 370 equivalent MIPS with respect to its adequacy as a measure of processor speed and its comparability across processors, see Cole et al. (1986, 41–42).

8. For a given manufacturer, within a family of processors (not shown in table) it is not unusual to find members with the same CPU cycle time rated at different MIPS. Models selected for inclusion in table 3.4 are those with the highest MIPS ratings in their family. Smaller (slower) members of a family are products made with less hardware. In these products, more CPU cycles are used to accomplish the same work done in one cycle of the bigger boxes.

Although the technological "race" is often discussed in terms of the fastest uniprocessor because it represents the shortest time to do any activity, it should be noted that manufacturers vary in their ability to lash multiple processors together to produce a single system image. During the 1980s, it was not uncommon to find that the manufacturer with the fastest uniprocessor was not the same as the one that made the fastest single system image. Similarly, manufacturers vary in their ability to design hardware that gets the most work done in one cycle.

Table 3.3   **Memory Chips Used in Maximum Main Memory Capacity Selected Large General Purpose Processors**

Year First Shipped	Maximum Memory Capacity	Memory Chip Included (bits/chip)
1975	8MB	2k, 4k
1979	16MB	2k, 4k
1980	16MB	2k, 4k, 16k
1981	16MB	64k
1982	32MB	64k
1983	32MB	64k
1984	32MB	64k, 256k
1985	32MB	1Mb
1986	1GB	1Mb
1987	1GB	1Mb
1988	1GB	1Mb
1989	1GB	1Mb, 4Mb

Note: These are maximum main memory capacities available on uniprocessors available in Dulberger's sample, 1975–84, updated through 1989. For single system images achieved with multiple processors, the maximum main memory is usually equal to the number of processors multiplied by the maximum for each. In 1986, a new member of the memory hierarchy called expanded storage was introduced. Expanded storage is composed of DRAMs, too, but is not within the same package as main memory. If included in the table, chip density of the maximum each year would be the same as shown, but maximum capacity would be much larger in 1988 and 1989.

Table 3.4   **Elements of Performance Improvements in Logic: Selected Large General Purpose Processors**

First Year Shipped	Mfr.	Model	CPU Cycle Time (ns)	Chip (ns)	Package (ns)	370 Equivalent MIPS
1973	IBM	168	80	40	40	2.3
1975	Amdahl	470	32			3.45
1978	IBM	3033	57	29	28	5.9
1982	IBM	3083	26	17	9	7.9
1982	Amdahl	580	26			13.0
1987	IBM	3090E	17.2			18.0
1987	NAS	XL60	18			21.0

Note: These are single processors, to be distinguished from multiple processors closely coupled in a single system image. ns = nanoseconds.
Sources: Entries for CPU cycle time, chip delay, and package delay for the years 1978 and 1982 are from Balderes and White (1989); 1973 values are from private discussions with D. Balderes (March 1990). 370 equivalent MIPS ratings are from Cole et al. (1986) updated thorugh 1987. CPU cycle times for Amdahl and NAS processors were taken from trade press reports.

than was the IBM 168 against which it competed, even though its CPU cycle time was more than 2.5 times shorter. Comparison of two competing processors with the same CPU cycle time, IBM's 3083 and Amdahl's 580, reveals that the 3083 was rated at executing 4.1 million fewer instructions in one second than the 580.

These comparisons illustrate that CPU cycle time is an inadequate measure of processor speed because it does not account for differences in design that affect speed. This inadequacy is true for products of the same manufacturer as well as across manufacturers. Furthermore, although a benchmark test such as that used in measuring 370 equivalent MIPS may be based on a work load not representative for some applications, such speed measures do provide a measure of each processor's ability to accomplish the same work.

Improvements in chips and packages are not always parallel. For example, for the processors in table 3.4, improvements made from 1973 to 1978 were about the same. But packaging improvements made from 1978 to 1982 were far greater. The importance of design and the proprietary nature of logic from the chips through the highest packaging level makes quality comparisons at lower levels most difficult.

At the chip level, density improvements in high-end (bipolar) logic have not kept pace with the rate of improvements in low-end (CMOS) logic. This was shown in figure 3.2 above. If it follows that quality-adjusted price declines in bipolar chips did not keep pace with CMOS chips, higher-level packaging improvements may make up a good part of the difference. Cole et al. (1986) offer some indirect evidence that logic packages in large general purpose processors did not decline in price quite as rapidly as did main memory. Their estimate of average price change was -21.0 percent for speed and -23.6 percent for main memory capacity during the period 1974–84. One would expect the difference to be greater after 1984, when the pace of technological improvement in CMOS memory and logic picked up.

3.2   Price Indexes for Selected Electronic Components

3.2.1   Publicly Available Price Indexes

Publicly available price indexes for the chip level, higher-level packages, and computer processors are shown in table 3.5. The price indexes for chips and higher-level packages are components of the PPI published by the Bureau of Labor Statistics (BLS). The processor price index is a component of the price deflator for office and computing equipment used by BEA in the NIPAs.

Table 3.5 shows the magnitude of inconsistency between price indexes of key inputs to computing equipment published by BLS and BEA's implicit price deflator for computer processors. The price changes in tables 3.1 and 3.2 above, although not aggregated into an index, suggest much more rapid price declines than are found in the PPI component. For example, the average price decline from 1984 to 1988 in the PPI component for MOS memories was 7.3 percent, while price declines (recorded in table 3.1) for the dominant chips of that period, the 64k and the 256k, were 16.0 and 38.6 percent, respectively. In the next section, additional evidence is compiled and explored.

Table 3.5   **Selected PPI Components and Implicit Deflator for Computer Processors (1982 = 100)**

Year	Chips		Higher-Level Packages	Final Product
	PPI: MOS memories (code 11784221)	PPI: Logic/ Microprocessors (code 11784225)	PPIR: Printed Circuit Boards and Circuitry on Passive Substrates (code PPU3679#H02)	Computer Processor Component of Price Index for Computing Equipment
1972				855.9
1973				924.5
1974				788.6
1975	. . .			703.7
1976	212.1			655.3
1977	. . .			473.6
1978	186.5			242.0
1979	168.8			204.9
1980	. . .			147.2
1981	. . .			118.6
1982	. . .	. . .	. . .	100.0
1983	. . .	96.3	99.9	93.9
1984	101.3	100.9	103.9	76.9
1985	73.4	. . .	106.5	51.2
1986	61.7	. . .	108.2	47.3
1987	63.5	80.4	110.2	40.3
1988	74.9	77.2	113.9	38.2
1989	82.8	80.3	115.4	36.3
Annual average rates of change				
1976–82	. . .	. . .	. . .	−26.9
1982–84	. . .	. . .	. . .	−12.3
1984–88	−7.3	−6.5	3.3	−16.0
1988–89	10.5	4.0	1.3	−5.0
1976–84	−8.8	. . .	. . .	−23.5
1976–89	−7.0	. . .	. . .	−20.0

Note: Ellipses points indicate one or missing data points within the year prohibiting the calculation of an annual average.

3.2.2 The Effects of Alternative Index Formulas

At this point, constructing some price indexes from the Dataquest data on MOS memory chips is helpful in illustrating the magnitude of price declines in these data and the sensitivity of price indexes for these products to the index number procedure employed. A logical starting point would be to replicate BLS methodology using these alternative prices, but, since BLS can release neither the weights nor the dates of entry of products embodying new technology into the index, we may construct a price index in the spirit of BLS procedure only.[9]

Dataquest Data

A brief description of the Dataquest data is worthwhile before proceeding. According to Dataquest analysts specializing in the semiconductor industry, the price data collected by chip and density are average prices paid compiled from interviews with purchasers. This source is used because producers are usually unwilling to provide prices.[10] These price "averages" need not refer solely to shipments of products manufactured in the United States. It is the opinion of these analysts that since, the prices by type and density vary so little (which makes sense for commodities), this procedure is not likely to produce misleading estimates of prices.[11]

The shipments data are collected from firms that produce them. Dataquest organizes the data by geographic location of the firm's headquarters, which is an increasingly poor approximation for production as this industry becomes more global. For example, the shipments from an establishment in Europe of a U.S.-based firm will be included in Dataquest's U.S. shipments.

In addition, shipments are those of merchant manufacturers only, which is important to note because captive production of these products is significant. As gathered, because these data differ from what is needed to calculate price indexes comparable to the PPI component, one would expect the value shares calculated to differ from those actually used by BLS. A comparison of the year-to-year relatives in the Laspeyres chain calculated from Dataquest prices and value shares (weights) from the Dataquest data and Census data is discussed later in section 3.2.2 and presented in table 3.9 below.

BLS Procedure for PPI Component

A short digression here to explore BLS procedure for estimating the PPI component for these products is helpful in understanding the nature of the published index and the basis for the index constructed in its spirit. The MOS memory component of the PPI is considered a "cell." This means that this is the lowest level at which a price index is calculated and then aggregated using a fixed weight. From December 1974 through June 1981, the index uses equal weights for all products for which prices are reported. For the period July 1981 through June 1986, the weights used would be based on the value share

9. BLS's refusal is based on concerns about violating the guarantee of respondent confidentiality. To encourage pursuit of the issues raised here, these data have been given to BLS on diskette.

10. With respect to data organization, however, prices for the same density do vary because organization affects the number of interchip connections required. A true price index of models with matched characteristics would require organization as a characteristic. The importance of organization as an attribute is minor compared with capacity. For additional discussion of organizations, see Flamm (chap. 5 in this volume).

11. Dataquest analysts generously provided their insights. The discussions took place throughout 1988.

of shipments of respondents in 1979. From July 1986 through the present, the weights are based on the value share of shipments in 1984. The published index is the result of chaining together three Laspeyres indexes, each with its own base period weights, and then normalizing the index to set it equal to 100 in 1982.

According to BLS, the weights as determined by importance of a particular product to the value of shipments of the respondents should approximate the product's importance as published by the Census Bureau in the Current Industrial Report (CIR). However, I was told that BLS does not routinely check its weights against those that could be calculated from Census data, and for these products such a check was not done.[12] Nor would BLS make available its weights for outside verification.

Price Indexes

Price indexes constructed from Dataquest data. It is clear that it would be preferable to use CIR rather than Dataquest to estimate the value shares needed for the price index calculations. However, detail by chip type and density were not shown in the CIR until 1984. In order to capture the spirit of BLS procedure and apply it to the Dataquest data on both prices and value share of shipments, I have proceeded as follows: (1) Treat the cell as the lowest level of detail for which data are available; for example, the price of the 256k DRAM will be weighted by its value share of the shipments in the year appropriate for the index formula. (2) For the period 1977–82, changes in a Laspeyres index with 1977 weights are used; thereafter, the index is Laspeyres with a 1982 base. This formula will be referred to as "Spirit" for the remainder of the paper and all tables.

Table 3.6 presents average compound growth rates for the period 1977–88 for each of five index formulas and six types of chips and aggregates. The formulas employed are Laspeyres, Paasche, Fisher Ideal, Tornqvist, and Spirit. The price indexes calculated are normalized to a reference year of 1982 and use Dataquest shipments as weights.

The similarity in average price change for all formulas except the Spirit is striking. In contrast, the price decline registered in the Spirit index is about half the rate of all the others. The most similar in formula, the Laspeyres chain and the Spirit, produce very different rates of price decline. The entire difference between these two is produced by the frequency with which the base period changes. The alternative chain formulas produce price declines that are more like each other for each chip type and across chip types than any of them compared with the Spirit.

The similarity across chip types is consistent with the fact that the dominant

---

12. This report of BLS methodology and how it is implemented for these products is a summary of discussions with James Sinclair and Brian Catron of BLS.

Table 3.6   Alternative Price Indexes, All MOS Memories by Chip Type, Average Annual Compound Growth Rates, 1977–88 (1982 = 100)

	Laspeyres Chain	Paasche Chain	Fisher Ideal Chain	Tornqvist Chain	Spirit
DRAMs	− 30.3	− 41.8	− 36.3	− 36.0	− 16.6
Slow SRAMs	− 20.2	− 33.4	− 27.1	− 26.3	− 7.5
Fast SRAMs	− 27.6	− 32.9	− 30.3	− 30.0	− 23.0
ROMs	− 23.8	− 32.8	− 28.5	− 28.5	− 12.6
EPROMs	− 30.1	− 40.2	− 35.3	− 34.7	− 18.4
EEPROMs	− 14.8	− 20.5	− 17.7	− 16.1	− 14.1
Total	− 26.5	− 38.0	− 32.5	− 32.0	− 12.3

Note: SRAM = static random access memory. ROM = read only memory. EPROM = electrically programmable read only memory. EEPROM = erasable electrically programmable read only memory.

forces in all are the same improvements in lithography. While the time frame in which the next generation within each type adopts the improvements will vary a little bit, overall one would expect that, over time, the effects on price would be close.[13]

Table 3.7 contains values for alternative price indexes for MOS memory chips aggregated across all types of chips. The lower panel of table 3.7 displays average price declines for selected subperiods for all index formulas shown in the upper panel. The PPI component falls at a much slower pace than even the Spirit index, for all subperiods shown. It appears that the index formula probably accounts for only part of the difference in the PPI component and these alternatives.

The effect of introduction delay on price indexes. These price indexes would be affected much more and the rates of decline would be much slower the greater the delay in introducing a chip with a new density into the index. Using DRAMs as an example, this point is illustrated in table 3.8. Compound growth rates for the period 1982–88 (a subperiod for DRAMs presented in table 3.6 above), calculated with introduction delays from zero to five years, are presented in the table. The earliest year in which entries by density appear in table 3.1 above correspond to an introduction delay equal to zero. A one-year delay means that each density first enters the index in the second year that it appears in table 3.1.

Table 3.8 shows that each additional year of delay reduces the rate of price decline. For all index formulas shown, a five-year introduction delay produces price indexes that fall at approximately one-tenth the annual rate of indexes in which products enter promptly. Indeed, the PPI component's 4.4 percent com-

13. For further discussion of lithography and its effect on semiconductor electronics, see Keyes (1977).

Table 3.7   **Alternative Price Indexes, All MOS Memories (1982 = 100)**

Year	Laspeyres Chain	Paasche Chain	Fisher Chain	Tornqvist Chain	Spirit	PPIR MOS Memories
1974	5,637.4	12,075.0	8,250.5	8,014.9	2,078.2	286.9[a]
1975	1,777.0	3,806.2	2,600.7	2,526.4	655.1	. . .
1976	1,087.6	2,329.7	1,591.8	1,546.3	393.0	212.1
1977	676.7	1,472.0	998.0	969.8	248.5	209.8[b]
1978	432.3	788.7	583.9	567.7	158.7	186.5
1979	383.9	640.2	495.8	480.4	163.3	168.8
1980	282.2	442.1	353.2	343.6	123.3	. . .
1981	146.6	188.7	166.3	164.6	100.6	. . .
1982	100.0	100.0	100.0	100.0	100.0	100.9[b]
1983	75.9	66.5	71.0	71.6	75.9	. . .
1984	66.5	45.2	54.8	56.7	74.4	101.3
1985	29.5	15.8	21.5	22.5	57.5	73.4
1986	20.5	9.0	13.6	14.2	48.4	61.7
1987	19.7	6.9	11.7	12.4	50.9	63.5
1988	22.7	7.6	13.2	14.0	58.6	74.9
Average annual rates of change: selected periods						
1977–82	−31.8	−41.6	−36.9	−36.5	−16.6	−5.4
1982–88	−21.9	−34.9	−28.7	−27.9	−8.5	−4.4
1977–84	−28.2	−39.2	−33.7	−33.3	−15.8	−4.3
1984–88	−23.5	−35.9	−30.0	−29.5	−5.8	−5.9
1977–88	−26.5	−38.0	−32.5	−32.0	−12.3	−4.9

Note: Ellipses points indicate value not calculated because fewer than eleven months available.
[a]December 1974 value (earliest value published).
[b]Average of values, January–November.

Table 3.8   **Effect of Late Introduction, Alternative Price Indexes, MOS Memories: DRAMs used in Main Memories of Selected Large General Purpose Processors, Compound Growth Rate, 1982–88**

Introduction Delay in Years	Laspeyres Chain	Paasche Chain	Fisher Chain	Tornqvist Chain
0	−27.5	−38.6	−33.3	−32.7
1	−26.2	−32.1	−29.2	−29.4
2	−24.7	−27.6	−26.2	−26.3
3	−19.9	−20.4	−20.1	−20.1
4	−7.1	−7.2	−7.1	−7.1
5	−1.8	−1.7	−1.8	−1.7

pound growth rate, 1982–88 (shown in table 3.7), would be matched by an introduction delay of between four and five years in the Dataquest data.

Furthermore, delaying introduction means that price changes in important products (in terms of market share in the lower panel of table 3.1) are not being measured directly and are estimated by price changes in products whose market share may be quite small. Consider the case of a three-year delay: the 64k chip does not enter until 1982, although its share was about 80 percent the prior year; the 256k chip would enter in 1986, although its market share was over 62 percent in 1985; and the 1Mb chip with over half the value of shipments in 1988 would not be in the index that year. One observes that the rate of price decline is most rapid for the products with the largest shares of the market. It is the products that are no longer important that register small price changes.[14] A comparison of the dates of entry into the PPI component of products having densities shown in table 3.1 with the dates of introduction in table 3.1 would be a useful undertaking for BLS to pursue.[15]

Limited Verification: Comparisons Using Dataquest and Census Data

Dates of product introduction and value shares used in the PPI component are needed to determine the source of the difference between the PPI for these products and the indexes shown here. However, the Census Bureau does publish some data in the MA36Q Current Industrial Report that can be used to judge the reasonableness of the weights derived from the Dataquest data set.

The entries in table 3.9 are the relatives that enter a Laspeyres chain calculation for DRAMs based on Dataquest data. Each entry is the ratio of the price index in each period divided by its value in the prior period. The calculations differ in the source and detail at which the weights (value shares) are calculated. The column heading "MA36Q" identifies the Census MA36Q reports as the source for weights used in calculating the relatives in the first column. The columns under the "Dataquest" heading use Dataquest estimates of shipments for U.S.-based manufacturers. Dataquest columns 1 and 2 differ in the level of detail at which one performs the calculations because Dataquest provides information in greater detail than is published in the MA36Q. Entries in Dataquest column 1 lump together the 256k and the 1Mb chips as is done in the seven-digit SIC. In Dataquest column 2, these densities enter separately, each with its own weight. For each of these three years, the relatives (and hence the price indexes that would be produced) are very much alike, lending some credibility to the rates of change in the price indexes offered in this paper.

3.2.3   Electronic Components Input to the Manufacture of Computing Equipment

Assessment of whether the quality-adjusted price declines in electronic products could result in the quality-adjusted price declines in the implicit de-

---

14. I am indebted to Jack Triplett for his suggestion to make explicit the effect of introduction delay.

15. Refreshing the sample more frequently has been suggested by BLS as a way to ensure that younger products are being priced. However, the time interval between new frontiers is not regular, and data reporters need not introduce products embodying the new technology at the same time. To be certain that products embodying new technology are identified early, data reporters could be asked to alert BLS to the introduction of such products.

Table 3.9   **Laspeyres Relatives with Alternative Weights, MOS Memories: DRAMs, Selected Years**

		Dataquest	
$t/t - 1$	MA36Q	(1)	(2)
$t = 1985$	.410	.382	.424
$t = 1986$	.718	.662	.772
$t = 1987$	.820	.825	.916

flator for computer processors requires an estimate of the importance of these products in materials consumed in the manufacture of processors. Ideally, one would use data on the consumption of each level package in the manufacture of the next level package up to processors. Unfortunately, such data are not available.

1987 Census of Manufactures: Office and Computing Equipment

The tabulation of the 1987 Census of Manufactures for industry 3571, electronic computers, in table 7, "Material Consumed by Kind," reveals that line items identifying the products described in this paper are missing. Selected line items from this table in the tabulation of the Census are shown in table 3.10, items in lines 367002–357003. Sixty-eight percent of the cost of materials consumed is accounted for by two line items. Ten line items account for 92 percent of the cost of materials consumed. The small value originally tabulated for line item 367002, whose definition included electronic components, suggested that a problem arose in the reporting of materials consumed data. According to the Bureau of the Census, the line item titled "Semiconductors" was intended to include chips. The title "Resistors, capacitors, transducers, and other electronic-type components and accessories, except semiconductors" was intended to include higher-level packages. After an investigation by the Census Bureau following the preliminary tabulation, it was decided that the values for these items would not be shown separately because, in many cases, respondents were not aware that line 367002 included complex electronic products such as printed circuit boards and consequently reported values for them in other lines such as those called "Parts . . ." (lines 357002, 357201, 357701, 357501, 366130, and 357003 in table 3.10) and the two line items for those materials not elsewhere listed (lines 970099 and 971000 in table 3.10). Indeed, the problem arose because respondents judged these other line items to have more appropriate descriptors.[16]

Data on the use of electronic components in the production of computer processors are needed to make appropriate input price indexes, and, without

16. Ken Hansen at the Bureau of the Census was responsible for the follow-up investigation that prevented the publication of meaningless data in the final report for this industry.

Table 3.10   **Industry 3571, Electronic Computers, Selected Materials Consumed by Kind**

1987 Material Code	Description	Delivered Cost ($billion)	% of Total
367408	Semiconductors	1.600	13.1
367002	Resistors, capacitors, transistors, transducers, and other electronic-type components and accessories, except semiconductors	6.740	55.2
357002	Parts for computers		
357201	Parts for auxiliary storage equip		
357701	Parts for input/output equip		
357501	Parts for computer terminals		
366130	Parts for communication interface equipment		
357003	Parts for other peripheral equipment		
970099	All other materials, components, parts, containers and supplies	1.575	12.9
971000	Materials, parts, containers, and supplies, n.s.k. (not specified by kind)	1.276	10.5
Sum		11.191	91.7
Materials, parts, containers, and supplies		12.205	100.0

reliable information, estimates of value-added cannot be made. We may ask, however, if the data presented thus far are consistent with the estimate of quality and price changes used for some of the products in the computer processor component of BEA's implicit price deflator in the NIPAs.

BEA Input-Output Tables

The input-output (I-O) tables for 1972, 1977, and 1985 published by BEA provide some information on the value of electronic products to the manufacture of the broad category office and computing equipment (OCE). A tabulation of selected elements from these I-O tables is given in table 3.11.

Total intermediate inputs excluding services used in producing OCE is mostly accounted for by two industries that make electronic products—electronic components and accessories and OCE itself. Indeed, the fraction was about .7, .6, and .6 in 1972, 1977, and 1985, respectively. It is reasonable to expect that for computer processors this fraction is substantially higher.

Value-added in the office and computing equipment industry as a share of output declined markedly between 1977 and 1985. This probably reflects in good part the move to assembly of parts away from the manufacture of those parts (Harding 1981, 649). Two distinct phases of production of computers have emerged: one is the fabrication of components, and the other is com-

Table 3.11   **Selected Elements of Inputs and Output of Office and Computing Equipment, I-O Tables: 1972, 1977, 1985 ($billions)**

Year	Output (1)	Value-Added (VA) (2)	VA/Output (3)	Total Intermediate Inputs Less Services (4)	Own Input (5)	Electronic Components Inputs (6)	([5] + [6])/(4) (7)
1972	8.518	3.495	0.41	2.911	1.212	0.765	0.68
1977	15.793	6.611	0.42	6.638	2.544	1.450	0.60
1985	58.324	16.870	0.29	27.780	10.108	6.411	0.59

monly known as BAT (bond, assembly, and test).[17] Some misconceptions and perhaps mismeasurement arise from the problem of determining which industries these belong in. Partly, this is due to the different views of an industry that one gets when looking at establishments rather than enterprises. In 1985, as is still true today, there was a wide range of activities performed across manufacturers of computer processors and other types of computing equipment as well.

Example

Using assumptions drawn from data presented in tables 3.2, 3.3, 3.10, and 3.11 above and based on conclusions drawn thus far, consider an example that uses realistic assumptions to assess the plausibility of price declines in computing equipment on the order of 25 percent per year since actual data required are not available.

For the purpose of example, consider the effect of quality-adjusted price declines in electronic components on the quality-adjusted prices of computer processors produced in two hypothetical establishments representing the extremes with respect to their use and own production of electronic components. It will be shown that, consistent with the estimates of price declines presented in this paper, I-O tables, and the Census of Manufacturers, quality-adjusted price declines in computer processors of about 25 percent per year may be the outcome at both extremes. This outcome may result from an establishment's own production and consumption of electronic components or from the effect of price declines and quality improvements in purchased electronic components. More of the value-added would be attributed to the computing equipment industry in the former case and to the electronic components industry in the latter.

Compare two hypothetical establishments. The output of establishment A is personal computers. Establishment A buys all the electronic products in its PCs. The output of establishment B is large general purpose processors; it

17. See the special commemorative issue of *Electronics*, 17 April 1980, 381.

purchases some and manufactures others of the electronic products it consumes in the final assembly of its output.

The values used in the example are chosen as follows: The ratio of value-added to output for establishment B is set to the 1985 value from the I-O table shown in table 3.11. It is set lower to .1 for establishment A because that is more appropriate for assembly-only activities.

The electronic components' share of materials consumed is set at the low value of .68 (the sum of semiconductors and resistors, capacitors, etc. in table 3.10) for establishment B. For establishment A, it is set at .92, the maximum computed in table 3.10.

A 26 percent reduction in the quality-adjusted price of output of establishment A is the outcome of a 33 percent reduction in the quality-adjusted price of its electronic inputs (much like the decline in price/kilobit in table 3.2 for the period 1977–85) and a 7 percent increase in the quality-adjusted price of all other inputs and its value-added:

(1) $.9[.92(.67) + .08(1.07)] + .1(1.07) = .7388.$

For establishment B, a quality-adjusted price reduction is set at 30 percent for both the electronics products it consumes and its own value-added. This marginally smaller rate of price change is consistent with the earlier conclusion that quality-adjusted price changes in more complex electronic packages did not quite keep pace with those of the simpler packages. The same 7 percent increase in the prices of all other inputs is used. The result is a 22 percent reduction in the quality-adjusted price of establishment B's output:

(2) $.7[.68(.70) + .32(1.07)] + .3(.70) = .7829.$

The example serves to illustrate that price declines and quality improvements in electronic components provided in this paper are consistent with quality-adjusted price declines in computer processors. The processor price decline may be passed along by establishments in the computer industry that contribute little (by comparison) value-added. Or, as in establishments like B, where complex electronic components are manufactured for own consumption, the quality improvements and price declines in the electronic components will take place in establishments in the computing equipment industry.

Companies whose main product is computing equipment often have establishments like both. Digital Equipment Corporation and IBM are examples (see Digital Equipment Corp. 1989). The magnitude of an enterprise's real value-added is very much determined by the degree to which it manufactures the electronic products that are key inputs to its products. Without actual data distinguishing assembly activities from those in which complex components are fabricated, allocating value-added between these two industries is not possible. The example serves to illustrate that electronic components are the important source of quality-adjusted price declines in computer processors and that the industry responsible may be either the electronic components industry or the computing equipment industry, depending on the degree to which the electronic components are produced for consumption within the same establishment.

3.3 Conclusion

Assessment of the limited data presented here on price declines and quality improvements in chips and the complex electronic components into which they are assembled offers some evidence that declines in quality-adjusted prices of semiconductor chips and, by way of example, higher-level packages, are not inconsistent with the processor component of the NIPA deflator for office and computing equipment.

Alternative matched-model indexes presented showed slower rates of price decline, with only two changes in the base year (weights) for the period 1975–88 as compared with rates of decline in price indexes constructed with consecutive changes in the base year (chained indexes), although the slower rates remained far more rapid than registered in the PPI component. More important, it was shown that, in the case of DRAMs, delaying the introduction of new products into the price index results in substantially smaller movements in the index. Indeed, delaying introduction between four and five years creates price index changes comparable to those observed in the PPI component. In addition, it was argued that these matched-model indexes for MOS memories would likely understate price declines in logic, where direct comparisons of quality are more difficult to measure.

There are two important implications to be drawn from the arguments and data presented: (1) the large differences in price changes within a cell for commodity products such as these suggest that price disequilibrium and associated errors in price measurement may be more widespread than is currently believed; and (2) shortening the sample refreshment cycle is likely to reduce the effects of introduction delay but is a solution that is second best to one that makes direct comparisons of quality.

Further, it was shown that price indexes for different types of chips registered similar and rapid price declines that did not differ greatly by choice of index formula. This finding illustrates the importance of improvements in technology, in this case lithography, on quality-adjusted prices.

In the absence of needed measures of value-added, an example was used to illustrate that price declines like those in the NIPA deflator for computer processors are consistent with quality improvements and price declines in electronic components. The source industry, however, may be either the electronic components industry or the computing equipment industry, depending on the degree to which establishments in the computing equipment industry purchase these key inputs or manufacture them for their own consumption.

References

Balderes, Demetrios, and Marlin L. White. 1989. Large general-purpose and super-computer packaging. In *Microelectronics packaging handbook,* ed. Rao R. Tummala and Eugene J. Rymaszewski. New York: Van Nostrand Reinhold.

Black, John R. H. 1986. Technology and market-trends in multilayer ceramic devices. *Advances in Ceramics* 19:3–11.

Cole, Rosanne, Y. C. Chen, Joan A. Barquin-Stolleman, Ellen Dulberger, Nurhan Helvacian, and James H. Hodge, 1986. Quality-adjusted price indexes for computer processors and selected peripheral equipment. *Survey of Current Business* 66 (1): 41–50.

Digital Equipment Corp. 1989. *Annual report.* Maynard, Mass.

Dulberger, Ellen R. 1989. The application of an hedonic model to a quality-adjusted price index for computer processors. In *Technology and capital formation,* ed. Dale W. Jorgensen and Ralph Landau. Cambridge, Mass.: MIT Press.

Harding, William E. 1981. Semiconductor manufacturing in IBM, 1957 to the present: A perspective. *IBM Journal of Research and Development* 25 (5): 647–58.

Keyes, R. W. 1977. Physical limits in semiconductor electronics. *Science* 195 (March): 1230–35.

Mayo, John S. 1986. Materials for information and communication. *Scientific American* 255 (October): 59–65.

Meindl, James D. 1988. Chips for advanced computing. *Scientific American Trends in Computing,* special issue, 1:98–107.

Noyce, R. N. 1977. Large-scale integration: What is yet to come. *Science* 195 (March): 1102–6.

Rajchman, J. A. 1977. New memory technologies. *Science* 195 (March): 1223–29.

Tummala, Rao R., and Eugene J. Rymaszewski, eds. 1989. *Microelectronics packaging handbook.* New York: Van Nostrand Reinhold.

4 Cost Function Estimation of Quality Change in Semiconductors

John R. Norsworthy and Show-Ling Jang

Semiconductor technology lies at the heart of the revolution in information technology. While the official price index in the national income and product accounts for computers has been revised to account for changes in the performance characteristics of computer systems (Cole et al. 1986), no comparable modification has been made to the price of semiconductor devices. Yet semiconductor devices incorporated in telecommunications equipment have been largely responsible for the technological change that led to deregulation of the telecommunications services industry. The rapid rate of adoption of advanced telecommunications equipment and the decline in cost (without a corresponding decline in quality) of telecommunications services are indirect qualitative evidence for embodied quality change in telecommunications equipment. Similarly, the new semiconductor devices have played an important role in the technological change of the computer industry. This empirical investigation is designed to develop quantitative evidence of quality change in semiconductor devices based on their use in computers and telecommunications equipment manufacture.

An econometric model, which consists of a revised translog variable cost function for quality adjustment, input demand functions, and an input quality-adjustment function, is developed and utilized in this study. The approach to quality adjustment, in the spirit of the hedonic approach, is based on two major characteristics of semiconductor products: the device density of DRAMs (dynamic random access memory) and the bit rating of microproces-

John R. Norsworthy is professor of economics and management at Rensselaer Polytechnic Institute and director of the Center for Science and Technology Policy. Show-Ling Jang is associate professor of economics at National Taiwan University.

The authors are grateful for comments from Ellen Dulberger, Kenneth Flamm, Marilyn Manser, and Jack Triplett in modification of the paper.

125

sors. Exponential weights for these technology indicator variables are estimated for the computer industry (SIC 3573), telephone and telegraph equipment (SIC 3661), and radio and television telecommunications equipment (SIC 3662).[1] In each industry, evidence for quality change in semiconductors is drawn from the input factor demand functions. All input factors are modeled jointly, rather than the demand for semiconductor input alone, as in the conventional hedonic model. That is, factor substitution information from other inputs—production- and nonproduction-worker labor, other purchased materials, purchased services—is brought to bear on estimation of the quality change in semiconductors used for the computer and telecommunications industries. Unlike the hedonic case, it is necessary to assume that the prices of semiconductor inputs are independent of the level of use by the decision makers who use them in production. This assumption is a standard (and minimal) one in production modeling.

In the computer industry, where output has been adjusted for performance change, it is also possible to obtain additional evidence for the characteristic-related quality change in semiconductors from the increase in the (computer) industry's total factor productivity associated with the use of semiconductors.

Within each of the industries, the quality-adjustment function is constrained to have the same parameters in all input demand functions and the cost function. However, a separate quality-adjustment function is estimated for each industry. It is found that the quality-adjusted prices for all three industries are similar but sufficiently different to reflect the different importance of the technological characteristics of semiconductors in the different industries. The results tend to confirm the approach.

The methods demonstrated here are for time-series data. The usual hedonic price index model relies heavily on cross-sectional data, often from special surveys or proprietary sources. Triplett (1989) provides an excellent summary of hedonic applications for the U.S. computer industry. It is often the case, however, that sufficiently long time series for product characteristics are either not publicly available or quite expensive to obtain.

No sources of quality change other than that associated with the quality of semiconductor input are recognized in this study. However, the specification of quality change is entirely associated with the semiconductor input as shown in equations (11) and (12) below, except in the computer industry, where an additional term is introduced. This term is introduced because the output of the computer industry is adjusted for quality change. It permits total and var-

---

1. SIC designations are from before the 1987 reclassification. The radio and television communications equipment industry (SIC 3662) is divided into seven categories: (1) communication equipment, except broadcast (SIC 36621); (2) broadcast, studio, and related equipment (SIC 36622); (3) alarm systems (SIC 36624); (4) search and detection, navigation, and guidance equipment (SIC 36625); (5) traffic control equipment (SIC 36626); (6) intercommunication equipment (SIC 36628); and (7) electronic systems and equipment not elsewhere classified (SIC 36629).

iable input factor productivity to change in association with the same semiconductor quality-modifying function used elsewhere in the model.

Section 4.1 of this paper shows how quality change can be estimated from industry input demand systems based on multiple characteristics or indicators of input technology. Section 4.2 explains the development of input and output prices and quantities from industry data sources at the Census Bureau and the Bureau of Labor Statistics (BLS). Section 4.3 discusses the mechanics of incorporating the technological characteristics of semiconductors in the cost function model of production. Section 4.4 presents and discusses the estimated results. Section 4.5 briefly discusses an agenda for future research based on the approach applied in the paper.

4.1 Indirect Measurement of Quality Change in Production Models

The translog cost function is a commonly used model of production that can be adapted to indirect measurement of quality change in an input.[2] The same general method can be incorporated in other functional forms. To illustrate the measurement of quality change embodied in an input in an econometric model, we first present (in sec. 4.1.1) a model without quality adjustment, consisting of a translog variable cost function and input demand equations, and then show (in sec. 4.1.2) the model with quality adjustment.

4.1.1 Translog Variable Cost Function without Quality Adjustment

This study empirically assesses the contribution of semiconductor inputs in the computer industry and two telecommunications equipment manufacturing industries. The translog restricted variable cost function model introduced by Brown and Christensen (1981) is used to model the production structure of these industries. The variable cost function recognizes disequilibrium in that the quantity of physical capital cannot be adjusted to achieve minimum total cost in the short run for a given set of input prices and the quantity of output. The conventional assumption of full equilibrium models such as the translog total cost function is simply not reasonable for industries such as semiconductors, computers, or telecommunications equipment characterized by rapid technological change.

The translog variable cost function for an industry is given by

$$
\begin{aligned}
\ln CV = {} & a_0 + \Sigma_i\, a_i \ln p_i + 1/2\, \Sigma_i \Sigma_j\, a_{ij} \ln p_i \ln p_j + b_Y \ln y \\
& + b_K \ln k + b_{ky} \ln k \ln y \\
& + 1/2\, b_{yy} \ln^2 y + 1/2\, b_{kk} \ln^2 k \\
& + \Sigma_i\, c_{iy} \ln p_i \ln y + \Sigma_i\, c_{ik} \ln p_i \ln_k,
\end{aligned}
$$

(1)

---

2. The explanation in this section is adapted from Jang and Norsworthy (1990a).

where i, j, are the variable inputs, p_i = price of variable input i, y = deflated real gross output, k = real capital input of structures and equipment, and CV = variable cost of production.

Based on Shepard's lemma and the assumption that variable cost is minimized for a given set of input prices, the cost share s_i for the translog variable cost function is given by

$$(2) \qquad \frac{\partial \ln \mathrm{CV}}{\partial \ln p_i} = s_i = a_i + \Sigma_j a_{ij} \ln p_j + b_{ik} \ln k + b_{iy} \ln Y.$$

Derivation of the variable cost function model and estimation of the equations for variable input cost shares with a residual error term e_i added jointly with the cost function itself are explained in Brown and Christensen (1981) and need not be repeated here. If an error term is added directly to equation (2), it will be in terms of value shares, however. In such a specification, input quality change not reflected in the price of input will be obscured because the error term contains both price and quantity components.

In order to separate price and quantity effects, the variable input demand equations can be estimated (jointly with the cost function) rather than the cost share equations. The demand equations are readily derived from equation (2); adding a classical normal error term to the demand equations yields

$$(3) \qquad q_i = \mathrm{CV} \cdot (a_i + \Sigma_j a_{ij} \ln p_j + b_{ik} \ln k + b_{iy} \ln Y)/p_i + \varepsilon_i.$$

Notice that the error term ε_i in equation (3) is in quantity units. We argue elsewhere that the input demand specification is preferable because errors in input quantity are minimized directly, thus leading to a better physical description of the technology of production (Norsworthy and Jang 1992, chap. 3). McElroy (1987) proposes an additive general error model based on estimation of input demand equations rather than price equations. The exact treatment specified by McElroy cannot be achieved when there are parameters that occur only in the cost function (e.g., b_y, b_k, in eq. [1]). However, the general approach and motivation for it are entirely consistent with that shown here.[3]

A major difference between the share equation and the demand equation systems is that one of the cost share equations is redundant, so that the variable cost function is estimated jointly with all but one share equation. That is, for any input r,

$$e_r = -\sum_{i \neq r} e_i.$$

---

3. This issue is explained in Norsworthy and Jang (1992, chap. 3). McElroy has verbally acknowledged the error.

For the demand equation system, each input equation has an independent error term. Consequently, estimation of the demand system increases the efficiency of the estimation because there are more degrees of freedom.[4]

Restrictions imposing symmetry and homogeneity of degree 1 in prices of variable inputs on the system of equations are as follow:

$$\Sigma_i \, a_i = 1,$$
$$\Sigma_j \, a_{ij} = \Sigma_i \, a_{ij} = 0, \quad \text{for all } i, j,$$
$$a_{ij} = a_{ji}, \quad \text{for all } i, j,$$

(4)
$$\Sigma_i \, c_{ik} = 0, \quad \text{for all } i,$$
$$\Sigma_i \, c_{iy} = 0, \quad \text{for all } i,$$
$$b_{yy} + b_{ky} = 0,$$
$$b_{kk} + b_{ky} = 0,$$
$$c_{ik} = -c_{iy}, \quad \text{for all } i.$$

4.1.2   Translog Variable Cost Function with Quality Adjustment Based on Multiple Technological Characteristics

The quality change of an input in the production model can be estimated by adjusting its quantity and price to their true values on the basis of some indicators of input technology. Either quantity or price may serve as the basis for empirical estimation of quality change in the model. The choice may affect the stochastic specification of the model, but both methods should yield similar results. Quality adjustment based on quantity of input and quality adjustment based on exogenous information such as TFP (total factor productivity) growth were developed and applied in our earlier studies (Jang and Norsworthy 1988, 1990a, 1990b). We assume here as in our earlier work that the quality of inputs is known by the producers; the task of our quality adjustment is to discovery why they behave the way they do in using the inputs. There is thus no problem of simultaneity in the estimation procedure outlined in this section.

The semiconductor input (q_s) is separated from other purchased physical materials (q_m), and purchased services (q_v) are separately treated as well. Suppose that the unmeasured quality change in semiconductor input q_s is proportional to the log of a quality-adjustment index I_s^α so that quality-adjusted input is

(5)
$$q_s^* = q_s \, I_s^\alpha, \quad \alpha > 0,$$

or

$$\ln q_s^* = \ln q_s + \alpha \ln I_s,$$

---

4. Degrees of freedom for estimation of a system of translog-based equations are given by the number of observations multiplied by the number of equations estimated.

where I_s is the technological characteristic index for the industry, α is an estimated coefficient, and (as before) q_s is measured semiconductor input.[5]

The corresponding quality-adjusted price for input s is

$$p_s^* = p_s/I_s^\alpha,$$

or

(6) $$\ln p_s^* = \ln p_s - \alpha \ln I_s.$$

The quality-adjustment index I_s is defined below in terms of semiconductor characteristics.

If the quality-adjusted price index of inputs declines faster than the official price statistics imply, then the coefficient α will be positive; the null hypothesis $\alpha = 0$ corresponds to no unmeasured quality change, positive or negative.

The quality-adjustment function may, of course, reflect multiple characteristics of the output(s) of the supplying industry. For example, let

(7) $$I_s^\alpha = f(t_1, t_2, \ldots, t_m),$$

where the t_i's are logs of technology indicators reflecting technological characteristics of input s. For the semiconductor industry, these indicators might measure performance characteristics such as device density, speed, power requirements, bit width of data and instruction paths in microprocessors, etc. For a first-order function,[6]

(8) $$I_s^\alpha = \Sigma_i w_i t_i, \quad i = 1, \ldots, m,$$

where w_i's are weights estimated in the input factor demand model for each of the m characteristics included in the function. (These are comparable to the characteristics coefficients in the hedonic model.) For clarity and comparability with the single index case, however, the quality-adjustment index may be written

(9) $$\alpha \ln I_s = \alpha [\sum_{i=1}^{m-1} z_i t_i + (1 - \sum_{i=1}^{m-1} z_i) t_m].$$

Equations (8) and (9) have the same number of independent parameters: exactly m. However, changing the parameterization so that $w_i = \alpha z_i$, $i = 1$, $\ldots, m - 1$, and $w_m = \alpha(1 - \sum_{i=1}^{m-1} z_i)$ permits us to estimate directly the

---

5. α may also be a function $\alpha = f(t) = c_t t$ or $\alpha = e^{ct}$, where t is the trend variable 1, 2, 3, $\ldots$, and the estimated coefficients c_t and c measure average annual augmentation of input s. Norsworthy and Jang (1989) argue that time trends may capture spurious effects collinear with time and that use of an alternative proxy for quality change that has economic content is preferable.

6. Higher-order functions, e.g., truncated qualities, are sometimes applied in the hedonic approach and could readily be accommodated in a sufficiently large and rich data set.

relative weights of the individual characteristics. These relative weights are readily interpreted because they sum to one.[7]

The estimated coefficient α is then directly comparable to the coefficient of the single indicator. The estimated coefficient z_i is the weight of technological characteristic i in the quality-adjustment function (9). Correspondingly, $\ln p_s$ is replaced by

$$(10) \qquad \ln p_s^* = \ln p_s - \alpha[\sum_{i=1}^{m-1} z_1 t_1 + (1 - \sum_{i=1}^{m-1} z_i)t_m]$$

in all its occurrences in the cost function.

Then the variable cost function in equation (1) can be rewritten incorporating the modified expression shown in equation (11) and the parameter α estimated as part of the cost function model:

$$
\begin{aligned}
(11) \quad \ln CV = \; & a_0 + \sum_{\substack{i \\ i \neq s}} a_i \ln p_i + a_s(\ln p_s - \alpha \ln I_s) + z_t(-\alpha \ln I_s) \\
& + 1/2 \sum_{\substack{i \neq s}} \sum_{\substack{j \neq s}} a_{ij} \ln p_i \ln p_j \\
& + \sum_{\substack{i \neq s}} a_{is} \ln p_i(\ln p_s - \alpha \ln I_s) \\
& + \sum_{\substack{j \neq s}} a_{js} \ln p_j(\ln p_s - \alpha \ln I_s) + 1/2\, a_{ss}(\ln p_s - \alpha \ln I_s)^2 \\
& + b_Y \ln Y + b_K \ln K + b_{KY} \ln K \ln Y + 1/2\, b_{YY} \ln^2 Y \\
& + 1/2\, b_{KK} \ln^2 K + \sum_i c_{iY} \ln p_i \ln Y \\
& + \sum_{\substack{i \neq s}} c_{iK} \ln p_i \ln K + c_{SY}(\ln p_s - \alpha \ln I_s)\ln Y \\
& + c_{SK}(\ln p_s - \alpha \ln I_s)\ln K,
\end{aligned}
$$

where $i, j = l, n, m, v$, for the variable inputs: production-worker labor (l), nonproduction-worker labor (n), purchased materials inputs (m), and purchased services (v).

The demand equation for the quality-adjusted input s then becomes

$$(12) \quad q_s^* = (CV/p_s/I_s^\alpha)[a_s + \sum_{\substack{j \neq s}} a_{sj} \ln p_j + a_{ss}(\ln p_s - \alpha \ln I_s)] + \varepsilon_s^*.$$

The substitution shown in equation (10) for the price of quality-adjusted semiconductor input is applied throughout the model, and the estimated coefficients α and z_i are constrained to be nonnegative. The first-order term $(-\alpha \ln I_s)$ with estimated coefficient z_t is the overall variable factor productivity gain or cost reduction effect associated with quality improvement in semiconductors (given the level of output and inputs). This effect can be reliably estimated only for the computer industry, where the output price has been

---

7. This reparameterization procedure was applied in earlier studies by Norsworthy and Jang (1991) and Norsworthy and Zabala (1990).

adjusted for quality change. Because adjustment for quality change has not been made for the price of output of either of the telecommunications equipment industries, there is a downward bias in measured total (and variable) factor productivity. Under these circumstances, any estimate of the effect of improvement in semiconductor quality on industry productivity would be unreasonably low; measured total factor productivity growth in the industries is very nearly zero, while true total factor productivity growth is certainly larger. This first-order term is therefore included only in the computer industry model.

The restrictions in equation (4) are not modified by the quality adjustment. The modified cost function with the restrictions applied is still homogeneous of degree 1 in input prices, including the modified price of semiconductor input. Estimates of a quality-adjusted price for semiconductor input may then be calculated after the estimation of the cost function (11) and the corresponding input demand equations.

Applying this procedure assumes that enterprises using input s do so on the basis of its technological characteristics; that is, the users perceive the input in terms of the quality-adjusted relation between price and quantity. Thus, the demand equation for the input s is stated in terms of *adjusted* quantity and price.[8]

In this framework, we can also test the hypothesis that $\alpha = 0$, that is, that there is no significant quality change except that reflected in the current official price index for semiconductors. The simplest test is based on the t-test; the significance of the contribution of the quality-based price adjustment to the estimated model as a whole may also be captured in a likelihood ratio test.

In the estimation procedure, the quantity demanded of semiconductor input, q_s^*, must be adjusted to agree with the quality-adjusted price, p_s^* from equation (10). We applied the following iterative estimation procedure:

1. For the initial value of α, compute q_s^* using equation (5).
2. Estimate α as part of a full information maximum likelihood (FIML) estimation of the cost function model.
3. Recompute q_s^* from (5) using the new value of α.
4. Reestimate α by FIML estimation of the cost function model using the parameter values from the prior iteration.

---

8. The dependent variable, and hence the error term, in the share equation for the quality-adjusted input s is invariant to the adjustment; i.e., s_s does not change in magnitude when quality adjustment for semiconductor input is introduced. However, while $s_s = s_s^*$, the dependent variable and error term in the demand equation for semiconductor input differ according to whether the input s is quality adjusted. That is,

$$q_s^* \neq q_s \quad \text{and} \quad \varepsilon_s^* \neq \varepsilon_s.$$

In other words, the stochastic specification of the model changes with the quality adjustment, necessitating the iterative estimation procedure described below.

Steps 3 and 4 were repeated until successive values of q_s^* for each year differed by a cumulative total of less than .05. This procedure converged in three iterations for SIC 3661, four for SIC 3662, and three for SIC 3573.

The final stage estimate of the quality-adjusted quantity of semiconductor input results in a larger q_s^* and smaller p_s^* than the initial estimate. The larger q_s^* changes the stochastic specification of the model by increasing the relative importance of errors in semiconductor input. The smaller p_s^* affects the elasticity of substitution estimates (through the a_{ij} coefficients), in principle for all pairs of inputs. Consequently, the iterative procedure is necessary.[9]

4.1.3   Comparison with the Standard Hedonic Approach

It is important to make clear how this approach relates to conventional hedonic studies of technology-intensive products, such as Dulberger (chap. 3 in this volume). Triplett provides a thorough statement of the hedonic approach to price deflation (Triplett 1987) and its applications to capital goods (Triplett 1989). The explanation that follows is keyed to the latter discussion.

The conventional hedonic function may be expressed as

$$(13) \qquad\qquad P = h(c),$$

where P is a vector of prices of n varieties of the good in equation (12), and c is a matrix measuring each of k characteristics of each of n varieties of the good (Triplett 1989, eq. [1], p. 128). The production function that corresponds in our study to Triplett's equation (2) (Triplett 1989, 130) is the short-run function

$$(14) \qquad\qquad y = f(q_L, q_N, q_M, q_V, q_S; K),$$

where y is output. K is fixed capital input, and q_i, $i = L, N, M, V, S$, are the variable inputs noted for equation (11) above. (Equation [11] above is the dual to eq. [14].) The quality adjustment of q_s, semiconductor input, is achieved by mapping q_s into semiconductor characteristics space:

$$(15) \qquad\qquad q_s = q(T_1, \ldots, T_m),$$

where the T_i, $i = 1, \ldots, m$, are the quantities of the various characteristics in the aggregate q_s. By estimating the function that carries out transformation (15) in the context of the production model, we obtain weights for the semiconductor characteristics embodied in the aggregate input q_s. These weights measure the marginal productivity in the industry being studied. This point is worth stressing: the weights obtained from the cost function for the industry

---

9. We utilized the FIML estimation procedure in program SORITEC. This procedure cannot update q_s^* shown in the demand equation for semiconductor input as part of the iterative process of determining parameter values, thus necessitating the iterative procedure.

are specific to the production technology used in that industry; they also reflect the mix of characteristics peculiar to input S in that industry.[10]

The quality-adjusted quantity of semiconductor input is thus denoted q_s^*, where

(16) $q_s^* = q_s \cdot I,$

and I is a quality index based on the transformation of the quantity of semiconductors into characteristics space. We specify the index I in logarithmic form:

(17) $\ln(q_s^*/q_s) = \ln I = (w_1 t_1 + \ldots + w_m t_m) = \Sigma_i\, w_i t_i,$

where t_i is the (log of the) representative measure of characteristic i for semiconductors. Its dimensions are units of characteristic i per unit of semiconductor input. (Ideally, t_i should represent the quantity of characteristic i in semiconductors input for the industry; however, that information was not available to us.) The coefficients w_i are estimated transformation coefficients and measure units of base year input S per unit of characteristic i. Consequently, the quality-adjustment expression for semiconductor input is given by

(18) $q_s^* = q_s \cdot \exp(\Sigma_i w_i t_i).$

The form in which equation (18) is estimated is altered somewhat to permit direct testing of the proposition that proportional changes in the characteristics lead to equal proportional changes in the quality of semiconductor input. Thus, for estimation, the log of the quality index in equation (17) is rewritten

(19) $\ln I = \alpha(\Sigma\, z_i t_i),$

where $z_m = 1 - \Sigma_{i=1}^{m-1} z_i$ and $w_i = \alpha z_i$.

We can then test the proposition that $\alpha = 1$ by computing the t-statistic for $\alpha - 1$ after estimation of the model.

The quality index I must preserve the cost of input s in nominal terms, that is,

(20) $p_s q_s = p_s^* q_s^*,$

where we obtain

(21) $p_s^* = p_s/I,$
                  $\ln p_s^* = \ln p_s - (w_1 t_1 + \ldots + w_m t_m).$

The right-hand side of expression (21) replaces $\ln p_s$ in the estimated translog model, equation (11) above.

The prices of characteristics may be obtained by simultaneously solving the system of simultaneous equations

---

10. There is no industry-specific information available to us to identify industry-specific composition of aggregate semiconductor input.

(22) $$p_i = [(\Sigma_i \, w_i T_i)/p_S^* - (p_S q_S - p_i T_i)]/T_i,$$

subject to the conditions that $p_s q_s = \Sigma_i \, p_i q_i$ and $p_i > 0$ for all i.

The formulation assumes that information is available that quantifies technological characteristics in the aggregate semiconductor input. In this application, we did not have that information; consequently, our estimates of the weights z_i (and the corresponding w_i) contain elements that reflect industry-specific adjustments not only for the transformation coefficients w_i but also for the T_i/q_s as well. Thus, in order to derive characteristics prices according to equation (22) from this application, it would be necessary to obtain estimates of T_i for each industry. A similar limitation applies to the technique used by Dulberger, as noted in section 4.4.2 below concerning industry-specific hedonic weights.

4.2 Data Sources, Measurement, and Concepts

The data used in this study are the historical U.S. time-series data at the four-digit SIC level for telephone and telegraph apparatus (SIC 3661), radio and television communications (other telecommunications) equipment (SIC 3662), and computers (SIC 3573).

To estimate the econometric models, the information required is total cost (TC), variable cost (CV), the price and quantity of output (Y), net capital stock (K), production-worker labor (L), nonproduction-worker labor (N), semiconductors (S), purchased services (V), and (other) intermediate input, "materials" (M).[11] These measures are derived and constructed on the basis of several data sources. The major sources are the Census of Manufactures (CM) and the Annual Survey of Manufactures (ASM) of the Census Bureau, the producer price index (PPI) program of the BLS, and *The Detailed Input-Output Structure of the U.S. Economy* (Bureau of Economic Analysis 1963, 1967, 1972, 1977). Following is a detailed description of the sources and methodology used to create the input, output, and price data for these industries.

4.2.1 Labor

Two components of labor input are distinguished in this study, namely, production-worker labor (L) and nonproduction-worker labor (N). Production workers are defined by the CM as workers (up through the line-supervisor level) closely associated with production operations at the establishment. The number of nonproduction workers is computed by subtracting the number of production workers from the number of all employees given in the CM or

---

11. Disaggregation of production and nonproduction labor in high-technology industries results in substantial improvement in the resulting model (Jang 1987) because the compensation and employment trends differ considerably for the two categories of workers. The Division of Productivity Research at BLS separates nonenergy intermediate input into purchased services and other materials because price and input trends for services are quite different, as William Gullickson of that agency has argued for many years.

ASM for each year; payroll for nonproduction workers is computed similarly. Supplemental labor costs are added into the payrolls of both production workers and nonproduction workers in proportion to their shares in total payroll. The augmented payroll of nonproduction workers divided by the number of nonproduction workers is the annual salary per nonproduction worker. (Employment of nonproduction workers is used as the unit of measure because hours of nonproduction workers are typically not measured, or not measured well.) The hours worked by production workers and their hourly wage rates based on the augmented production-worker payroll are derived from the CM and ASM and used as the quantity and price of production workers, respectively.

4.2.2 Semiconductors

From a technological perspective, semiconductors are one of the most important materials in the manufacture of communications equipment and computers. We separate semiconductors (SIC 3674) from other intermediate materials, which includes all physical materials and electric and gas utilities, shown in the CM and ASM. The ratio of expenditure on purchased semiconductors to expenditure on total intermediate materials is taken from the input-output tables in the CM years. These ratios are interpolated for each year. The price index for semiconductors comes from gross output deflators developed in the BLS economic growth program.

4.2.3 Materials

The levels of annual materials expenditures excluding semiconductors (and most purchased services) are taken directly from the five-year CM and the ASM. The real quantity of materials input is obtained by deflating materials expenditure. The aggregate price deflator for materials, P_M, is constructed as follows:

$$P_M = \sum_{i=1}^{n} W_i P_i, \quad i = 1, \ldots, n,$$

where i designates a particular materials input category. Twenty to thirty-five categories of materials and services inputs together were treated, depending on the industry. On the basis of the detailed input-output table, all physical materials and services purchased from the manufacturing sector and electric, gas, water, and sanitary services are included. The prices (P_i) of these detailed materials are obtained from the producer price indexes of BLS. The weight (W_i) of each individual material in aggregate intermediate input in these industries is computed from the input-output tables. First, we compute the weight from the input-output tables of 1958, 1963, 1967, 1972, and 1977; then we interpolate these weights to obtain the approximate weights for each year. The 1982 CM was used to extend the weights for materials.

4.2.4 Purchased Services

The services provided by the transportation, communications, wholesale and retail trade, finance, insurance and real estate, and government sectors, especially computer services, have become more and more important in the production process, but the cost of materials measured in the CM and ASM does not include the cost of these purchased services.

The ratio of purchased services expenditures to total cost for each industry is taken from the input-output tables for the CM years, and the ratio is interpolated between these values for each intermediate non-CM year. Using the approach applied to materials, we developed the price index for purchased services by aggregating the detailed purchased services shown in the input-output tables.

4.2.5 Variable Costs after Adjustment for Holding Inventories

Besides the direct costs of variable input factors such as labor, semiconductors, materials, and purchased services discussed above, manufacturers must pay the costs of holding work-in-process inventories. These costs can be measured in terms of holding related variable inputs. We thus compute the total cost of holding the work-in-process inventories by multiplying the quantity of the inventories in current dollars by the rate of return in the industry. This cost is then distributed to the individual variable inputs by their shares in total variable cost. Thus, the cost of holding raw materials inventories is added to total materials expenditures after deflation to obtain the real quantity of materials inputs. Thus, the price of materials is increased by the cost per unit of materials input of holding work-in-process inventory. The cost of holding the work-in-process inventory is thus treated as part of the cost of the variable inputs, with the cost allocated according to the shares in the variable cost of production. Semiconductor and other materials inputs are treated the same since there is no separate information on inventories of semiconductors and other materials.

4.2.6 Capital Stocks for Physical Assets and Financial Assets

The quantities of capital stocks of equipment and structures in these industries were computed by the perpetual inventory method. Investment data series are taken from the ASM and CM. The rates of economic depreciation applied for different types of producers' durable equipment and for private nonresidential structures from Hulten and Wykoff (1981) are used here as in many productivity studies, notably Jorgenson, Gollop, and Fraumeni (1987). The Hulten-Wykoff asset depreciation rates are not specific to industries, nor do they change through time. Depreciation rates for capital stock in these industries are developed as follows. First, the shares of the different types of durable equipment and structures in total expenditures on capital goods for each industry are computed on the basis of the capital flow tables for 1963, 1967, 1972, and 1977 from the associated input-output studies. These shares are interpolated between CM years. Using these shares as weights, the depreciation rates are summed for all types of equipment and structures from the Hulten-Wykoff study to obtain more reasonable depreciation rates for these two elements of the capital stock for each industry. The depreciation rates vary through time because and only because the weights change.

To compute the service prices of capital equipment and structures, we use Jorgenson et al.'s approach, somewhat modified. Besides equipment and structures, other assets, especially financial assets, are also important in most manufacturing industries. These financial assets must also earn a normal return. Their omission from calculation of the rate of return on physical assets imparts an upward bias to that rate of return. Interindustry differences in rates of return on capital should in principle reflect productivity differences. However, differences in rates of return measured in this way will result not only from differential productivity of physical assets but also from different requirements for financial assets.

The rate of return on capital, which includes equipment and structures as well as other assets—financial assets and all types of inventories—is computed by dividing total property income by the sum of nominal values of all assets at the end of the prior year. The values of equipment and structures are the products of their asset prices and quantities, respectively, which are derived as described above. The value of financial assets is estimated by multiplying the ratio of financial assets to the physical assets in the industry by the value of the physical assets. The ratios are taken from the financial statements in the Compustat data base for SIC 3661 and 3573. Balance sheets of nonfinancial corporate business from the Federal Reserve Board of Governors is used as a proxy for SIC 3662, for which Compustat lists no companies at all. A serious deficiency in coverage arises with the financial data for both industries because AT&T, a major producer of both types of equipment as well as of computers, is not listed in either SIC 3661, SIC 3662, or SIC 3573 in the Compustat data base. The omission of AT&T financial data amounts to assuming that the capital requirements for production of telecommunications equipment in that company are the same as those of nonfinancial corporations in general. While this assumption is dubious, the resulting correction for the return to financial assets is surely better than the assumption that they earn no return at all.

4.2.7 Total Cost and Output

The sum of shipments and changes in inventories of finished goods in current prices that come from the CM and ASM is the total cost before adjustment for the cost of holding financial assets and inventories. The cost of holding financial assets and inventories is measured by multiplying the amounts of financial assets and inventories by the rate of return in the industry. To get the true total cost for production, the costs of holding financial assets and finished goods are subtracted from the sum of shipments and changes in inventories.

Production of output is thus separated from production of shipments, and the two are priced separately. The quantity of real output is the deflated value of total revenue after the adjustments noted above. Output is deflated using the appropriate BLS price indexes from the PPI.

The quantities and prices of variable inputs are normalized to 1.00 in 1977. Quantity indexes are then obtained by dividing expenditures on the input by the normalized price.

4.3 Semiconductor Characteristics for Quality Adjustment in a Cost Function Model

Appendix table 4A.1 shows the technology frontiers chosen to represent the seventy-fifth percentile of performance for two types of semiconductor devices: DRAMS and microprocessors. The original data went back only to 1972; extrapolations to 1968 were based on the perceived history of the industry and have not been objected to in discussions with semiconductor specialists.[12] (These data were not adjusted to "tune" the estimation results.) Polynomial smoothing (a quadratic function of time) was applied to reflect the mix of devices of both types. It would be most appropriate to use value weights for the mix of DRAMs and microprocessors used in each industry applied to the indicators. We judged that such a procedure would result in roughly comparable smoothing. From 1968 to 1977, the normalized performance indicators move about the same distance (from -3.4 to 0), although in different patterns. After 1977, the depicted advance in DRAM characteristics is about four times faster than that of microprocessors. The two series of technological characteristics clearly show different patterns, however imprecise they may be.

In a study based on cross-sectional as well as time-series data, a much richer description of semiconductor technology than employed here would be possible. Such a study could be based in part on plant-level data from the Longitudinal Research Data file at the Census Bureau. In terms only of the number of characteristics included, this study is inferior to the conventional hedonic approach. However, the model explains more than 99 percent of the observed variation in input demand.

This approach has innovative features that compare favorably with the usual hedonic study, however. The weights of the characteristics of semiconductor devices are permitted to change by industry. (While we have not yet done so, we would expect to reject the hypothesis that the quality-adjustment functions are the same across industries.) Second, the interaction of semiconductors with other major categories of inputs is incorporated into the model through the joint estimation of the input demand functions and the cost function. Third, in the case of the computer industry, it is also possible to include evi-

---

12. However, we regard the 1968–71 data as preliminary.

dence for the semiconductor quality adjustment from the effect on total factor productivity in the industry. An ideal approach, in our view, would combine cross-sectional data with the cost function–based model applied here, enabling the analysis of more technological characteristics.

4.4   Empirical Application to Three Industries

4.4.1   Estimation Results

The cost function estimations outlined above were carried out for the telecommunications equipment and computer manufacturing industries SIC 3661, 3662, and 3573 by the FIML method in the SORITEC econometrics package. The results for each of these industries are shown in tables 4A.2, 4A.3, and 4A.4, respectively.

The coefficients of the estimated variable cost function models suggest that most of the model characteristics are satisfactory.[13] All variable input demand curves slope downward at all points, except as noted below, based on the BY parameters.[14] All industries show increasing returns to scale (in varying degrees) as expected; scale measures are in "credible" ranges: greater in computers, reasonably close to one elsewhere. Second-order parameters are reasonable in size; models characterized by overfitting often show second-order parameter values exceeding one.

With the exception of the demand for production-worker labor in industry 3662, the input demand functions are concave in their own prices, as the elasticities in table 4A.5 show. The shadow cost of capital, b_k, however, is effectively zero. The coefficient, b_k, was constrained to be nonpositive in all models. As noted in the data section, the absence of financial data for AT&T from the industry aggregate makes the capital results for SIC 3661 and 3662 less than complete. Because there are parameter constraints connecting the capital and output coefficients, this problem may also affect the estimates of economies of scale, which show increasing returns of about 40 percent in SIC 3661. The Durbin-Watson statistics (after first-order autocorrelation correction in SIC 3661) indicate that there may be downward bias in the estimated standard errors owing to serial correlation of the residuals for SIC 3662 and 3573.

13. It may be that the method for computing standard errors and *t*-statistics in FIML estimation results in downward bias in the standard errors when our iterative method of estimation is applied. A characteristic of many FIML estimation techniques is that the standard errors of the estimated coefficients are determined empirically on the basis of changes in the provisional coefficient estimates just prior to convergence. In consequence, when the estimation tolerance is extremely small—a practice to ensure reproducibility of the results and comparability across models—the variance-covariance matrix of the estimated coefficients gets quite small, and the *t*-statistics explode. In this constrained choice set, we chose the accuracy of the parameter estimates over that of their standard errors in order better to identify the interindustry differences among the quality-adjustment functions. It may be possible to correct this deficiency in the near future.

14. The parameters in the appendix tables have been rewritten as uppercase entities because of the limitations of computer software.

We did not expect the rates of quality augmentation inferred from the three industries to be the same. Lancaster's (1971) theory of demand based on characteristics of goods represents an individual product as a bundle of characteristics. As an example, device density and microprocessor capacity[15] for semiconductor inputs could be expected to yield different advantages in different kinds of communications equipment and computers. (In fact, this appeared to be so, but with little effect on the correlations of the resulting quality-adjusted prices.) Further, a considerable number of different devices are grouped together as output of the semiconductor industry, with large differences in function and prices per unit. Because our technology indicators include only two characteristics, DRAM density and microprocessor bit width, we thought it reasonable that the effects of embodied technical change might differ significantly in value per unit among the three industries. This proved to be the case, but the differences are somewhat smaller than we expected.

Estimates of the coefficients for quality adjustment of semiconductor input in this study for the three industries are shown in tables 4A.2–4A.4. The estimated coefficients alpha (α) are quite close for the telecommunications equipment industries. Computer manufacture is similar to telephone and telegraph equipment, but with even higher weight for DRAMs. That is, the values of α are 1.34 for SIC 3661, 1.38 for SIC 3662, and 1.28 for SIC 3573.[16] As table 4A.6 shows, the weights for the DRAM and microprocessor characteristics are about ⅔ and ⅓, respectively, in telephone and telegraph equipment and computers (SIC 3661 and 3573) and are reversed for other telecommunications equipment (SIC 3662). Preliminary discussion with semiconductor and telecommunications industry sources suggests that the relations among the weights for the three industries are plausible.[17] The great similarity between the manufacture of computers and the manufacture of telecommunications switching devices has been widely noted (e.g., Flamm 1989). The similar weights for technological characteristics found in the patterns of usage by the two industries confirm that observation. In contrast, microprocessor performance seems to be more important in other telecommunications equipment (SIC 3662).

The t-statistics reported in tables 4A.2–4A.4 are biased upward as a consequence of the iterative estimation procedure and are therefore inappropriate for testing hypotheses concerning the effect of quality change on the models.

15. Microprocessor capacity is expressed as "bit width"—our own term (not to be confused with "band width," which is only tangentially related). Integrated circuit technology has packed more functions on successively larger microprocessor "CPUs" (central processing units) so that bit width is an indicator of circuit integration and microprocessor speed as well as the data path and instruction repertoire that bit width directly measures.

16. The overall effect in computers is much larger despite the smaller value for alpha because an additional term, z_t, is included, representing the effect on total factor productivity in the industry.

17. Conversations with Jerry Junkins, chief executive officer, and Vladmire Catto, chief economist, Texas Instruments.

In order to test the hypothesis that adding quality adjustment to the models *does not* improve their explanatory power, we adopt the likelihood ratio test (see, e.g., Judge et al. 1985, 182–84). The test statistic is

$$\lambda = 2(U - R),$$

where U is the log of the likelihood function (LLF) of the unrestricted model (the model with technology-based quality adjustment, and R is the LLF of the restricted model (the model without quality adjustment). The test statistic λ has a chi-squared distribution with degrees of freedom equal to the number of parameter restrictions: two each for the telecommunications equipment industries and three for the computer industry. The LLF for the unrestricted model is based on the first pass of the iterative estimation procedure because the left-hand side of the model is changed in subsequent passes. Thus, the unrestricted LLFs reported in the text table below (showing hypothesis tests for effects of quality change in semiconductors) are not comparable to those reported in tables 4A.2–4A.4:

Industry	Unrestricted	Restricted	df	λ	$\chi^2(.05)$
3661	216.21	195.17	2	42.08	5.99
3662	121.95	116.32	2	10.63	5.99
3573	85.31	63.82	3	42.98	7.81

The overall effect of semiconductor quality improvement in computers is much larger than in telecommunications equipment because a term is included in the model representing the variable input factor productivity effect of improvement in the quality of semiconductors. This effect is about 6.3 percent per year, as table 4A.6 shows. Such an effect is quite large: for U.S. manufacturing as a whole, total factor productivity growth is about 1 percent per year before removal of scale effects. The coefficient estimated in table 4A.4 that leads to the effect reported in table 4A.6 is adjusted for scale effects because the scale coefficient b_y is estimated as part of the same model.

It is interesting to speculate why the exponential weights for the quality-adjustment functions are all greater than one. That is, the implied input demand effects (including substitution and, in the computer industry, cost reduction) of semiconductors are greater than DRAM density and microprocessor bit width changes would imply. This result may be interpreted as the effect of omitted characteristics. Dulberger (chap. 3 in this volume) suggests that the answer may lie in improved "packaging" of the devices: adaptation of the techniques that combine the semiconductor devices with other components and each other in the construction of complete systems. Whatever the cause, however, it is remarkable that the evidence from all three industries suggests that the growth in performance characteristics of semiconductor devices as measured here *understates* the growth in their comparative value in production of computer and telecommunications equipment.

Table 4A.7 shows the resulting quality-adjusted semiconductor prices for these three industries as well as the official price index for the computer industry (Cartwright 1986). The price index for computers used in the GNP accounts described by Cartwright is adjusted for quality change using a hedonic approach introduced by Cole et al. (1986). In comparison with this computer price index, our estimated prices of semiconductor devices used in all industries decline much more rapidly. Such a pattern would result in correspondingly higher growth of real output and productivity in the semiconductor industry than the measures obtained from the official price statistics.

Table 4A.8 shows the correlation coefficients for the quality-adjusted price indexes and their changes, expressed both in levels and in natural logarithms. While the correlation coefficients are all extremely high, the adjusted prices nevertheless exhibit rather different behavior. Quality adjustment for computer industry use of semiconductors shows the largest decline over the period studied, with the decline about twice as rapid both before and after the index year 1977, compared to the adjusted price of input to other telecommunications equipment. Another source of differences in quality-adjusted prices among industries could result from the adjustment of semiconductor input prices to reconcile production and shipments costs. (It should be noted that we made no postestimation or "feedback" adjustment of any of the model data to "tune" the results.) However, comparison of tables 4A.8 and 4A.9 shows that the quality-adjusted semiconductor prices are more highly correlated across industries than are the prices of semiconductor input before quality adjustment.

Table 4A.10 shows the effects of changes in performance characteristics of semiconductors on production costs in the U.S. computer industry for the period 1969–86 and for three subperiods. The cost-reducing effect declines from an annual rate of more than 2 percent in 1969–73 to about 0.67 percent in 1979–86. However, the value of the cost reduction increases from the earliest to the latest period because the total volume of sales in the computer industry increases.

4.4.2   Comparison with Dulberger's Method

It is useful to compare this approach with that applied by Dulberger (chap. 3 in this volume). (Note that Dulberger's analysis is based on data that were not available to us during the course of our study.) The Dulberger hedonic price index can be applied to deflate semiconductor input to an industry only if the detailed composition of that input is known in terms of characteristics. In other words, if the Dulberger deflator is applied to deflate input to the computer industry (SIC 3573) or telecommunications industries equipment (SIC 3661 and 3662), then the deflation will be based implicitly on the composition of the hedonic sample in the absence of data on composition of the semiconductor input in that specific industry. Unlike the hedonic deflator from the Dulberger application, the deflator derived from our approach reflects the technology of production in each of the industries studied, and the hedonic weights reflect the input demand transactions carried out by each industry. That is, the Dulberger hedonic index, like the Lancaster formulation, reflects the combinations of characteristics in the buyer's opportunity set but is mute concerning the buyer's actual choices. Our variant reflects the results of the buyer's choices but does not identify the original opportunity set.[18]

4.5   Conclusions and Implications for Future Research

This study examines three related equipment manufacturing industries that are central in different ways to the information revolution. Our key findings are as follows.

1. Advances in semiconductor technology have profoundly influenced the patterns of production in telecommunications equipment and computer manufacture. These technological advances are captured in physical characteristics of semiconductors.

2. These technological advances constitute largely unmeasured quality change in semiconductors. After adjustment, the prices per unit of performance fall dramatically (table 4A.7) and—as expected—faster than quality-adjusted prices of computers.

3. Consequently, the producer price indexes for semiconductor devices greatly understate quality change and thus the quantity of semiconductor input of constant performance.

4. The relative weights of DRAM device density and microprocessor word size vary among industries and are highest for DRAMs in the computer industry. (All three industries might be better understood and modeled as multiproduct industries so that the roles of the semiconductor inputs could be clarified by estimation of separate parameters linking them to different output categories in the using industries.)

5. Cost function–based estimation of hedonic price indexes offers substantial promise for finding industry-specific price deflators. The required assumption that producers minimize the short-run variable cost of production is

---

18. Despite the data limitations that our application necessarily reflects, the resulting input deflators are industry specific and perhaps not implausibly different from one another. There is no doubt, however, that a more specific data set in the particulars noted would improve our method. Our method has been applied in a recent doctoral dissertation at Rensselaer Polytechnic Institute (Pitt 1991). In that application, technological characteristics of aircraft are the basis for obtaining airline-specific indexes of the quality of the fleet of aircraft. Each fleet year for each carrier is represented by a vector of technological characteristics based on the composition of the fleet in that year. (The current value of the aircraft is used to weight its contribution to overall fleet technological characteristics.) Thus, in that case, where the data were available, the method applied here used detail of the type represented in Dulberger's analysis.

also required to interpret conventional hedonic price indexes as reflecting value in use.

6. Finally, cost function–based estimation of hedonic price indexes permits the unambiguous attribution of cost changes and associated productivity changes to quality change in the subject input, as demonstrated above for the U.S. computer industry.

We believe that the methods applied here also hold considerable promise for investigation of quality change in other industries. Particularly if applied to pooled plant-level time-series/cross-sectional data, these methods could accommodate a wider range of technological characteristics and thus provide more detailed and more reliable results than industry time-series data can support. (As noted in sec. 4.4, there is evidence for unmeasured characteristics.) A major strength of the approach is that identifying information for the value of different technological characteristics is derived from demand for other inputs as well as the one under study and from the cost function itself. There are literally dozens of studies in the past twenty years that attest to the improvement that interrelated factor demand models bring to studies of production. Much of this promise can be realized in quality-adjusting input factors for unmeasured quality change, that is, in adapting a hedonic or characteristics-based approach in cost function modeling.

The role of technological change in telecommunications equipment on telecommunications would be better understood through a study of the telecommunications services industry itself. Such a study could incorporate descriptions of the technological advances embodied in telecommunications equipment as this study uses DRAM density and microprocessor word size to describe the performance of semiconductors. Jang and Norsworthy (1990b) have outlined a method for assessing the effect of technological change in telecommunications equipment on telecommunications services. Such a study could provide an improved estimate of quality change of telecommunications equipment and thus an improved estimate of real output in SIC 3661. That information in turn would permit estimation of the contribution of semiconductors to the (quality-adjusted) growth of total factor productivity in telecommunications equipment, in the fashion applied to the computer industry in this paper. We are currently conducting such a study for the New York State Public Service Commission.

In the broader context of analysis of technological change, such a study would represent an important addition to the vertical tracing of the effects of semiconductor technology through equipment manufacture to the delivery of information services. A comparable study of the role of computers in financial and other services as well as manufacturing would complement the telecommunications sequence nicely.

Ultimately, however, studies from currently available data sources cannot substitute for the systematic collection of data for quality adjustment of products whose technological characteristics are rapidly evolving. For the detailed sort of information required to permit the PPI and CPI programs to keep up with accelerating technological change, considerably more resources will be required both for data collection and for empirical research based on those data. Studies such as this, and even those possible with the Census Bureau's Longitudinal Research Data file, can provide only "targeting" information for industries where technological change has outrun industrial price measurement programs. Certainly, the semiconductor industry is one such.

Appendix

Table 4A.1   **Technological Characteristics of Semiconductors Used for Quality-Adjustment, Natural Logarithms (1977 = 0)**

	DRAM		Microprocessor	
Year	Density Smoothed	Density Indicator	Word Size Smoothed	Word Size Indicator
1968	− 3.38946	− 3.46574	− 3.22815	− 3.46574
1969	− 3.00345	− 3.46574	− 2.74520	− 3.46574
1970	− 2.61980	− 3.46574	− 2.29332	− 2.07944
1971	− 2.23849	− 2.07944	− 1.87251	− 2.07944
1972	− 1.85953	− 2.07944	− 1.48276	− 0.693147
1973	− 1.48292	− 2.07944	− 1.12408	− 0.693147
1974	− 1.10867	− 0.693147	− 0.796460	− 0.693147
1975	− 0.736761	− 0.693147	− 0.499908	0.00000
1976	− 0.367206	− 0.693147	− 0.234421	0.00000
1977	0.000000	0.00000	0.000000	0.00000
1978	0.364855	0.00000	0.203356	0.00000
1979	0.727360	0.00000	0.375646	0.00000
1980	1.08751	0.693147	0.516871	0.00000
1981	1.44532	0.693147	0.627031	0.00000
1982	1.80077	2.07944	0.706125	0.693147
1983	2.15388	2.07944	0.754154	0.693147
1984	2.50463	2.07944	0.771117	0.693147
1985	2.85303	2.07944	0.757015	0.693147
1986	3.19908	3.46574	0.711848	1.38629

Table 4A.2   **Estimated Translog Variable Cost Function, U.S. Telephone and Telegraph Apparatus Industry (SIC 3661), Quality Adjustment Based on Technological Characteristics of Semiconductors**

Coefficient Name	Value of Coefficient	t-Statistic
AO	4.27823	2,825.12
AN	0.185892	179.697
AM	0.536192	521.608
AS	-0.162901E-01	-19.3494
ALPHA	1.3416	$-2,692.00$
ZR	0.64450	3,039.89
AV	0.790003E-01	47.3942
ANM	-0.345065E-01	-48.9988
ANS	-0.408186E-03	-0.895394
ANV	0.137574	369.008
AMS	-0.546782E-02	-8.69463
AMV	-0.374891E-01	-12.7577
ASV	-0.408221E-02	-4.20729
ANN	0.332749E-01	87.7688
AMM	0.684195E-01	142.557
ASS	-0.552270E-02	-9.58593
AVV	-0.444951E-01	-359.275
BY	0.720430	1,038.59
BK	-0.893981E-05	-0.0943134
BEK	-0.592812	$-2,767.58$
CNK	0.249345E-01	14.6355
CMK	-0.187211E-03	-0.163427
CSK	0.125610E-01	18.5945
CVK	-0.265574E-01	-16.9188
RL	-0.739801E-01	-127.501
RN	-0.478550	-706.962
RM	-0.178418	-140.741
RS	1.10119	1,541.58
RV	0.475493	524.840

LLF = 123.15

	R^2	D = W
Variable cost function	0.9980	1.0850
Input demand equations:		
Production workers	0.8607	0.9811
Nonproduction workers	0.9103	0.9726
Materials	0.9949	0.9249
Semiconductors	0.9203	0.3198
Purchased services	0.9795	0.8463

Table 4A.3   **Estimated Translog Variable Cost Function, Other Communications Equipment (SIC 3662), Quality Adjustment Based on Technological Characteristics of Semiconductors**

Coefficient Name	Value of Coefficient	t-Statistic
AO	4.96015	115485
AN	0.267009	512.181
AM	0.327592	683.261
AS	0.649659E-01	294.571
ALPHA	1.3843	−49,596.3
ZR	0.582204	6,450.42
AV	0.153946	624.417
ANM	0.691214E-01	368.229
ANS	−0.475510E-02	−20.2399
ANV	0.439374E-01	279.605
AMS	−0.773440E-02	−16.0016
AMV	−0.904379E-01	1,275.38
ASV	−0.937887E-02	−60.5852
ANN	−0.547744E-01	1,616.57
AMM	0.523390E-01	590.507
ASS	0.953483E-02	101.642
AVV	0.796024E-01	1,619.52
BY	0.964603	40,780.1
BK	0.141558E-03	32.4336
BEK	−0.401418	−89,902.6
CNK	0.311857E-01	1,271.62
CMK	0.185577E-01	206.153
CSK	−0.257856E-01	−69.4602
CVK	−0.251170E-01	143.386

LLF = 110.28

	R^2	D = W
Variable cost function	0.9949	1.0850
Input demand equations:		
Production workers	0.6358	0.9811
Nonproduction workers	0.9442	0.9726
Materials	0.9798	0.9249
Semiconductors	0.9999	0.3198
Purchased services	0.9963	0.8463

Table 4A.4   **Estimated Translog Variable Cost Functions, U.S. Computer Manufacturing (SIC 3573), Quality Adjustment Based on Technological Characteristics of Semiconductors**

Coefficient Name	Value of Coefficient	t-Statistic
AO	6.11539	36,859.8
AN	0.345391	328.308
AM	0.272393	176.175
AS	0.402017E-01	45.8208
ALPHA	1.28181	2,991.85
ZR	0.830143	585.567
ZT	−0.629755E-01	−226.155
AV	0.175130	154.050
ANM	−0.210291E-01	−10.2198
ANS	−0.250516E-01	−30.6193
ANV	0.189820	275.013
AMS	0.926313E-02	8.85685
AMV	0.579878E-01	121.829
ASV	−0.856720E-02	−16.5092
ANN	−0.591376E-01	−145.826
AMM	−0.190384E-01	−61.8067
ASS	−0.533597E-02	−14.8061
AVV	−0.236525	−2,681.77
BY	0.468209	121.687
BK	−0.477556E-01	−197.401
BEK	−0.717143E-01	−38.8456
CNK	0.957002E-01	125.170
CMK	−0.185323E-01	−12.7616
CSK	0.427278E-02	4.47603
CVK	−0.318193E-01	−39.7112

LLF = 46.426

	R^2	D = W
Variable cost function	0.9981	1.307
Input demand equations:		
Production workers	0.9529	1.499
Nonproduction workers	0.9550	1.250
Materials	0.9934	1.393
Semiconductors	0.9957	1.499
Purchased services	0.9961	1.053

Table 4A.5   **Own Price Elasticities of Inputs, Quality-Adjustment Models Based on Technological Characteristics of Semiconductors,[a] (1967–86)**

	SIC 3661	SIC 3662	SIC 3573
Production-worker labor	0.1552	− 0.1778	− 1.7692
Nonproduction-worker labor	− 3.2001	− 3.4818	− 2.4502
Materials	− 0.6445	− 1.6033	− 2.9221
Semiconductors	− 106.9720	− 12.9657	− 29.1951
Purchased services	− 23.0867	− 1.8441	− 12.9602

[a]From models reported in tables 4A.2–4A.4.

Table 4A.6   **Coefficients of Quality-Adjustment Function for Semiconductor Inputs in Telecommunications Equipment and Computer Industries[a]**

	SIC 3661	SIC 3662	SIC 3573
Alpha (α)	1.3416	1.3843	1.2818
DRAM density (Z_s)	0.6445	0.5822	0.8301
Microprocessor word size	0.3555	0.4178	0.1699
TFP growth (annual from Z')			0.056

[a]The estimated variable cost function does not include the capital input so that we have no way of estimating the capital saving associated with improvement in the quality of semiconductors. Accordingly, we have assumed no capital saving and reduced the estimated variable factor productivity increase in accordance with the share of capital in total cost: about 14.2 percent.

Table 4A.7   Semiconductor and Computer Price Indexes after Quality Adjustment (1977 = 100)

Year	PPI	Quality-Adjusted Prices Based on Technological Characteristics of Semiconductors Used In:			Official Computer Price Index
		SIC 3661	SIC 3662	SIC 3573	
1969	93.54	4,912.9	5,074.5	11,458.3	309.11
1970	92.29	2,845.1	2,825.0	3,476.1	276.46
1971	91.46	1,673.0	1,511.2	2,884.0	237.26
1972	89.99	987.2	934.3	1,539.6	204.36
1973	91.29	607.1	571.7	866.3	184.93
1974	99.75	406.5	383.0	528.0	145.77
1975	101.75	256.8	247.2	300.4	132.75
1976	100.06	158.1	154.0	170.4	115.72
1977	100.00	100.0	100.0	100.0	100.00
1978	99.16	63.4	65.5	59.0	84.78
1979	100.16	41.4	33.9	36.3	73.21
1980	107.21	29.0	33.2	23.8	58.84
1981	106.57	19.0	23.2	15.0	53.78
1982	103.29	12.3	16.1	9.2	50.08
1983	109.44	8.8	12.4	6.3	38.61
1984	113.15	6.2	9.7	4.4	34.30
1985	112.11	4.2	7.3	2.9	. . .
1986	113.72	3.0	5.7	2.1	. . .
Average annual rate of change (%)	.47	−17.86	−16.39	−20.76	−5.97

Table 4A.8   Correlation Matrices for Quality-Adjusted Prices of Semiconductor Inputs for Three Using Industries, 1969–86[a] (price indices: 1977 = 1)

SIC	Levels			Changes		
	3661	3662	3573	3661	3662	3573
3661	1.0			1.0		
3662	0.9996	1.0		0.9993	1.0	
3573	0.9943	0.9969	1.0	0.9947	0.9977	1.0

[a]Changes are correlated from 1970–86.

Table 4A.9   **Correlation Matrices for Prices of Semiconductor Inputs before Quality Adjustment for Three Using Industries, 1969–86[a] (price indices: 1977 = 1)**

	Levels			Changes		
SIC	3661	3662	3573	3661	3662	3573
3661	1.0			1.0		
3662	0.9986	1.0		0.9923	1.0	
3573	0.9847	0.9881	1.0	0.9304	0.9309	1.0

[a]Changes are correlated from 1970–86.

Table 4A.10   **Technological Characteristics of Semiconductors and Effects on Computer Industry Cost, Average Annual Rates of Change,[a] Selected Periods, 1969–86**

	1969–86	1969–73	1973–79	1979–86
Average change in DRAM density	36.4855	38.0132	36.8380	35.3103
Average change in microprocessor word size	20.3355	40.5281	24.9954	4.8028
Cost effect of DRAM density	−0.9275	−1.3886	−1.0334	−0.5733
Cost effect of microprocessor word size	−0.2904	−0.6705	−0.3252	−0.0435
Average total effect of semiconductors	−1.2180	−2.0591	−1.3586	−0.6169

[a]Computed by differences in logarithms.

References

Brown, R. S., and L. R. Christensen. 1981. Estimating elasticities of substitution in a model of partial static equilibrium: An application to U.S. agriculture, 1947 to 1974. In *Modeling and measuring natural resources substitution,* ed. E. Berndt and B. Field. Cambridge, Mass.: MIT Press.

Bureau of Economic Analysis. U.S. Department of Commerce. Various years. *The detailed input-output structure of the U.S. economy.* Washington, D.C.

Cartwright, D. W. 1986. Improved deflation of purchases of computers. *Survey of Current Business* 66 (March): 7–11.

Cole, R. E., Y. C. Chen, J. Barquin-Stollman, E. R. Dulberger, N. Helvacian, and J. H. Hodge. 1986. Quality-adjusted price indexes for computer processors and selected peripheral equipment. *Survey of Current Business* 66 (January): 41–50.

Crandall, R. W., and K. Flamm, eds. 1989. *Changing the rules: Technological change, international competition and regulation in communications.* Washington, D.C.: Brookings.

Flamm, K. 1989. Technological advance and costs: Computers versus communications. In Crandall and Flamm 1989.

Hulten, C. R., and F. C. Wykoff. 1981. The measurement of economic depreciation. In *Depreciation, inflation and the taxation of income capital,* ed. C. R. Hulten. Washington, D.C.: Urban Institute.

Jang, S.-L. 1987. Productivity growth and technical change in the U.S. semiconductor, computer and telecommunications equipment industries. Ph.D. diss., Rensselaer Polytechnic Institute.

Jang, S.-L., and J. R. Norsworthy. 1988. Scale economics, learning curves and downstream productivity growth: A study of technology in the U.S. microelectronics and computer industries. Technical Report no. 02-88. Center for Science and Technology Policy, School of Management, Rensselaer Polytechnic Institute.

————. 1990a. Measurement methods for technological change embodied in inputs. *Economics Letters* 32 (4): 325–30.

————. 1990b. Productivity growth and technological change in U.S. telecommunications equipment manufacturing industries. In *Competition and the regulation of utilities,* ed. Michael Crew. Boston: Kluwer Academic.

Jorgenson, D. W., F. M. Gollop, and B. M. Fraumeni. 1987. *Productivity and U.S. economic growth.* Cambridge, Mass.: Harvard University Press.

Judge, G. G., W. E. Griffiths, R. C. Hill, H. Lutkepohl, and T. Lee. 1985. *The theory and practice of econometrics.* 2d ed. New York: Wiley.

Lancaster, K. 1971. *Consumer demand: A new approach.* New York: Columbia University Press.

McElroy, M. B. 1987. Additive general error models for production cost, and derived demand or shared systems. *Journal of Political Economy* 95 (4): 737–57.

Norsworthy, J. R., and S.-L. Jang. 1989. A new framework for measuring and analyzing productivity and technology in service industries. Paper presented at the conference of the Pacific Telecommunications Council, Honolulu, January.

————. 1992. *Empirical measurement and analysis of productivity and technological change.* New York and Amsterdam: North-Holland.

Norsworthy, J. R., S.-L. Jang, and W. Shi. 1991. Productivity in the U.S. postal service: Variations among regions. In *Privatization in postal services,* ed. M. Crew and P. Kleindorfer. Boston: Kluwer Academic.

Norsworthy, J. R., and C. A. Zabala. 1990. Worker attitudes and productivity: Hypothesis tests in an equilibrium model. *Economic Inquiry* (January): 57–78.

Pitt, I. 1991. Technical change and investment in commercial aircraft. Ph.D. diss., Rensselaer Polytechnic Institute.

Triplett, J. E. 1987. Hedonic functions and hedonic indexes. In *The new Palgrave: A dictionary of economics,* ed. J. Eatwell, M. Milgate, and P. Newman. New York: Stockton.

————. 1989. Price and technological change in a capital good: A survey of research on computers. In *Technology and capital formation,* ed. D. Jorgenson and R. Landau. Cambridge, Mass.: MIT Press.

5 Measurement of DRAM Prices: Technology and Market Structure

Kenneth Flamm

Semiconductor memory is an example of a good undergoing continuing, rapid technological change, with historical price declines even more dramatic than in the (now well-documented) case of computers.[1] Indeed, declines in the cost of memory are most likely a major cause underlying the striking behavior of computer prices.

A twenty-year downward spiral in memory prices came to an abrupt halt in 1987. For the first time in the recorded history of the chip industry, substantial and sustained increases in memory costs were noted in 1987 and 1988. Although the reason for these increases is not the focus of this paper, it is reasonable to suspect that the negotiation of the Semiconductor Trade Arrangement (STA) between the United States and Japan, which became operational in late 1986, may have catalyzed this abrupt reversal of historical trends (see Flamm 1989, 1990, 1993).

This paper was motivated by my difficulties in determining exactly what happened to memory prices in 1987 and 1988 and what the probable effect of these price increases was on computer systems prices. It is concerned primarily with the task of analyzing price indexes for the computer memory chip type that accounts for the vast bulk of the market, the so-called dynamic random access memory (DRAM). Existing data on DRAM prices suffer from many deficiencies, most of which are detailed below (although not all are remedied). Producer price indexes prepared by the Bureau of Labor Statistics

Kenneth Flamm is a senior fellow at the Brookings Institution, Washington, D.C.

Without implicating them in his errors, the author thanks Marilyn Manser, Jack Triplett, Ellen Dulberger, Philip Webre, Doug Andrey, and Mark Giudice for their useful comments and suggestions and Yuko Iida Frost for very helpful research assistance. The views expressed in this paper are the author's alone and in no way represent those of the officers, trustees, or staff of the Brookings Institution.

1. For a comprehensive survey and synthesis of studies of computer prices, see Triplett (1989a).

(BLS) suffer from critical problems described below and in Dulberger (chap. 3 in this volume). By default, estimates prepared by the market consulting firm Dataquest are the most commonly used source of price data in this industry (they are used by Dulberger and even published in the official *Statistical Abstract of the United States*).

For this reason, I examine the methodology underlying the Dataquest price estimates in some detail in this paper. Rather than rely on the Dataquest figures, this paper develops new time-series data on DRAM prices from data on individual transactions and presents an econometric analysis of pricing practices within the market that enables us to control for relevant characteristics of the product and the transaction. Approximate Fisher Ideal DRAM price indexes using this new data are also constructed; these research price indexes may be of use in future work on this important industry.

I begin with a discussion of the nature of the product, its technology, and the industrial organization of the DRAM market. Then follows an examination of existing data on DRAM pricing and the strengths and weaknesses of different statistical sources. This is followed by an econometric analysis of a sample of actual DRAM contracts, from which both a price index and some suggestive analysis are then extracted.

5.1   The Product and Its Technology

Memory chips are the largest single segment in the U.S. semiconductor market, accounting for 28 percent of sales in 1989; they accounted for 34 percent of integrated circuit (IC) consumption.[2] The dominant product (with almost two-thirds of memory sales) was the DRAM, which by itself accounted for 20 percent of American IC consumption in 1989.

The first widely used commercial DRAM was the 1K memory (K means 1,024 bits of information), introduced in 1970 by American semiconductor companies. A new generation chip (with four times the capacity of the last generation) has been introduced approximately every three years since the mid-1970s.

At center stage in the continuing saga of technological improvement in DRAMs sits continuing advance in semiconductor manufacturing processes. Improvements in fabrication technology have steadily reduced the size of electronic circuit elements and stimulated development of fabrication processes for novel types of physical microstructures implementing standard electronic functions.

The principal and overwhelmingly important characteristic of a DRAM from the point of view of its consumers is its bit capacity, the amount of infor-

---

2. These figures are based on U.S. market estimates from *Electronics,* January 1990, 83. Note that only a small fraction of DRAMs consumed are manufactured within the United States; DRAMs account for a much smaller share of the value of U.S. production.

mation it can hold. The effect of technical improvement is typically measured in cost per bit. Greater density would be more desirable even in the absence of reduction in bit cost, however, because fewer chips must be interconnected within a system, lowering system manufacturing costs.

Faster access speed is also of importance to users but, like manufacturing cost per bit, is highly correlated with circuit density over the long run. Higher density parts are generally considerably faster than older parts; the shorter lengths of connections between circuit elements improve speed.

DRAMs are generally designed with some "standard," average speed specification in mind. Typically, the result of the fabrication process is a bell-shaped distribution around the specified speed, at which the chips perform adequately. The chips residing in the left tail of the distribution are identified through testing; those not meeting the design specifications have their speed ratings reduced and are sold at a discount.

As fabrication technology continuously improves, chip size is shrunk. Three or more such "die shrinks" may typically occur over the life cycle of a given capacity DRAM within a single company. A desirable side effect of incrementally smaller chips is gradually improved speed. Thus, the speed of the "standard" 256K DRAM produced by most manufacturers went from 150 to 120 nanosecond (ns) access time over the period 1987–88, the result of die shrinks. Even improvements in manufacturing processes for an existing design have often been associated with changes in product specifications large enough to lead to reclassification as new product types.

Chips also use power, and lower power consumption is desirable. It means less costly power supplies, and costs for heat dissipation, within systems that use chips. Beginning with the 64K generation, a lower-power chip technology known as CMOS (complementary metal-oxide semiconductor) gradually began to displace an older technology (known as NMOS [n-channel metal-oxide semiconductor]) in DRAM manufacture. The introduction of the 1M (for megabit, 1,024K) DRAM marked the almost complete displacement of NMOS by CMOS technology in DRAM manufacture, so power consumption is rarely an important factor in selection among current generation chips.

Because improvements in virtually all the desirable characteristics of DRAMs have been positively correlated with lower bit cost, cost per bit can probably be regarded as an upper bound on a suitably defined index of quality-adjusted chip cost. Data presented later in this paper show that, over at least some time periods, changes in simple cost per bit, for chips of given memory capacity, have not diverged greatly from a superlative DRAM price index accounting for technical improvements in speed and organization as well.

A crucial point to make is that virtually all technological improvement in DRAMs has been embodied in the introduction of distinct and identifiable new products, as opposed to more subtle qualitative improvement in existing chips. Because of this, construction of a price index that properly identifies and accounts for the introduction of new, improved products will also correctly capture the effect of technological advance (and other factors) on the cost of that input.

5.1.1 Product Differentiation

DRAMs—and other memory chips—have a reputation as the "commodity" product par excellence within the semiconductor industry: a high-volume, standardized good, with almost perfect substitution among different manufacturers' offerings the norm. Chips from different manufacturers use the same array of package types, pins, and have many common minimal technical specifications. They mainly use the same speed classifications (rated in nanoseconds average access time to a bit). Products with appropriate specifications from different manufacturers may be substituted within a given piece of equipment. Although DRAMs are in this sense a "commodity" product, the actual physical design of the chip's internal structures and many subtle aspects of its performance vary by manufacturer.

Because of subtle but important variation across producers in DRAM electrical and physical performance parameters, large manufacturers typically put a device through an extensive and expensive qualification process.[3] Some retesting is required every time the manufacturing process for a chip is changed. These costs provide an important economic incentive for systems manufacturers to limit the number of qualified suppliers for a particular application. Quality standards maintained by a manufacturer reduce the need to test components after purchase, and DRAMs are generally shipped to large customers in boxes with quality seals to guarantee factory-set standards (physical handling of chips is a major cause of failure or degradation). Purchasing chips from a new supplier, or outside manufacturer-controlled sales channels,[4] will generally lead to expensive additional testing.

Until recent years, DRAM manufacturers did not differentiate their products much in any dimensions other than speed and quality/reliability. This began to change in a significant way with the 64K generation of DRAMs, first shipped in 1979 (see Flaherty and Huang 1988, 12). The organization of chips (the way in which memory is accessed) began to diversify: a 1M DRAM, for example, may now be purchased in 1M × 1 or 256K × 4 configurations. New, specialized addressing structures were increasingly offered.[5] And specialized, proprietary DRAM designs with application-specific features became increasingly common: line buffers for television and video use,

---

3. Merely qualifying and testing a second source for a part already in use was estimated by one industry source to cost $120,000. Qualification costs were large enough to prompt at least one group of relatively large computer manufacturers to form a cooperative chip qualification joint venture, in order to pool these costs. Within the electronics purchasing community, talk of the economic pressure to reduce the number of suppliers is a staple of everyday conversation.

4. Unless, as sometimes happens, the chips can be purchased in boxes with the original factory quality seals intact.

5. Manufacturers of DRAMs now typically offer products with "page," "fast page," "nibble," and "static column" addressing modes.

multiple-ported buffers for computer graphics applications, bidirectional data buffers. Finally, a bewildering alphabet soup of package types is now used to encase a finished DRAM. There are many types of single-chip plastic casing for DRAMs,[6] ceramic cases, and various kinds of multichip memory module packages.

Organization, addressing structures, and application-specific designs mark off substantially different products. Although they may be created on the same production line, different tooling, fabrication steps, and manufacturing problems characterize these products. Packaging, on the other hand, can probably be regarded as a nonessential difference among chips. At a relatively late stage in the fabrication process, decisions can be made to change the mix of packages used for the product. Indeed, competition among manufacturers works to drive costs for a DRAM toward the market price for that DRAM in the standard plastic case, plus some incremental add-on reflecting the cost to the producer of additional packaging options. If demand for a single specific package type exceeds supply, pushing price up, manufacturers can easily switch output to that package type quite late in the production process.

Note that the relative prices of DRAMs of varying sizes and organizations are quite volatile and do not seem to be linked by a particularly stable relation, even within the course of a single year. In particular, faster parts are typically introduced at a substantial premium relative to lower-speed components; this premium rapidly erodes over time, however, as the mix of output shifts toward faster chips, for reasons discussed next. Figure 5.1 shows the retail prices of various DRAMs relative to a garden variety 265K × 1, 120 ns part, as reported in advertisements by one Los Angeles–area mail-order vendor over the course of a year.[7] Relative prices fluctuated quite a lot (note the rapid erosion in fast 60 ns 256K × 1 and 80 ns 64K × 4 chip prices relative to more mature products).

5.2 Industrial Organization of the DRAM Market

Different classes of consumers purchase DRAMs through different sets of marketing channels. The distinctions are important: over the last half decade, price movements in each of these distinct market segments have varied greatly. Government policies seem to have accentuated these differences and created sharp regional (i.e., the United States, Europe, Japan, Asia, etc.) price differentials in what seems to have been a previously well-integrated

6. The most common was the familiar dual in-line pin (DIP), but there is also the single in-line pin package (SIPP), the zig-zag-in-line pin (ZIP), the small outline J-leaded (SOJ) case, and the plastic-leaded chip carrier (PLCC).

7. The vendor is L.A. Trade, and the source for these prices is the publication *Computer Shopper*. Scrutiny of dated advertisements elsewhere in this publication suggests a two-month lag between submission of advertising copy and the month of publication for the magazine. The prices shown here are assigned to their inferred *submission* dates.

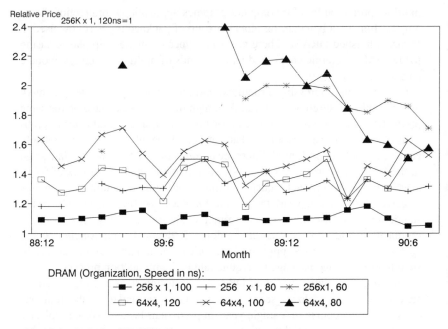

Fig. 5.1   Relative DRAM prices

market. Finally, user-supplier relations appear to play an important but poorly understood role in determining market prices for DRAMs.

5.2.1   Market Organization

There are three basic purchasing channels linking the supplier with users of ICs. First, large electronic equipment manufacturers (so-called OEMs, original equipment manufacturers) who purchase large volumes of product deal directly with chip manufacturers. Transactions in this market are generally labeled *contract* pricing. It is not unknown for OEMs to contract for large purchase volumes in order to qualify for volume pricing discounts, then resell the surplus over their actual needs to brokers.

Second, chip manufacturers maintain a formal distribution network through "authorized distributors" to service lower-volume customers. Chip manufacturers warrant the product distributed through this channel and often play an important role in the technical support and quality assurance programs offered to the customers. Given the historical fact of a continuous yet relatively volatile decline in chip prices, manufacturers have historically offered their authorized U.S. distributors "price protection," the assurance that distributors lowering their sales prices to meet market competition will receive a credit reflecting the difference between the distributor's purchase price and the lower sales price to the final consumer. The risk related to price uncertainty is then assumed by the chip manufacturer. Pricing generally seems to be on a spot basis, although there can be a substantial lead time between orders and deliveries in times of buoyant demand, and distributor prices take on a "contract" aspect.

Finally, there is the so-called grey, or spot, market. Independent distributors, brokers, and speculators buy and sell lots of chips for immediate delivery. There is also a significant retail market selling directly to computer resellers and users wishing to upgrade computer systems or replace defective parts. Supplies of chips on the American grey market come from chip manufacturers, OEMs, and authorized distributors selling their excess inventories and also from Japanese trading companies and wholesalers purchasing directly from Japanese DRAM manufacturers (see, e.g., USITC 1986, A-12). Grey market product is *not* warranted by the manufacturer and has frequently been subjected to unknown handling and quality assurance procedures.

In 1985, U.S. industry sources estimated that authorized distributors accounted for about 30 percent of chip manufacturers' DRAM sales (USITC 1985, A10–A11). Since grey market sales are often resales of product originally sold through OEM contracts or authorized distributors and double count chips flowing into the grey channel from sources other than chip manufacturers, one must be careful in calculating the share of these different channels in sales to final users. One 1985 estimate held that 20 percent of "the market" (presumably, end users) is accounted for by the grey channel in times of shortage.

This is roughly in sync with more recent estimates. In early 1989, one industry source estimated that perhaps 70 percent of DRAM sales were "contract" sales made directly by producers to large users, 15 percent went to final users through authorized distributors, and an additional 15 percent went through the grey market.[8]

5.2.2   Government Policy and Regional Segmentation of the Market

A final factor complicating discussion of DRAM prices was the appearance of significant regional price differentials in 1987 and 1988, after the signing of the STA. In response to the STA, the U.S. and Japanese governments began to set floor prices for export sales of DRAMs by Japanese companies. Initially, different standards were set for sales to the U.S. market and other ("third-country") export markets; after U.S. protests, the systems were later unified. (In response to European protests, the pricing guidelines were separated again in 1989.)

Regulation of Japanese export sales ultimately involved four elements. First, an export licensing system was adopted. This system required de facto government approval of the export price, which was to be set above minimum

---

8. The estimate is that of Don Bell, of Bell Microproducts Inc., whom I thank for spending the morning of 16 February 1989 attempting to educate me in the intricacies of the DRAM market.

norms established by Japan's Ministry of International Trade and Industry (MITI). Second, foreign purchasers of Japanese chips were required to register with MITI. Third, all export transactions required a certificate provided by the original chip manufacturer attesting to the fact that the chips in question were actually manufactured by that producer. Fourth, MITI established informal regional allocation guidelines to ensure that supplies were not diverted from one export market to favor another.

By most accounts, MITI's guidance was quite effective in setting minimum pricing standards for Japanese DRAM manufacturers' direct export sales. (Because Japanese manufacturers were by this time responsible for between 80 and 90 percent of world DRAM sales, this effectively worked as a floor on price in the global market.) The intent of the second and third elements was clearly to reduce access by foreign purchasers to Japanese grey market channels not under the direct supervision and control of Japanese chip manufacturers. Predictably, prices in the unregulated Japanese market soon dropped below foreign export prices. In 1988, articles in the Japanese business press (see the references to them in Flamm [1993]) suggested that the differential between domestic and export pricing was quite large.

5.3   Historical Data on DRAM Prices: A Review and Comparison

At a relatively aggregate level of detail, BLS publishes matched-model producer price indexes for integrated circuits, including an estimated index for MOS memory. It is obvious to all those familiar with pricing behavior in the industry, however, that the BLS price indexes grossly underestimate price declines in entire classes of semiconductor products subject to rapid technological change, such as memory chips. (For example, the BLS producer price index for MOS memory ICs declines by about 50 percent over the five-year period from June 1981 to June 1986, implying an annual rate of price decline of only 13 percent.)

The most significant reason for this bias is probably the infrequent updating of the sample of products covered and recalibration of their relative weights. (Also, in recent years, fierce competition had led many U.S. producers to withdraw from producing certain of the products with the steepest price declines, so the slow decline of the BLS IC price indexes may also reflect in part a shift in the product mix of U.S. producers toward chips undergoing less rapid price declines.) Figure 5.2 sketches out a stylized view of the typical price trajectory over time for a new generation of memory chip—very steep initial declines, followed by much less rapid decline. Assume, for simplicity, that the mix of shipments quickly shifts to the new generation of chip when its cost per bit declines below that of the older generation chip, at time T_1, but that very small quantities of the older generation chip are shipped for long periods afterward. An approximation to an exact price index would then look something like line ABC and would catch most of the rapid fall in the initial

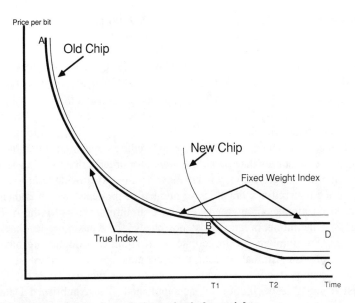

Fig. 5.2   Effect of delay in updating price index weights

stages of the new generation part's life cycle. Delaying updating of the sample, and adjusting weights for a price index, until time T_2, as is probably the empirical case, would result in the index traced out by line *ABD*, which substantially underestimates the true decline.

Until the mid-1980s, there is essentially only one published source of historical price data on DRAMs: Dataquest, an American market research firm. Dataquest publishes quarterly estimates of DRAM production, by bit capacity, and an aggregate worldwide "average selling price" (ASP) for every capacity chip then in large-scale production. ASP is a "billing" price; that is, it reflects bills sent out when product is actually shipped. Because there is often a lag between when a sale is negotiated ("booked") and when product actually ships under the agreed terms, current "billing" price was the "booking" price in an earlier period when the purchase was negotiated. There are several indications that the Dataquest ASP estimates have become less reliable in the period after 1985.[9]

Since 1985, Dataquest ASP estimates have been supplemented by quarterly contract booking price data based on a survey conducted elsewhere within the Dataquest organization. While the methodology used to construct both sets of numbers has apparently never been formalized, or published,[10] interviews

9. Further analysis of price data supporting this statement is available on request from the author.
10. The published methodology for quarterly contract booking prices consists of the following: "Dataquest collects price information on a quarterly basis from North American suppliers and major buyers of these products. North American bookings price information is analyzed by SUIS

with various Dataquest staff members in 1989–90 provided some basic idea of the general procedures used at that time to construct these two series.

Prior to 1985, the Dataquest ASPs were apparently based exclusively on "informal inquiries" and "ongoing dialogue" on pricing trends with both producers and users of semiconductors. After 1985, when Dataquest began its quarterly survey of U.S. booking prices for semiconductor purchasing contracts, these quarterly U.S. booking prices have been the starting point for a more systematic estimation procedure for average selling (billing) prices worldwide. In essence, the estimation procedure applies considerable judgmental input to survey data on U.S. *booking* (or order) price for a few standard parts, in order to derive a very much more detailed worldwide *billing* (or shipping) price matrix for a much larger number of products, which is then used to produce estimates of aggregate revenues, in turn the basis for the ASP estimates.[11] If the numbers fail consistency checks, or if customer feedback suggests that the numbers are inaccurate, or if significant doubts are otherwise raised, either the original booking price estimate based on survey data or the various pricing structure assumptions used to construct the ASPs, or both, is adjusted until "reconciliation" is accomplished. Thus, published Dataquest ASPs are a complex hybrid of limited survey data, analyst judgments, and informal dialogue with Dataquest's customers.

The feedback from manufacturers and users may very well serve to improve these estimates of average quarterly billing prices. Comparable numbers are readily available within most chip producers' sales and chip consumers' purchasing departments. For this reason, the aggregate billing price estimates are probably more accurate than the quarterly booking price data, despite the fact that the latter, not the former, are what is actually measured in Dataquest surveys.

The quarterly price survey (of U.S. booking prices), apparently the only semiformal survey instrument used by Dataquest analysts in constructing their worldwide ASPs, is sent to approximately eighty to ninety U.S.-based companies, of which approximately 60 percent are manufacturers and 40 percent users. It covered 140 different types of parts in 1989 (of which a very small

---

[Semiconductor User Information Service] analysts for consistency and reconciliation. The information finally is rationalized with worldwide billings price data in association with product analysts, resulting in the current forecast" (I thank Mark Giudice, of Dataquest, for providing me with this on 11 July 1990).

11. Conversation with Fred Jones, Dataquest Semiconductor Industry Service, 20 July 1990. The bookings price reported by the quarterly survey is "adjusted" to an equivalent billings price on the basis of an analyst's estimate of the lag between bookings and billings, the effects of ongoing renegotiation of current (and write-downs of backlogged) orders under older contracts, and sales to the spot market. Estimates of product mix price differentials are then applied to a "base" billing price to get a price structure for a much larger number of products (other speeds, other organizations, other packaging) than is covered by the survey. Still more analyst estimates and judgments of regional price differentials are combined with detailed estimates of quantities shipped by region, then aggregated over regions, to arrive at a worldwide estimate of revenues and (after dividing by worldwide shipments) ASPs.

number were DRAMs).[12] Respondents are asked to provide estimates of their average booking price, for given products and volumes. The quarterly booking price estimate is then constructed as a weighted average of these responses, with weights based on annual aggregate semiconductor production by responding producers and the estimated annual aggregate semiconductor procurement of surveyed consumers. Conceptually, therefore, it is neither an input, nor an output, nor a consumer price index. The survey covers only U.S.-based suppliers and purchasers.

Apparently in response to the creation of the "monitoring" system associated with the STA in 1986, price floors, and significant regional price differentials, Dataquest began a new program reporting regional contract pricing for a sample of twenty-five semiconductor components, on a biweekly basis. These data (the "Dataquest Monday Report") are based on a survey of six to ten respondents, primarily chip manufacturers, in each of six geographic regions.[13] For DRAMs, the survey asks for the current contract price negotiated in three different volumes: 1,000, 10,000, and volume (over 100,000).[14] If producers have not concluded any contracts for a particular volume, they are asked to estimate the price that would have been negotiated on a contract of that size. Japanese producers do not report a contract price, and Japanese price data refer to "large volume wholesale" prices.

The data discussed thus far have largely ignored DRAMs sold by distributors and in the spot market. This misses an important dimension of the change in market conditions after the signing of the STA. To remedy this situation, I have constructed time series showing retail spot prices for memory chips, beginning in the spring of 1985. To do so, I collected weekly data on sales prices by one of the largest retail vendors of memory chips in the United States.[15] The advertised prices are dated (an important point since there is typically a substantial lag between the submission of advertising copy and its publication). Contacts with this vendor have also made it clear to me that these are real prices; that is, in-stock product is actually available at these prices. The contrast with contract prices is striking: spot retail prices for 256K DRAMs quadrupled between early 1987 and early 1988, while U.S. contract prices (as measured by the Dataquest Monday series) merely increased by 60 percent!

The conclusion that emerges from a comparison of the bits and pieces of information available on DRAM pricing is that, prior to 1985, various available price series are roughly consistent and tend to move relatively closely together. Significant regional differentials were not important. All this changed after 1987; it became much more important to disaggregate by sales

12. By the spring of 1990, the survey had been expanded to cover 211 types of parts.

13. I thank Mark Giudice, of Dataquest, who, in various conversations in 1989 and 1990, provided the description of the Dataquest Monday Report Survey given here.

14. In some published Dataquest reports, it is stated that "volume" prices mean greater than 20,000 parts, not 100,000; the definition of *volume* for DRAMs is apparently an exception to this rule.

15. A detailed analysis of these data may be found in Flamm (1993).

channel and region in tracking DRAM prices actually faced by users. For example, assume that the grey market accounted for 15 percent of consumption by volume and 25 percent of consumption by value in some base year. If grey market sales prices quadruple (to construct a not-so-hypothetical example) while prices in other sales channels merely double, the increased cost to chip consumers will be about 25 percent greater than what is shown by a price index based solely on sales through non–grey market channels!

5.4   The Economic Role of Contract Pricing

Given that perhaps 70 percent of DRAM sales are initially made as direct "contract" sales to large users, it is useful to examine the nature of these contracts in detail. An econometric analysis of contract prices will permit one to control for detailed characteristics of DRAMs and DRAM contracts and more accurately measure a "quality-adjusted" price for DRAMs. The analysis will be applied in constructing Fisher Ideal price indexes in the next section of this paper.

Typically, "contract" sales are commitments to supply some quantity of parts, at some specified price, beginning at one future date, and ending at another future date. However, they rarely seem to be legally binding commitments. The prices specified in these long-term contracts generally appear to hold when shipments under the contract begin but often do not persist over the life of the contract. Many contracts contain explicit provisions for renegotiation of price downward, at the purchaser's option, in response to changing market conditions; purchasers also successfully demand downward price adjustments even when no such provision is explicitly made.[16]

Furthermore, because the system of price floors for DRAMs put into place by the U.S. Commerce Department in 1986 specified that the prevailing floor price at the time a legally binding contract was drawn up and signed remained in force throughout the life of the contract, despite expected future declines in DRAM prices, there was an additional disincentive to producing a formal, legally binding document. On the other hand, suppliers generally seem to respect contract prices as a de facto ceiling on prices charged their customers (although, during the unprecedented increase in memory chip prices of 1987–88, some purchasers apparently did face cancellation or reduction of prescribed contract volumes at the negotiated price).

If contract prices are generally not legally or practically binding much beyond the original beginning date for the contract, what then is the purpose of entering into one of these informal, "handshake" commitments? Interviews with OEM purchasing managers suggest that assuring the *quantity* of DRAMs

---

16. An interesting compendium of DRAM contract "horror" stories—users and producers repudiating oral and written price commitments in response to changing market conditions—may be found in USITC (1986, A-75–A-82).

to be purchased from suppliers is the major objective of these arrangements. In fact, purchasers frequently suggest that the critical issue in times of extreme shortage is not necessarily pricing but getting adequate supplies. Spot market purchases may create other significant costs for the chip consumer that extend beyond the purchase price. Additional qualification costs or extensive additional testing may be required for purchases from new sources or grey market suppliers.

Producers of DRAMs face a different logic. Significant "learning-curve" effects lead to a sharp increase in the output of any given initial investment in DRAM production capacity over the product life cycle of that generation of DRAM. Producers must be concerned about volatility in demand for the increasing quantities of DRAMs that will be flowing off of existing fabrication lines in future periods. Quantity commitments lock purchasers into deliveries of a given producer's output and reduce the odds that large volumes of chips emerging from ever more productive factories will have to be liquidated in the grey market.

My working hypothesis, then, is that long-term chip contracts represent the marriage of quantity commitments to a forward price in force at the beginning of the contract. Over the remaining life of the contract, however, contract buyers seem to enjoy something like the "price protection" offered to distributors.

5.4.1   Econometric Analysis of Contract Pricing

I collected confidential data on OEM DRAM contracts covering the period 1985–89 from industry sources. The data are drawn from contracts negotiated by a small number of European and North American electronic equipment OEMs; the bulk of the reported contracts refer to purchases by European users. Characteristics of the contracts that were collected include negotiation date, start date for shipments, period over which shipments are to be delivered, total quantity commitments over this period, contract price, nationalities of chip vendors (American, European, Korean, and Japanese) and purchasers, chip organization and packaging, and chip speed (access time). After discarding contracts for which speed measures were unavailable (or covering parts with a mixture of speeds), parts that used packages other than plastic dual in-line pin (DIP), plastic-leaded chip carrier (PLCC, in the case of 256K DRAMs only) and small outline cases (SO, in the case of 1M DRAMs only),[17] and chips with relatively uncommon organization,[18] a sample of 83 agreements for 64K DRAMs, 174 for 256K DRAMs, and 128 for 1M DRAMs remained. A growing variety of chip organizations and packaging in this

17. These involved a small number of observations divided among a relatively large group of other packages. Only 256K DRAMs with access times of 120 ns, or faster, were packaged in PLCC cases in the contracts in this sample.

18. Chip organizations other than 64K × 1, 256K × 1, 1M × 1, or 256K × 4 (the latter two are 1M DRAM types) appeared only in a relatively small number of contracts in my sample.

sample, with each new generation of DRAM, confirms my earlier observations about increasing product differentiation in the DRAM market.

I examined the distribution of these contracts by lead time (months from negotiation date to start date) and length (duration of contract, months from start date to end date). It was readily apparent that the vast bulk of these contracts begin with a very short period after their negotiation. The contract lengths cluster around three-, six-, and twelve-months' duration. More than 40 percent of the contracts for 64K and 256K DRAMS and 29 percent of those for 1M DRAMs could be considered "spot": shipments were scheduled to begin in the month they were negotiated. A large but smaller fraction (38 percent of the 1M, 28 percent of the 256K, 14 percent of the 64K) were to begin in the month following the contract's negotiation. All remaining contracts began within two to six months for 64K parts; 2 percent of 256K DRAM and 7 percent of 1M DRAM contracts began more than six months later.

The distributions for 64K and 256K DRAM agreements before and after September 1986 suggest that contracts negotiated after that date tended to have longer lead times and to last longer. A formal chi-square test comparing pre- and post-STA distributions generally confirmed these casual impressions.[19] (But note that the period prior to the signing of the STA was one in which markets saw abundant supplies and generally declining prices, while 1987 and 1988 were generally marked by firm or rising prices and tightening supplies.)

My analysis treats observed prices as being derived from some "base" market price for a standard DRAM in a plastic DIP case, corrected for the incremental costs of more complex packaging (recall the discussion of "packaging arbitrage" above). Discussions with electronics purchasing personnel suggest that this is, indeed, how price is conceptualized when contracts are negotiated (i.e., projections of the prevailing prices for the "base" product are added to the cost of specialized packaging). Quantity discounts (presumably reflecting fixed selling costs) and vendor nationality effects (which may reflect perceptions of quality by chip consumers or distinctive sales strategies by groups of firms) will also be considered as possible reasons for deviation from prevailing "base" DRAM prices. Prices paid by European and American customers will also be permitted to differ in the statistical analysis, in order to test for the apparently increasing regional segmentation of DRAM markets after 1986. Specification of the determinants of this "base" price is the subject to which I next turn.

5.4.2   An Econometric Model of Forward Pricing in DRAMs

My starting point is the notion that these "contract" prices are forward prices, reflecting expectations at the negotiation date for spot DRAM prices at

---

19. Rejecting a null hypothesis of no change at the 5 percent level, I conclude that both lead times and lengths of contracts signed for the newer 256K DRAMs seem to have increased after the STA was signed, while lead times increased for more mature 64K chips (but I did not reject the hypothesis of no change in the distribution of lengths).

the start date for the contract. The 40 percent of contracts that start immediately are true "spot" prices. If these contract prices were truly binding over the life of the contract, then one would further expect this price to decline with contract length, in a regime of falling DRAM prices, since the fixed price would have to be adjusted down to leave a purchaser indifferent between a longer contract and a sequence of shorter-term forward contracts. (The opposite, of course, would occur in a regime of rising DRAM prices.) Length of contract has been included as an explanatory variable in order to test the null hypothesis that contract length plays no significant role in price determination, in accordance with the a priori perception that initial contract price is generally renegotiated as soon as there are significant reductions in DRAM prices.

My approach is borrowed from the literature on futures prices.[20] The basic identity is

$$(1) \qquad f_s^r = E_r[P_s] + \xi_s^r,$$

where f_s^r is forward price at time r for period s, $E_r[P_s]$ is the expectation—conditional on information available at time r—of spot price in period s, and ξ_s^r is defined as bias, the difference between forward price and expected spot price.

If the forward price is "unbiased," then the ξ term will be zero. On the other hand, a risk-averse speculator requires a positive return to buy forward contracts and accept the risk associated with uncertainty about future prices, so the ξ term may be negative. The latter situation was described by Keynes as his theory of "normal backwardation." Whether future prices generally are unbiased, or exhibit normal backwardation, or possibly even a positive bias, is the subject of heated debate and will be treated as an empirical question in what follows.[21]

At a minimum, I shall assume that, for any generation of chip, market participants' expectations about supply and demand fluctuations are generated by some "model" that remains constant over the product life cycle of that chip and that a fixed stationary term structure of forward contract prices prevails, that is, that the bias term in equation (1) is given by a function of delivery lead time, $s - r$ (aside from random, mean zero disturbances). This means that we can rewrite (1) as

$$(2) \qquad f_s^r = E_r[P_s] + \xi(s - r).$$

Deviations of forward prices from expected spot price at delivery are given by a set of constants, with exactly one corresponding to each possible value of lead time to delivery.

---

20. The primary distinction between a futures price and a forward price is that the futures market is relatively large and well organized, with a high degree of standardization of contracts and commodities, well-refined tools and procedures to make contracts legally enforceable, and government regulation of trading behavior.

21. For a spectrum of different approaches to this issue, see Chari and Jagannathan (1990), Stein (1987, chaps. 1, 2), Newbery (1987), Houthakker (1987), and Williams (1986).

As an alternative approach to specification, we start with Stein's model of futures markets (see Stein 1987, chap. 2). Bias is proportional to the conditional (at time r) variance of spot price at delivery time s, $V_r[P_s]$:

$$(3) \qquad f_s^r = E_r[P_s] - \frac{h_r V_r[P_s]}{u},$$

with h representing net hedging pressure (the excess supply of forward contracts were forward price set equal to the expected future spot price), and u a function of such market characteristics as degree of risk aversion and relative numbers and types of different classes of market participants.[22] The latter can reasonably be taken as relatively constant; the behavior of net hedging (as measured empirically in traditional commodities future markets) has also not been particularly volatile (Stein 1987, 63). In what follows, I assume that, over the relatively short time periods examined in this paper, the hedging pressure h can be taken as randomly varying around some fixed mean H, that is,

$$(4) \qquad h_t = H + \eta_t,$$

with the η_t i.i.d., mean zero random disturbances.

If we then take the additional step of assuming that conditional variance $V_r[P_s]$ is approximately proportional[23] to $s - r$, lead time (with constant of proportionality σ^2), we then have

$$(5) \qquad f_s^r = E_r[P_s] + b(s - r) - \frac{\sigma^2}{u}(s - r)\eta_r,$$

with $b = -H\sigma^2/u$.[24]

If forward prices are unbiased, b is zero; if they exhibit normal backwardation, b is negative. This specification effectively imposes a series of linear constraints on the less restrictive specification of a fixed, stationary term structure of forward contract prices set out in equation (2), that is, that $\xi(s - r) = b(s - r)$, and can therefore be tested.[25]

To actually estimate (5), we may add on a mean zero random disturbance term, v_r, and (incorporating [4]) rewrite it as

22. Other approaches to modeling futures prices can also yield a bias in forward price proportional to the conditional variance of price (see Newbery and Stiglitz 1981, chap. 13; and Newbery 1987, 445).

23. Because $V_r[P_r]$ must equal zero, I have constrained the intercept of a linear approximation to equal zero.

24. Or, with a deterministic supply and price given by adding permanent random shocks onto a deterministic inverse demand function, a conditional variance $V_r[P_s]$ proportional to $s - r$ can be explicitly derived.

25. That is, if the coefficient of the lead time dummy variable for a contract with a two-month lead time is constrained to equal two times the coefficient of the dummy variable for a contract with a one-month lead time, the coefficient of the dummy variable for a three-month lead time is constrained to equal three times the coefficient of the dummy variable for a contract with a one-month lead time, etc., we produce specification (5).

$$(6) \quad f_s^r = P_s + b(s - r) + \{E_r[P_s] - P_s\} - \frac{\sigma^2(s - r)\eta_r}{u} + v_r.$$

Assuming rational expectations, the expression in braces will on average equal zero, and we might wish to incorporate it, and all terms to its right, into a random disturbance term and not explicitly model the formation of expectations. However, the difference between conditional expectations and their future realization (the expression in braces in [6]), which becomes part of the error term in a regression equation, will generally be correlated with P_s and therefore calls for more complex estimation strategies. My approach will be to use instrumental variables. Note as well that the random disturbance term in (6) is explicitly heteroskedastic.

I do not actually have data on spot prices for large user contracts; however, I did construct the time-series data on spot retail prices in the United States described earlier. Large-volume U.S. spot contract prices were assumed to be related to U.S. retail spot prices by the relation

$$(7) \quad\quad\quad\quad\quad P_s = c + dR_s,$$

where R_s is retail spot price at time s. The presumed constancy of this relation in the U.S. market can be used to identify changes in price differentials between U.S. and European markets, with the use of appropriate dummy variables (i.e., shifts in parameter c), even if no U.S. contract data are actually available, in a sample composed exclusively of European contracts. If any U.S. contracts *are* available in the sample, actual differentials (distinct levels for the United States and Europe), as well as changes over time, are identified when (7) is substituted into (6). Thus, even if data on U.S. contract data are unavailable over periods when price differentials between the United States and Europe are believed to have changed, we can still check for such changes by regressing European contract prices on U.S. retail spot prices.

Finally, note that the semiconductor industry habitually analyzes its prices on diagrams with logarithmic scales. I shall regard contract prices, and models of pricing, as being set and analyzed in the logs of prices and will undertake the econometric analysis of chip prices using logarithmic functional forms. In equations (1)–(7), then, f, P, and R should be read as the logarithms of the respective prices; the analysis is otherwise unchanged.

5.4.3 Estimation

The model to be estimated, which relates forward prices, by delivery date, to actual spot prices on that delivery date, assumes DRAM base price is described by (7) and (6), modified to take into account possible economies of scale in purchasing, costs of special packaging, and possible price differentials specific to producer and consumer geographic region. This specification is given by

(8) $\ln(f_s^r) = \beta_0 + \beta_1 \ln(Q) + \beta_2(s - r) + \beta_3 \text{ Length} + \beta_4 \ln(R_s)$
$+ \beta_5 \text{ Package} + \sum_k \beta_k \text{ ven}_k + \sum_l \beta_l \text{ eurt}_l + u,$

with u a statistical disturbance term, and Q purchase volume in thousand units. "Package" is a dummy variable for specialty packaging (PLCC for 256K DRAMs, small outline for 1M DRAMs); "ven" are dummy variables that denote Korean, European, and American vendors (expressing price differentials as deviations from the price quoted by a Japanese vendor); and "eurt" are dummy variables introduced to measure differentials in prices paid by European consumers (relative to the North American market) over discrete periods of time. Retail spot prices lagged n periods and earlier were used to instrument R_s, with n chosen to exceed the maximum lead time $(s - r)$ before a contract began in the actual sample (to ensure that all instruments precede R_r and can reasonably be regarded as predetermined).

Because the retail spot price series were constructed for only a single speed of DRAM for each density of chip, and because earlier analysis suggested that price changes over time varied substantially by speed of chip for any given density, analysis was restricted to those contracts for which U.S. retail spot price data relating to the appropriate speed had been constructed. Results are organized and discussed by chip density.

256K DRAMs

Because time-series data were constructed only for retail spot prices for 120 ns, 256K × 1 DRAMs (extended back to 1984 by linking to the International Trade Commission spot 256K DRAM price data), a subset of eighty-seven contracts covering 120 ns DRAMs, in DIP and PLCC packages, was used to estimate equation (8). The limited availability of historical time-series data on monthly spot prices meant that sample size was maximized by further restricting the exercise to contracts with lead times of up to four months (two observations with seven-month lead times were eliminated from the sample as a result), leaving eighty-five observations in the sample. Seventy-nine of the contracts were with European customers and six with American chip consumers. Six contracts were with Korean vendors, six with European producers, twenty-two with American firms, and the balance with Japanese companies.

Coefficient estimates and asymptotic standard errors are shown in table 5.1. Only instrumental variable estimates are shown, but OLS parameter estimates were in all cases quite close to the instrumental variables estimates. Available data permitted the use of prices lagged from five to eight months prior to the contract start date (since the maximum contract lead time was four months) as instruments.

Examination of the Dataquest regional contract price estimates led me to use four dummy variables to capture European price differentials prevailing at different contract start dates: EUR, a base Europe-U.S. differential dummy

Table 5.1   Econometric Analysis of 256K DRAM Contracts (two-stage least squares regression)

	With Contract Length Variable		Without Contract Length Variable	
Dependent variable	LogPRICE		LogPRICE	
Mean of dep. var.	1.047		1.047	
SE of regression	0.205		0.205	
No. of observations	85		85	
SD of dep. var.	0.326		0.326	
Sum of sqrd. residuals	3.575		3.575	

	Results Corrected for Heteroskedasticity			
	Coeff.	SE	Coeff.	SE
Constant	0.917	0.208*	0.921	0.204*
LogQUAN	−0.0376	0.0237	−0.0374	0.0235
LENGTH	0.000470	0.00624	. . .	. . .
LEAD	−0.0364	0.0210***	−0.0363	0.0207***
PLCC	0.103	0.0409**	0.104	0.0390*
LogSPOT	0.282	0.0737*	0.282	0.0717*
Vendor dummies:				
EURVEN	−0.0732	0.0514	−0.0738	0.0525
KORVEN	0.0791	0.0561	0.0791	0.0559
USVEN	0.0139	0.0806	0.0138	0.0804
Time-period dummies:				
EUR	−0.147	0.121	−0.148	0.118
ETA	−0.118	0.0704***	−0.116	0.0721
ETB	0.00116	0.0783	0.00268	0.0815
ETC	0.170	0.135	0.171	0.135

H0: No Europe-U.S. price differentials: Wald statistic, $\chi^2(4) = .2208$

*Reject hypothesis of equality with zero, two-tailed test, 1 percent significance level.
**Reject hypothesis of equality with zero, two-tailed test, 5 percent significance level.
***Reject hypothesis of equality with zero, two-tailed test, 10 percent significance level.

variable with a value of one for European contracts throughout the sample period (August 1985–January 1989), zero elsewhere; ETA, a dummy variable with a value of one for European customers during period A (September 1986–February 1987, the beginning of the STA through the end of a period when Dataquest shows European prices somewhat lower than U.S. prices), zero in all other cases; ETB, equal to one for European contracts starting over March 1987–June 1988 (where the Dataquest data show European and American prices moving more or less together), zero elsewhere; and ETC, equal to one when European customers' contracts started during period C (July 1988–

April 1989, when Dataquest showed European prices significantly higher than U.S. prices), zero elsewhere.

An initial specification test did not lead me to reject the null hypothesis of linearity in lead time (although not shown, a version of the model corresponding to equation [2]—with an unrestricted term structure, using individual monthly lead time dummies—was first estimated).[26] Because heteroskedastic disturbance terms are a distinct possibility (individual contract sizes ranged from five thousand to 8.9 million chips), heteroskedasticity-consistent standard errors were calculated.

The coefficient of contract length was quite small and statistically indistinguishable from zero at any reasonable significance level. (Two-tailed tests of significance were used for all coefficients.) The second half of table 5.1 shows the resulting estimates when this hypothesis is maintained; the coefficient estimates show virtually no change.

The coefficient of lead time was negative (suggesting bias in the forward price) and statistically significant at the 10 percent level but not at the 5 percent level, with forward price declining 3.6 percent with every additional month of lead time before delivery. None of the European price differential dummies were statistically distinguishable from zero at these significance levels. Indeed, the point estimates of European price differentials were generally negative, except in period C, and most negative in period A, right after the signing of the STA. The grossly higher European 256K DRAM prices shown by Dataquest data from July 1988 through early 1989 contrast with a much smaller estimate of this differential (about 2 percent higher in Europe) within my sample of contracts. A Wald test for the hypothesis that there were no price differentials between the United States and Europe, before and after the STA, does not permit us to reject this conjecture.[27]

Quantity discounts do not seem to be a significant factor. The statistically insignificant coefficient for units to be shipped suggests that increasing contract volume tenfold produces a roughly 8 percent decline in unit price, a modest discount. I interpret this to mean, not that purchase volume is irrelevant to pricing, but that the relatively large companies in my sample get the benefit of the largest volume discounts based on their overall status as a volume account, not on the details of individual contract transactions. Plastic-leaded chip carrier (PLCC) packaging is associated with a statistically significant premium.

My point estimates indicate that Korean producers seem to have charged 8 percent more for their 256K DRAMs than Japanese vendors over the entire period, but the estimated standard error is quite large, and the hypothesis of

---

26. The Wald statistic was .0654, with three degrees of freedom; the null hypothesis cannot be rejected at any reasonable significance level.

27. The Wald statistic, with four degrees of freedom, was .221; the null hypothesis cannot be rejected at any reasonable significance level.

no difference in pricing cannot be rejected at the 5 percent level. American and European producers also show pricing differences with Japanese competitors that are statistically insignificant at this level.

1M DRAMs

For 1M DRAMs, the retail spot price time series that I have constructed covers 1M × 1 chips with 100 ns access times, in DIP packages, and extends back to June 1986. Available contract data for these chips in either DIP or small outline (SO) packages covered sixty-two observations, with the first two beginning in July 1986 and another eight negotiated before June 1987. Sample size was maximized by dropping these ten observations and including only the subset of fifty-two contracts with lead times under eight months; the first contract in this reduced sample started in June 1987, after the STA had been signed.

Results appear in table 5.2 and are basically similar to those for 256K parts; heteroskedasticity-consistent standard errors were again calculated.[28] Examination of the Dataquest regional contract price estimates led me again to construct four dummy variables to capture European price differentials for 1M DRAMs at different contract start dates. First, a base Europe-U.S. dummy variable for the entire sample period (June 1987–January 1989) was constructed. Over most of this post-STA epoch, Dataquest showed European and American 1M DRAM prices moving more or less together. Other periods, when regional price differentials seem to show up in the Dataquest data, were accounted for by constructing additional dummy variables: these included period A, June 1987–July 1987 (fragmentary Dataquest data show European prices somewhat lower than U.S. prices at the beginning of this period); period B, November 1987–January 1988 (where the Dataquest data again show European prices falling below American prices); and period C, April 1988–October 1988 (when Dataquest showed European prices significantly higher than U.S. prices).

The European price differential dummies for the entire sample period and period A were relatively large, negative, and statistically significant at both the 5 and the 1 percent levels, while the dummy for period B was small and statistically insignificant. The dummy for period C was positive and statistically significant (at the 5 or 1 percent levels) but would imply that European prices were slightly lower over this period. Thus, if one were to accept the notion of regional price differentials, European 1M prices generally appear to

28. As before, only instrumental variable estimates are shown; OLS parameter estimates were in all cases relatively close to the instrumental variables estimates. Available data permitted the use of prices lagged from eight to eleven months prior to the contract start date as instruments. Eleven of the contracts were with American customers, forty-one with European customers. Four of the contracts were with Korean chip producers, three with American companies, three with European vendors, and the balance were Japanese. Once more, an initial specification did not lead to rejection of the null hypothesis of linearity in lead time, at the 5 percent significance level. The Wald statistic was .100, with six degrees of freedom.

Table 5.2   Econometric Analysis of 1M DRAM Contracts (two-stage least squares regression)

	With Contract Length Variable		Without Contract Length Variable	
Dependent variable	LogPRICE		LogPRICE	
Mean of dep. var.	2.861		2.861	
SE of regression	0.0838		0.0860	
No. of observations	52		52	
SD of dep. var.	0.144		0.144	
Sum of sqrd. residuals	0.365		0.385	
	Results Corrected for Heteroskedasticity			
	Coeff.	SE	Coeff.	SE
Constant	2.378	0.377*	2.431	0.343*
LogQUAN	−0.0209	0.0165	−0.0213	0.0165
LENGTH	−0.00724	0.00353**	. . .	. . .
LEAD	−0.0110	0.00609***	−0.0110	0.00584***
SOJ	0.0270	0.0324	0.0345	0.0325
LogSPOT	0.219	0.109**	0.188	0.0997***
Vendor dummies:				
EURVEN	−0.0127	0.0366	−0.0162	0.0385
KORVEN	0.108	0.0521**	0.106	0.0507**
USVEN	0.0363	0.0243	0.0512	0.0258**
Time-period dummies:				
ESTA	−0.156	0.0482*	−0.145	0.0485*
ETA	−0.187	0.0545*	−0.219	0.0506*
ETB	0.00532	0.0375	−0.0133	0.0404
ETC	0.0946	0.0359*	0.103	0.0325*

H0: No Europe-U.S. price differentials: Wald statistic, $\chi^2(4) = .3036$

*Reject hypothesis of equality with zero, two-tailed test, 1 percent significance level.
**Reject hypothesis of equality with zero, two-tailed test, 5 percent significance level.
***Reject hypothesis of equality with zero, two-tailed test, 10 percent significance level.

have been somewhat lower than those in the United States and very much lower in the summer of 1987. Using a joint test statistic, however, the hypothesis that there were no price differentials throughout the sample period could not be rejected.[29]

64K DRAMs

For 64K DRAMs, the retail spot price time series that I created covers 64 × 1 chips with 150 ns access times, in DIP packages, goes back to May

29. The Wald statistic (four degrees of freedom) was .304; one cannot reject at any reasonable significance level.

1985, and ends in mid-1987. This series was extended back to February 1982 by linking to data tabulated by the International Trade Commission (ITC) in the course of an antidumping investigation; it was extended forward to 1989 by linking to a wholesale price series based on data found in *Nihon Keizai Shimbun*, converted into dollars at prevailing exchange rates.[30] (I judge this composite index to be a significantly less accurate indicator of movements in the U.S. retail spot market than the series used for 1M and 256K DRAMs, and this caveat should be borne in mind when interpreting my results.) Available data for these chips in DIP packages covered fifty-one contracts, with the first one beginning in April 1985 and the last in February 1989. Maximum lead time was six months, so I was able to use all observations in this sample. Forty-four of the purchasers were European companies, the balance American. Two of the contracts involved vendors who were Korean, three were with European producers, eleven dealt with American firms, and the balance were with Japanese companies.

Results are displayed in table 5.3 and again, are basically similar to those for 256K DRAMs.[31] Available data permitted the use of prices lagged from seven to ten months prior to the contract start date as instruments. Since no Dataquest regional contract price estimates are available for 64K DRAMs, the same four dummy variables used to capture European price differentials for 256K DRAMs at different contract start dates were used for 64K DRAMs.

All four European price differential dummies were statistically significant at the 10 percent level, and two were statistically significant at the 1 percent level. The pattern of differentials associated with these estimates is of European 64K DRAM prices falling almost 20 percent lower than U.S. prices prior to the signing of the STA, then gradually rising to a level almost 20 percent greater by early 1989.

Summary

An econometric analysis of DRAM contract price data for three successive generations of memory chips has supported several general propositions. First, the simple model of the term structure of forward prices that I am using seems quite consistent with these data: formal statistical tests did not reject it, and estimated coefficients were largely unaffected by imposition of this set of constraints. Second, my a priori suggestion that, beyond the initial purchase at the contracted price, these contracts mainly represent quantity commitments is supported by the generally small magnitudes and statistical insig-

30. Quarterly ITC data for spot-market sales of 64K DRAMs in quantities of under 10,000 chips were imputed to the middle month of every quarter, and data for the remaining months of each quarter were produced by interpolation between these mid-quarter observations. Because my retail spot price series began in May 1985, only a small number of observations relied on these interpolated ITC data.

31. As before, an initial specification test leads one not to reject the null hypothesis of linearity in lead time, at any reasonable significance level. The Wald statistic was .389, with five degrees of freedom. Heteroskedasticity-consistent standard errors were again calculated.

Table 5.3   Econometric Analysis of 64K DRAM Contracts (two-stage least squares regression)

	With Contract Length Variable		Without Contract Length Variable	
Dependent variable	LogPRICE		LogPRICE	
Mean of dep. var.	−0.0191		−0.0191	
SE of regression	0.177		0.178	
No. of observations	51		51	
SD of dep. var.	0.368		0.368	
Sum of sqrd. residuals	1.604		1.610	
	Results Corrected for Heteroskedasticity			
	Coeff.	SE	Coeff.	SE
Constant	−0.241	0.153	0.232	0.152
LogQUAN	−0.0156	0.0221	−0.0113	0.0206
LENGTH	0.00669	0.00827	. . .	. . .
LEAD	−0.0644	0.0185*	−0.0671	0.0183*
LogSPOT	1.248	0.449*	1.359	0.398*
Vendor dummies:				
EURVEN	0.0343	0.104	0.0466	0.106
KORVEN	0.313	0.136**	0.332	0.134**
USVEN	−0.0196	0.0722	−0.0293	0.0688
Time-period dummies:				
EUR	−0.205	0.0868**	−0.201	0.0868**
ETA	0.245	0.0698*	0.256	0.0671*
ETB	0.307	0.0954*	0.294	0.0951*
ETC	0.449	0.225**	0.390	0.208***
			H0: No Europe-U.S. price differentials: Wald statistic, $\chi^2(4) = .5392$	

*Reject hypothesis of equality with zero, two-tailed test, 1 percent significance level.
**Reject hypothesis of equality with zero, two-tailed test, 5 percent significance level.
***Reject hypothesis of equality with zero, two-tailed test, 10 percent significance level.

nificance of the coefficients of contract length as a determinant of contract pricing.

Analysis of price differentials faced by American and European purchasers of DRAMs suggested much smaller differentials than had been indicated by the Dataquest Monday contract price data, and, overall, I could not reject the null hypothesis of no regional differences. The sign of point estimates of these differentials was generally consistent with the pattern suggested by Dataquest's numbers, however.

The general pattern that emerged of Korean vendors, selling their product at somewhat higher prices is consistent with anecdotal observations by market participants.[32] It suggests that Korean producers were following an opportunistic pricing strategy focused on short-run rent extraction in marginal demand not covered by long-term contracts with other producers, rather than the establishment of long-term relationships with a stable set of customers. In effect, in a period of scarcity, the Korean producers may have charged a higher price than the long-term contract price, approaching the spot grey market price, while, in a period of glut, the Koreans would charge a lower price, again approaching the spot grey market price. Since Korean product in my sample was shipped only during periods of relatively tight markets (i.e., after 1986, through early 1989), this would explain the positive differential on contracts for Korean product. This analysis is also consistent with the reports in the trade press on Korean producer Samsung's dealing with its American distributors.[33]

In my model, the coefficient of lead time measures the "bias" in forward prices. My empirical results supported the presence of "normal backwardation" in forward contract prices for DRAMs. My point of departure was a model in which bias in forward prices serves to compensate purchasers for the transfer of risk to them by producers. The rather dramatic decline of the bias term from the 64K generation of DRAMs, to the 256K generation, to the 1M generation, suggests that the market viewed prices for current generation chips as considerably less volatile than previous generations of chips. This, of course, was precisely what the administrative pricing guidelines and mechanisms imposed on the DRAM market with the advent of the STA would have been expected to accomplish.

5.5 Improved Price Indexes for DRAMs

The econometric results presented above can be used to address several of the many problems in existing data on DRAM prices surveyed earlier. Leaving aside data and sampling issues, those problems can be grouped into two distinct categories: problems related to product heterogeneity and problems related to the aggregation of prices over time.

This first problem is the variety of products and distribution channels. While at one time DRAMs of given density were a relatively homogeneous product, the proliferation of organizations, packaging, and speeds has meant

32. One Korean producer—Samsung—was responsible for the vast majority of Korean DRAM sales over the period covered in this sample.
33. At the peak of the DRAM shortage, in the summer of 1988, Samsung attempted to hike its prices to levels that its American distributors protested left them uncompetitive and temporarily ended price protection for distributors (see *Electronic News*, 15 August 1988, 47; 27 February 1989, 27; 3 April 1989, 35). When prices turned down sharply in early 1990, Samsung shocked its American distributors by doing away with the customary "price protection" altogether. American distributors complained bitterly about Samsung's "broker mentality" (see *Electronic News*, 22 January 1990, 34; 5 February 1990, 38; 2 July 1990, 32).

that the volume-weighted averages published by industry sources now aggregate over a large variety of different parts, so that changes in product mix within a sample—as well as transaction size if there are quantity discounts—may produce significant changes in average prices. The existence of multiple distribution channels—larger user volume contracts, authorized distributors, and grey market brokers—means that shifts among distribution channels may also affect average prices in unpredictable ways.

The second complication stems from the fact that chip sales are often embedded in forward contracts, so we can associate a chip sales price with both negotiation and delivery dates. From the standpoint of measuring company revenues or a producer price index, for example, one might choose to measure average sales or billing prices, the actual average price received per chip shipped in a given period. These are essentially shipment-weighted averages of prices on contracts booked both in the past (subject to some revision) and in the current period.

However, for an economist interested in the cost of chips as an input to the production of other products, it may be useful to have some notion of current market cost, at the margin, of additional supplies of that input. The current "average" booking price will not do; it is actually a weighted average of the current market price for spot contract deliveries and expected market prices in future periods when deliveries on contracts with future delivery dates will begin, further complicated by the possible existence of discounts in pricing for future delivery due to "normal backwardation." An ideal measure of current input cost arguably would measure the price of the input for immediate delivery only (with booking price equal to billing price) since this is the true opportunity cost relevant to a consumer of the product at the moment of use.

I turn next to the construction of price indexes that address both sets of concerns, using the empirical results of the preceding section. Since virtually all the technological improvements in DRAMs—in the form of greater density, novel organizations, smaller power consumption, and faster speeds—have been embodied in the introduction of distinctive new product types, dealing in a satisfactory way with the effect of product differentiation is equivalent to constructing a quality-adjusted price index for DRAMs.

5.5.1   Construction of Average Billing Prices

The first step was to calculate the average sales price for as many distinct types of DRAMs as possible, for which contract data were available in relative abundance (so a reasonable approximation to a time series could be constructed). For 1M and 256K DRAMs, this meant using data for " × 1" organized chip types of two speeds and " × 4" organized chip types of one speed, in DIP, SO, and PLCC packages. For 64K DRAMs, this meant using data on " × 1" organized DRAMs of two distinct speeds, in DIP packages. Altogether, 116 contracts for 1M chips, 196 contracts for 256K chips, and 71 contracts for 64K chips were used to construct quarterly price indexes spanning the period from the second quarter of 1985 to the first quarter of 1989.[34]

In constructing my price indexes, two adjustments were made to the original data, to control for variance in price attributable to quantity and packaging. All prices were adjusted to a quantity 100,000 basis, using the estimated coefficients reported in the empirical results above. (Although the estimated coefficients for quantity discounts were small and had relatively large standard errors, a priori knowledge suggests the existence of some discount.) These coefficients were assumed to apply to all chips of the same density, including those with speeds and organizations different from those used for the econometric analysis. (A 256K × 4, 100 ns 1M DRAM, e.g., was assumed to face the same quantity discount structure as a 1M × 1, 120 ns DRAM.) Also, chips packaged in PLCC and SO cases were adjusted to a DIP package basis using the coefficients estimated above.[35]

It was further assumed that product shipped under a contract was delivered at the start of the contract at the negotiated price. (Renegotiation of price was assumed to affect only deliveries after this initial delivery.) Thus, for every contract, the negotiated price was attributed to the quarter in which product was first shipped. Individual contract prices were weighted using total contract quantity divided by the length of the contract (an estimate of average monthly delivery volume under the contract), to produce a weighted average quarterly shipment price for each type of chip.[36] The products of these average prices (after "adjustment" to a quantity 100,000, DIP package basis) and their quantity weights were then used to produce estimates of total (adjusted) expenditure shares on chips of various types within this sample.

Table 5.4 shows how rapidly the distribution of (adjusted) expenditure shifted historically within the sample, as new types of chips were brought to market. The extraordinary speed with which these expenditure shares shift

34. For 1M DRAMs in DIP or SO packages, 62 observations on 100 ns 1M × 1 parts (52 of which had been used in the econometric analysis of the last section), 26 observations on 120 ns 1M × 1 parts, and 28 observations on 120 ns 256K × 4 chips were used. For 256K DRAMs in DIP or PLCC packages, there were 87 observations on 120 ns 256K × 1 chips (85 of these observations had been used in our econometric sample), 75 contracts for 150 ns 256K × 1 chips, and 34 observations for 120 ns 64K × 4 parts. For 64K DRAMs in DIP packages only, there were 51 observations on 150 ns 64K × 1 chips and 21 contracts for 120 ns 64K × 1 chips. One extreme outlier for 120 ns 64K DRAMs was discarded in the belief that package type had been incorrectly reported, resulting in a total of 71 contracts used to construct price indexes for 64K DRAMs.

35. Obviously, this assumes a fixed price differential between DIP and these other packaging types.

36. Note that, because the coefficient estimates are derived from a model linear in *logarithms*, I am actually adjusting the log of price, then taking the antilog, in deriving an estimate of price. As an experiment, price indexes were also calculated using total volume over the entire length of the contract as the quantity weight for a contract price associated with the quarter in which first shipments occurred; these alternative weights had only a slight effect on the actual indexes.

Table 5.4   **Estimated Distribution of (Adjusted) Expenditure: Percentage of Sample Total, by Chip Density**

	Period				Entire 4 Years, 85:2–89:1
	85:2–86:1	86:2–87:1	87:2–88:1	88:2–89:1	
1M DRAMs:					
256K × 4,120 ns		N.A.	0.11	0.22	0.20
1024K × 1,120 ns		0.19	0.03	0.08	0.07
1024K × 1,100 ns		0.81	0.87	0.71	0.72
256K DRAMs:					
256K × 1,150 ns	0.79	0.41	0.15	0.05	0.22
256K × 1,120 ns	0.21	0.59	0.81	0.62	0.58
64K × 4,120 ns	N.A.	N.A.	0.04	0.33	0.20
64K DRAMs:					
64K × 1,150 ns	0.80	0.71	0.76	0.55	0.71
64K × 1,120 ns	0.20	0.29	0.24	0.45	0.29

Note: N.A. = not available. Chip prices adjusted to 100K quantity, DIP package basis, and are weighted using average monthly contract volume, to calculate adjusted expenditure. Contract prices are assumed to be in effect in the month in which contract deliveries start. No adjustment for regional price differentials or lead time has been made.

suggests that very frequent updating of products sampled is essential in constructing accurate price indexes for semiconductors.

The weighted average quarterly prices produced by the procedure outlined above are averages for the entire sample of contracts. Implicitly, their construction maintains the hypothesis of no regional price differentials between European and American DRAM consumers. As we have seen, however, the econometric evidence suggests that significant regional differentials may very well have existed.

An alternative average price for every type of chip may be calculated by further "adjusting" all prices in the sample to either an American or a European basis. This was accomplished by using the regional/time-period dummy variables' estimated coefficients from the econometric analysis described earlier, either to adjust all prices reported by European buyers to an American equivalent to produce a U.S.-basis price or, conversely, to convert American contract prices to a European equivalent.[37] The three sets of volume-weighted,

37. This procedure was slightly more complicated in the case of 1M DRAMs because the econometric sample began after the start of the STA. Rather than assume that the initial post-STA U.S.-Europe differential was identical to that of the pre-STA period, only prices reported by American customers were used to construct the US.-basis series for quarters prior to the beginning of the sample used in the econometric analysis. Similarly, only actual European contract prices were used to construct the European-based indexes for quarters prior to the start of the statistical analysis. For this reason, the U.S.- and European-basis price indexes for 1M DRAMs are available for differing time periods prior to June 1987.

adjusted average contract prices so produced will be referred to as being on a "sample basis," "U.S. basis," or "European basis."

A final issue to be addressed was how to weight average billing prices for different types of chips of a given density to produce a single price index for that given density. The question was complicated by the sporadic absence of data for some particular types of DRAMs in a particular quarter, which made some sort of imputation procedure to deal with missing data necessary.

The solution adopted in addressing this problem was to divide the overall sample into four periods of four quarters, with each period ending in the first quarter of one of the years 1986–89 (these are the same periods shown in table 5.4). In the final quarter of each of these subperiods (i.e., in 1986:1, 1987:1, 1988:1, and 1989:1), data were fortuitously available for all chip types actually consumed over the four-quarter period. The final quarter of each of these four periods was therefore taken to be a "base" period. The share of cumulative expenditure on different types of DRAMs (reported in table 5.4) over the four adjacent quarters ending in this "base" quarter was judged to be an acceptable estimate of the actual expenditure shares in the general population of DRAM contracts for chips of that density in the final "base" quarter. Thus, average prices and estimates of expenditure shares on each type of DRAM sold in significant numbers, for 64K, 256K, and 1M DRAMs, respectively, were constructed for four quarters spaced one year apart, from 1986:1 to 1989:1.

This is precisely the information needed to calculate a Fisher Ideal price index, which Diewert (1978) has shown to be a "superlative index"—a second-order approximation to a true, exact price comparison between two periods derived from microeconomic theory. Because virtually all technical innovation in DRAMs has been embodied in the introduction of distinctive new products, a Fisher Ideal price comparison between two periods, if available, will provide a good approximation to the economic effects of technological change. That is, technological advance in DRAMs has mainly been reflected in the rapid cheapening of newer, more advanced products relative to older products, and a Fisher Ideal index will capture the economic effects of this technical improvement (as well as whatever other factors may affect prices) on DRAM producers or consumers. The Fisher Ideal price index giving price in period 1 relative to period 0 is

$$\sqrt{\sum_i (\frac{p_i^0 q_i^0}{\sum_i p_i^0 q_i^0}) \cdot \frac{p_i^1}{p_i^0} \Big/ \sum_i (\frac{p_i^1 q_i^1}{\sum_i p_i^1 q_i^1}) \cdot \frac{p_i^0}{p_i^1}}.$$

I thus calculated Fisher Ideal price indexes for DRAMs of varying organizations and speeds, for any given density, in order to produce a quality-adjusted measure of DRAM cost. The rates of change for DRAM cost associated with the Fisher Ideal index are in table 5.5, contrasted with an index

Table 5.5   **Annual DRAM Price Changes: Fisher Ideal Comparisons versus Volume-Weighted Averages (percentage rate of change, average-selling-price basis estimates of first shipment contract price)**

DRAM	1986–87	1987–88	1988–89
1M:			
E basis:			
Vol. weighted Average	NA	8.70[a]	5.31
Fisher ideal	NA	8.81[a]	3.91
U basis:			
Vol. weighted Average	NA	NA	0.83
Fisher ideal	NA	NA	−0.57
S basis:			
Vol. weighted Average	NA	15.37[a]	2.42
Fisher ideal	NA	18.19[a]	1.50
256K:			
E basis:			
Vol. weighted Average	8.72	25.20[a]	56.18
Fisher ideal	21.61	29.60[a]	54.84
U basis:			
Vol. weighted Average	11.29	18.63[a]	38.32
Fisher ideal	16.60	15.17[a]	38.39
S basis:			
Vol. weighted Average	3.28	29.86[a]	59.87
Fisher ideal	11.69	29.93[a]	59.18
64K:			
E basis:			
Vol. weighted Average	35.17	24.44	75.40
Fisher ideal	33.61	24.53	67.72
U basis:			
Vol. weighted Average	4.64	19.80	59.35
Fisher ideal	3.51	20.17	52.57
S basis:			
Vol. weighted Average	34.64	24.49	58.98
Fisher ideal	33.04	24.68	54.99

Note: All year-to-year changes are from first quarter of the first year to first quarter of the second year. All reported contract prices have been adjusted to a quantity 100,000, DIP package basis using the econometric results described above. "Average-selling-price basis first shipment contract price" means the volume-weighted average (using average quarterly contract volume, for given chip characteristics) of contract prices for contracts with first shipments scheduled for a given quarter, with no adjustment for variation of lead time from contract negotiation date to first shipment date. Volume-weighted average price is an average for all chips of a given density, including chips of varying speeds and organizations. Fisher Ideal indexes are calculated with the Fisher ideal price index formula, using separate volume-weighted average prices for chips of differing densities, speeds, and organizations. Expenditure share weights have been approximated as the cumulative four-quarter sum (through a given first quarter) of adjusted (for quantity and packaging variation) contract price times average quarterly contract volume, for contracts with first shipments beginning over that four-quarter period. E, U basis: Reported prices adjusted using time/region dummy variables to European and U.S. customer basis. S basis: No adjustment made to reported price in sample other than to 100,000 quantity, DIP package basis. NA = not available.

[a]Not a true Fisher Ideal because of missing price for products introduced over this period. Missing prices are implicitly assumed to change exactly as a subindex based only on chips with available price data changes. As discussed in the text, this probably adds a positive bias to the estimated rate of change.

of price per bit, a simple volume-weighted index often reported within the industry.[38]

Although table 5.5 correctly computes a Fisher Ideal price comparison between 1988:1 and 1989:1 and between 1986:1 and 1987:1, the numbers shown for 1988:1 relative to 1987:1 are likely to be biased upward in the case of both 256K and 1M DRAMs. This is because new products were introduced in my samples after 1987:1 and a price for these products was not reported in 1987:1 and earlier.[39] The unobserved price (the product was most likely available, but only in small or sample quantities) was therefore assumed to move as the weighted average of the observed prices (using end-period expenditure weights). Because prices for new products may generally be expected to fall more rapidly (or increase less quickly) than prices for more mature products within this industry, the denominator in the expression for the Fisher Ideal index (a Paasche index comparing period 0 with period 1) would in this case be biased downward and the resulting index number therefore biased upward.

Since a price index based simply on price per bit, or per chip, for given density effectively ignores quality change associated with improvements in chip speed and organization, table 5.5 also shows what sort of price is paid in terms of bias when these additional quality adjustments are not made. The answer, over the rather unusual historical period portrayed in table 5.5 (with prices generally rising), is that unadjusted price per chip behaved very much like the Fisher Ideal price index, subject to occasional large errors. Remarkably, the rate of change of simple, current volume-weighted price per chip was within 5 or 10 percent of the quality-adjusted Fisher Ideal comparison for DRAMs of that density, most of the time.[40] Occasional large divergences are apparent, however, suggesting that chained price indexes based on simple average sales price would generally be less reliable shortcut approximations to Fisher Ideal indexes than straight comparisons between pairs of periods.

5.5.2   Construction of Spot-Basis Contract Prices

Earlier, I noted that the billing price in a chip contract can be interpreted as an estimate at the time a contract was negotiated of the spot price of the chip

---

38. Note that, for chips of any given density, average cost per bit is a scalar multiple of average cost per chip. Thus, a price index giving price in period 1 relative to price in period 0, based on cost per either bit or chip, amounts to

$$\sum_i \frac{q_i^1}{\sum_i q_i^1} p_i^1 \bigg/ \sum_i \frac{q_i^0}{\sum_i q_i^0} p_i^0.$$

39. As Diewert (1987) notes, the theoretically correct procedure is to use the imputed (but unobserved) price that would have just reduced consumption to zero, if consumption is truly nil.

40. One exception is a comparison of 1986:1 to 1987:1, for 256K DRAMs, where there is a substantial difference. Further examination suggests this was due to an unusual mix of chip types purchased in 1986:1 within my sample, one that differed substantially from the mix in the other quarters within this period.

at its shipping date, less a possible discount reflecting the transfer of risk from seller to buyer (normal backwardation). It is the spot price at shipment that determines the true current opportunity cost of an input to a consumer, however, and this may be a more useful measure of price for studies of input use.

One way to estimate what contract price applied to spot transactions is to restrict the sample of contracts to those in which shipments began in the same month as the negotiations concluded. Recall that 44 percent of the contracts for 64K parts, 41 percent of the contracts for 265K DRAMs, and 29 percent of the 1M contracts were to begin in the month negotiated. Because such "spot" contracts accounted for well under half the contracts in this sample, however, an index calculated from such a subset of the data would have many "holes" and require much ad hoc linking to other quarters using subsets of the products in the index.

The model of contract pricing used in the econometric work suggests an alternative procedure that makes more complete use of available data. Suppose we were able to estimate the risk premium embedded in a particular contract (based on the lead time to first delivery for that contract), which in turn is subtracted from a reported contract price in order to produce an estimate of the forecast future spot price implicit within the contract price. The assumed rationality of price expectations implies that a weighted average of forecasts of future spot price derived from contracts for some given shipment date will be an unbiased predictor of the actual spot price at the shipment date.[41] Inspired by this logic, the econometric results were used to calculate "zero lead time" equivalents of observed contract prices. These adjusted "spot-basis" contract prices for first shipments of DRAMs in any given quarter were combined with actual "spot" contract prices in price index numbers constructed using the procedures described above; rates of change are shown on a sample, American, and European basis in table 5.6.

Because both table 5.5 and table 5.6 are based only on data for shipments on contracts beginning in a given quarter, they may be expected to show less

---

41. More formally, let F^r_{si} be an "implicit" forecast of spot price at time s derived from observation i on forward contract price negotiated at time r, and an adjustment for normal backwardation. Assuming rational expectations, $E_r[F^r_{si} - P_s] = 0$. The estimator that I am constructing for P_s is $\Sigma_r\Sigma_i w_i F^r_{si}$, the quantity-weighted average of these adjusted forward prices, with $w_{ri} = Q_{ri}/\Sigma_r\Sigma_i Q_{ri} < 1$, $\Sigma_r\Sigma_i w_{ri} = 1$, and Q_{ri} quantity associated with contract i negotiated at time r (for adjusted, "spot-basis" period-s price F^r_{si}). A substantial number of these contracts involve $r = s$; i.e., I assume that actual "spot" prices reported contracts vary randomly around some unobserved "market" price. The bias of this estimator of P_s is

$$E[(\Sigma_r\Sigma_i w_{ri} F^r_{si}) - P_s] = \Sigma_r\Sigma_i w_{ri} E(F^r_{si} - P_s) = \Sigma_r\Sigma_i w_{ri} E[E_r(F^r_{si} - P_s)] = \Sigma_r\Sigma_i w_{ri} E(0) = 0.$$

Thus, a weighted average of conditionally unbiased estimates of spot price at time s will produce an unbiased estimate of P_s.

Since the econometric model that I have actually used is specified in the logs of prices, not actual prices, and my coefficient estimates are consistent but not unbiased, I am limited to claiming asymptotic virtues for my procedure, i.e., that plim $\Sigma_r\Sigma_i w_r F^r_{si} - E(P_s) = 0$.

Table 5.6   **Annual DRAM Price Changes: Fisher Ideal Comparisons versus Volume-Weighted Averages (percentage rate of change, spot-basis estimates of first shipment contract price)**

DRAM	1986–87	1987–88	1988–89
1M:			
E basis:			
Vol. weighted Average	NA	9.42	5.75
Fisher ideal	NA	9.62	4.45
U basis:			
Vol. weighted Average	NA	NA	1.19
Fisher ideal	NA	NA	− .10
S basis:			
Vol. weighted Average	NA	16.17	2.83
Fisher ideal	NA	19.10	2.01
256K:			
E basis:			
Vol. weighted Average	9.57	27.48	57.57
Fisher ideal	20.04	33.28	56.20
U basis:			
Vol. weighted Average	12.48	20.29	39.89
Fisher ideal	15.39	17.91	39.86
S basis:			
Vol. weighted Average	4.25	31.92	61.47
Fisher ideal	10.39	33.32	60.73
64K:			
E basis:			
Vol. weighted Average	50.33	16.93	84.07
Fisher ideal	46.65	17.97	74.94
U basis:			
Vol. weighted Average	16.38	12.57	67.22
Fisher ideal	13.55	14.00	59.11
S basis:			
Vol. weighted Average	49.78	16.97	66.63
Fisher ideal	46.08	18.14	62.05

Note: As in table 5.5, with the following exception. "Spot-basis first shipment contract price" means the volume-weighted average of contract prices for contracts with first shipments scheduled for a given quarter, with an additional adjustment for variation of lead time from contract negotiation date to first shipment date. A discount for future delivery at later dates, reflecting "normal backwardation," is used to "gross up" actual contract price. The resulting average may be interpreted as the average expected spot price for all contracts written with some given future first delivery date.

"inertia" than a producer price index derived from shipments on all contracts, including any older contracts from previous quarters whose terms have not been revised during the current quarter. Table 5.6 further "grosses up" those prices negotiated in advance of actual shipments to include the implicit discount due to "normal backwardation," in order to estimate the spot market price.

Time-series data on DRAM prices would also be quite useful for empirical research, and to construct these I implemented a procedure suggested recently by Triplett (1989b), to calculate what he terms "Times-series Generalized Fisher Ideal" (TGFI) price indexes. Fixed expenditure weight price indexes for "spot-basis" contract prices were calculated using each of the base quarters within our four periods as the base for a price index. Over the four quarters from one base quarter to another, the index calculated using the initial quarter as the base (and source of data for expenditure weights) is the Laspeyres price index, the index using the end quarter as the base is a (rebased) Paasche price index, and the geometric mean of these two indexes is Triplett's TGFI index. Base quarter to base quarter TGFI price indexes were then linked at base quarters to form a single price index over all sixteen quarters. The indexes so constructed are shown in table 5.7, on an unadjusted (sample) basis, along with adjustments made to reflect regional price differentials in European or American markets.

For base quarter to base quarter comparisons, the TGFI is identical to a Fisher Ideal index and therefore is a superlative price index. For the quarters in between, the TGFI is not a second-order approximation to an exact price index, however, and is merely the geometric mean of fixed-weight price indexes bounding the true price comparison. Rates of change between the first-quarter (base-period) index numbers shown in table 5.7 produce the Fisher Ideal comparisons given in table 5.6.

The TGFI that I have calculated is "approximate," in at least three senses. First, I have already noted that newly introduced chips were assumed to decline at the same rate as a weighted average of older products, before their entry into the sample, a procedure that, as argued, probably induces some positive bias in estimated rates of change in such periods. Second, cumulative expenditure by type of chip over the four-quarter period ending in the base quarter is being used as an estimate of the true expenditure weights for the base quarter. Finally (and inevitably, given the relatively small size of the sample), price and quantity data on particular products were sometimes lacking even after they had first been introduced within the sample. In these cases, the Laspeyres or Paasche price indexes were chained to an adjacent quarter, using a subset of prices available in both adjoining quarters and the corresponding expenditure weights for this subset of prices.[42]

The same set of procedures could also be applied without any correction for lead time to delivery, producing an estimated TGFI price index for average selling prices (or billing prices) of first shipments from sample contracts, by quarter of first delivery. The TGFI indexes on an "average-selling-price basis" are compared with the "spot-basis" indexes in figure 5.3, for 256K and 1M DRAMs. The differences are small in most quarters. This probably reflects the relatively short lead times in most contracts, the generally small estimated

---

42. This is noted in table 5.8 below. When chaining to an adjacent quarter, I adopted the convention of chaining in the direction of the base quarter for the index being chained.

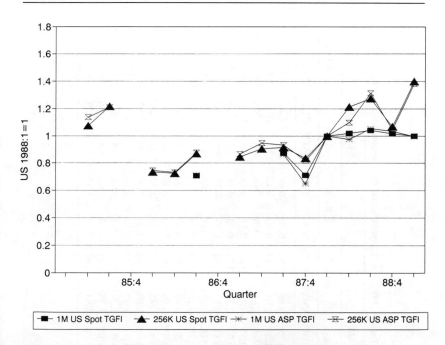

Fig. 5.3   Average selling price vs. spot basis, first shipped price

effects of "normal backwardation," and the fact that implicit short-term expectations about future price movements generally seem to have been relatively accurate (i.e., true "spot" contract prices were quite close to "adjusted" spot-basis prices in contracts negotiated in earlier quarters).

Finally, the price indexes constructed here, combined with the coefficients from the econometric analysis, can be used to analyze price differentials between the U.S. and the European markets. This is done by setting U.S. price in the first quarter of 1988 equal to one, then using the estimated differential between European and American prices in the third quarter of 1988 (which is completely encompassed in one of the region/time-dummy variables used in the econometric models) to link the European price index to the American price index in that quarter. The results of this procedure are also shown in figures 5.4 and 5.5 and are contrasted with the regional price differentials shown by Dataquest in its Monday contract prices over the same period. Both Dataquest and the estimates constructed here show slightly lower prices in Europe in 1987. Where Dataquest shows substantially higher prices in Europe in 1988 for 1M DRAMs (and huge differentials for 256K DRAMs), however, the present sample's data indicate only marginally higher European prices.

I conclude that the price indexes constructed for this paper do not diverge significantly from Dataquest's prior to 1987 but show some significant differences after that period. European-U.S. differentials, in particular, seem quite

Table 5.7 Approximate Time-Series Generalized Fisher Ideal DRAM Price Indices, 1988:1 = 1, ("spot-basis" first shipment contract prices)

| | 1M DRAM | | | | | | 256K DRAM | | | | | | 64K DRAM | | | | | |
| | E Basis | | U Basis | | S Basis | | E Basis | | U Basis | | S Basis | | E Basis | | U Basis | | S Basis | |
	VWCP	TFGI	VWCP	TGFI	VWCP	TGFI	VWCP	TGFI	VWCP	TGFI	VWCP	TGFI	VWCP	TGFI	VWCP	TGFI	VWCP	TGFI
1985:2	NA	NA	NA	NA	NA	NA	0.89	0.91[c]	0.91	1.08[e]	0.90	0.99[e]	0.50	0.49[i]	0.67	0.66[i]	0.50	0.49[i]
1985:3	NA	NA	NA	NA	NA	NA	1.05	1.05	1.06	1.22	1.05	1.13	0.50	0.47[j]	0.67	0.63[j]	0.50	0.47[j]
1985:4	NA	NA	NA	NA	NA	NA	NA	NA	NA	NA	NA	NA	NA	NA	NA	NA	NA	NA
1986:1	NA	NA	NA	NA	NA	NA	0.72	0.63	0.74	0.73	0.73	0.68	0.57	0.58	0.76	0.77	0.57	0.58
1986:2	NA	NA	NA	NA	NA	NA	0.86	0.78[f]	0.70	0.72[f]	0.77	0.75[f]	0.72	0.74	0.97	0.99	0.75	0.76
1986:3	NA	NA	0.68	0.71[a]	0.75	0.71[a]	0.86	0.74	0.88	0.87	0.87	0.81	0.79	0.77	1.05	1.03	0.79	0.77
1986:4	NA	NA	NA	NA	NA	0.84[m]	NA	NA	NA	NA	NA	NA	NA	NA	NA	NA	NA	NA
1987:1	0.91	0.91[m]	NA	NA	0.86	0.84[m]	0.78	0.75[n]	0.83	0.85[n]	0.76	0.75[n]	0.86	0.85	0.89	0.88	0.85	0.85
1987:2	0.78	0.80[m]	NA	NA	0.74	0.74[m]	0.96	0.89[n]	0.86	0.90[n]	0.89	0.89[n]	0.80	0.80	0.81	0.81	0.79	0.79
1987:3	0.77	0.78[b]	0.86	0.87[b]	0.73	0.73[b]	0.85	0.85[n]	0.87	0.91[n]	0.86	0.88[n]	0.60	0.48[k]	0.60	0.48[k]	0.60	0.48[k]
1987:4	0.71	0.72[b]	0.70	0.71[b]	0.67	0.67[b]	NA	0.81[g]	NA	0.83[g]	NA	0.82[g]	1.23	1.32[l]	1.23	1.32[l]	1.12	1.20[l]
1988:1	1.00	1.00	1.00	1.00	1.00	1.00	1.00	1.00	1.00	1.00	1.00	1.00	1.00	1.00	1.00	1.00	1.00	1.00
1988:2	1.06	1.01[c]	1.02	1.02[c]	1.02	0.97[c]	1.17	1.15[h]	1.21	1.21[h]	1.19	1.17[h]	1.54	1.52	1.54	1.52	1.53	1.48
1988:3	1.17	1.17	1.04	1.04	1.11	1.10	1.24	1.35	1.26	1.27	1.26	1.37	NA	NA	NA	NA	NA	NA
1988:4	1.13	1.14[d]	1.01	1.02[d]	1.10	1.10[d]	1.29	1.17[h]	1.18	1.07[h]	1.35	1.21[h]	NA	NA	NA	NA	NA	NA
1989:1	1.06	1.04	1.01	1.00	1.03	1.02	1.58	1.56	1.40	1.40	1.61	1.61	1.84	1.75	1.67	1.59	1.67	1.62

Table 5.7   (continued)

Note: See the text. The Time-series Generalized Fisher Ideal price index uses the first quarter of each year as a benchmark quarter, then takes the geometric mean of quarterly Paasche and Laspeyres indexes between adjoining benchmark quarters. Four-quarter sequences of TGFI indexes are then linked at benchmark quarters; comparisons between adjoining pairs of benchmark quarters are true Fisher Ideal comparisons. Underlying Paasche and Laspeyres index numbers cannot be calculated when some needed price data are missing or unavailable; available data has been used to impute unobserved price changes and chain to adjacent quarters when possible. Unless otherwise noted, the Laspeyres (starting-quarter weights) index is chained back to the previous quarter; the Paasche (ending-quarter weights) index is chained forward to the following quarter. This procedure imputes a rate of change for missing prices equal to the weighted average of available prices, and has been applied as follows:

[a]Chained to 1988:1 using 120 ns, 1M × 1;

[b]Chained using 100 ns, 1M × 1;

[c]Chained using 100 and 120 ns, 1M × 1;

[d]Chained using 100 ns, 1M × 1;

[e]Chained to 1985:3 using 150 ns, 256K × 1;

[f]Chained using 150 ns, 256K × 1;

[g]Chained to 1987:3 using 100 ns, 256K × 1;

[h]Chained using 120 and 150 ns, 256K × 1;

[i]Chained to 1986:1 using 150 and 120 ns, 64K × 1;

[j]Chained to 1986:1 using 150 ns, 64K × 1;

[k]Laspeyres chained to 1987:2, Paasche to 1988:1, using 120 ns, 64K × 1;

[l]Laspeyres chained to 1987:2, Paasche to 1988:1 using 150 ns, 64K × 1.

In 1987, the Paasche index cannot be calculated for some quarters in which new products introduced that year were not purchased by firms in the sample. In this case, a subindex for products excluding the newly introduced item was calculated and used (as discussed in the text, this probably creates some positive bias). The following two products were excluded in these cases:

[m]120 ns, 256K × 4 excluded;

[n]120 ns, 64K × 4 excluded.

VWCP = Volume weighted contract price, all chip types; TGFI = approximate Time-series Generalized Fisher Ideal price index; E = European customer basis; U = United States customer basis; S = sample basis.

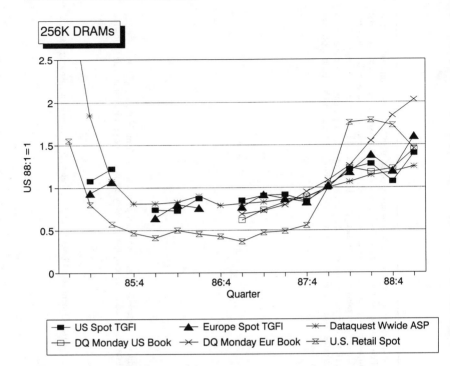

Fig. 5.4   256K DRAMs: U.S.-Europe price indexes and differentials

exaggerated in the Dataquest figures, and the timing of 1988 increases in 1M DRAM contract prices seems to lag the present estimates somewhat. Table 5.8 displays two variants of annual price indexes based on Dataquest's estimated average selling prices for 256K DRAMs with another consulting firm's average-selling-price estimates and a "spot-basis" booking price series developed in this paper. As can be seen, the billing price estimates from Integrated Circuit Engineering (ICE) and my price index generally track each other better than either price index based on Dataquest estimates.[43]

5.6   Conclusion

Semiconductor memory is thought to have experienced one of the most rapid rates of decline in quality-adjusted price yet measured by economists, exceeding even that of computers. Examination of this question is complicated by the extraordinary rate of introduction of new products embodying technical change and by the complexity of the sales channels and contractual

43. Note that the (unweighted quarterly average) Dataquest price for 256K DRAMs used by Dulberger, and reproduced in this table for direct comparison with my price index, behaves very differently from Dulberger's "MOS memory" price index as reproduced in Triplett's comparison table in this volume.

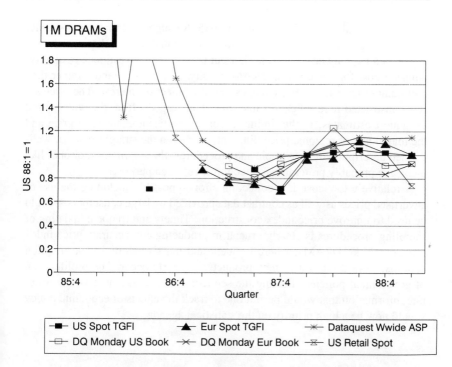

Fig. 5.5   1M DRAMs: U.S.-Europe price indexes and differentials

Table 5.8   **Comparison of Alternative Price Indexes for 256K DRAMs**

	Dulberger/Dataquest (simple quarterly avg)	Dataquest (q wtd. quarterly avg.)	ICE (annual avg. sales price)	Flamm TGFI (avg of Q2, Q3, U.S. weights)
1985	216	164	159	145
1986	100	100	100	100
1987	102	102	107	114
1988	132	132	171	156

Sources: Dulberger/Dataquest form Dulberger (chap. 3 in this volume, table 3.1). Dataquest quantity weighted average of quarterly prices calculated by author using data supplied by Dulberger. ICE calculated by author using data from Integrated Circuit Engineering, *STATUS 1992* (Scottsdale, Ariz., 1992), fig. 6–81, p. 6–58. Flamm TGFI is simple average for quarters 2 and 3, "spot-basis" contract price, U.S. weights, table 5.7.

arrangements used to market these products. In this paper, results of an econometric analysis of a sample of actual sales contracts for DRAMs have been used to produce suitably disaggregated estimates of price change that capture most of the effect of technological improvements and deal with the complexity of sales arrangements for this crucial product.

The empirical results for the period 1985–89 suggested that using simple, volume-weighted average cost per chip, aggregated across chip speeds and organizations, may be a tolerable shortcut in producing an estimate of quality-adjusted cost for some given DRAM density, if long-run trends, rather than particular quarter-to-quarter changes, are the object of interest. The price series constructed here differ in some important respects from the widely used Dataquest estimates, in the timing of some significant changes in price and the magnitude of regional price differentials. Given the straightforward, well-defined description of my sample and procedures, these estimates, or ones like them, are probably preferable for economic research purposes.

A relatively low-cost data collection effort—possibly including the use of advertised prices as well as contract data provided by large consumers—could be used to improve price index construction. Timely and frequent updating of sampling procedures is clearly crucial in producing any accurate price index for a good like DRAMs, where frequent and massive shifts in consumption patterns, toward innovative new products, regularly occur. The proliferation of government policies affecting the semiconductor market means that accurate information that would permit one to track the effects of economic policy should now be a high priority on the statistical agenda.

References

Chari, V. V., and Ravi Jagannathan. 1990. The simple analytics of commodity futures markets: Do they stabilize prices? Do they raise welfare? *Federal Reserve Bank of Minneapolis Quarterly Review* (3): 12–24.

Diewert, W. Erwin. 1978. Superlative index numbers and consistency in aggression. *Econometrica* 46: 883–900.

———. 1987. Index numbers. In *The new Palgrave: A dictionary of economics,* ed. John Eatwell, Murray Milgate, and Peter Newman. London: Macmillan.

Flaherty, M. Therese, and Kathryn S. H. Huang. 1988. The myth of the shortening product life cycle. Harvard Business School. Typescript.

Flamm, Kenneth. 1989. Policy and politics in the international semiconductor industry. In *Information services seminar 1989.* Mountain View, Calif.: Semiconductor Equipment and Materials Institute.

———. 1990. Semiconductors. In *Europe 1992: An American perspective,* ed. Gary C. Hufbauer. Washington, D.C.: Brookings.

———. 1993. *Mismanaged trade? Strategic policy in semiconductors.* Washington, D.C.: Brookings.

Houthakker, H. S. 1987. Futures trading. In *The new Palgrave: A dictionary of economics,* ed. John Eatwell, Murray Milgate, and Peter Newman. London: Macmillan.

Newbery, D. M. G. 1987. Futures markets, hedging, and speculation. In *The new Palgrave: A dictionary of economics,* ed. John Eatwell, Murray Milgate, and Peter Newman. London: Macmillan.

Newbery, D. M. G., and J. E. Stiglitz. 1981. *The theory of commodity price stabilization.* Oxford: Clarendon.

Stein, Jerome L. 1987. *The economics of futures markets.* London: Blackwell.

Triplett, Jack E. 1989a. Price and technological change in a capital good: A survey of research on computers. In *Technology and capital formation,* ed. Dale W. Jorgenson and Ralph Landau. Cambridge, Mass.: MIT Press.

―――. 1989b. Superlative and quasi-superlative indexes of price and output for investment goods: Office, computing, and accounting machinery. Discussion Paper no. 40. Washington, D.C.: Bureau of Economic Analysis.

U.S. International Trade Commission (USITC). 1985. *64K dynamic random access memory components from Japan.* Publication no. 1735. Washington, D.C.

―――. 1986. *64K dynamic random access memory components from Japan.* Publication no. 1862. Washington, D.C.

Williams, Jeffrey. 1986. *The economic function of futures markets.* Cambridge: Cambridge University Press.

Comment   Jack E. Triplett

This session contains three studies of a single product. Estimating the trend of semiconductor prices is of interest in itself, owing to the role of semiconductors as carriers of much of the high-tech electronic revolution of the last thirty years.

The session also provides evidence on a major puzzle of government price statistics—the contradictory and anomalous behavior of the Bureau of Economic Analysis (BEA) computer price index and producer price index (PPI) semiconductor price indexes. The PPI for semiconductors declines at a modest rate that is clearly inconsistent with the dramatic decline of computer prices (see the left-hand columns of table C.2). Semiconductors are major inputs to the computer industry. They are also important technological contributors to the advances in computer capability. To paraphrase Denison (1989), how can computer prices fall so fast if the prices of semiconductor inputs to the computer industry do not? Are the computer price indexes in error, as Denison suggests, or are there problems in the semiconductor price indexes?

Alternatively, we might ask this question another way. If the PPI semiconductor price measures are right, an enormous increase in productivity in the computer industry is implied by the computer price indexes that are prepared by the BEA; is this plausible? The first section that follows discusses the price index issues; the second turns to the productivity questions.

Jack E. Triplett is chief economist of the Bureau of Economic Analysis, U.S. Department of Commerce.
Copyright is not claimed for this comment.

Table C.2   **Comparison of Price Indexes for U.S. Computers and Semiconductors (1982 = 100 unless specified)**

		PPI Semiconductors					Flamm (DRAM) (1988:1 = 100)	
	NIPA Computer Price Index	3674	3674P	MOS	Dulberger, MOS Memory	Norsworthy and Jang	256K[a]	1M[a]
Year	(1)	(2)	(3)	(4)	(5)	(6)	(7)	(8)
1974	789	110		287	8,251	5,739		
1975	704	113		NA	2,601	3,265		
1976	665	107		212	1,592	1,852		
1977	474	101		210	998	1,087		
1978	242	95		187	584	641		
1979	205	94		169	496	395		
1980	147	101		NA	353	259		
1981	119	101	NA	NA	166	163		
1982	100	99	96	101	100	100		
1983	94	101	96	NA	71	68		
1984	77	107	101	101	55	49		
1985	51	107	95	73	21	32	108	NA
1986	47	108	94	62	14	23	72	71[b]
1987	40	108	92	63	12	NA	90	87[b]
1988	38	108	93	75	13	NA	121	102
1989	36	108	92	. . .	NA	NA	140[c]	100[c]

Sources: Column 1: Bureau of Economic Analysis, unpublished price index for computer processors (mainframes). Column 2: Producer price index, Bureau of Labor Statistics, LABSTAT series PCU 3674# (includes secondary products and miscellaneous receipts). Column 3: Producer price index, Bureau of Labor Statistics, LABSTAT series PCU 3674#P (primary products only). Column 4: Producer price index, MOS memory (taken from Dulberger, chap. 3 in this volume, table 3.7). Column 5: Dulberger (chap. 3 in this volume, table 3.7; Fisher Ideal chain index). Column 6: Norsworthy and Jang (chap. 4 in this volume, table 4A.7 [price index for semiconductors used in SIC 3575, computer manufacturing], rebased to 1982 = 100). Column 7: Flamm (chap. 5 in this volume, table 5.7), Time-series Generalized Fisher Ideal indexes for U.S. DRAM customers.

Note: NA = not available.

[a]Second quarter of the year, unless otherwise specified.

[b]Third quarter.

[c]First quarter.

Price Index Issues

Is the Semiconductor PPI Right?

All three studies present evidence suggesting that the PPI for semiconductors is not right, that correctly measured price indexes for semiconductors would fall rapidly, perhaps as fast as computer prices (see table C.2). Two of the three studies (Dulberger; Norsworthy and Jang) present price indexes for semiconductors for fairly long time series. Both studies show enormous drops in semiconductor prices; these drops contrast sharply with the modest declines that are recorded in the PPI.

Comparing these research price indexes with the PPI for semiconductors does present some comparability problems. The PPI index for the semiconductor industry (SIC 3674, col. 2 in table C.2) is an output price index; Norsworthy and Jang compute a price index (col. 6) for semiconductors used as inputs in other SIC four-digit industries (computers and communications equipment). It is well established that the theoretical concepts that underlie an output price index differ from those that underlie an input price index: each index is based on a different aggregation, for example, and each employs a different concept of quality change. Yet conceptual differences between Norsworthy and Jang's indexes and the PPI cannot account for more than a small fraction of the enormous empirical differences between them.

Dulberger's comparisons are precisely focused on a single product—MOS (metal oxide semiconductor) memory chips. The PPI MOS memory index (col. 4) declines more rapidly than the aggregate semiconductor PPI.[1] Yet Dulberger's MOS memory price index (col. 5) falls from eight *thousand* to thirteen, a decline that differs so greatly from the relatively modest decline shown in the PPI MOS index that the two indexes might be measuring different phenomena. Again, there are potential comparability problems. For example, the Dulberger index includes, but the PPI excludes, production outside the United States. However, it is difficult to believe that overseas production explains more than a small part of the empirical difference between the two indexes. Dulberger's work indicates, as does Norsworthy and Jang's, that PPI semiconductor indexes have failed to record the full price decline in semiconductors.

Dulberger and Norsworthy and Jang tell us that, during the past fifteen years or so, semiconductor prices have decreased more rapidly than computer prices. In contrast, the PPI indexes indicate that semiconductor prices have decreased more slowly than computer prices. Technological information from the computer and semiconductor industries as well as anecdotal evidence and experiences of computer users all support the picture provided by the price indexes in these papers. The PPI seems in error.

Flamm's intensive study of the relatively short period following the U.S.-Japan semiconductor agreement concludes that the agreement reversed—and quite suddenly—the long historical trend detailed in Dulberger and in Norsworthy and Jang (table 4.1, cols. 7, 8). The PPI also seems to have missed the turnaround in semiconductor prices.

What Are the Difficulties in Pricing Semiconductors for the PPI?

The authors give a variety of answers. Dulberger notes that controlling only for density (bits per chip) produces a biased measure. Other attributes of semiconductors, such as miniaturization, are also important. Flamm notes the cor-

---

1. I presume that the disconcerting gaps in the historical series in col. 4 are caused by the number of reporters falling below the PPI disclosure rule—I believe that the minimum number of reporters for publication is three—rather than by true discontinuity in the series.

relation of other attributes with decreasing price per bit; miniaturization in semiconductors has its own advantages, quite apart from chip density. Controlling for all the relevant quality characteristics in semiconductors is difficult and leads to specification errors in the price index. Flamm also raises the issue of contract price. Does the PPI get true transaction prices?

However, the overwhelmingly persuasive criticism of the PPI comes from Dulberger's demonstration that the point at which new chips are introduced into the price index for semiconductors determines the price decline that is recorded in the index. When new chips are introduced into the index to coincide with their introduction into the market, the price index drops 33 percent per year; when the lag in introducing new chips is three years, the price decrease recorded in the index is cut to 20 percent, and a five-year introduction lag nearly eliminates the price decrease. In the following, I refer to the bias caused by delay in introducing new chips into the semiconductor index as "new introductions" bias.

Flamm's figure 5.2 illustrates new introductions bias in graphic fashion; he clearly demonstrates that new chips must be introduced into a price index at the point of their introduction into the market, not at some later time when most of the initial price decline has already occurred. This is particularly important in the semiconductor industry because new products quickly account for a substantial portion of the market and because they are uniquely the vehicles for price change in the industry.

Under present PPI procedures, however, it is difficult to bring new semiconductor chips into the PPI rapidly enough. The PPI has a sampling procedure in which a particular chip, or chips, is selected by probability methods when a semiconductor producer is "initiated" into the index. In subsequent months, prices are collected for the same chips that were chosen at initiation. A new probability selection of chips will occur only on the PPI's reinitiation cycle, currently five years (certain other circumstances may trigger a resampling and, therefore, reduce the cycle in practice). As noted above, Dulberger shows that a five-year lag in introducing new chips into the PPI virtually assures that the index will record only modest price decreases, even when semiconductor prices are in fact falling rapidly.

New introductions bias poses a fundamental challenge to the entire PPI survey design. The PPI's elaborate probability sampling mechanism was put into place to ensure that the index was representative of price change and to permit the construction of measures of sampling error. The change toward scientific sampling surely is to be commended.

However, we want the PPI to be based on a probability sample of *current* price *changes*. The present PPI sampling methodology approximates a probability sample of *sales* in the *initiation* period.[2] A probability selection of

---

2. The PPI methodology only approximates a probability selection of sales because the PPI sample design, like that of all Bureau of Labor Statistics (BLS) surveys, is based on a sampling

initiation-period sales may be adequate when little change occurs in the range of products that are for sale, when yesterday's products are pretty much the same as today's. Or the PPI sampling procedure may work fairly well when the prices of any new products that are introduced move more or less consistently with those of established products. Otherwise, however, the elaborate and expensive PPI probability sampling methodology does not work and may in fact give severely biased measures of price change.

Empirically, these three papers indicate that the PPI sampling mechanism does not work in the PPI semiconductors indexes. The sampling mechanism is also problematic for pricing computers, and it is inadequate in the PPI for prescription drugs, where new introductions show price movements that differ substantially from those for established drugs (Berndt, Griliches, and Rosett 1992). Although there is no PPI for CT scanners, the hedonic index that is presented in a paper by Trajtenberg (1990) resembles hedonic price indexes for computers far more than it resembles the PPI for medical equipment, which shows only modest declines.

All these cases are ones of technologically dynamic industries that are characterized by aggressive product competition. In semiconductors and computers, and possibly in the other two as well, the technology gives us new products at a cost so far below the cost implied by the old technology that the new products simply take over the market from the established ones. The prices of the established products never fall sufficiently to make them competitive with the new products. A price index that records only price movements in established products misses much of the price change that occurs in the industry.

The new introductions bias can be thought of as a "quality problem" in the price index, but it is not a quality *adjustment* problem. New introductions bias has nothing to do with the adequacy of the methods that are used for quality adjustment when new products are encountered in the normal production of the index, although inadequate quality adjustment methods can exacerbate the problem. It also has nothing directly to do with Laspeyres or Paasche (or even superlative index number) weighing schemes, although aspects of weighing problems may be present, may also exacerbate the problem, and may inappropriately influence the sample design process. New introductions bias is a sampling problem, a case where rapid technological change creates a sample that is not representative of current price change in the industry.

The present PPI sampling methodology forces the BLS to measure technologically dynamic industries with a sample of old products. Reducing the interval between reinitiations may produce somewhat better numbers (the magnitude of the improvement is suggested by Dulberger's table 3.8); however, more frequent initiations will never eliminate the problem and may not reduce

---

frame that contains only the establishment's employment, not its sales. The data on the sales of the establishment are in the Census Bureau's records, which illustrates one of the deficiencies of the irrationally organized U.S. "decentralized" statistical system.

new introductions bias to an acceptable level. What is needed is a complete rethinking of the PPI sampling methodology and possibly as well some rethinking of the purposes of the PPI and the objectives of the PPI program.[3]

Traditional PPI Methods and Hedonic Methods

Hedonic methods provide an alternative to traditional PPI methods. It is quite well established that hedonic methods can be used to develop price (and output) indexes for technologically dynamic industries, and, despite some problems, they are better than conventional methods for measuring technologically dynamic products. For a review of hedonic methods from the practical vantage of a statistical agency environment, see Triplett (1990). For a review of their application to a particular high-tech industry, see Triplett (1989).

Hedonic methods can be used to construct price and output indexes for the computer industry, and for some other technological industries, because data are available annually on *all* the product varieties that the industry produces; hedonic indexes thus incorporate all the new products in the period in which they are introduced into the market. New introductions bias is, accordingly, absent. Hedonic methods can also be used to analyze the effects of the various ways of introducing new products into the index (see Dulberger 1989; Berndt et al. 1992).

However, hedonic price indexes are often quality-adjusted *list price* indexes because the most readily available cross-sectional price information usually consists of published list prices. Some transaction price errors are inevitable in hedonic indexes when discounts from list prices change.[4]

As noted above, the PPI sampling methodology can, in principle, get the transactions prices right, but using this methodology incurs a substantial new introductions bias. Hedonic price indexes using list prices eliminate the new introductions bias but may result in a transactions price error.

The obvious solution is to use a combination of both approaches. If the PPI sampling methodology were reoriented to collect the average discount by class of product, then these discounts could be employed to correct the he-

---

3. For example, in a monthly index that serves as contract escalator, it may be difficult to introduce new information that may be available only annually, or with a lag, into the measure. If the purpose of the index is analytic, gathering information on new products and the date when they were introduced leads naturally to revising the index when additional information becomes available. The present PPI is designed as if its objectives were solely of the first type; analytic objectives always, or usually, give way when conflict arises.

4. However, the error introduced by missing discounts must be small relative to new introductions bias and quality-change errors in the long-term trend, at least for high-tech goods such as computers. When rebased to 1982 = 100, the computer processor index in Triplett (1989) begins at over 76,000 in 1953, falls to 856 in 1972, and winds up at 77 in 1984—i.e., the quality-adjusted (list) price index indicates that computer prices in 1984 were *one-tenth of 1 percent* of their level thirty years before. No conceivable change in discounts will perceptibly affect one's views of the price change in computers over this period. Changes in list prices and transactions prices may be more important in measures of quarterly or monthly price change.

donic indexes for movements in the ratio of list prices to transactions prices. The French statistical agency is proposing to use this combined method to estimate computer prices (INSEE 1991). A similar reorientation of the traditional PPI approach to price index numbers might also be fruitful in the United States.

Productivity and Technical Change Questions

What Have We Learned about the Allocation of Productivity Change?

The introduction to this comment asked whether the enormous productivity increase recorded in the computer industry was overstated. These three papers suggest that it is. The new price indexes for semiconductors that are produced by these three studies will reallocate some of the *measured* multifactor productivity change from the computer industry to the semiconductor industry.[5] The faster semiconductor prices decline, the greater will be the growth in the deflated (quantity) measure of semiconductor inputs used in the production of computers, and thus the slower the growth in computer industry multifactor productivity. Some of the computer industry's reduced productivity will be transferred, in turn, to the semiconductor industry because its deflated output measure will grow more rapidly when the new price indexes for semiconductors replace the PPI. These new price indexes for semiconductors will more accurately allocate the total productivity contribution of these two technologically dynamic industries.

There is a corollary question that is often discussed. Why is the productivity increase (price decrease) for computers so much greater than the productivity increase (price decrease) for other semiconductor-using industries, particularly communications equipment?

Dulberger emphasizes differences in the technology of the processes that are used by each industry. Innovations are observed in the characteristics of semiconductors (e.g., density) and also in their manufacturing processes. A second stage of technical innovation concerns the packaging of semiconductors on computer cards and boards (her table 3.4 shows the relative contributions of chips and packaging to the reduction in delay time). She also emphasizes the great differences between logic chips and memory chips. The computer and communications equipment industries use different semiconductors, or use these chips in differing proportions, and will, therefore, benefit differentially.

5. Provided that multifactor productivity studies employ *output* in the numerator of the productivity ratio (the left-hand side of the production, or cost, function), rather than computing "value-added" productivity. Output, not value-added, is the appropriate variable for production analysis. To paraphrase a remark that Evsey Domar made thirty years ago, one wants a measure of the productivity of the computer industry, not the productivity of making computers without semiconductors.

Norsworthy and Jang also conclude that the use of different semiconductors accounts for the differences in the productivity increases of these two using industries. They estimate cost functions for the two using industries and find that the quality-adjusted semiconductor prices paid by the two industries differ. They give as an explanation that computers and communications equipment in fact use different semiconductors.

Flamm has addressed this issue elsewhere (Flamm 1989). He rejects the analogy that says that computers and communications equipment both simply move information from one place to another. In fact, the technology that each one uses is different, and the computer industry has been able to take advantage of technological changes in electronics more quickly than the communications equipment industry. This, of course, might change in the future.

Aggregation Issues in Studying Quality Change

The semiconductors that are used in computers differ from those used in communications equipment, as Dulberger and Norsworthy and Jang conclude, and it is plausible that these different semiconductors have different price movements. Those facts, however, transparently constitute an argument against aggregating the output of the semiconductor industry, as Norsworthy and Jang have done. Norsworthy and Jang form an aggregate semiconductor industry output measure (SIC 3674). They then employ this aggregate semiconductor industry *output* measure as an *input* in the computer industry and in the communications equipment industry.

If computers and communications equipment use different semiconductors that have different price movements, or if they use them in differing proportions, one should disaggregate semiconductors into components. Then the semiconductors that are actually used in, say, communications equipment can be employed in the using-industry cost function for that industry; working with an *output* price index for the SIC 3679 industry-wide aggregation introduces misspecification. I suspect that the authors might agree and that, in a "second round," they might pursue a more disaggregate approach.

A similar point can be made about their treatment of semiconductor characteristics. Norsworthy and Jang's equation (18) suggests that the two semiconductor characteristics (density for DRAM chips and band width for microprocessor chips) should be combined with weights that are obtained from the using industry's cost function in order to get an aggregate measure (α) that they call "quality change."

To understand this "quality change" measure, suppose that communications (z) and computers (c) each use only one type of semiconductor (S_z and S_c, respectively). Assuming that only these two types of semiconductors exist, the volume of the output of the semiconductor industry is the quantity $P_z S_z + P_c S_c$) where P_z and P_c designate the prices for the two semiconductors.

Norsworthy and Jang seek a "quality-adjusted" price (P^*) so that the output of the semiconductor industry ($P_z S_z + P_c S_c$) can be used as an *input* to the communications industry or the computer industry. The quality-adjusted price P^* for communications semiconductors is thus defined by

(1) $$(P_z S_z + P_c S_c)/P^* = S_z.$$

In words, the quality-adjusted price P^* is the "deflator" that reduces the value of the semiconductor industry's *output* to make it an appropriate measure of the communication equipment industry's input. Since in this example the communications industry uses only S_z, this "deflator" must eliminate entirely the part of the semiconductor industry's output that is not used in communications equipment (i.e., $P_c S_c$). A similar statement applies to computer industry semiconductor inputs.

In addition, as Norsworthy and Jang assume, and as Dulberger and Flamm show, if the prices of the two types of semiconductors (P_z and P_c) are mismeasured, the computation of the price P^* must also correct for any measurement errors in the output of the semiconductor industry. Norsworthy and Jang's estimating procedure, however, is as much an adjustment for the differing compositions of industry output and of using-industry input as it is as an adjustment for what we usually term *quality change*.

This point indirectly brings up an important, but often neglected, point about the PPI. The revised PPI is based on the idea of *output* price indexes—it produces measures that are aggregated for the output of SIC four-digit industries, such as the semiconductor industry. Yet many of the uses of price indexes require input aggregations—for example, semiconductors as inputs to computers, or inputs to communications equipment, and so forth. As equation (1) and the previous discussion suggests, the price index for industry output may be inappropriate for input uses of price indexes. The PPIs for SIC four-digit industries may not meet the requirements of analytic data users who need alternative aggregations.

Worse, data users cannot form their own aggregations of product-code PPI indexes because the detailed indexes are not always available or because there are gaps in them (see table C.2), because aggregations other than the SIC four-digit PPIs are not produced (lower-level semiconductor aggregations might ameliorate some of the discontinuity problem shown in table C.2), and because the PPI product codes often do not match the detailed Census Bureau seven-digit product codes with which the detailed PPIs would be used. Users must, therefore, use econometric procedures (such as those of Norsworthy and Jang) that would not be necessary if the PPI program were more oriented than it is now to the needs of analytic data users.

Estimating cost functions for high-tech industries is a valuable approach for determining the relative contributions to productivity of various stages of production. I am convinced, however, that extension of the direct, tool-making approach of Dulberger and of Flamm has more potential for *price index estimation* than econometric models to correct the inadequate presentation of data from government statistical agencies.

Conclusion

These are three valuable papers. Dulberger, Flamm, and Norsworthy and Jang have presented results that add to an emerging body of research on technological change and on price change in high-tech industries. Most of this research shows very large price reductions for technologically dynamic industries. Like some of the other studies, these three suggest that there are substantial deficiencies in the methodology that has traditionally been used in the PPI, certainly when it is employed on technologically dynamic products. At some point, it will be necessary to reconsider PPI methodology and to search for other methodologies that better match the economics, the technology, and the marketing practices of technologically dynamic industries.

References

Berndt, Ernst R., Zvi Griliches, and Joshua Rosett. 1992. Auditing the producer price index: Micro evidence from prescription pharmaceutical preparations. NBER Working Paper no. 4009. Cambridge, Mass.: National Bureau of Economic Research, March.

Denison, Edward F. 1989. *Estimates of productivity change by industry: An evaluation and an alternative*. Washington, D.C.: Brookings.

Dulberger, Ellen R. 1989. The application of an hedonic model to a quality-adjusted price index for computer processors. In *Technology and capital formation*, ed. Dale W. Jorgenson and Ralph Landau. Cambridge, Mass.: MIT Press.

Flamm, Kenneth. 1989. Technological advance and costs: Computers versus communications. In *Changing the rules: Technological change, international competition, and regulation in communications*, ed. Robert W. Crandall and Kenneth Flamm. Washington, D.C.: Brookings.

Institut National de la Statistique et des Etudes Economiques (INSEE). 1991. Hedonic price indexes for microcomputers in France. Paris: Division Prix de Vente Industrials, May.

Trajtenberg, Manuel. 1990. Product innovations, price indexes and the (mis)-measurement of economic performance. NBER Working Paper no. 3261. Cambridge, Mass.: National Bureau of Economic Research, February.

Triplett, Jack E. 1989. Price and technological change in a capital good: A survey of research on computers. In *Technology and capital formation*, ed. Dale W. Jorgenson and Ralph Landau. Cambridge, Mass.: MIT Press.

———. 1990. Hedonic methods in statistical agency environments: An intellectual biopsy. In *Fifty years of economic measurement: The jubilee of the Conference on Research in Income and Wealth*, ed. Ernst R. Berndt and Jack E. Triplett. Studies in Income and Wealth, vol. 54. Chicago: University of Chicago Press (for the National Bureau of Economic Research).

III Quality-Change Issues in Consumer Prices

6 Adjusting Apparel Indexes in the Consumer Price Index for Quality Differences

Paul R. Liegey, Jr.

The consumer price index (CPI) measures the average change in the prices paid by urban consumers for a fixed market basket of goods and services. One of the more difficult conceptual problems faced in constructing the price index is the accurate measurement and treatment of quality change that arises from frequent changes in product specifications. This paper examines the effect on apparel indexes of adjustments for differences in quality between substitute items. The adjustments are based on parameter estimates developed with hedonic regression techniques.

The sample of prices that compose the CPI is for goods and services such as food, shelter, apparel, transportation, and entertainment: goods and services that people buy for everyday living. Price change is measured by repricing essentially the same market basket of goods and services at regular intervals and comparing current prices with prices of the previous period. The CPI is designed to measure price change, holding constant the quality of the goods and services priced. When an item that is priced in the index is no longer available for consumer purchase, it must be replaced by another item of the same quality in order to maintain the integrity of the CPI. However, in practice, substitute items of comparable quality are not always available.[1]

Paul R. Liegey, Jr., is a staff economist in the Office of Prices and Living Conditions, Bureau of Labor Statistics, U.S. Department of Labor.

The author gratefully acknowledges the insightful comments furnished by Paul A. Armknecht and Allan H. Young. Both were extremely helpful by providing suggestions that improved the overall consistency and clarity of the paper. Graphic illustrations were provided by Patricia Hanson.

Copyright is not claimed for this paper.

1. Triplett's (1971) notion of quality most clearly embodies the notion of quality used in this paper. He contends that "quality itself is, in some ultimate sense, not a variable or measurable entity at all. But it is a kind of shorthand reference to the characteristics [of the good or service], and characteristics are, in principle, observable and measurable. Furthermore, even if there is no objective phenomenon identifiable as 'quality,' the employment of the notion of characteristics,

Finding replacement apparel commodities with the same level of quality as discontinued ones is a particularly serious problem in the CPI because of frequent and widespread variation in fashions and styles. Almost 70 percent of apparel commodities in the CPI are marketed seasonally, with new items introduced at the beginning of the fall/winter and spring/summer fashion seasons. Such commodities are usually introduced at high regular prices and subsequently discounted at "sale" prices throughout their season or selling life. Since these items seldom undergo price increases after introduction, it is when they are introduced into the markets that the manufacturer and retailer pass along any price increases.[2]

The CPI should measure only price change of apparel commodities of constant quality. Price increases passed along to the consumer by apparel manufacturers and retailers are not directly reflected in the CPI when replacement items with different quality levels are selected for discontinued items. Instead, an imputed price change is used to bridge the gap between discontinued and replacement items. This imputed price change is equivalent to the average price change of all commodities within the same stratum that have quality characteristics similar to the substitute item in the current period. Many of the price changes that are used in the imputation process are for items sold year round (over 30 percent of the sample) that show little or no price change from month to month. About half the sample for seasonal items (almost 35 percent) cannot be used for imputation because the items are not available for pricing (e.g., fall/winter items are not in stores during the spring/summer selling season). Price changes for seasonal items that are used for imputation and still available in the current season (e.g., in-season items that do not require substitution) reflect discounted "sale" prices because these items were left over from the previous fashion year. Therefore, replacing large price increases by manufacturers and retailers with the average of relatively small or no price changes from previously priced items may introduce an index bias.

An approach to eliminating this price index bias caused by low-price replacement items (called substitutions) is to attempt a measurement of the quality difference between items. One direct way to implement this approach would be to collect information from producers about the retail value of changes in each specific characteristic of each product. However, the large number of products and producers makes this impossible to accomplish in the time span required for producing a monthly price index. The use of a hedonic regression to measure the implicit price of a quality change is more feasible.

---

and the idea that 'quality' involves the disaggregation of goods into constituent characteristics, permits us to say meaningful and useful things about situations which are usually felt to involve quality comparisons and which, without this approach, are difficult to subject to analysis" (p. 14). Further discussion may be found in Triplett (1986).

2. For more detailed discussions of rates of product substitution in the CPI and the pricing practices of U.S. apparel manufacturers and retailers, see Armknecht and Weyback (1989), Armknecht (1984), and Pashigian (1988).

Griliches justifies the hedonic model: "The 'hedonic,' or, using a less value-loaded word, characteristics approach to the construction of price indexes is based on the empirical hypothesis (or research strategy) which asserts that the multitude of models and varieties of a particular commodity can be comprehended in terms of a much smaller number of characteristics or basic attributes of a commodity and that viewing the problem this way will reduce greatly the magnitude of the pure new commodity or 'technical change' problem, since most (though not all) new 'models' of commodities may be viewed as a new combination of 'old' characteristics" (1971, 4).

In the CPI, recent investigations on the use of hedonic modeling have concentrated on the apparel area. The empirical findings from hedonic models for apparel items have led to two types of enhancements that have increased the number of constant quality price comparisons used in index calculations. (1) The collection documents, known as checklists, have been revised to enable field representatives to better capture a complete set of measurable quality characteristics for each item priced. This procedural change alleviated a previously troublesome problem regarding the identification of comparable quality substitutes for some discontinued apparel commodities. (2) The decision rules used to determine whether an item is a comparable quality substitute have been improved by incorporating information from the hedonic models on the importance of item characteristics.[3]

This paper builds on this earlier work at the Bureau of Labor Statistics (BLS) by extending the hedonic regression techniques to develop measures of price change for substitute items of different quality that approximate market price changes better than current BLS methodology. Section 6.1 outlines the methodology. Section 6.2 compares the published CPI apparel indexes with those calculated in this study. Concluding remarks are presented in section 6.3.

6.1 Methodology

The price adjustments for substitute items of different quality developed in this study are based on hedonic parameter estimates, or implicit prices, calculated for characteristics found in two strata of women's apparel. These strata are labeled in the CPI as *women's coats and jackets* and *women's suits*. The choice of these strata was motivated both by index behavior reflecting minimal and even declining price changes over a long period and by the presence of more substitutions with dissimilar-quality items in these strata than in other apparel strata.[4]

---

3. Prior to this study, another investigation was conducted, culminating in Georges and Liegey (1988). Other internal studies involving the use of hedonic regression techniques have been undertaken and are currently under investigation for a number of CPI goods and services.

4. Consumer price indexes are primarily published at the stratum level, which consists of groupings of similar items. The regression models have usually been constructed at lower levels for

6.1.1   Data Source

The characteristics and prices used in the study were collected by BLS field staff on checklists. Checklists are designed for a particular genus of goods or services and specify a broad range of characteristics. When data are collected for an individual item, characteristics on the checklist that are applicable to the item are noted and serve as a description of the item. This checklist permits the BLS field representative (in the next data collection period) to locate the same item or, if it is discontinued, to locate a suitable substitute item. Both strata of women's apparel in this study use the checklist format enhanced by hedonic regression to improve the probability of selecting a comparable-quality replacement if substitution is necessary. To facilitate the choice of comparable-quality substitutes by field staff, the specified characteristics on this type of checklist are divided into three groups or "tiers." The first tier contains major price-determining characteristics, the second tier minor price-determining characteristics, and the third tier product identifiers.[5]

6.1.2   The Hedonic Model and Parameter Estimates

The hedonic approach to deriving implicit prices for characteristics of a commodity is as follows. The price of an item (P) is expressed as the sum of the product of implicit characteristic prices (b_i) times the quality characteristics (X_i):

$$P = b_o + \Sigma\, b_i X_i + e_i.$$

The functional form used in this study is the semilog form. The dependent variable is the natural logarithm of price so that the b_i coefficients measure the ceteris paribus percentage change in price caused by a unit change in the quality characteristic, X_i. The intercept, b_o, is the value of the base, or fundamental, model of the item excluding the additional quality characteristics.[6]

The data cover March and April 1989.[7] The fiber content of an apparel item

---

individual classes called *entry level items* (ELIs) or smaller subclasses called *clusters*. The apparel commodities chosen for this study happen to consist of one cluster per ELI. Additionally, these two ELIs are the only ELIs in their respective strata. The task of quality adjusting all eligible substitutions in a multiclustered ELI, a stratum with more than one ELI, or both requires the formulation of hedonic regression models at the cluster level.

5. For more information about tiered checklists, consult Armknecht and Weyback (1989).

6. The disturbance term, e_i, is assumed to satisfy the basic properties of classic regression models constructed by the method of ordinary least squares.

7. Armknecht and Weyback explain how data bases for (apparel) commodities are created. Basically, "two months [of cross-sectional data] are needed to include all local areas in the CPI because apparel is priced bimonthly in many areas. Characteristics and prices were integrated into a database containing the entire sample (separate databases were created for each stratum in this study). Any imputed prices as well as 'sale' prices were then replaced by the item's last regular reported price using historical price data. This approach enables both fall/winter and spring/summer seasonal items to be fully and equally represented" (1989, 15). Another study is currently under consideration in which at least two or more cross-sectional samples would be pooled together to create one data base. Differences in time periods would be accounted for by dummy variables. As more tiered checklist data become available, this option of calculating parameter estimates on the basis of pooled cross-sectional samples will become more viable.

is represented by continuous variables with discrete values from 0 to 100. Each of the remaining characteristics is represented by a binary dummy variable. Control variables for city size, region, and type of business were included to capture the effects of price variations across urban areas and sectors of the country and business pricing practices. Results pertaining to the coefficients' magnitude, direction, and significance for women's coats and jackets and for women's suits are reported in tables 6.1 and 6.2, respectively. These tables are arranged by quality characteristic, as described in the CPI data collection documents; they show the characteristics included in the base model and parameter estimates for the statistically significant price-influencing characteristics.

Determination of the best set of characteristics to explain price for each stratum is naturally limited to physical attributes. This is a serious limitation with apparel because of the influence that fashion has on price. This subjective measure *fashion* is difficult to capture quantitatively since it relies strictly on (industry) opinion. To some extent, nonetheless, fashion can be captured peripherally with such characteristic categories as type, design, brand/label, and closure found in tables 6.1 and 6.2. Other characteristic categories such as lining and fiber are more obvious candidates for inclusion in the regression models since their existence is so fundamental to the price of an apparel item. All these characteristics can be physically observed and tested to see the degree of influence, if any, they exert on price. The parameter estimates calculated in each of the full linear regression models presented in tables 6.1 and 6.2 are of considerable theoretical importance since their inclusion in the models makes logical sense and conforms with a priori expectations.

Several tools were utilized to corroborate the determination of the best set of characteristics in terms of explanatory power and acceptable collinearity levels. Forward stepwise regressions were used to examine the relative importance and significance of both continuous and dummy variables. In these stepwise regressions, as each variable was added to the model, existing variables remained statistically significant. Also, the relations between the variables were analyzed using a correlation matrix to help guard against multicollinearity in the regression models. Finally, price-determining characteristics were examined for frequency in the sample to ensure against the inclusion of variables for which there were few observations and that had no direct influence on price.

Within a characteristic category, specific characteristics contributed differently to price depending on factors such as durability, comfort, general market supply, etc. The importance of a characteristic is indicated by the magnitude of its coefficient relative to the coefficients for the other characteristics in the category. For instance, inspection of tables 6.1 and 6.2 will reveal that luxurious fibers such as cashmere and silk were found to influence price more than ordinary fibers such as wool and cotton. Other results pertaining to table 6.1 indicate that coat and jacket characteristics such as trenchcoat, all weather, and heavyweight styles are more price determining than lightweight, shirt

Table 6.1   Women's Coats and Jackets—Regression Model

Characteristic	Parameter Estimate	t-Statistic
Intercept	3.7487	45.383
Type:		
All-weather	0.3945	7.118
Raincoat	0.2344	3.332
Heavyweight	0.2858	5.311
Lightweight	base	
Closure:		
Single-breasted	−0.1902	−3.961
Double-breasted	base	
Design:		
Shirt jacket	−0.1546	−2.588
Windbreaker	−0.5099	−8.043
Balmacaan	0.2036	3.787
Parka	base	
Trenchcoat	0.3709	6.166
Fiber:		
Cashmere	0.0214	6.069
Wool	0.0078	10.680
Cotton	0.0023	3.925
Manmade	base	
Leather	0.0127	10.101
Lining:		
With	0.3103	5.662
Without	base	
Control:		
Full-service family	0.1417	2.353
Discount department	−0.4569	−7.451
Full-service/ready to wear	base	
Northeast	0.0963	2.114
South	0.0886	2.117
West	base	
A-size city	0.1539	4.106
B-size city	base	
D-size city	−0.1347	−2.213

$R^2 = .60, N = 904$

Note: All variables except those for fiber content are dummy (0, 1) variables. Since the dependent variable is the logarithm of price, the parameter estimates for each characteristic can be interpreted as the percentage change in price associated with the presence of the particular characteristic. For the fiber specifications, the variables are continuous, with values from 0 to 100. The parameter estimates can be interpreted as the percentage change in price associated with a 1 percent change in the content of a particular fiber.

Table 6.2   **Women's Suits—Regression Model**

Characteristic	Parameter Estimate	t-Statistic
Intercept	3.9224	23.768
Fiber:		
Silk	0.0062	2.847
Wool	0.0023	3.610
Cotton	−0.0036	−2.269
Polyester	−0.0057	−7.836
Rayon/nylon	base	
Brand/label:		
Store/private	base	
National/regional	0.1575	3.233
Exclusive brand	0.7286	6.006
Composition:		
Jacket or coat	0.3056	−2.076
Shirt or pants	base	
Lining:		
With	0.7231	11.006
Without	base	
Control:		
Discount/ready to wear	−0.2523	−2.213
Full-service/ready to wear	base	
A-size city	0.0855	1.931
B-size city	base	
	$R^2 = .58, N = 430$	

Note: All variables except those for fiber content are dummy (0, 1) variables. Since the dependent variable is the logarithm of price, the parameter estimates for each characteristic can be interpreted as the percentage change in price associated with the presence of the particular characteristic. For the fiber specifications, the variables are continuous, with values from 0 to 100. The parameter estimates can be interpreted as the percentage change in price associated with a 1 percent change in the content of a particular fiber.

jacket, and windbreaker styles. These results also are to be expected; they make sense when considering the durability and comfort, especially in cold, wet weather, that these characteristics provide. The closure characteristic group is more influenced by fashion than other groups. The closure characteristics for women's coats and jackets indicate that single-breasted construction detracts from price, indicating that, while double-breasted construction may not cost more to manufacture, it is a feature that fashion-oriented consumers prefer to single-breasted construction.

The regression model in table 6.2 reveals that the presence of an exclusive brand contributes more to price than a national/regional brand. This result is realistic when considering that the price of a London Fog–brand coat (national/regional) will inevitably be less than the price of a Gucci-brand coat (exclusive) if other characteristics are the same. The presence of a lining, which lends durability and comfort, in commodities in both strata is—as expected—a positive price-determining characteristic. Finally, the signs of the coefficients were found to be reasonable for both strata. For example, the parameter estimates for discount stores are negative, while those for full-service stores are positive.

The parameter estimates in tables 6.1 and 6.2 measure the value added to the item by the presence of a particular quality characteristic. For the continuous variables, the parameter estimate represents the percentage contribution to the price of the item of a 1 percentage point increase in the content of a particular fiber. For the dummy variables, the parameter estimate represents the percentage contribution to the price of the item of the presence of a particular characteristic.

To calculate the quality-adjusted price, the parameter estimates were used in the following manner. Assume that a woman's coat without lining containing 20 percent wool and 80 percent polyester (a base variable) was no longer available for pricing and was replaced in the sample by a coat with lining containing 40 percent wool and 60 percent polyester, ceteris paribus. In this example, the value of a lining and 20 percent wool would be added to the price of the old item so that constant-quality prices could be compared. Since in this example polyester is considered to be a base variable (i.e., it neither adds to nor subtracts from the value of the coat), the value of 20 percent polyester is not subtracted from the price of the old item.

6.1.3 Determination of Eligible Substitution Data

Data for a full year—from November 1988 to October 1989—were used for both strata. Product specifications, arranged by collection period and apparel stratum, were analyzed. Substitutions eligible for price adjustment based on quality differences were determined by the following criteria:[8]

1. All pertinent characteristics were reported for both items.
2. The characteristics for an item were not contradictory.
3. Parameter estimates existed for all characteristics that varied between the discontinued item and its replacement.[9]

---

8. I gratefully acknowledge the contribution of Melinda K. McAllister during this phase of the study. She devoted numerous hours deciphering thousands of characteristics. Her efforts culminated in abridged listings that highlighted the degree of relevant characteristic variation for all substitutions evaluated in this study. These abridged characteristic listings greatly simplified determination of substitutions eligible for quality adjustment.

9. An exception to this criterion existed for characteristics considered to be "base" variables. Theoretically, base variables neither add to nor subtract from the value of the item; i.e., they represent the quality level to which others are compared. These base variables are explicitly excluded from hedonic regression models and not represented by parameter estimates as are price-determining variables. Only those pertinent characteristics that were significantly correlated with price and varied between the substitute items were used in the adjustment process.

Substitutions that met the three criteria were eligible for adjustment. Table 6.3 shows the number of ineligible and eligible substitutions by collection period for each stratum, with the eligible substitutions in two groupings. The first group contains replacement items that possess identical price-determining characteristics. This group is labeled COMPARE. The second group contains replacement items that differ in one or more of the price-determining characteristics. This group is labeled ADJUST.

Table 6.4 shows the breakdown of ineligible substitutions in terms of the three criteria. These criteria were applied sequentially in the order shown above in the text. The third criterion—lack of parameter estimates—was by far the major reason for substitutions being declared ineligible for price adjustment.

6.1.4   Adjusting Apparel Prices for Quality Differences

The COMPARE group simply required direct price comparison between items. Theoretically, the types of substitutions found in this group should have been deemed comparable when they were originally reviewed for use in the CPI since the major price-contributing characteristics were identical for both items. However, in practice, price change is monitored, and, if the price change generated by two items with comparable characteristics exceeds established thresholds, it may be edited from index calculations and replaced by an imputed price change as discussed above for substitutions with items of differ-

Table 6.3   **Breakdown of Substitutions**

	Women's Coats and Jackets			Women's Suits		
Month	Ineligible	Compare	Adjust	Ineligible	Compare	Adjust
Nov. 1988	30	5	16	7	0	4
Dec. 1988	19	1	11	2	3	0
Jan. 1989	6	0	6	4	1	0
Feb. 1989	19	3	11	6	4	6
Mar. 1989	32	10	34	13	5	11
Apr. 1989	30	7	20	12	2	12
May 1989	10	1	6	4	2	7
June 1989	3	1	8	1	2	1
July 1989	2	1	2	1	0	5
Aug. 1989	18	5	8	6	1	1
Sep. 1989	29	11	27	10	3	12
Oct. 1989	39	15	24	13	3	9
Total	237	60	173	79	26	68

Note: Ineligible substitutions did not meet the criteria listed in the methodology section of the text. Eligible substitutions in which the replacement items possess identical price-determining characteristics are accounted for in the COMPARE column; those in which the replacement item differs in one or more price-determining characteristics are accounted for in the ADJUST column.

Table 6.4   Percentage of Substitutions Ineligible for Price Adjustment, by
                   Criteria

	Pertinent Characteristics Not Reported	Contradictory Characteristics	Parameter Estimates Unavailable	Other	Total
Women's coats and jackets	14.5	1.5	32.6	1.8	50.4
Women's suits	3.5	1.2	41.0	0	45.7

Note: The three criteria were applied sequentially in the order shown in the text in sec. 6.1.3. A substitution determined ineligible under the first or second criterion was not evaluated under the remaining criteria.

ent quality. This type of price editing results mainly from BLS concerns that the checklist may fail to capture some aspects of the quality of the item priced. BLS is thus applying a "reasonableness" check based on the price differential. Product substitution of this nature is prevalent for apparel commodities owing to the difficulties encountered when trying to define and quantify notions of fashions and style. The COMPARE group accounted for approximately 26 percent of all substitutions eligible for adjustment in both strata.

Calculating price change for substitutions in the ADJUST group required an assessment of the quality difference between the old and the new items using the hedonic parameter estimates. The characteristics for both items were compared, and, when a major or tier 1 difference occurred, the price of the discontinued item was adjusted on the basis of the difference in characteristics. This adjusted price was then used in index recalculation.

For example, assume that the discontinued item was an exclusive brand suit while the replacement item was a national/regional brand suit and that all other characteristics of the two items were the same. The discontinued item's price would be adjusted by subtracting the "exclusive brand" quality effect and adding the "national/regional brand" quality effect. A numeric example is presented in table 6.5.[10]

10. As noted at the beginning of this section, the natural logarithm of price was used to calculate the parameter estimates in this study. Therefore, an antilogarithmic conversion of these estimates was necessary so that "same scale" price changes could be observed between the discontinued and the replacement items. In particular, the price of the old item was adjusted such that

$$P_{(old, adjusted)} = P_{(old)} \times e^x.$$

In the text example, x represents the national/regional brand value less the exclusive brand value and is computed by subtracting the parameter estimate for the exclusive brand quality, the discontinued item, from the parameter estimate for the national/regional brand quality, the replacement item. The resulting adjusted price for the discontinued item can be compared with the replacement item's price to produce a (theoretically) constant-quality price change that can be used for index calculation. The choice of the exponential function for parameter estimate conversion follows from the relation

$$x = e^{\ln(x)}.$$

The exponent, x, as indicated in the example above, represents the aggregate value of all varying replacement item characteristics, as represented by the sum of their parameter estimates, minus

Table 6.5   **Derivation of Estimated Price Change from Observed Prices for Exclusive and National/Regional Brands of Women's Suits**

Observed Prices ($):	
Discontinued exclusive brand in period 1	262.50
Substitute national/regional brand in period 2	157.50
Parameter estimates (table 6.2):	
Exclusive brand characteristic	0.7286
National/regional brand characteristic	0.1575
Difference	−0.5711
Price in period 1 adjusted for quality difference ($), (262.50) * $e^{-.5711}$	148.29
Estimated constant-quality price change (%), [(157.50/148.29) − 1.0] * 100	6.2

6.1.5   Recalculating Apparel Indexes with the Adjusted Data

For each apparel stratum, four indexes were developed. The first index, labeled PUBLISHED, reproduces the not seasonally adjusted CPI-U (the urban population CPI). The second, labeled COMPARE, includes the substitutions described above in which a direct price comparison without any quality adjustment was possible. The third, labeled ADJUST, includes the substitutions in which the hedonic parameter estimates were used to develop a quality adjustment. The fourth, labeled COMPARE/ADJUST, includes both types of substitutions.

To compute the indexes for each group, COMPARE, ADJUST, and COMPARE/ADJUST, the adjusted prices were entered into a Statistical Analysis System (SAS) program simulating an actual CPI estimation. Indexes were computed for each group by collection period and stratum. Aggregated price change was then calculated for each stratum, reflecting the quality-adjusted data. The aggregate price change is the ratio of the weighted sum of prices in the current period to the weighted sum of prices in the previous period for a specific item stratum within a market basket (index area). Generally speaking, the weight for each price quote is the estimate of the average expenditure for the stratum in a retail outlet as determined from the Consumer Expenditure Survey (CEX) and Point of Purchase Survey (POPS). Price changes for the U.S. city level, such as those examined in this study, are obtained by summing price changes over all index areas using aggregation weights derived from the CEX.[11]

---

the aggregate value of all counterpart discontinued item characteristics, as represented by the sum of their parameter estimates. In general, as this difference in aggregate parameter values becomes larger, the difference between the logarithmic quality-adjusted price and the "true" quality-adjusted price becomes much larger. Failing to account for this antilogarithmic conversion will result in distorted price change results between the discontinued and replacement items. I am grateful to Marshall B. Reinsdorf for bringing this matter to my attention.

11. The SAS program that simulates index computation was devised by Kenneth J. Stewart. Without this program, it would have been virtually impossible to observe and measure the effect of the constant-quality price changes. Stewart's advice and comments throughout the development of this paper are also greatly appreciated. Additional information on the estimation of expenditure and population weights are provided in BLS (1988, chap. 19).

Given recalculated price changes, new index numbers were computed. For each stratum and group, the published CPI index number recorded one collection period prior to the start of the study period was used as a beginning point. Since the study period began in November 1988, the published index number for October 1988 was multiplied by the stratum-level price change recalculated for November 1988. The resulting index number, rounded off to three decimal places, was then recorded as the recalculated index number for November 1988. This recalculated index number was then multiplied by the new price change calculated for December 1988 to obtain the recalculated index number for December. This process continued for each month of the study period. The results are presented in table 6.6 and figure 6.1 for women's coats and jackets and table 6.7 and figure 6.2 for women's suits.

6.2   Empirical Findings

The results presented in this section measure both the effect of replacing edited price changes with observed price changes for substitute items with the

Table 6.6   **Indexes for Women's Coats and Jackets**

Month	Published	Compare	Adjust	Compare/Adjust
Oct. 1988	110.337	. . .	. . .	. . .
Nov. 1988	108.650	108.666	107.065	107.082
	(−1.5)	(−1.5)	(−3.0)	(−3.0)
Dec. 1988	104.546	104.614	102.491	102.560
	(−3.8)	(−3.7)	(−4.3)	(−4.2)
Jan. 1989	100.219	100.285	98.262	98.328
	(−4.1)	(−4.1)	(−4.1)	(−4.1)
Feb. 1989	104.554	104.604	102.893	102.948
	(+4.3)	(+4.3)	(+4.7)	(+4.7)
Mar. 1989	112.780	111.358	110.512	110.831
	(+7.9)	(+6.5)	(+7.4)	(+7.7)
Apr. 1989	114.409	114.316	110.947	112.462
	(+1.4)	(+2.7)	(+.4)	(+1.5)
May 1989	110.067	109.898	105.869	107.235
	(−3.8)	(−3.9)	(−4.6)	(−4.6)
June 1989	106.439	105.579	101.479	102.110
	(−3.3)	(−3.9)	(−4.1)	(−4.8)
July 1989	102.053	101.983	100.252	101.604
	(−4.1)	(−3.4)	(−1.2)	(−0.5)
Aug. 1989	104.197	105.347	104.258	106.603
	(+2.1)	(+3.3)	(+4.0)	(+4.9)
Sept. 1989	112.726	113.879	114.894	117.453
	(+8.2)	(+8.1)	(+10.2)	(+10.2)
Oct. 1989	116.205	117.389	117.587	120.473
	(+3.1)	(+3.1)	(+2.3)	(+2.6)

Note: The indexes correspond to the not seasonally adjusted CPI-U. Percentage change is given in parentheses.

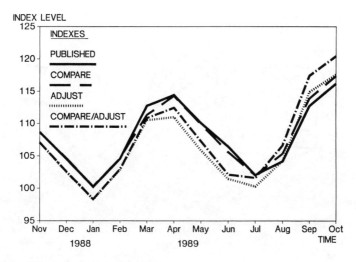

Fig. 6.1   Women's coats and jackets

Table 6.7   Indexes for Women's Suits

Month	Published	Compare	Adjust	Compare/ Adjust
Oct. 1988	126.035	. . .	. . .	. . .
Nov. 1988	122.467	122.467	122.332	122.332
	(−2.8)	(−2.8)	(−2.9)	(−2.9)
Dec. 1988	120.133	122.995	120.000	122.859
	(−1.9)	(+0.4)	(−1.9)	(+0.4)
Jan. 1989	116.075	119.454	115.947	119.322
	(−3.4)	(−2.9)	(−3.4)	(−2.9)
Feb. 1989	117.258	121.832	114.950	119.455
	(+1.0)	(+2.0)	(−0.9)	(+0.1)
Mar. 1989	139.524	146.914	135.572	142.795
	(+19.0)	(+20.6)	(+17.9)	(+19.5)
Apr. 1989	135.962	143.299	131.780	138.933
	(−2.6)	(−2.5)	(−2.8)	(−2.7)
May 1989	128.061	135.271	124.753	131.789
	(−5.8)	(−5.6)	(−5.3)	(−5.1)
June 1989	119.991	126.453	116.834	123.138
	(−6.3)	(−6.5)	(−6.3)	(−6.6)
July 1989	114.157	120.305	109.552	115.463
	(−4.9)	(−4.9)	(−6.2)	(−6.2)
Aug. 1989	121.180	127.646	116.423	122.647
	(+6.2)	(+6.1)	(+6.3)	(+6.2)
Sept. 1989	132.411	140.791	125.510	132.692
	(+9.3)	(+10.3)	(+7.8)	(+8.2)
Oct. 1989	133.937	141.782	126.415	133.061
	(+1.2)	(+0.7)	(+0.7)	(+0.3)

Note: The indexes correspond to the not seasonally adjusted CPI-U. Percentage change is given in parentheses.

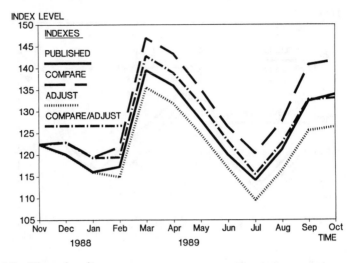

Fig. 6.2   Women's suits

same characteristics and the effect of using hedonic regression models to adjust apparel prices for quality differences in substitute items with different price-determining characteristics. Interpretations and conclusions drawn from these empirical findings are limited in scope. More general conclusions concerning the effects of using hedonic models in quality adjustments for all CPI apparel commodities will require further research when more resources can be allocated to the project.

Test indexes replicating the published apparel CPIs located in tables 6.6 and 6.7 indicate that the annual October 1988–October 1989 index change for women's coats and jackets and women's suits are +5.3 and +6.3 percent, respectively. The results for the two strata including the new information gleaned from the hedonic models reveal the differences between the published indexes and those developed for each of the test groups—COMPARE, ADJUST, and COMPARE/ADJUST.

6.2.1   COMPARE Group Results

The results of hedonic models permit the development of a consistent set of criteria for making the decision about substitution comparability. For women's coats and jackets, use of these criteria results in the annual price change being +1.1 percentage points greater than that for the published index (COMPARE, +6.4, vs. PUBLISHED, +5.3). In the case of women's suits, this effect is even larger, with the annual price change +6.2 percentage points greater (COMPARE, +12.5, vs. PUBLISHED, +6.3). Thus, uncertainty about quality change versus price change resulted in some price change being excluded from the published index for both strata.

6.2.2   ADJUST Group Results

The parameter estimates from the hedonic models are used to make price adjustments based on quality differences when sufficient information on the price-determining quality characteristics of the discontinued and substitute items are available. For women's coats and jackets, this results in the adjusted annual price change being +1.3 percentage points greater than that for the published index (ADJUST, +6.6, vs. PUBLISHED, +5.3). This implies that, over the test period, some price change was treated as quality change and excluded from the published index. For women's suits, the effect of using the parameter estimates from the hedonic model for adjusting price on the basis of quality differences was the reverse. The adjusted annual price change was 6.0 percentage points lower than the published change (ADJUST, +0.3, vs. PUBLISHED, +6.3). This result implies that some quality change was treated as price change and included in the published index.

6.2.3   COMPARE/ADJUST Group Results

When the two individual approaches are combined, the effects become interactive because of the method of CPI estimation. This is a result of the imputation procedure used for items that do not have current price information because they are out of season, temporarily out of stock, or discontinued— that is, when a noncomparable substitution occurs. When more items are deemed comparable, as with the COMPARE group, more information is used in index estimation. The new information includes both the new price changes and the new average price change used for imputation. The same holds true when more price changes are used owing to quality adjustments, as in the ADJUST group. When both groups of information are used together, they have an interactive effect on the average price change used for imputation.

In the case of women's coats and jackets, the combined effects result in an annual price change that is +3.9 percentage points above that for the published index (COMPARE/ADJUST, +9.2, vs. PUBLISHED, +5.3). This indicates that a downward bias may exist in the published index owing to price change being treated as quality change and excluded from the (published) index. In the other case, the combined effects for women's suits result in an annual change that is 0.7 percentage points below that for the published index (COMPARE/ADJUST, +5.6, vs. PUBLISHED, +6.3). This indicates that an upward bias may exist in the published index owing to quality change being treated as price change and included in the (published) index.

6.2.4   Interpretation of Test Group Results

The most striking difference in the results between the apparel strata is the difference in the direction of the potential bias in the price indexes. In the case of coats and jackets, the difference between published and test indexes indicates a positive quality change. By contrast, the case of women's suits indicates a negative quality change between published and test indexes.

Results of this nature may be directly linked to the complexity of the commodity (or service) under consideration. Women's suits, which are frequently composed of at least two, and sometimes three, components, are difficult to keep constant from discontinued to replacement item because of the great number of characteristics. Consequently, the published index for women's suits may have reflected more quality change than the (published) index for women's coats and jackets because it is more difficult to capture quality factors for the former than the latter. As a result, test indexes may not perform consistently when the degree of quality "creep" varies for published indexes.

Given the description of the apparel market presented earlier (i.e., that manufacturers and retailers pass along any price increase when new items are introduced at the beginning of the fall/winter and spring/summer selling seasons), the test results for women's coats and jackets should be more indicative of what should occur when other commodities are tested.

6.2.5   Additional Sources of Explanation for Index Behavior

The different behavior of these test indexes may also be attributable to the following factors.

First, the "success" of test index behavior is greatly determined by the "accuracy" of the implicit characteristic prices. A measure of this accuracy is the explanatory power, R^2, of the models. The models presented possess implicit prices explaining approximately 60 percent of the variation in (the natural logarithm of) price. Given the nature of these commodities—that is, the inherent difficulty associated with quantifying fashion—explanatory powers of 60 percent are "reasonable." However, when using these models to determine the dollar value of quality differences between substitute items, it should be recognized that test indexes may not always behave alike. Models for commodities possessing characteristics that, unlike fashion, are easily quantified would display greater explanatory power.

Second, the actual number of substitutions adjusted for quality differences in the samples available for this study may have been inadequate to produce consistent test index behavior. The two primary reasons for exclusion of substitutions in this study, noted in table 6.4 above, were missing characteristics and unavailable parameter estimates for characteristics that varied between items. Lack of parameter estimates was by far the major reason for substitutions being declared ineligible for price adjustment. Unfortunately, little headway has been made in developing parameter estimates for quality factors or characteristics that appear infrequently in the CPI data base. Therefore, quality adjustment of these characteristics is effectively precluded. A method for treating characteristics without parameter estimates must be devised in order to reduce this potential source of substitution ineligibility.

The explanations outlined above are meant to convey possible reasons for differences in behavior of the test indexes. These explanations are plausible owing to their intrinsic links to the quality-adjustment procedure. Continuing efforts focused on reducing the number of ineligible substitutions will further decrease potential index bias.

6.3 Summary

Historically, eliminating potential index bias generated when substitute items of different quality have been selected for use in the CPI has been a difficult task. Nowhere has this bias been more suspect than with apparel commodities whose indexes have reflected minimal price changes or even declining prices over long periods. Revision of data collection procedures and materials has been oriented toward increasing the likelihood that a comparable item will be chosen by the CPI data collection staff as a replacement for the discontinued item. However, in situations when selection of a noncomparable item is unavoidable, action must be taken so that constant quality price change is captured.

This paper has outlined the empirical results of applying an important tool to provide better estimates of price change. Adjustment of substitute items of different quality using parameter estimates developed for apparel commodity characteristics from hedonic regression techniques has been demonstrated. Greater emphasis must be placed on developing models that explain those factors that influence the prices of goods and services. Also, continued enhancement of collection documents and review procedures is needed to minimize the possibility of missing important data on quality characteristics. Pursuit of these broad goals will lead to a more adequate separation of price and quality change when items are replaced with substitutes of different quality.

6.4 Postscript

Since January 1991, BLS has employed about twenty hedonic regression models to assist with the production of published consumer price indexes for apparel commodities in the manner described in this article. Further research to examine the consistency of index performance among these different commodities could be conducted by removing the hedonic price adjustment effect from the CPI data. At least a twelve-month period should be analyzed in order to include both spring/summer and fall/winter selling seasons. Research of this depth, which would require more resources than were available for this study, would provide more conclusive evidence.

References

Armknecht, P. A. 1984. Quality adjustment in the CPI and methods to improve it. In *American Statistical Association, Proceedings of the Business and Economic Statistics Section, 1984*. Washington, D.C.: American Statistical Association.

Armknecht, P. A., and D. E. Weyback. 1989. Adjustments for quality change in the U.S. consumer price index. *Journal of Official Statistics* (2): 107–23.

Bureau of Labor Statistics (BLS). 1988. Consumer prices. In *BLS handbook of methods*. Bulletin no. 2285. Washington, D.C.: U.S. Department of Labor, Bureau of Labor Statistics.

Georges, E. V., and P. R. Liegey, Jr. 1988. An examination using hedonic regression techniques to measure the effects of quality adjustment on apparel indexes. Internal report. Washington, D.C.: U.S. Department of Labor, Bureau of Labor Statistics.

Griliches, Z. 1971. Introduction: Hedonic price indexes revisited. In *Price indexes and quality change,* ed. Z. Griliches. Cambridge, Mass.: Harvard University Press.

Pashigian, B. P. 1988. Demand uncertainty and sales: A study of fashion and markdown pricing. *American Economic Review* 78: 936–53.

Triplett, J. E. 1971. The theory of hedonic quality measurement and its use in price indexes. Staff Paper no. 6. Washington, D.C.: U.S. Department of Labor, Bureau of Labor Statistics.

———. 1986. The economic interpretation of hedonic methods. *Survey of Current Business* 66 (January): 36–40.

7 The Effect of Outlet Price Differentials on the U.S. Consumer Price Index

Marshall Reinsdorf

A major trend in the twentieth-century marketplace has been the replacement of small independent "mom-and-pop"-style retailers with large retail establishments owned by chains. Since prices at the large cash-and-carry self-service stores were often much lower than prices at the small independent stores that they supplanted, Denison (1962, 162) suggested that, over the long term, the "revolutionary changes in establishment type that have taken place in retail trade" may have caused a substantial upward bias in the U.S. consumer price index (CPI). Key in Denison's argument was an analysis of the effect of the Bureau of Labor Statistics (BLS) linking procedure for incorporating new stores into CPI outlet samples.

The present paper examines whether there exists a systematic tendency that is not reflected in the CPI for consumers to shift their retailer patronage patterns in ways that reduce the average prices they pay and hence their cost of living. Oi (1990, 15) documents the postwar trends away from higher-priced small independent food retailers, calculating, for example, that, between 1940 and 1980, the number of households per food store rose from 78 to 481 while the chains' share of food sales grew from 35.2 to 46.7 percent. Moreover, the effect of retail industry evolution on the CPI is not a matter of solely historical interest: trends of market share gains by lower-priced retail industry segments are continuing. The April 1989 *Progressive Grocer* annual report on the industry shows that the trends identified by Oi persisted up to 1988, as

Marshall Reinsdorf is an economist in the Office of Economic Research, Bureau of Labor Statistics, U.S. Department of Labor.

The views expressed in this paper are those of the author and do not reflect positions of the Bureau of Labor Statistics. The author is grateful to Diane Primont for helping him obtain and understand CPI data sets, to Leslie Platt and Philip Case for research assistance, and to Murray Foss and Marilyn Manser for helpful suggestions.

Copyright is not claimed for this paper.

food stores went on declining in numbers and growing in average size while the chains increased their market share to almost 50 percent. Furthermore, both low-priced economy format food stores and very large "extended format" food stores experienced such rapid growth between 1979 and 1988 that their combined market share grew from about 31 percent to about 50 percent of the industry. Equally noteworthy is the rise in off-price food sales by wholesale clubs, general merchandise discounters, and drug stores. When in February of 1988 *Grocery Marketing* decided to begin including wholesale clubs in its annual industry profile "Who's Who in the Grocery Marketplace," the Price Club, founded in 1976, had a 1987 national food market share rank of eighteenth, and Sam's Wholesale Clubs had a rank of twenty-sixth despite having existed for fewer than five years.[1] Finally, even within the class of traditional, full-service supermarkets, the phenomenal gains of the low-priced chain Food Lion, whose market share rank climbed from forty-second in 1980 to thirteenth in 1987 (see *Grocery Marketing,* February 1988; and Business Guides 1980), suggest that stores pursuing low-price strategies may collectively be capturing an increased market share.

Gains by lower-priced retailers at the expense of traditional vendors are not limited to food retailing. In general merchandise retailing, Wal-Mart, which generally offers much lower prices than the small town independent retailers it has often replaced, has now supplanted Sears as America's largest retailer. Off-price "mill outlet" retail centers such as Potomac Mills near Washington, D.C., and budget-priced home furnishings sellers such as Ikea are also capturing business from higher-priced competitors. In some cases, the ascendance of price-oriented discounters at the retail level has purportedly even led to pressure on manufacturers' prices. For example, in a 30 July 1990 article on Briggs and Stratton entitled "Discount Trend's Ripple Effect," the *New York Times* reports, "Because of a fundamental change in American retailing—the move by consumers away from full-line, full-price department stores and neighborhood merchants to discount specialty stores and discount mass merchants—lawn mower prices have been falling steadily in recent years. Those price declines have greatly benefited shoppers around the country but have dragged [Briggs and Stratton's] profits down with them."

The empirical results reported in the present paper suggest that the bias in the food and gasoline components of the CPI arising from changes in consumers' patronage patterns could potentially have been large during the 1980s. For food at home, one method of determining an upper bound for outlet substitution bias yields an astoundingly large estimate of 2 percent per year. For unleaded gasoline, that method gives an upper bound estimate of nearly 1

1. About 35 percent of the sales of the wholesale clubs are to consumers (*Wall Street Journal,* 7 November 1990). Therefore, even though their overall market share overstates their importance for the consumer population whose costs are tracked by the CPI, the wholesale clubs are still important enough to influence the average prices that consumers pay for food and other merchandise significantly.

percent per year, although, if the reduction in the average price paid attributable to the shift to self-service is not counted, the estimate falls to about 0.5 percent per year. A second estimator gives more moderate values of 0.25 percent per year for both food and gasoline.

7.1   Consumers' Seller Substitution Behavior

A prerequisite for consumer benefits from cost-reducing seller substitution to exist and yet not be reflected in the CPI is the presence of persistent price dispersion in retail markets. If on the entry of a low-priced competitor into a retail marketplace the other sellers' prices decline sufficiently to match the entrant's prices after a "quality" adjustment for any differences in the value of the retailer's services, convenience, or ambience,[2] then an index that tracks only incumbents' price changes will remain unbiased. Such complete price matching may occur rarely, however. As Denison observes, similar products may simultaneously be sold by high-priced and low-priced retailers because time lags are required for market disequilibria to resolve themselves rather than because their quality-adjusted prices are identical. Indeed, the pattern of consistent gains in market share by retailers with lower-priced formats is evidence that they offer consumers superior value. In addition, the academic literature on the role of costly information in consumer markets indicates that price dispersion in a market need not be a very short-term phenomenon. Stigler (1961), who reports sizable price variation in samples of Chevrolet and coal dealers, argues that price dispersion is generally present in retail markets because information is not costless for consumers. Pratt, Wise, and Zeckhauser (1979) and Carlson and Pescatrice (1980) find substantial price dispersion for larger samples of consumer products. Successful tests of costly information models of retail price dispersion by Marvel (1976), Dahlby and West (1986), and Van Hoomissen (1988) furnish empirical evidence that outlet price differentials are at least partly real rather than merely reflective of differences in quality.

The entry of lower-priced outlets is not the only possible source of shifts in consumers' patronage toward outlets whose prices are lower. Consumer search theory implies that consumers may substitute outlets in response to changes in the distribution of the prices offered by incumbents or even—as Anglin and Baye (1987) observe—in response to changes in their own search costs.[3] Nevertheless, change in the composition of retailing industries is the

2. In the price index literature, any attribute of an item that affects its value to consumers is regarded as a component of the item's "quality." Outlets may offer a number of services and features in conjunction with the goods they sell that are valued by consumers. Erlich and Fisher (1982) emphasize the provision of information, while Betancourt and Gautschi (1988) also discuss convenience of location, depth and breadth of product assortment, guarantee of product delivery, and appealing ambience.

3. In the case of an increase in search costs, outlet substitution will, of course, increase the average price paid. However, in equilibrium, sellers' responses to changes in consumers' search

most important reason for concern about the effects of outlet substitution by consumers because such change may be associated with substantive long-run bias in the CPI.

Closely related to outlet substitution are brand and variety substitution by searching consumers. Variety substitution occurs because even a given brand of a given good may come in more than one size, style of packaging, or potency. In addition, changes between different variations of a product, such as switching from an XT-type personal computer to an AT or from a conventional tape player to one with digital technology, may be considered variety substitutions. Because the brands or varieties of a good are near-perfect substitutes, only one of them will generally be purchased by a consumer on a given occasion. Thus, brand or variety substitution may be treated as a result of a search process just as outlet choice is. Furthermore, many of the results of outlet substitution are equally applicable to brand substitution. Consumers may realize cost savings through the substitution of brands or manufacturers just as they may from outlet substitution, and manufacturers may gain market share through offering a lower quality-adjusted price than competitors just as outlets may; consider, for example, the gains of generic products in ethical drug markets. Moreover, in the U.S. CPI, the rotation of outlets and of brands and varieties is generally simultaneous because, when a new sample of outlets is drawn, a new sample of brands and varieties is drawn as well.

Since the focus of the present paper is outlet substitution, in the discussion that follows it will be convenient to refer only to outlet substitution even though often the comments could also apply to brand and variety substitution. It should be noted, however, that, despite the many analogies that exist between outlet and brand/variety substitution, two important differences exist between these phenomena in the CPI. First, in certain cases, there is more scope for very large gains in quality in the case of new varieties; examples are important product innovations from the fields of electronics and medicine. Second, when a product variety is dropped by a retailer or modified by its manufacturer, it is sometimes possible to adjust the price of the variety substituted for it in the CPI sample for quality differences using data on its characteristics. In contrast, when one outlet replaces another in the CPI sample, overlap price linking is always employed.

7.2 BLS Outlet Sampling and Linking Procedures

In order to see how the systematic displacement of high-priced outlets (and brands) by low-priced ones of equal quality would bias the CPI upward, it is

---

costs will largely neutralize any effect of such changes on market shares. For example, simulations of the effect of search cost changes in a modified version of the Carlson and McAffee (1983) equilibrium price dispersion model in Reinsdorf (1988) show that outlets adjust their prices so that their market shares are approximately preserved.

necessary to understand BLS outlet sampling and linking procedures. Pricing the same varieties at the same outlets over time would be most consistent with the Laspeyres fixed-weight philosophy of the CPI, but it is not feasible. As outlets and varieties disappear, the sample size would become inadequate, while the evolution of consumer patronage patterns would make such a sample increasingly unrepresentative for tracking changes in consumers' cost of living. Consequently, BLS continuously refreshes its CPI outlets samples, with about one-fifth of U.S. cities undergoing sample rotation in any year. The outlet sampling frame comes from the Continuing Point of Purchase Survey (CPOPS), with an outlet's probability of selection usually proportional to its share of consumers' expenditures for the good in question. Once an outlet has been selected to furnish prices for a good, each brand and variety sold by the outlet has a probability of selection proportional to its sales.[4] This procedure yields current, representative outlet and variety samples that provide unbiased estimates of the average price that consumers pay for an item at the time they are drawn. Nevertheless, just as when varieties are substituted, incorrect treatment of outlet quality differentials when the outlet sample changes could bias the CPI.

When an outlet disappears from a CPI sample in month t, the average price of the item in month $t - 1$ is recalculated without that outlet's price quote. Then, when the item's average price in month t is compared to its average price in month $t - 1$ in calculating the CPI, identical sets of outlets and unique items will be represented in both months. Similarly, when CPI outlet samples are rotated, collection of prices from both the new and the old sample of outlets in the month before the new outlet sample prices are first used in the index allows a comparison over time of identical sets of outlets and items. In the overlap pricing month, the average price change in the old sample of outlets is used to move the index, while, in the following month, only comparisons of prices from the new outlet sample to their former values enter the index. Thus, when one outlet replaces another in the CPI sample, an implicit adjustment for a change in quality occurs based on the percentage difference between prices at the two outlets in the overlap pricing month. For example, if in that month the newly sampled outlet charges $0.80 for at item sold for $1.00 at the outlet that it is to replace, dividing the prices from the new outlet by 0.8 and then comparing them to prices from the old outlet will give the same values for the CPI that linking with overlap prices does. If the "law of one price" held so that all contemporaneous differences in prices in fact represent quality differentials, this would, of course, be correct. Even entry by lower-priced, more efficient competitors would not bias the CPI because prices at the incumbent outlets in the CPI sample would quickly fall to match those competitors' quality-adjusted prices.

---

4. Occasionally, merchants are unable to furnish sales data, and fall-back methods, which are discussed in the *BLS Handbook of Methods* (U.S. Department of Labor 1988, 162–66), are used.

Persistent price dispersion arising from costly information appears to be quite common in retail markets, however. Moreover, those outlets offering genuinely lower prices can be expected to increase their market shares over time, resulting in gains for consumers but the removal of interoutlet price differentials from the CPI means that these gains will not be counted.

Current BLS procedures may, of course, be the best feasible. Even if comparing only prices in successive months of identical brands and varieties from the same outlets leads to bias, this practice probably reduces the mean square error of the index by removing the variance caused by stochastic changes in quality. Moreover, when the average price level paid by consumers changes as a result of systematic outlet substitution, the average quality level of retailer services is also likely to change. Absent a method to control for such quality changes, simply letting the CPI reflect the outlet price differential when consumers substitute outlets could also result in bias.

7.3   The Theory of Outlet Substitution Bias in the CPI

Bias in a cost-of-living (COL) index from consumers' substitution of sellers is in many ways analogous to the textbook problem of bias arising in fixed-weighted COL indexes from consumers' commodity substitution. (Theoretical studies of commodity substitution bias date from Konus [1939]; for a textbook treatment, see Layard and Walters [1978].) Commodity substitution by utility-maximizing consumers responding to changing relative prices of goods leads to upward bias in a Laspeyres price index, such as the CPI, and to downward bias in a Paasche price index.[5] These biases arise because consumers decrease their relative consumption of those goods whose prices have risen fastest and increase their relative consumption of the goods whose relative prices have fallen. Commodity substitution bias in COL indexes has long attracted economists' attention, and careful empirical estimates of its magnitude exist for the United States.[6]

In order to develop a simple theory of outlet substitution bias in the CPI, assume that consumers search for low prices but do not engage in commodity substitution. Under this condition, the true COL index is a weighted average of price indexes for individual commodities, so we can focus on the bias in a price index for a single representative product. An additional simplification is to focus on a single representative consumer.[7] Under these assumptions, a

5. In a Laspeyres price index, reference or "base" period commodity quantities are used for evaluating both reference and comparison period prices, while, in a Paasche price index, comparison period quantities furnish the price weights.

6. Examples of such studies are Manser and McDonald (1988), Braithwait (1980), and Christensen and Manser (1976).

7. It is usual to discuss a single homogeneous group of consumers in deriving results in COL indexes from economic theory because difficult problems arise in aggregating across diverse consumers. In the present paper, this "representative consumer" approach is exemplified in the assumption that all consumers face the same price of search. Although the identical consumers

COL index that incorporates fixed reference period outlet weights and search costs will be greater than or equal to the true search-based COL index. This result corresponds to the familiar upward bias property of Laspeyres price indexes resulting from commodity substitution when relative prices of goods change.

Let the marginal cost of search at time t be c_t, and let the vector of prices offered by the n outlets in the market for the quantity of the good that consumers purchase be $\mathbf{p}_t$.[8] Denote the consumers' expected cost of acquiring the good under the optimal search strategy by $M(\mathbf{p}_t, c_t)$, and denote the associated vector of probabilities of buying from each outlet by $\mathbf{w}_t = w^*(\mathbf{p}_t, c_t)$. Finally, define a total cost of search function $C(\mathbf{w}_t^T \mathbf{p}_t, c_t)$ as c_t times the minimum expected number of searches necessary to achieve an expected price at least as low as $\mathbf{w}_t^T \mathbf{p}_t$. For example, if $\mathbf{w}_t^T \mathbf{p}_t$ is greater than or equal to the unconditional expected price $E(\mathbf{p}_t)$, then $C(\cdot)$ will equal c_t. If $\mathbf{w}_t^T \mathbf{p}_t$ equals the mean of the v lowest prices—as it might if $\mathbf{w}_t$ reflects a reservation price strategy—then $C(\cdot)$ would equal $c_t n/v$.

The next step is to note that, since $\mathbf{w}_t$ emerges from an economically optimal search of the distribution of offered prices $\mathbf{p}_t$, for any different set of outlet selection probabilities $\hat{\mathbf{w}}$, $\hat{\mathbf{w}}^T \mathbf{p}_t + C(\hat{\mathbf{w}}^T \mathbf{p}_t, c_t) \geq M(\mathbf{p}_t c_t)$. But the reference period weighted index is

$$L(\mathbf{p}_t, \mathbf{w}_t, c_t, \mathbf{p}_0, \mathbf{w}_0, c_0) = \frac{\mathbf{w}_0^T \mathbf{p}_t + C(\mathbf{w}_0^T \mathbf{p}_t, c_t)}{M(\mathbf{p}_0, c_0)}$$

(1)
$$\geq \frac{\mathbf{w}_t^T \mathbf{p}_t + C(\mathbf{w}_t^T \mathbf{p}_t, c_t)}{M(\mathbf{p}_0, c_0)}$$

$$= \frac{M(\mathbf{p}_t, c_t)}{M(\mathbf{p}_0, c_0)},$$

where the last expression in (1) is the "true" COL index.

In the more general case of search for many substitutable goods, two sources of complication arise. First, as Anglin and Baye (1987) observe, substitution possibilities make the optimal reservation price in each market dependent on the outcome of search in other markets. Second, comparisons of "true" indexes of the expected cost of living with fixed commodity and outlet weight COL indexes will necessarily reflect both commodity substitution bias

---

assumption appears innocuous in the present context, for some problems this approach is not suitable. In particular, Reinganum (1979) finds that, if all consumers are identical, including having the same marginal search costs, sequential search strategies with no learning are consistent only with dispersed price equilibria in which no one chooses to search.

8. In one of the cases examined below, food markets, it is more realistic to think of consumers as searching for the store offering the lowest price for an entire market basket rather than the lowest price for a single good. In this case, the elements of $\mathbf{p}_t$ can be interpreted as the purchase price of the desired market basket at each of the n food outlets because, in the present analysis, every good is assumed to be purchased in a predetermined quantity.

and outlet substitution bias. The difference between a fixed-commodity-weight index and an index in which both commodity and outlet weights are fixed may be regarded as a pure measure of outlet substitution bias, however, and this approach has the advantage of avoiding the problem of reservation prices that are ex ante stochastic. Since a fixed-commodity-weight COL index can be expressed as a weighted average of individual commodities' relative prices (or, in the case of searching consumers, commodities' relative acquisition costs), it is straightforward to generalize equation (1) to show that, in the multiple good case, outlet substitution bias is also nonnegative.

It is worth noting that equation (1) implies that upward bias may occur in a fixed-outlet-weight price index even if the amount of price dispersion in the market is unchanged. The present inquiry into whether consumers reduce their cost of living in a way not measured by the CPI by substituting one outlet for another when outlets' comparative prices change thus concerns the indirect implication of price dispersion for the CPI. The direct effect of changes in the amount of price dispersion on consumers' cost of living is explored in Reinsdorf (1990), which finds that increases in price dispersion may cause a short-term upward bias in COL indexes employing fixed outlet weights.

7.3.1 Indexes That Exclude Costs of Search

Because measuring the costs of search itself is generally impossible, properties of a feasible search-based COL index covering only prices paid are of as much interest as those of a complete searcher's COL index. Generally, an index of searchers' prices paid will also be upwardly biased when fixed reference period outlet share weights are used, although, for certain changes in the distribution of offered prices, this need not be so. Manipulating equation (1) shows that

$$(2) \qquad \mathbf{w}_0^T \mathbf{p}_t - \mathbf{w}_t^T \mathbf{p}_t \geq C(\mathbf{w}_t, \mathbf{p}_t, c_t) - C(\mathbf{w}_0, \mathbf{p}_t, c_t).$$

As long as the effort devoted to search is nondecreasing over time, the fixed-outlet-weight index will rise faster than the average price paid by consumers. A decrease in the benefits and hence the quantity of search due to a drop in price dispersion in period t could, however, cause $\mathbf{w}_0^T \mathbf{p}_t / \mathbf{w}_0^T \mathbf{p}_0$ to be less than $\mathbf{w}_t^T \mathbf{p}_t / \mathbf{w}_0^T \mathbf{p}_0$. For example, if the highest-priced outlet lowers its price, reducing any fixed-weighted average of offered prices, its market share may increase by enough to cause the average price paid to *rise*. (This rise will, of course, be less than the decrease in average search expenses.) Yet a faster increase in the average price paid than in the average price that searching consumers would have paid had they not altered their outlet purchasing patterns is likely to occur rarely. When the offered price distribution changes enough to reduce consumers' desired amount of search significantly, outlets' price rankings will generally be altered. Such rearrangements of outlets' price rankings will almost certainly have a greater effect on searchers' outlet selection probabilities than any reductions in the amount of search. Consumer search will thus normally result in outlet substitutions that reduce consumers' average price paid along with their cost of living.

7.3.2   Effects of Outlet Entry and Exit

Consumer search theory implies that, among a set of continuously existing outlets, those whose comparative prices decline will capture increased proportions of consumers' purchases. Nevertheless, shifts of consumer patronage caused by searchers' responses to the evolution of price relations among a set of continuously existing outlets can cause relatively little long-term bias in the CPI because gaps between competitors' prices cannot grow indefinitely. Substantial long-term bias could, however, arise from a process of gradual but steady replacement of higher-priced retail establishments by lower-priced entrants. As was noted in the introduction, the revolutionary changes in the retailing industries created in part by declines in the real price of transportation, housing, refrigeration, and mass communication (see Oi [1990] and, for the effect of mass advertising, Steiner [(1973) 1976]) have evidently involved such a process. Moreover, the structure of many retail industries still seems to be evolving in favor of lower-priced outlets. Finally, consideration of economic theory implies that firms whose expected costs are lower than incumbents' are most likely to enter, while exit is most likely for the firms with higher than average costs. Given an association between high costs and high prices, this implies a tendency for low-priced retailers (as well as manufacturers) to replace high-priced ones in the marketplace.

7.4   Price Level Differences between Old and New POPS-Based Outlet Samples

The empirical evidence on price differentials between the outlets entering and those leaving CPI samples is discussed in this section and in section 7.5 below. The analysis is limited to two classes of goods, food and energy, because of data availability and price comparability considerations. If migration of consumer patronage to lower-priced outlets indeed occurs, it should be reflected in prices that are on average lower in newly sampled outlets. Moreover, a finding of such a pattern would be evidence that outlet substitution bias exists in the CPI: even though lower prices may often be associated with lower quality, systematic gains by lower-priced outlets should occur only if their price savings exceed the value of any retailer services or ambience that their customers must forgo.

Two approaches are possible for testing for the existence of outlet substitution bias in the CPI. The first is to compare price levels in outgoing and incoming CPI outlet samples, and the second—discussed in section 7.5 below—is to compare the evolution over time of unlinked sample average prices and their linked CPI component index counterparts.

Since outlets' probabilities of sample selection are proportional to the expenditures reported for them in the CPOPS, the new outlet samples will reflect the evolution of consumer outlet choices over the preceding five years. In particular, obsolescence of the CPOPS share estimates is probably negligible in the few months that elapse before BLS first collects prices from the outlet samples reflecting those estimates, so that mean prices in new samples of outlets provide unbiased estimates of the average prices paid by consumers. Consumer search behavior and entry by lower-priced outlets should thus result in lower prices on average in newly sampled outlets than in the ones they replace.

The qualification "on average" is important for three reasons. First, changes in the quality of the outlets or the brands and varieties priced will undoubtedly occur. In some cities, increases in average outlet or brand quality will be reflected in a higher price in the newly drawn sample. Second, even if outlets whose current prices are high have low market shares and low probabilities of sample selection, they will sometimes be selected instead of the high-probability, low-priced outlets. Although sampling according to size provides an unbiased estimate of the average price paid by consumers, the estimate for any particular city will have a high variance. Pooling across cities is probably necessary to get a reliable estimate of the bias in the CPI due to consumer outlet substitution behavior.

Third, for goods usually purchased close to home, a potential source of noise in the estimation of outlet substitution effects may be differences between the neighborhoods in a city selected for sampling in successive CPOPS waves. Since 1984, clustered sampling has been used for the CPOPS (U.S. Department of Labor 1988, 164). Furthermore, in some cases, definitions of sampling areas have changed to reflect their growth. In particular, in 1987, Norwalk was included in the New York/Connecticut suburbs sample area, while, in 1988, San Jose was added to the San Francisco area, and San Bernardino was added to the Los Angeles suburbs area.

Unfortunately, comparisons of old and new CPI outlets samples are not purely tests for the effects of consumer outlet substitution. New samples of item brands and varieties are necessarily drawn at the same time that new outlet samples are drawn, so, for many goods, effects of brand and variety substitution will also be reflected in sample comparisons. A simultaneous test for outlet and brand/variety substitution is itself of interest since consumer search among brands of an item is in many ways analogous to search among outlets selling an item. Rising incomes and the introduction of improved products could, however, lead to unmeasured growth in average brand or variety quality and an underestimate of the magnitude of outlet and brand substitution bias in the CPI.

7.4.1 Testing for Sample Differences in the Location of the Price Distribution

The form of an efficient estimator of the mean price level change between the old and the new CPI outlet samples is largely determined by the way the data are collected. When rotating CPI outlet samples, BLS field representatives visit each outlet in the new sample twice before the old sample is dropped. The first visit, which is primarily to choose the brands and varieties to be priced, occurs three to six months prior to the link month for the area in which the newly selected outlet is located. The first set of observations from a new sample of outlets is thus spread out over a period of three or four months.

These scattered observations can be utilized by deflating each new sample price quote by the mean price in the old sample for the corresponding good, size, and month. A geometric rather than an arithmetic mean of the old sample prices is used so that rates of change can be calculated by taking logarithms: logarithms of new sample prices that were deflated by arithmetic means would have a negative expected value even under the null hypothesis that prices come from the same distribution in both samples.[9] Separate means are utilized for deflating different sizes or size classes to control for this important dimension of variety quality because, even after expressing all prices on a par ounce basis, for most items size appeared to affect price.

Collection of data in two months while the old outlet sample is still being priced and collection of prices for more than one item in many outlets mean that the data sets contain multiple price quotes from each new sample outlet. For food, 3,106 quotes from 584 newly sampled outlets imply an average of 5.3 quotes per outlet, while, in the fuel data set, 516 quotes from 131 newly sampled outlets imply an average of 3.9 quotes per outlet. Since observations coming from the same outlet are unlikely to be independent, a simple mean of all the price changes in the data is not the minimum variance estimator of the mean price change between samples. Moreover, nonindependent data lead to a downward bias in the ordinary formula for the standard error of the mean.

The efficient estimator of the mean price change and a consistent estimator of its standard error are easily derived in an error components framework. Let the logarithm of the jth deflated price quote from the ith outlet in the new sample be $p_{ij} = \mu + u_i + v_{ij}$, where u_i and v_{ij} are independent outlet and quote-specific error components having constant variances, and where μ represents the mean logarithmic price change between outlet samples. Also, denote the number of observations from the ith outlet by N_i, and let there be I outlets. The variance of p_{ij} is $E(u_i^2) + E(v_{ij}^2) \equiv \sigma_u^2 + \sigma_v^2$, but the variance of $\bar{p}_i \equiv \Sigma_{j=1}^{N_i} p_{ij}/N_i$ equals $\sigma_u^2 + \sigma_v^2/N_i$. If σ_u^2 is positive because outlet effects are present, then the ordinary mean of the deflated new sample prices is an inefficient estimator of μ because it equals a weighted mean of the $\bar{p}_i$ in which the weights are N_i/N, where $N \equiv \Sigma_{i=1}^{I} N_i$. The efficient weight for any $\bar{p}_i$ is inversely proportional to its variance. Define w_i as $1/\text{var}(\bar{p}_i)$. Then

9. Taking logarithms of the relative prices has two benefits. First, the logarithmic variable has a convenient interpretation as the percentage change in price levels between old and new samples. Second, price distributions tend to be right skewed, and, indeed, in the present study, the skewedness of the price logarithms was much closer to zero than was that of the prices themselves. The transformed data were thus less likely to suffer from heteroskedasticity and were more suitable for hypothesis testing using Student's t-distribution.

(3) $$w_i = N_i/(N_i\sigma_u^2 + \sigma_v^2).$$

The minimum variance estimator of μ is

(4) $$\hat{\mu} = \frac{\Sigma_{i=1}^I w_i \bar{p}_i}{\Sigma_{i=1}^I w_i}.$$

The variance of this estimator is simply

(5) $$\text{var}(\hat{\mu}) = \frac{1}{\Sigma_{i=1}^I w_i}.$$

It is, of course, necessary to have values for σ_v^2 and σ_u^2 in order to utilize these estimators. Values of σ_v^2 and σ_u^2 can be estimated on the basis of the separate means for each outlet. The variance of p_{ij} remaining after outlet effects are removed provides an estimate for σ_v^2, an approach known as Henderson's (1953) Method 3 in the statistics literature. That is,

(6) $$\hat{\sigma}_v^2 = \Sigma_{i=1}^I \Sigma_{j=1}^{N_i}(p_{ij} - \bar{p}_i)^2/(N - I).$$

The "total sum of squares" (TSS) is $\Sigma_i \Sigma_j (p_{ij} - \bar{p})^2$. Its expected value is

(7) $$E\text{ (TSS)} \equiv E\left[\Sigma_{i=1}^I \Sigma_{j=1}^{N_i} (p_{ij} - \bar{p}^2\right]$$
$$= \sigma_u^2[N - (\Sigma_i N_i^2/N)] + \sigma_v^2(N - 1).$$

Therefore, σ_u^2 can be estimated as

(8) $$\hat{\sigma}_u^2 = [\text{TSS} - \hat{\sigma}_v^2(N - 1)]/[N - (\Sigma_i N_i^2/N)].$$

Note that (8) can be interpreted as dividing the portion of the total variance of p_{ij} attributable to u_i by the appropriate degrees of freedom. Substituting $\hat{\sigma}_u^2$ and $\hat{\sigma}_v^2$ for σ_u^2 and σ_v^2 in equations (4) and (5) results in the "feasible generalized least squares" estimator of the mean effect on collected prices of rotating outlet samples and its standard error.

7.4.2 Empirical Results on the Effect of Sample Rotation on Price Levels

Estimates of the price level differences in old and new outlet samples in cities undergoing CPOPS outlet rotation are presented in tables 7.1 and 7.2. The food and gasoline items used are described in the appendix. The time periods included in the analysis are all twelve months of 1987 and July 1988–June 1989. Clearly, much longer periods would have been desirable in order to study the long-run effects of structural change in the retailing industry. Unfortunately, because CPI data are not collected for research purposes, archival files are accessible only with great difficulty, and data collected before 1987 are inaccessible.

The new food outlets' mean rates of change from old outlet sample price levels appear in table 7.1. Pooling all food products in all cities results in an estimate of -1.23 percent for μ, the mean price level change when outlet

Table 7.1   **Effect of CPI Outlet Sample Rotation on Food Price Levels, 1987–89[a]**

Area	Mean % Change[b]	t-Statistic[c]	Median % Change[d]	No. of Outlets	No. of Quotes
All areas pooled	−1.23	−1.89**	−.99	584	3,106
Boston	−4.83	−1.72**	−4.47	48	265
Buffalo	4.56	2.29***	2.09	22	129
Cleveland	−0.15	0.01	−1.95	42	133
Denver	1.60	0.48	0.02	24	132
Ft. Dodge	−0.34	−0.10	−0.93	7	191
Honolulu	−4.41	−1.35*	−4.22	21	137
Los Angeles suburbs	−1.50	−0.69	−0.76	62	213
Miami	−4.99	−1.96**	1.44	31	109
Milwaukee	2.03	0.51	3.04	20	70
Minneapolis	−2.14	−0.55	−0.09	21	141
New York and Conn. suburbs	−3.71	−2.53***	−3.81	79	519
Philadelphia	−0.77	−0.51	−0.87	84	505
Raleigh	−2.63	−0.89	−4.02	23	98
San Francisco	3.96	2.06***	0.65	61	204
Seattle	−2.47	−0.70	0.96	16	127
Tampa	3.30	1.29	2.62	23	133

[a]Effect variable is log $(P_i^N/\bar{P}^O)$, where P_i^N is the ith new sample price quote for a particular size of a particular item, and $\bar{P}^O$ is calculated as a geometric mean of the obsolete outlet sample price quotes for the item and size that it is to deflate.
[b]Each outlet mean observation is weighted by its inverse variance.
[c]One asterisk denotes significance at the 10 percent level in a one-tailed test, two asterisks denote significance at the 5 percent level in a one-tailed test, and three asterisks denote significance at the 1 percent level in a one-tailed test.
[d]Computed using SAS default definition (see *SAS User's Guide: Basics,* Version 5 ed., p. 1187).

samples are rotated. If the average quality of the outlets and varieties is comparable in the new and five-year-old samples, this estimate implies an upward bias due to outlet substitution in the food at home component of the CPI of 0.25 percent per year. This figure is slightly larger than Manser and McDonald's (1988) point estimate of 0.18 percent per year for the average commodity substitution bias in a Laspeyres price index for U.S. consumers, but it may possibly overstate the true outlet substitution bias because average quality in the new samples may have declined along with average prices. After correcting as described above for the effects of nonindependence of repeated observations from the same outlet, the t-statistic for the pooled mean is −1.9. The null hypothesis that price levels at newly sampled outlets are no lower than in outlets chosen five years before is thus rejected at the 5 percent level in a one-tailed test.

Use of the efficient estimator given by (4) instead of the ordinary unweighted mean has only a small effect on the point estimate of the effect of

Table 7.2   Effect of CPI Outlet Sample Rotation on Motor Fuel Price Levels, 1987–89[a]

Area	Mean % Change[b]	t-Statistic[c]	Median % Change[d]	No. of Outlets	No. of Quotes
All areas pooled	−1.29	−1.59*	−3.19	131	516
Boston	0.78	0.44	0.02	19	93
Buffalo	10.23	4.77**	12.24	3	18
Cleveland	−3.88	−1.24	−6.96	18	54
Denver	−0.79	−2.08*	−0.44	4	16
Ft. Dodge	−1.89	−0.94	−0.26	4	20
Honolulu	3.50	0.89	6.71	4	18
Los Angeles suburbs	−7.91	−3.43***	−9.51	10	33
Miami	−3.71	−2.28***	−4.10	21	47
Milwaukee	1.84	0.31	−3.52	3	8
Minneapolis	−7.84	−2.95**	−6.15	3	14
New York and Conn. suburbs	4.53	1.05	4.90	8	44
Philadelphia	−0.92	−0.45	−3.19	15	80
Raleigh	−2.65	−1.29	−0.98	5	15
San Francisco	2.41	0.37	−5.01	7	20
Seattle	−1.92	−4.45*	−0.44	3	18
Tampa	0.06	0.02	0.86	4	18

[a]See table 7.1, n. a.
[b]See table 7.1, n. b.
[c]See table 7.1, n. c.
[d]See table 7.1, n. d.

outlet rotation on price levels. In particular, for the pooled cities, the un-weighted mean price change is −1.32 percent. In contrast, correcting for the correlation of observations from the same outlet does have a major effect on the estimated t-statistics: the ordinary formula would have implied a t-statistic of −3.0 for the pooled mean.

The median difference between food outlet price averages is −1 percent. The median is, of course, a less efficient statistic than the mean, both because it does not take magnitudes of observations into account and because it treats all outlet observations identically regardless of how many quotes they average.

Table 7.2 reports mean percentage differences between price levels in new and old samples of outlets for motor fuel. The items included are various grades of gasoline and diesel fuel. The pooled estimate for the mean outlet price difference between samples is −1.29 percent, which also implies an upper-bound estimate for CPI outlet substitution bias of about 0.25 percent per year. Yet, despite the similarity of this estimate to the food result, its t-statistic of −1.6 does not quite attain the −1.645 cutoff for significance at the 5 percent level in a one-tailed test. The lower t-statistic for motor fuel is evidently a result of a much smaller sample size: the standard deviation of fuel outlet price differences was actually lower than the standard deviation of food outlet differences. Yet, even for fuel, sizable variation in deflated new outlet price levels is indicated by the dispersion of the individual city means. This is not surprising given that outlets with a small market share are nevertheless likely to be selected for the CPI samples in at least a few cases. In addition, there may be noise due to variations in outlet, brand, and neighborhood quality, as discussed above. Large samples of outlets are evidently necessary to achieve highly significant results because of the modest magnitude of the outlet substitution bias effect and the large variation in prices between outlets and brands and varieties that cannot be explained or is due to unmeasured random changes in quality.

7.5 Inflation Rate Differences between BLS Average Price Series and CPI Components

The second way of testing whether a potential exists for outlet substitution bias in the CPI is to compare the growth of the average price (AP) series published by BLS with that of corresponding components of the CPI. The AP series for an item tracks the price paid on average for a representative variety by the all-Urban CPI population of U.S. consumers. There should be little quality variation due to changing varieties in the AP series because a single variety is typically chosen to represent an item in that series. Narrow variety specifications are adopted by the AP program in order to minimize variation in quote quality: the "link with overlap price" procedure for controlling for quality changes is not appropriate because dollar values rather than index numbers are published. Instead, when new outlets enter the sample, any prices that they furnish for a variety eligible for the AP program are simply utilized without quality adjustment. This approach can be viewed as polar to the overlap price linking of the CPI: whereas the CPI linking procedure implicitly assumes that there is no price dispersion between outlets, an index based on the AP series implicitly assumes the absence of outlet quality dispersion. If the average outlet quality chosen by consumers has declined, the difference in growth rates between AP series and comparable CPI component indexes would thus exaggerate the gains realized by consumers via the substitution of outlets. Nevertheless, slower growth of average prices would indicate that outlet substitution is present in the CPI since endogenous market share gains by the lower-quality outlets would be caused by greater-than-compensating price differentials.

Utilizing published AP series offers the major advantage of allowing examination of the effects of outlet substitution over a nine-year period rather than the short two-year period for which the price quote data themselves were available. Another advantage of the AP comparisons is that they include the effects of outlet disappearances: if the outlets that exit are disproportionately ones whose costs and prices are uncompetitively high, the estimates of outlet substitution bias based on outlet rotation effects will ceteris paribus be biased downward. Both food and gasoline retailing experienced notable declines in number of establishments during the 1980s, so it is likely that outlet disappearance effects are important. In the case of gasoline, the *National Petroleum News Factbook Issue* figures for numbers of retail establishments in 1980 and 1990 reveal that *net* gas station closures during the 1980s amounted to 30 percent of the industry!

Nevertheless, three limitations of the AP series comparisons are worthy of note. First, since the AP series are based on quotes for a single variety of each good, differences in the long-run evolution of the prices of different varieties of the same good could cause CPI component indexes to behave differently from indexes based on AP series. Second, there could be variation over time in the average outlet or brand quality of the individual items furnishing price quotes for the AP program. Third, comparisons between the AP series and the CPI component series may reflect price differences from geographic movements of population as well as from outlet substitution. For some purposes, price declines due to the migration of population to lower-priced areas should be considered; for example, migration in the past decade to cities with lower prices and wages may have led to overly pessimistic conclusions regarding the progress of workers' real earnings or incomes in studies that use the U.S. CPI for deflation. In estimating the effect of outlet substitution on average prices paid, however, any effects of the shifting geographic composition of the samples on their average prices would distort comparisons of changes in AP and CPI time series: because of linking, the CPI does not reflect price level changes due to geographic changes in sampling or weighting.

7.5.1   Empirical Results on Differences between AP and CPI Inflation Measures for Food

Table 7.3 compares changes in AP series for food items with changes in the most closely corresponding CPI expenditure class index. The changes are measured by the ratios of the January 1989 value in each series to the January 1980 value. The results are again consistent with the existence of significant outlet substitution bias in the CPI. Of fifty-two food items, all but four show greater inflation in their CPI indexes, and, in three of those instances (T-bone steak vs. sirloin steak, rib roast vs. chuck roast, and chicken breast vs. chicken parts), the lack of comparability of the CPI index seems likely to have been important. Moreover, means of the relative CPI food indexes weighted according to importances of the items in the CPI show an average annual increase of 4.2 percent, while the weighted mean of the average prices grows at a rate of only 2.1 percent per year. This implies an outlet substitution bias for food in the CPI of about 2 percent per year during the 1980s.

Such an extraordinarily large estimate raises the question of whether the differences in table 7.3 could themselves suffer from a large upward bias due

Table 7.3   Comparison of Changes in Average Prices and the CPI for Foods

Average Price Series Item	Jan. 1989 Avg. Price Relative[a]	CPI Expenditure Class	Jan. 1989 CPI Relative Value[a]	CPI Change Minus Avg. Price Change
Flour, white, all purpose	1.123	Flour and prepared flour mixes	1.302	0.179
Rice, white, long grain, uncooked	1.010	Rice, pasta, and cornmeal	1.391	0.381
Bread, white, pan	1.303	White bread	1.506[b]	0.203
Bread, french	1.493			
Cookies, chocolate chip	1.478	Cookies, fresh cakes, cupcakes	1.663	0.185
Ground chuck, 100% beef	0.992	Ground beef, excluding canned	1.011	0.019
Chuck roast, U.S. choice, bone-in	1.017	Chuck roast	1.138	0.121
Round roast, U.S. choice, boneless	1.054	Round roast	1.082	0.028
Round steak, U.S. choice, boneless	1.127	Round steak	1.173	0.046
Sirloin steak, U.S. choice, bone-in	1.190	Sirloin steak	1.330	0.140
Steak, T-bone, U.S. choice, bone-in	1.431	Sirloin steak	1.330	−0.101
Rib roast, U.S. choice, boneless	1.406	Chuck roast	1.138	−0.268
Frankfurters, all meat or all beef	1.239	Other beef and veal	1.396	0.157
Bologna, all beef or mixed	1.124	Other beef and veal	1.396	0.272
Bacon, sliced	1.242	Bacon	1.376	0.134
Pork chops, center cut, bone-in	1.417	Pork chops	1.496	0.079
Ham, canned, 3 or 5 lbs.	1.191	Ham	1.374	0.183
Pork shoulder picnic, bone-in, smkd.	1.114	Other pork, including sausage	1.376	0.262
Pork sausage, fresh, loose	1.357	Other pork, including sausage	1.376	0.019
Chicken, fresh, whole	1.295	Fresh whole chicken	1.494	0.199
Chicken breast, bone-in	1.568	Fresh and frozen chicken parts	1.528	−0.040
Chicken legs, bone-in	1.109	Fresh and frozen chicken parts	1.528	0.419
Turkey, frozen, whole	1.026	Other poultry	1.224	0.198
Tuna, light, chunk	1.034	Canned fish and seafood	1.421	0.387
Eggs, grade A, large	1.071	Eggs	1.366	0.295
Milk, fresh, whole, fortified	1.208	Fresh whole milk	1.227	0.019
Milk, fresh, low fat	1.187	Other fresh milk and cream	1.239	0.052

(*continued*)

Table 7.3 (continued)

Average Price Series Item	Jan. 1989 Avg. Price Relative[a]	CPI Expenditure Class	Jan. 1989 CPI Relative Value[a]	CPI Change Minus Avg. Price Change
Butter, salted, grade AA, stick	1.187	Other dairy prod, incl. butter	1.332	0.145
Ice cream, prepackaged, regular	1.451	Ice cream and related products	1.422	−0.029
Apples, red delicious	1.316	Apples	1.668	0.352
Bananas	1.235	Bananas	1.321	0.086
Oranges, navel	1.537	Oranges, including tangerines	2.115	0.578
Orange juice, frozen concentrated,	1.503	Fruit juices, incl. frozen	1.606	0.103
Grapefruit	1.355	Other fresh fruits	2.129	0.774
Lemons	1.308	Other fresh fruits	2.129	0.821
Pears, anjou	1.251	Other fresh fruits	2.129	0.878
Lettuce, iceberg	2.243	Lettuce	2.769	0.526
Tomatoes, field grown	1.134	Tomatoes	1.695	0.561
Cabbage	1.439	Other fresh vegetables	1.985	0.546
Celery	1.235	Other fresh vegetables	1.985	0.750
Carrots, short trimmed and topped	1.241	Other fresh vegetables	1.985	0.744
Onions, dry yellow	1.667	Other fresh vegetables	1.985	0.318
Peppers, sweet	0.898	Other fresh vegetables	1.985	1.087
Radishes	1.527	Other fresh vegetables	1.985	0.458
Cucumbers	1.558	Other fresh vegetables	1.985	0.427
Beans, green, snap	1.429	Other fresh vegetables	1.985	0.556
Potatoes, frozen, french fried	1.423	Frozen vegetables	1.573	0.150
Sugar, white, 33–80 oz. pkg.	1.405	Sugar and artificial sweeteners	1.416	0.011
Shortening, vegetable oil blends	1.240	Fats and oils	1.370	0.130
Cola, nondiet, can, 72 oz. 6 pk.	1.056	Carbonated drinks	1.297	0.241
Coffee, 100% ground roast	0.924	Coffee	1.032	0.108
Potato chips	1.369	Snacks	1.582	0.213
Weighted mean	1.202		1.450	0.248

Source: LABSTAT.

[a]January 1980 = 1.000.

[b]Fresh other breads CPI relative value is 1.519.

to the declines in average prices from shifting geographic representation. This does not appear to be the case. Primont and Kokoski (1990) find that overall food price levels differ relatively little between cities in the continental United States; furthermore, they report relatively low food prices for some of the Rust Belt cities losing population in the 1980s and high prices for some Sun Belt cities that grew. In fact, their lowest multilateral food price index for a specific urban area was 93.3 for Pittsburgh/Beaver Valley, and their highest (excluding Anchorage and Honolulu) was 106.8 for fast-growing Atlanta. Even under an implausible "worst-imaginable-case" scenario, the average food price comparisons would not suffer much upward bias from geographic effects. Supposing that the entire gain of about 3 percentage points in the weight of the Sun Belt during the 1980s occurred because population shifted from New York City, whose index of 106.7 was the second highest, to Miami–Fort Lauderdale, whose index was a very low 95.25, implies a cumulative bias over the nine-year period studied of only 0.34 percent. Additional evidence that geographic effects play at most a small role in the table 7.3 results comes from figure 7.1. The major jump in the Sun Belt's weight occurred in 1986, but figure 7.1 shows a consistent upward trend of the difference between the CPI food indexes and indexes based on AP series.

It thus appears that a considerable portion of the discrepancy between the

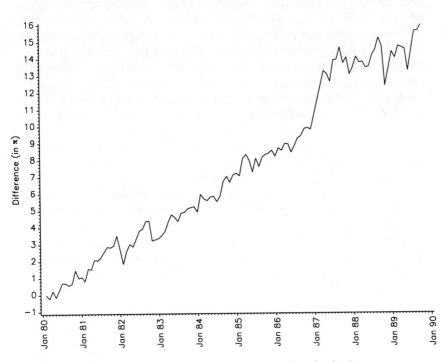

Fig. 7.1   Difference in growth of CPI and average prices for food

CPI measure of food price inflation and inflation in average food prices is due to changes in the food retailing industry's structure and systematic market share gains by lower-priced competitors. Structural changes in the industry include the continued trend of disappearances of small and independent stores, the replacement of traditional format supermarkets by warehouse and other economy format food stores (*Progressive Grocer*'s April 1988 annual report shows that their market share rose from 3.8 percent in 1979 to 15.2 percent in 1988), gains by off-price but traditional format supermarkets such as Food Lion, the emergence of the wholesale club format as a national market force, and increasing off-price food sales by retailers in other lines of business such as general merchandise discounters and drugstores. These trends that lowered the prices that consumers paid were evidently not offset by a continued trend of gains by convenience stores.

In indicating that structural changes in the food retailing industry and systematic patronage gains by lower-priced stores had a significant effect on the prices that consumers paid, table 7.3 shows that outlet substitution does reduce consumers' cost of living in a way that the CPI cannot reflect. Yet, because many of the cheaper store formats offer consumers fewer services, less selection, or less ambience than the formats they have tended to replace, quality adjusting the average food price indexes might well reduce their discrepancy with the CPI food price changes. The adjustment for changing outlet quality would not eliminate the discrepancy because consumers' willingness to alter their patronage patterns indicates that they value the outlet services that they forgo less than the price difference between the store types.

Unfortunately, data with which to attempt a direct outlet quality adjustment to the BLS average price series are lacking. It is possible that little adjustment for declining outlet quality is necessary: the negative effect on average outlet quality from gains by the off-price formats may be offset by several quality-augmenting trends in the food retailing industry. Selections of items and varieties available in a single store have grown dramatically as supermarkets have become larger and added features such as in-store bakeries, delicatessens, salad bars, and fresh fish markets. Convenience stores, which may be regarded as higher quality due to their extended hours and accessible locations, also grew in importance: their proportion of food sales rose from 5.6 percent to 7.8 percent between 1980 and 1988. Moreover, even within the economy format class, there was a trend toward greater breadth and depth of assortment. Finally, some of the shifts in consumer patronage patterns during the 1980s—such as the rapid climb of Food Lion noted above—do not appear to present quality-adjustment issues even though they probably did reduce average prices paid by consumers.

Changing brand quality is a potential source of bias in the outlet sample price comparisons of tables 7.1 and 7.2 despite the attempt to hold variety constant in the average price program. Since the end of the 1982 recession, however, the shares of cheaper generic and private label brands have steadily declined. Food brand quality is thus unlikely to have fallen in recent CPI samples, and it may even have increased.

7.5.2 Empirical Results on Differences between AP and CPI Inflation Measures for Fuel

Table 7.4 reports comparisons between price changes in CPI and AP time series for energy. It also shows faster growth of the CPI than of corresponding average prices, but the discrepancies are about half the size of the mean discrepancy in table 7.3. Unleaded regular gas fell at a 2.3 percent average annual rate in the AP series but at only a 1.4 percent rate in the CPI, while leaded regular gasoline fell at a 2.35 percent rate in the AP series but at a 1.2 percent rate in the CPI series. Since large numbers of gas stations closed during the 1980s, these dramatic discrepancies probably result in part from a tendency for the stations that went out of business to have had higher prices than the stations that remained or that opened. One change in outlet format that contributed to this was the growing importance of low-cost "pumper" stations with multiple self-service pumps and no repair services available.

Another trend that depressed the average gasoline price in the CPI samples is the increasing penetration of self-service, which grew from about a 50 percent market share to about an 80 percent market share between 1980 and 1989 (according to the 1990 *National Petroleum News Factbook Issue*). The average differential between full-service and self-service prices for regular unleaded gasoline in the 1984 *National Petroleum News Factbook Issue* is about 15 percent. Had self-service maintained a constant 50 percent market share, the January 1989 average price relative for regular unleaded gasoline would thus have been higher by a factor of about 1.075/1.03, and its average annual rate of change would have been − 1.82 percent. Approximately half the total discrepancy between the average price percentage change and the CPI percentage change can therefore be attributed to the growth of self-service. Yet whether a significant adjustment is therefore necessary in the discrepancies in table 7.4

Table 7.4   **Comparison of Changes in Average Prices and CPI Components**

Average Prices item	Jan. 1989 Avg. Price Relative[a]	CPI Expenditure Class	Jan. 1989 CPI Relative Value[a]	CPI Change Minus Avg. Price Change
Fuel oil #2	.950	Fuel oil	.978	0.28
Utility gas (therm.)	1.541	Utility (piped) gas	1.608	.067
Electricity	1.491	Electricity	1.634	.143
Gasoline, all types	.850	Gasoline	.898	.048
Gasoline, leaded regular	.807	Gasoline, leaded regular	.898	.091
Gasoline, unleaded regular	.812	Gasoline, unleaded regular	.881	.069

Source: LABSTAT.

[a]January 1980 = 1.000.

to arrive at the value of consumers' gains from outlet and variety substitution is not clear. Little net quality decline may be associated with forgoing the services of the station attendant because self-service reduces consumers' time cost for refueling.

For fuel oil, the discrepancy in average annual growth rates is a more modest 0.3 percent per year, which is close to the overall outlet substitution bias estimates of tables 7.1 and 7.2. It is also evident from table 7.4 that, when products differ greatly in price across regions, shifting geographic weights can seriously distort the AP series comparisons. Both piped natural gas and electricity exhibit lower inflation in their average prices than in their CPI indexes even though outlet and variety substitution possibilities are minimal for these utilities. In the case of electricity, virtually all the discrepancy is the result of shifting geographic composition of the sample giving more importance to lower-priced Sun Belt cities in 1985 and 1986. Nevertheless, the potential for geographic shifts to cause a significant upward bias in the discrepancies between AP and CPI changes appears to be just as small for gasoline as for food. Neither the amount of geographic reweighting nor the amount of interarea variation in gasoline prices in the continental United States is large. Eleven of fifteen urban areas for which BLS calculated average gasoline prices in 1989 had prices that differed by no more than 11 percent from one another, and the highest price level was found in an urban area that grew rapidly in the 1980s— Washington, D.C., and its suburbs.

Figure 7.2 depicts the evolution of the difference between CPI and average price inflation for unleaded gasoline. For the most part, it displays a persistent upward trend rather than the trendless pattern interrupted by large vertical jumps that might be expected from geographic reweighting. Geographic effects may, however, be evident in figure 7.2: near the end of 1984, there is an upward vertical jump in the AP-CPI discrepancy of 1.4 percent, and, in early 1986, there is a downward drop of 2 percent. A seasonal effect also seems to have occurred in the early years, with much of the CPI-AP discrepancy accumulating during the summer climbs in gasoline prices.

7.5.3   The Performance of Retail Industry Productivity Measures

The question of outlet substitution bias in the CPI was first raised by Denison in a discussion of the downward bias it would cause in retail productivity indexes. In fact, the BLS productivity index for food retailing exhibits such a poor performance—declining, for example, by 7 percent between 1977 and 1986—that Baily and Gordon (1988) characterize the industry as an apparent "basket case" and seek a reason for mismeasurement. The large disparities between average food price inflation and CPI measures of inflation for foods in table 7.3 indicate that the outlet substitution bias identified by Denison could account for much of the implausibly poor performance of the food retailing indexes. However, certain increases in quality also play a role: Baily and Gordon suggest that, in addition to long-term quality-improving trends

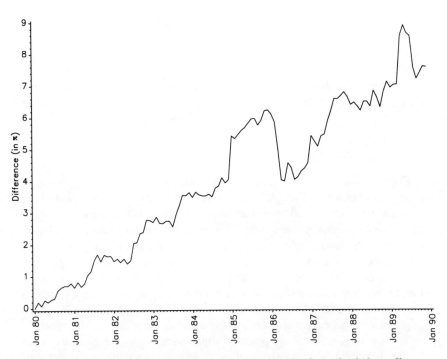

Fig. 7.2   Difference in growth of CPI and average price for unleaded gasoline

such as the expansion of item assortments and the extension of opening hours, in the 1980s food stores added "labor-intensive services valued by consumers, including full-service deli and seafood counters [and] salad bars" (1988, 411). Although quality improvements embodied in newly opened stores could be expected to raise the AP indexes in table 7.3, in the case of quality improvements from the provision of new goods the AP indexes will only reflect any increased margin on other goods that the stores offering the new goods are able to charge because of the additional store traffic that the new goods generate. Table 7.3 is not, therefore, inconsistent with this kind of quality improvement playing a role in the poor performance of the food retailing productivity index; both outlet substitution bias and a bias due to a changing mix of goods sold may simultaneously be present in the food retailing productivity index. Yet offering store-baked bread and delicatessen and salad bar meals is not primarily a case of outlet quality improvement but rather a case of adding high-quality goods for which labor contributes a high proportion of total costs. Apparent declines in labor productivity in the retail food industry are, in effect, partly a result of the substitution of labor for materials costs.

The productivity story for gasoline retailing is very different from that for food retailing. Because of the large decline in the number of gas stations per car, the changing format of the stations, and the growth of self-service, gains in service station productivity averaged nearly 4.2 percent per year from 1980 to 1987, according to the productivity index figures in LABSTAT, the BLS on-line data base. Thus, no "declining productivity" puzzle exists for gasoline retailing. Nevertheless, even if one wishes to remove the effect of the growth of self-service, table 7.4 suggests that enough productivity gains from the disappearance or replacement of less efficient outlets may have occurred to make the true productivity growth figure perhaps 0.4 percent per year higher.

7.6 Conclusion

Comparisons of new and obsolete outlet sample prices and comparisons of changes in published average prices with changes in CPI components both indicate that outlet substitution bias affects the food and fuel components of the CPI. Moreover, the magnitude of the outlet substitution bias may be large. For foods, the linked indexes from the CPI program rise a full 2 percent per year faster than the corresponding AP time series, and for unleaded gasoline the AP series grow about 0.9 percent per year faster. Nevertheless, it is important to interpret these estimates with caution. In particular, the differences between the growth of sample average prices and corresponding CPI series ought to be regarded as upper bounds for outlet substitution bias since there is no attempt to control for the possibility that average outlet quality may have declined. Furthermore, another method of estimating a bound for outlet substitution bias—comparing prices from newly selected outlets with prices from their predecessors—implies only a 0.25 percent per year outlet substitution bias for food and gasoline.

Eliminating outlet substitution bias may be possible by directly comparing the prices from new and old samples of outlets after quality adjustment, just as the downward bias in the women's apparel index created by linking of seasonal fashions was mitigated by increasing the number of direct price comparisons (see Armknecht and Weyback 1989). This would require collecting detailed data on characteristics of outlets and items priced so that hedonic regressions could be used to control for changes in item characteristics and in the types of outlets represented in CPI samples. Note, however, that hedonic adjustments to allow comparisons of prices from different types of outlets are more complicated than hedonic adjustments for changes in variety characteristics because they must allow for the existence of temporary market disequilibria and a distribution of preferences across consumers. In particular, large shifts in market share in favor of discounters indicate that the inframarginal consumers making such outlet substitutions experience increased consumer surplus. The average value of this increased consumer surplus depends on the distribution of preferences across consumers, which could be estimated if data providing equilibrium market shares at various price differentials between outlet types were available.

Collecting the necessary data to control for outlet substitution bias may, of course, be very expensive. Nevertheless, the evidence of outlet substitution bias in the CPI is sufficiently strong to warrant further study of the effects of overlap price linking when new samples of outlets are introduced into the CPI on the basis of a CPOPS or in order to replace outlets no longer in business.

Appendix

Table 7A.1   **Food and Fuel Items Used in Tables 7.1 and 7.2**

BLS Item Code	Description	BLS Item Code	Description
Foods		12011	Potatoes
01011	Flour	12021	Lettuce
01031	Rice	12031	Tomatoes
02011	White bread	13011	Frozen orange juice
02021	Bread other than white		
02061	Crackers	14021	Canned beans other than lima beans
03011	Ground beef	14022	Canned cut corn
03021	Chuck roast		
03031	Round roast	15021	Sugar and artificial sweeteners
03051	Round steak		
03061	Sirloin steak	16011	Margarine
		16014	Peanut butter
04011	Bacon		
04021	Pork chops	17011	Cola drinks
04031	Ham (excluding canned)	17012	Carbonated drinks other than cola
04042	Pork sausage		
		17031	Roasted coffee
05011	Frankfurters	17302	Instant and freeze-dried coffee
06011	Fresh whole chicken	*Fuels*	
		47012	Regular leaded gasoline
08011	Eggs	47013	Premium leaded gasoline
		47014	Regular unleaded gasoline
09011	Fresh whole milk	47016	Premium unleaded gasoline
		47017	Diesel
10011	Butter		
11011	Apples		
11021	Bananas		
11031	Oranges		

References

Anglin, Paul M., and Michael R. Baye. 1987. Information, multiprice search, and cost-of-living index theory. *Journal of Political Economy* 95 (December): 1179–95.

Armknecht, Paul A., and Donald Weyback. 1989. Adjustments for quality change in the U.S. consumer price index. *Journal of Official Statistics* 5:107–23.

Baily, Martin Neal, and Robert J. Gordon. 1988. The productivity slowdown, measurement issues and the explosion of computer power. *Brookings Papers on Economic Activity,* no. 2:347–420.

Betancourt, Roger, and David Gautschi. 1988. The economics of retail firms. *Managerial and Decision Economics* 9 (June): 133–44.

Braithwait, Steve D. 1980. The substitution bias of the Laspeyres price index. *American Economic Review* 70 (March): 64–77.

Business Guides, Inc. 1980. *1980 directory of supermarket, grocery and convenience store chains.* New York.

Carlson, John A., and R. Preston McAffee. 1983. Discrete equilibrium price dispersion. *Journal of Political Economy* 91 (June): 480–93.

Carlson, John A., and Donn R. Pescatrice. 1980. Persistent price distributions. *Journal of Economics and Business* 33 (Fall): 21–27.

Christensen, Laurits R., and Marilyn E. Manser. 1976. Cost-of-living indexes and price indexes for U.S. meat and produce, 1947–1971. In *Household production and consumption,* ed. Nestor Terleckyj. Studies in Income and Wealth, vol. 40. New York: Columbia University Press (for the National Bureau of Economic Research).

Dahlby, Bev, and Douglas S. West. 1986. Price dispersion in an automobile insurance market. *Journal of Political Economy* 94 (April); 418–38.

Denison, Edward. 1962. *The sources of economic growth in the United States and the alternatives before us.* New York: Committee for Economic Development.

Erlich, Isaac, and Lawrence Fisher. 1982. The derived demand for advertising: A theoretical and empirical investigation. *American Economic Review* 72 (June): 366–88.

Henderson, C. R. 1953. Estimation of variance and covariance components. *Biometrics* 9:226–52.

Konus, Alexander A. 1939. The problem of the true index of the cost of living. *Econometrica* 7 (January): 10–29.

Layard, P. Richard G., and Alan A. Walters. 1978. *Microeconomic theory.* New York: McGraw-Hill.

Manser, Marilyn, and Richard McDonald. 1988. An analysis of the substitution bias in measuring inflation, 1959–1985. *Econometrica* 56 (July): 909–30.

Marvel, Howard P. 1976. Retail gasoline price behavior: An empirical analysis. *Journal of Political Economy* 76 (October): 1033–59.

Oi, Walter Y. 1990. Productivity in the distributive trades: The shopper and the economies of massed reserves. Paper presented at the National Bureau of Economic Research/Conference on Research Income and Wealth Conference on Output Measurement in the Services Sector, Charleston, S.C.

Pratt, John W., David A. Wise, and Richard J. Zeckhauser. 1979. Price differences in almost competitive markets. *Quarterly Journal of Economics* 93 (May): 189–211.

Primont, Diane F., and Mary F. Kokoski. 1990. Differences in food prices across U.S. cities: Evidence from survey data. Washington, D.C.: U.S. Bureau of Labor Statistics. Typescript.

Reinganum, Jennifer F. 1979. A simple model of equilibrium price dispersion. *Journal of Political Economy* 87 (July/August): 851–58.

Reinsdorf, Marshall. 1988. Consumer information and industrial probability in an

equilibrium price dispersion model. Working Paper no. 178. Washington, D.C.: U.S. Bureau of Labor Statistics.
——. 1990. Multi-good search and cost of living indexes: Theory and evidence. Working Paper no. 201. Washington, D.C.: U.S. Bureau of Labor Statistics.
Steiner, Robert L. [1973] 1976. Does advertising lower consumer prices? Reprint no. 37. Washington, D.C.: American Enterprise Institute, January.
Stigler, George J. 1961. The economics of information. *Journal of Political Economy* 69 (June): 213–25.
——. 1988. *BLS handbook of methods.* Bureau of Labor Statistics Bulletin no. 2285. Washington, D.C.: U.S. Government Printing Office.
Van Hoomissen, Theresa. 1988. Price dispersion and inflation: Evidence from Israel. *Journal of Political Economy* 96 (December): 130–314.
Who's who in the grocery marketplace. 1988. *Grocery Marketing* (February): 36–41.

Comment   Joel Popkin

By analogy with Alfred Marshall's low-key definition of economics as the study of mankind in the ordinary business of life, price measurement economics is the study of price statisticians going about their ordinary work of deciding when and how to link.[1] To link or not to link is the most frequent decision a price index compiler makes and comprises the class of decisions that can potentially have the most significant ongoing effect on the behavior of price indexes.[2] Thus, the jumping-off point for this conference is the issue of linking. That is what is addressed in both the papers I have been asked to discuss. And it is a sensible place to begin.

The papers differ in subject matter—Liegey's deals with linking prices of seasonal women's clothing, while Reinsdorf's focuses on linking new outlets into the CPI to replace older ones. In one, the analysis proceeds with the use of the regression tool; in the other, alternative statistical approaches are used. Each paper has strengths and weaknesses of its own, but the intersection of these two pieces of research provides direction for future improvements in the procedure used to link price data in compiling indexes. I hope to make that intersection apparent in the course of my discussion.

Joel Popkin is president of Joel Popkin & Co., an economic consulting firm. He was formerly assistant commissioner for prices and living conditions, Bureau of Labor Statistics, U.S. Department of Labor.

1. In its simplest form, linking is a process of introducing a substitute item or the same item priced in a substitute outlet into a price index. It is accomplished by collecting the price of both the outgoing and the incoming item for the same period and moving the price of the outgoing item by the relative of change in the new one. By implication, the two items or outlets are treated as though they were of equivalent quality.

2. Issues of index concept, such as how housing should be measured in the CPI, can have a large effect as well, but they tend to emerge as discrete rather than continuous issues.

Liegey's paper on the quality adjustment of two (entry-level) items of women's clothing—uses regression analysis to detect biases that can result whenever there is a high turnover of individual items priced within an entry-level-item category. Clothing presents an egregious case of such turnover because of the change in seasons and in fashions, particularly for women's suits and coats and jackets, which are the two items investigated. The regression for each item is estimated from monthly data covering a full calendar year in which there are two distinct clothing seasons, fall/winter and spring/summer. To the individual observations actually used in the official published indexes for each item are added two kinds of observations that were collected but not used. One (COMPARE) consists of data that did not differ in specification but for which the reported price was discarded as an outlier. The second (ADJUST) consists of prices that were not used in the official index because they had noncomparable quality characteristics. Three indexes are constructed from regressions using the published index observations plus COMPARE (1), plus ADJUST (2), and with both COMPARE and ADJUST (3). Each is compared with the published index. There are some anomalies among the three regression results that need to be explored further.[3]

Of more interest to me, however, is the picture that the results yield of possible longer-run bias due to quality adjustment. For women's suits, the published index ends the year at the same level as the index that combines directly compared and regression adjusted items. But, for coats and jackets, the latter ends the year 3.7 percent higher than the former. That is a large difference to cumulate in such a short period of time, especially since Liegey indicates that the quality-adjustment uncertainties are greater for suits.[4]

Despite these and other imperfections that arise when regressions are used for quality adjustments, two of Liegey's conclusions are justified and important. The first is that regression analysis can be valuable not merely for ex post adjustment to make price data comparable but also for selecting, ex ante, the characteristics of items that are to be priced and of substitutes for these items. Thus, regression techniques can be used to define the specification to be used in price collection. The second is that the more robust of the regression coefficients can be used on an ongoing, timely basis to adjust prices used in the compilation of the monthly indexes, without delaying their publication.

Liegey's paper provides a nice bridge to Reinsdorf's paper on linking out-

3. For example, while the author notes that interactive effects can be present, I find disquieting the results in table 6.6 for coats and jackets in which the index based on the combination of COMPARE and ADJUST ends the year about 3 percent higher than each of the two indexes that treat COMPARE and ADJUST price sets separately.

4. Not all possible quality characteristics are used in the regressions. Those selected are based on correlations between price and characteristics that the Bureau of Labor Statistics (BLS) collects. Such likely quality determinants as fabric weight and stitches per inch are not among the information that the BLS can collect.

lets. Both apparel regressions contained dummy variables for outlet types. For coats and jackets, there was a 60 percentage point differential between prices charged for the same item by the outlet categories "full-service family" and "discount department."[5] Small wonder the outlet linking issue needs attention.

In Reinsdorf's paper, two kinds of calculations show that the outlet substitution bias for food and gasoline items appears to be large. It is at least 0.25 percent per year, and by some measures even higher. Clearly, some structural effect on price movements is afoot. But, before policymakers seize on these results (as they are trying to do in some areas of service-sector pricing) to claim that their policies to control inflation are more effective than they appear, the weaknesses of this research need to be cited. The author mentions these weaknesses as well. My comments are designed merely to alter the weights accorded them.

The first is that outlet substitution and item substitution occur simultaneously. That is, when a new outlet is initiated about six months before an old one is abandoned, a somewhat different item may be selected for pricing in the new outlet than in the old. That is permitted in the so-called entry-level-item (ELI) approach, one with which I do not disagree. But it would permit the pricing of a store label cereal in a new outlet as a substitute for a brand name cereal in an old one. Clearly, that kind of substitution could explain some of the author's findings that price indexes of directly compared outlets drift down vis-à-vis published indexes.

The second issue that needs more prominence in this paper is that of defining and measuring the "quality" associated with the services provided by different outlets.

We cannot examine the issues of substitution and quality, whether they refer to items or to outlets, without reference to the CPI concept. While the unifying framework for dealing with practical questions that arise in compiling the CPI is the cost-of-living index, the CPI is calculated using the Laspeyres formula. Thus, item and outlet substitution bias is something inherent in the CPI. Nonetheless, their quantitative effect needs to be monitored.

To do this for outlet substitution, the regression analysis approach of the first paper could be introduced into the second, permitting the determinants of outlet quality change to be understood and measured. Regression analysis could be used both to determine the adjustment that may be appropriate when outlets roll over and to shed light on the effect of switching to the ELI approach from the more narrowly defined specification formerly imposed on respondent outlets.

Fortunately, the data base for such research exists. It is the point-of-purchase survey (POPS), a survey to which I devoted considerable energy to obtaining funding for as part of the 1978 CPI revision program, precisely

5. The outlet differential range was 25 percentage points for suits.

because it seemed obvious that outlets could make a difference. Thus, regression work incorporating POPS data would strengthen research both on outlet substitution effects and on the quality adjustment of item prices. The results would also be useful when the BLS begins to compile industry-sector price indexes for the four-digit SIC industries in retailing.

IV   Transaction Prices

8 The Problem of List Prices in the Producer Price Index: The Steel Mill Products Case

Thomas Betsock and Irwin B. Gerduk

The failure of list prices to reflect the reality of transaction price movement in the steel industry, especially over the course of the business cycle, was a problem that had long been recognized by the Bureau of Labor Statistics (BLS). When the Bureau began to publish steel industry price indexes under its revision methodology for the producer price index (PPI) in July 1982, it hoped to overcome this well-known weakness as well as others, including the bias due to the reliance on "volume sellers." The introduction of the new indexes occurred in the closing months of the deep 1981–82 economic recession. However, the attempts by BLS to improve the type of steel price reported in the 1980s were largely unsuccessful. The problem of obtaining valid price indexes became acute as the domestic steel industry's output and employment crumbled over the period from 1982 to 1985 and discounting below list became intense. In January 1986, the major steel producers raised net transaction prices while substantially lowering list prices. The latter was reflected in a 4.2 percent decline in the index for PPIR (Producer Price Index Revision) Code 3312. These divergent movements were sufficiently severe to cause the credibility of the index to be questioned.

This paper is a case study of the problems encountered in obtaining transaction prices for the PPI. It seeks to provide some insight into the issues and problems encountered by statistical agencies. What makes this case study interesting is its apparent simplicity. The steel index problems were well known before BLS instituted its revision methodology. There were no theoretical measurement issues involved. This paper not only discusses the July 1982

Thomas Betsock and Irwin B. Gerduk are economists at the Bureau of Labor Statistics, U.S. Department of Labor.

Copyright is not claimed for this paper.

revision but also reviews the changes in price collection procedures made for the most recent sample of the steel industry, the results of which began publication in January 1990. The subsequent index movement provides definitive proof that the pricing problems have been fully resolved.

Section 8.1 summarizes PPI index methodology. Section 8.2 provides an overview of the issues involved in steel industry pricing. Section 8.3 deals with practical operating problems faced by BLS following the introduction of the 1982 sample. Section 8.4 describes the approach taken to resolve the pricing problem in the industry resampling completed in January 1990 and looks at the results obtained from the new sample.

8.1   Index Methodology

The PPI measures average changes in price received by domestic producers for their output in the following sectors of the economy: (1) agriculture; (2) fishing; (3) forestry; (4) mining; (5) manufacturing; and (6) gas and electric services. In addition, the PPI is expanding coverage into the transportation, communication, and services sectors. Imports are not within the scope of the PPI because the index is limited to the output of domestic industries.

There are three primary systems or structures of indexes within the PPI program: stage-of-processing indexes; indexes for the net output of industries and their products; and commodity indexes (U.S. Department of Labor 1988). The stage-of-processing structure organizes products by class of buyer and degree of fabrication. The entire output of various industries is sampled to derive price indexes for the net output of industries and their products. The commodity structure organizes products by similarity of end use or material composition.

The PPI is a modified Laspeyres index and is based on the fixed input-output price index (FIOPI) model (Archibald 1977). The assumptions of the model, which govern the conceptual design of the PPI, include perfect competition, fixed technology, profit maximization, and fixed quantity and type of inputs. In addition, the Laspeyres approximation to the FIOPI holds fixed output quantities at the base period levels. PPI procedures, however, allow for periodic reweighting to a new weight base. Currently, the index uses value of shipments data from the 1987 Census of Manufactures to weight the index.

The Laspeyres index is obtained by multiplying the current period and the base period prices of each item by the quantity of that item shipped in the base period:

$$I_c = \frac{\sum P_{ic}Q_{ib}}{\sum P_{ib}Q_{ib}} \times 100,$$

where Σ = the sum over all the items in the index, I_c = index in the current period, P_{ic} = current period price of the ith item, P_{ib} = base period price of the ith item, and Q_{ib} = base period quantity of the ith item.

Most data used to calculate the indexes are obtained through the systematic sampling of four-digit SIC industries. The PPI revision involved probability sampling of approximately five hundred industries in the mining and manufacturing sectors in the period 1978–85. Final publication of the completed revision occurred with the release of the January 1986 index. At roughly seven-year intervals, each industry will be sampled in an ongoing index maintenance program. By the summer of 1990, we were over two-thirds through our second cycle of probability sampling. BLS uses probability-proportionate-to-size (PPS) sampling techniques first to select sample units and second to select unique items within the unit for inclusion in the sample. Sample units are separate profit-maximizing centers engaged in one predominant economic activity. They consist of one or more operating establishments. Item selection involves selecting a unique product or other revenue-generating activity with unique terms of sale. An iterative PPS random selection technique based on sales revenue is used by BLS at this stage (U.S. Department of Labor 1986).

The price of the selected item should represent revenue received by the producer at the time of the sale in the base period and should reflect subsequent month-to-month movements. To achieve this, a continuous "price basis" must be established. This requires holding the physical characteristics of the product unchanged or adjusting for quality changes should they occur. In addition, all terms of transaction, such as the shipment size or type of buyer, must be specified and held unchanged in subsequent months. Any change in terms of transaction must be either adjusted for, if possible, or linked out of the price series. The latter procedure treats the price difference as a quality difference, and no change is shown in the index.

BLS strongly encourages cooperating companies to supply actual transaction prices at the time of shipment. Prices are normally reported monthly by mail questionnaire for the Tuesday of the week containing the 13th. Price data are always provided on a voluntary and confidential basis; no one but sworn BLS employees is allowed access to individual company price reports. The Bureau publishes price indexes instead of unit dollar prices. All producer price indexes are routinely subject to revision once, four months after original publication, to reflect the availability of late reports and corrections by respondents.

Weights used in the PPI come from two sources. Item weights are derived from the sample unit's value of shipments and are equal to

$$1/p \times 1/n \times \text{MHF} \times S,$$

where p = the reporting unit's probability of selection, n = the number of items for which BLS tried to obtain prices initially, MHF = multiple hit factor (when the same item is selected more than once),[1] and S = the reporting unit's value of shipments.

---

1. The "multiple hit factor" indicates the number of times a unique item is selected when the BLS agent visits the company and is given access to the company books.

Weights for cell indexes are derived from the Census of Manufactures. Item weights affect the calculation at the cell index level, that being the most detailed index level. The aggregation of many cell indexes to calculate a higher level index also utilizes weights from the Census.

8.2 Pricing Steel in the 1980s

In 1978, BLS undertook a fundamental revision of the PPI. Work in the iron and steel area (SIC codes 3312, 3315, 3316, and 3317) began in 1981 (the appendix lists the SIC structure, major product lines, and commodity groupings affected by this initiative). The specific goals for this sector were improved sampling techniques to select producers, products, and transactions and greater efforts to obtain actual transaction prices. The latter was a commitment to a greater effort to secure such prices rather than a change in methodology.

At the outset, the American Iron and Steel Institute (AISI), acting primarily on behalf of the larger steel companies, indicated that companies would be extremely hesitant to provide the necessary data needed for PPS sampling procedures. AISI and BLS agreed to retain Price Waterhouse to secure the desired information from most of the larger steel companies, who were generally members of AISI. BLS trained Price Waterhouse personnel in PPS sampling techniques, which Price Waterhouse used to obtain revenue data by product and to select the number of items within product lines for inclusion in the index. For the Price Waterhouse segment of the sample, BLS field office personnel were relegated to the role of collecting the detailed product specifications and terms of transaction for the preselected products. Data for the remainder of the industry, mainly the smaller companies, were collected entirely by BLS.

The major benefit of the new sampling was that a much broader array of steel items was selected for pricing; this would reduce the volume-seller bias found in the old index. However, at this stage, the prices obtained continued to be primarily book prices in the critical product areas of flat-rolled carbon steel. Flat-rolled carbon steel includes such products as hot-rolled carbon sheet, cold-rolled carbon sheet, galvanized sheet, carbon plate, strip, and tinplate. These products are made mainly by the large, integrated mills and account for nearly 40 percent of the weight of the overall steel index.

The question may be asked, Why did BLS accept the use of list prices in the steel industry index not only for the 1982 revision but also for earlier periods? Despite repeated requests for transaction prices, nearly all the major steel companies adamantly refused to provide anything but book prices. At the time of the 1981–82 revision, the major steel companies sold a much wider product range than they do now, and not to have had their price data would have produced serious gaps and rendered many PPI cells unpublishable. At that time, a strictly transaction price index would have been a reflection of price movement in only a few areas, such as concrete reinforcing bar, where transaction prices could readily be obtained by BLS.

The Bureau felt that it had to accept book prices if it was to meet user demands for a continually published steel index. While recognizing that an index based on book prices would fail to capture discounting in recession years, BLS thought that such an index would at least track the trend in prices over a long period of years.

There was some support for such reasoning from the Stigler-Kindahl study on industrial pricing, in which a supposedly transaction price index for steel was constructed in the years 1957–66. Comparing their index with the BLS index for finished steel products, Stigler-Kindahl found that "the BLS and the [Stigler-Kindahl] prices of steel products move together so closely that a description of one is a description of the other. . . . Neither index displays a noticeable cyclical movement in either expansion or contraction" (Federal Trade Commission 1977, 172).

But contrary evidence came from a 1977 Federal Trade Commission (FTC) report on the steel industry that concluded that "the BLS data are not reflective of post-1967 actual prices on a cyclical basis." The FTC report cited numerous trade journal articles about steel price discounting during business slumps. One study cited in the FTC report constructed an index, based on trade journal articles, of percentage discounts from list in 1973–75. For major mills, this study concluded that, while there was no discounting in all of 1974 and in the first quarter of 1975, large discounts appeared subsequently: a 12 percent average in the second quarter, 13 percent in the third quarter, and 5 percent in the fourth quarter (Federal Trade Commission 1977, 193).

On the basis of this report and our own reading of trade journal articles, it did not seem entirely unreasonable in 1981 to accept once more a list price index. If BLS was implicitly thinking in terms of a mild recession, a list price index, although inaccurate on a month-to-month basis during a steel slump and early recovery period, at least at some point in the expansion would get close to a correct transactions price level. In addition, there was no alternative if the Bureau was to publish. Steel discounting in 1981, when most of the work for the first revision was done, appeared from press reports to be in the 5–10 percent range. However, neither the Bureau nor forecasters generally anticipated the prolonged steel industry recession that was to occur and was to result in a distortion of BLS steel price measurement.

From January 1982 through 1986, record losses aggregating $11.7 billion were recorded by the steel industry. From 1982 through 1987, approximately 440 steel manufacturing and related facilities closed. Average annual employment declined from 390,000 to 175,000 during this period. Raw steel production fell from 121 million tons to 86 million tons.[2]

2. Income, employment shipments, and production data based on selected AISI annual statistical reports and Census reports.

In 1984, the Reagan administration adopted a policy of negotiating voluntary restraint agreements (VRAs) with countries whose exports to the United States had allegedly increased through subsidies, dumping, or other unfair trade practices. Import penetration had reached a record level by this date, accounting for nearly 27 percent of apparent steel consumption in 1984. Twenty countries negotiated VRAs with the United States. The program's goal of limiting imports to 20.2 percent of domestic consumption was not realized since other countries increased their shipments in this period. Imports were still 23.6 percent of consumption in 1986. Additionally, duties on many products were increased, and orderly marketing agreements were negotiated with seven countries.

To compete, U.S. integrated mills were forced to modernize or close obsolete facilities. For example, continuous cast steel, which was only 20 percent of raw steel in 1980, accounted for over 60 percent in 1988. Labor productivity improved by over 30 percent from 1980 to 1988. Foreign investment in U.S. steel operations, either through joint ventures or through outright purchase, funded much of the capital improvement. Perhaps the major structural change in the industry was the growth of the minimill sector, which wrested control of the hot-rolled bar, light structural, rebar, and wire rod markets from both the big domestic firms and import competition.

Again, it should be noted that the problem of unrepresentative book prices occurred chiefly in the carbon flat-rolled products area, which is dominated by the large, integrated producers. Certain areas of the index, such as merchant bar, rebar, light structurals, and most of the stainless steel indexes, were based heavily or entirely on net transaction prices. Nearly two-thirds of the price quotes collected in SIC 3312 for the first sample were for net transaction prices, but these carried less than half the index weight. The higher-level index was inaccurate chiefly because of the uncooperative price-reporting policies of the integrated mills.

According to a *Wall Street Journal* story in September 1985, the major producers, led by U.S. Steel Corporation, were preparing to revise book prices to be effective in January 1986 (Russell 1985). The adjustment was to be accomplished through a formula that both lowered the book price and significantly reduced discounts. Net transaction prices were thought to be as much as 30 percent below book prices by late 1985. Data presented in figure 8.1 strongly support this.

Figure 8.1 provides three different measures of steel prices. First is the price series published in the *American Metal Market's* annual statistical report, converted to index numbers to reflect book price movement for standard carbon steel products. Second is the PPI index for this group of products, which reflects a mixture of list and transaction prices but is heavily weighted toward list prices. Finally, we prepared an index for those steel items in the PPI based on actual transaction prices.

While this graph is only suggestive of the problem, it is clear that list price

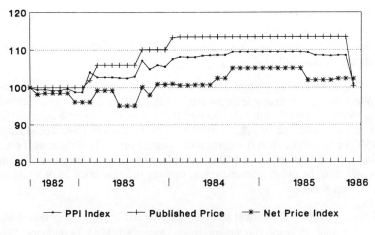

━•━ PPI Index   ─┼─ Published Price   ─✳─ Net Price Index

Published price, American Metal Market

Fig. 8.1   Three measures of price movement of hot-rolled carbon sheet: Published prices, PPI index, net prices

displayed a clear upward bias from mid-1982 to December 1985. The January 1986 list price adjustment appears to have reestablished the list/net transaction price relation that existed in June 1982. A note of caution is in order. The net price index reflects very few observations, and each price quote reflects one negotiated price transaction for the month.

While it was widely anticipated in the press that a downward realignment of list prices would occur in January 1986, it was also anticipated that U.S. Steel would simultaneously attempt to increase transaction prices (Larue 1985). Import prices were expected to increase because of the strength of the dollar in late 1985. Several major domestic producers felt that domestic transaction prices could be raised in tandem with import prices. Since price leadership was common in the industry, U.S. Steel was expected to raise its transaction prices, with some but not all major producers following in January. If this happened, the PPI steel index would be falling at a time when market prices were believed to be increasing. In fact, our steel mill index, SIC 3312, fell by 4.2 percent in January 1986.

8.3   Operational Issues and the 1986 Price Adjustment

As the January 1986 day of reckoning approached, it became clear that BLS had to resolve the issue of reflecting short-term index accuracy versus correcting the index level. This section will clarify the options available and illustrate why any solution was bound to be less than satisfactory.

Once there is an upward bias in the index, there can be no painless solution. Many of the integrated mills changed their pricing structures in January 1986 by lowering list prices. While list prices were lowered, however, market prices were actually rising as discounts were reduced. As reported by Mark Russell (1985) in the *Wall Street Journal,* an example of how U.S. Steel would adjust prices is as follows:

> U.S. Steel's pricing system would work in this way: Highest quality cold-rolled sheet, for example, now has a list price of $563 a ton. But with discounts a typical customer can buy that ton of steel for at least $100 less than list. Under the new U.S. Steel system, that ton of steel would list for $503 or $40 more than the current discounted price. To determine the new discount, the difference of $40 is multiplied by 40%, which yields $16; that is added to the old discounted price, making the new price $479 a ton, or a 3.5% increase.

There were two theoretical options open to BLS. The first option was to show the market price movement from December 1985 to January 1986, which was thought by industry experts to be an overall price increase. This would have provided short-term accuracy by reflecting the discount reductions that, according to press reports, occurred in January. But this option was unrealistic since we could not obtain net transaction prices. Indeed, BLS had made a second, and again unsuccessful, effort earlier in 1985 to persuade the major steel companies to report market prices. More important, while this option would have provided an accurate one-month measure of price change had we been able to obtain market prices, the January transaction price increases would have further elevated an already upwardly biased index level.

BLS decided instead that the better choice was to correct the index level by using the list prices reported in January 1986, which reflected very large list price reductions by the integrated mills, thereby reducing the upward bias caused by tracking book prices from July 1982 to December 1985. As a result, the steel mill product index (commodity code 1017) dropped from a level of 104.3 in December 1985 to 99.5 in January 1986. The index reflected a substantial one-month decline when, in fact, market prices were actually rising. Index level decreases were concentrated in those indexes covering sheet and plate.

8.4   The Recent Resampling of the Steel Industry

The primary goal for the current steel index, which began publication in January 1990, was to gather only net transaction prices. We decided not to accept book prices, despite the risk of not publishing certain indexes. Fortunately, the major steel companies were now generally willing to provide net transaction prices. The collection process, conducted by the two national office steel analysts and a small number of BLS field personnel, generated some interesting reactions from company personnel. In some cases, the same individuals who nine years before had insisted on providing book prices are now providing net transaction prices, freely conceding that only the latter can accurately reflect steel price movement. Companies have generally provided this price data with little hesitation. While in 1981–82 nearly every major steel company insisted on using book prices, the current sample has only one company that refused because of our insistence on net transaction prices.

It is difficult to account for the turnaround in the steel industry's willingness to provide transaction prices. Possibly, after years of seeking trade protection and other government assistance, the industry has a greater respect for good economic data. Possibly, various refinements in BLS collection techniques helped. Data collection for this sample was handled by a smaller staff, which was generally better informed of steel pricing problems than was the case in 1981–82. The use of average prices lagged one month helped, although this option existed for the 1981–82 sample and was insufficient to gain cooperation. Certainly, much of our success with the current sample is due to the improvement in automated record-keeping systems at most of the companies. Several reporters told us that records of net transaction prices were not available, at least not on a timely basis, in 1982.

The use of lagged average prices is a necessary compromise if we are to obtain net transaction prices from the major mills. As noted in section 8.1, BLS generally prices specific transactions as of the specific pricing date and asks that these prices be returned for processing within two weeks. The major steel mills, most of which were generally being asked to price a large number of items, simply could not work that quickly, forcing us to accept a one-month lag in their prices.

We found that the most obtainable price was an average price. Many company marketing departments, through which we generally collect prices, often produce average net transaction price reports for specific products. Companies liked the average pricing option since it required no additional formatting of price records and avoided revealing any buyer-specific details. BLS finds average pricing acceptable since each reported price generally reflects scores or even hundreds of transactions of a unique item and reflects all discounts and surcharges applied to that transaction. The drawback to average pricing is that it may involve a mix of types of buyers. But, on the basis of our early meetings with the companies, we believe that the buyer mix for specific products is fairly constant, at least over the length of time a particular sample is asked to supply data.

The results of the current revision have been good. Of the eighty-two companies in the SIC 3312 sample, sixty-nine are providing us with price data. Six companies refused to cooperate at the outset, half as many as in the 1982 sample. Two companies have since requested to leave the program. The remaining sample units that are not supplying prices are the result of closings, mergers, or misclassifications.

Two-thirds of the carbon sheet producers, representing over two-thirds of the index weight for this sector, are providing us with net transaction price data. One producer of carbon sheet would provide us only with list prices and so was excluded from the program. Two other carbon sheet producers initially agreed to cooperate but then decided that they had insufficient staff to assemble the data.

Cooperation by specialty steel mills and minimills remains good, with over 90 percent of these sectors' respective index weights represented in the index. All are providing net transaction prices.

Figure 8.2 tracks the annual movement of SIC code 3312311 (hot-rolled carbon sheet) since the June 1982 base date. The index plainly shows the artificial increase caused by list prices from 1982 to 1985, the downward adjustment of January 1986, the subsequent increase in list prices that occurred in the 1987–89 steel recovery, and the decrease in steel transaction prices that began in late 1989 and has continued with only slight interruptions into the spring of 1992.

The 1990s may have ushered in a new era in steel price reporting. Figure 8.3 shows the monthly movement of the BLS index for hot-rolled carbon sheet since December 1989 and the contrasting movement of book prices. The book prices are not now being reported to BLS but are taken from *American Metal Market,* a trade source. They represent a nonsystematic sampling of those major producers presumed to be price leaders by the press. In the latter part of the 1980s, most of the large producers of sheet steel were still reporting book prices to BLS. In December 1989, the book price for hot-rolled carbon sheet was $445 per ton. Three subsequent increases in book prices—in January 1990, January 1991, and October 1991—brought the book price to $495. In the meantime, however, the transactions prices, which were being reported to BLS, were showing a general downward drift. In October 1991,

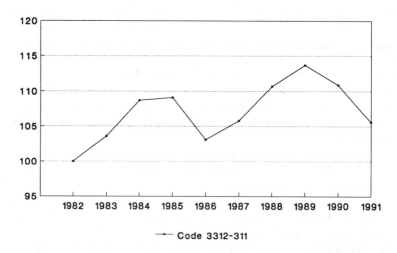

Fig. 8.2   Index of hot-rolled carbon sheet prices, annual average, 1982–91

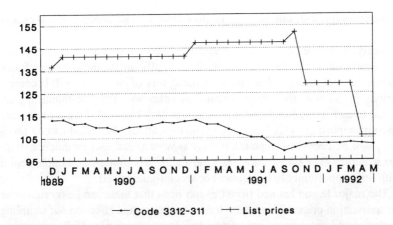

Fig. 8.3   List and transaction prices, hot-rolled carbon sheet, December 1989–May 1992

they were some 12 percent below their December 1989 level, a sharp contrast with the 10 percent rise shown by book prices over the same period.

In November 1991, two of the major mills lowered their book price to $345 per ton, a reduction that was repeated by the remaining integrated steel companies in April 1992. Transaction prices rose a little in the fall of 1991 but were little changed in the first five months of 1992. The levels of the two indexes in the spring of 1992 were quite close, but the change in the nature of reporting by steel producers spared BLS a repetition of the January 1986 experience.

Most of our other indexes for flat-rolled carbon steel—hot-rolled strip, cold-rolled sheet and strip, hot-dipped galvanized sheet, and plate—show similar downward movements for the past two years. Electrogalvanized sheet prices have also fallen, although this decline has been somewhat moderated by the greater prevalence of contract pricing. Tinplate, which is sold to the relatively stable can stock market, has maintained its price level.

8.5   Conclusion

The analysis presented in this paper shows that list prices are unsuitable for use as proxies for net transaction prices for measuring month-to-month price change in the steel industry and are of questionable value for measuring long-term price movement. Figure 8.1 shows a consistent upward bias in list prices, which eventually forced a steep adjustment. The case study shows that users cannot have confidence in a price-reporting system characterized by dramatic adjustments to list prices to correct for a large multiyear unidirectional bias. Since the mission of a statistical agency is to provide comprehensive index coverage with suitable quality, the use of net transaction prices is clearly needed.

Analysis of index behavior subsequent to the resampling of the steel industry completed in 1990 shows that we have finally turned the corner on index quality in steel pricing. Whether a changing mix of customers will become a serious problem in the future remains an unknown. The one-month lag referred to earlier appears to have been a necessary trade-off if we are to secure discount reporting. This lag, which primarily affects flat-rolled carbon products, will be deemed acceptable if there is widespread user confidence in index accuracy. The statistical agency must choose a strategy and implement it with little opportunity to experiment or second-guess itself.

The major lesson learned from this has been that there can be no substitute for transaction prices. This lesson has had a substantial effect on our sampling strategies and procedures, reflecting a heightened awareness of the unsuitability of accepting list prices for the index. This is having a significant effect in the PPI's initiative in obtaining prices in the service sector.

Appendix

SIC Structure

3312: Blast furnaces and steel mills
    33121: Coke oven and blast furnace products
    33122: Steel ingots and semifinished shapes and forms
    33123: Tin mill products, hot-rolled sheet and strip
    33124: Hot-rolled bars, plates, and structural forms
    33125: Steel wire
    33126: Steel pipe and tubes
    33127: Cold-rolled sheet and strip
    33128: Cold-finished bar
3315: Steel wire
3316: Cold-rolled sheet, strip, and bars
3317: Steel pipe and tubes

SIC's 3315, 3316, and 3317 differ from 3312 in that they involve production of goods from purchased material. (The industry definitions derive from the 1987 SIC manual put out by the Office of Management and Budget. The four-digit industries are further defined into five-, seven-, and sometimes nine-digit categories on the basis of Census of Manufactures data.)

Commodity Index

1017: Steel mill products

Code 1017 encompasses SIC codes 3312, 3315, 3316, and 3317. For example, production of cold-rolled carbon sheet would fall under commodity code 101707 and also under either 33127, if the company both melted and rolled the metal, or 33167, if the company rolled sheet from purchased slab.

References

Archibald, Robert. 1977. On the theory of industrial price measurement: Output price indexes. *Annals of Economic and Social Measurement* 6 (Winter): 57–72.

Federal Trade Commission. 1977. *Staff report on the United States steel industry and its international rivals: Trends and factors determining international competitiveness.* Washington, D.C., November.

Larue, Gloria T. 1985. Analysts assess steel pricing. *American Metal Market,* 6 December.

Russell, Mark. 1985. Steel concerns study U.S. steel move on pricing. *Wall Street Journal,* 23 September.

U.S. Department of Labor. 1986. *Producer price measurement—concepts and methods.* Washington, D.C.: Bureau of Labor Statistics, June.

———. 1988. *The Bureau of Labor Statistics handbook of methods.* Bulletin no. 2285. Washington, D.C., April.

9 Does Government Regulation Inhibit the Reporting of Transactions Prices by Business?

Murray F. Foss

Sometime in the mid-1980s, the Bureau of Labor Statistics (BLS) completed a major overhaul of the producer price index (PPI). The Bureau made several important improvements in the PPI, notably the introduction of probability sampling, and broadened coverage not merely in terms of industries but also in terms of types of sellers and transactions. It promised greater efforts at enlisting cooperation from businesses so that the index would reflect transactions (shipments) prices rather than list prices. A big problem for which BLS made no promises was the quality problem—in the sense of changing commodity characteristics—because it recognized that much more research was needed. Quality was the one remaining major issue for which a ready solution was still not at hand.

What got me started on this particular paper—the behavior of steel prices in the first half of the 1980s—suggested that quality was not the only big problem still outstanding. I had read newspaper reports that, under the depressed market conditions in the steel industry, particularly from 1982 to 1985, market prices for steel were well below list prices. I was curious to see how the newly revamped PPI was reflecting this weakness in demand.[1] To my surprise, the PPI for steel showed relatively little response, as I indicate further on. I say "surprise" because I thought that the Bureau's efforts to obtain

Murray F. Foss is a visiting scholar at the American Enterprise Institute.

The author is indebted to many individuals for help with this paper: from the Bureau of Labor Statistics, William Alterman, Curtis Jacobs, Marvin Kasper, Richard Pratt, Elliott Rosenberg, Al Schwenk, Thomas Tibbetts, Allen Tupek, and Jeannette Van Belleghem; from the Bureau of the Census, Allan Meyer, Paula Muroff, Ron Piencykoski, and Charles Waite; from the Office of Management and Budget, Jerry Coffey; from the Federal Trade Commission, Terry Calvani and Michael Sibarium; and also Marvin Kosters, James C. Miller, Milton Moss, and Marius Schwartz. Robert M. Klein of the American Bar Association was very helpful, as were a number of other attorneys. The author alone is responsible for errors and other shortcomings of this paper.

1. The index for steel mill products was revamped in July 1982.

transactions prices, if not eradicating this problem, had greatly diminished its importance. I believe now that BLS was overly sanguine in its expectations regarding the transactions–list price problem; indeed, I think that this old problem is still very much with us, although improvements have occurred and some major changes in the reporting of steel prices were introduced in 1990.

The reason that this problem does not go away has to do with the sensitive nature of much price information, particularly as it is affected by law and regulations. I believe that the existence of the Robinson-Patman Act, a law directed against price discrimination that has been on the books for more than half a century, is a significant impediment to the reporting of transactions prices by business. I must emphasize that I cannot prove this point. Stigler and Kindahl mentioned the Robinson-Patman problem about twenty years ago, but no one seems to have pursued it. I can only suggest its importance by providing some figures on survey response rates, discussing the Robinson-Patman Act and business response to it, and discussing how a rational businessman might react to government requests for price data.

I believe that, even in the last decade of the twentieth century, we still do not measure prices well at the producer level. This is an old story that many have written about. Much is at stake, in terms of both theory and measurement. The apparent rigidity of prices and wages is at the heart of the controversy in macroeconomics that has been going on for some two decades and perhaps half a century.

Through most of the period that has seen the rise and partial eclipse of the Keynesian macroeconomic system, there has been a series of empirical studies demonstrating the rigidity of prices in recessions and attempting to explain it by concentration, industrial structure, and the like. Keynesians have tended to be more accepting of the facts of rigid prices and the explanations of them. In contrast, the newer rational expectations macroeconomists have been somewhat more skeptical of the facts of rigid prices, often raising many questions about the validity of the data in support of rigidity.

The past ten years have seen the emergence of new theories that reject the new macroeconomics and attempt to solve the Keynesian dilemma. The late Arthur Okun and others developed theories that accept price rigidity as a normal aspect of the relations between buyers and sellers (Okun 1981). Wage and price stickiness is at the core of what has been called the "new Keynesian" economics (Gordon 1990). In addition, recent empirical work by Dennis Carlton (1986) based on prices paid by individual buyers (from the Stigler-Kindahl [1970] study) finds a great deal of rigidity in prices, especially where there is a long-term relationship between buyer and seller. He raises the question of whether economists have been right in believing that prices and prices alone serve as allocators of resources. In a more recent article, Carlton suggests that nonprice methods as well as prices are used to allocate goods (Carlton 1989, 943).

The issue involves more than cyclical movements in prices. Inadequacies in our producer price measurements may also give a distorted view of the long-run movement of prices. If, because of Robinson-Patman, businesses are uncertain about the legality of the price cutting that they may employ to establish themselves in new markets or to improve market shares, they may be chary about reporting to BLS, or the prices they do report may not be accurate reflections of true transaction prices. Thus, the prices that are reported may have an upward bias.

This paper is organized as follows. First I give a brief historical review of the criticisms of the PPI (formerly the wholesale price index [WPI]), focusing on the list–transactions price problem. The big 1979–86 revamping of the PPI was a major undertaking. The expansion in sample size and the shift to probability sampling for four-digit industries were important responses to many of the earlier criticisms. However, the best sample design can be frustrated if companies refuse to cooperate or, when they do, if they fail to submit the desired transactions prices. In the second section, I provide some information on cooperation or what I refer to as *response rates*. Measured by the number of companies who submit price reports to the BLS, the nonresponse to the PPI appears to be substantial. In this section, I provide no information about the nature of the price quotations that companies do report, that is, whether they are true transactions prices. In the third section, I hypothesize that the Robinson-Patman Act may be a significant influence affecting the nature of the price information that BLS obtains from business. After a brief review of this law and criticisms of it, I speculate about how its existence may affect both the willingness of firms to cooperate in the BLS price program and the nature of the prices they do submit.

I am aware that government agencies are at a serious disadvantage when they conduct voluntary surveys that are affected by or impinge on government laws and regulations. The agencies see discussion of such matters as exceedingly delicate, if not impossible. At the very least, outside economists should recognize and discuss such problems. In section 9.4, I offer a few suggestions that take some account of the U.S. regulatory environment. I believe that BLS is not following optimal policies for obtaining information about price behavior in producer markets. Where response is not good, BLS should be willing to accept a different kind of price reporting, which might elicit better cooperation in terms of numbers of firms and a closer approximation of transactions prices.

9.1   The Bureau of Labor Statistics and Its PPI Critics

The Bureau of Labor Statistics has been aware of the problem of accurate price measurement from the very beginning. John Flueck (1961, 419–20) quotes Wesley C. Mitchell from a 1915 BLS bulletin (no. 173, *Index Numbers of Wholesale Prices in the U.S. and Foreign Countries*) that goes to the heart of the matter:

[The] reliability of an index number obviously depends upon the judgement and accuracy with which the original price quotations were collected. This field work is not only fundamental, it is also laborious, expensive, and perplexing beyond any other part of the whole investigation. Only those who have tried to gather from the original sources quotations for many commodities over a long series of years appreciate the difficulties besetting the task. . . . To judge from the literature about index numbers, one would think that the difficult and important problems concern methods of weighing and averaging. But those who are practically concerned with the whole process of making an index number from start to finish rate this office work lightly in comparison with the field work of getting the original data.

During the 1930s, the validity of price quotations became a prominent issue after Gardner Means published his famous study on price inflexibility based on BLS wholesale prices (Means 1935). In the hearings of the Temporary National Economic Committee, rigid prices were drawn into the debate over the causes of the 1937–38 recession, one side maintaining that rigid prices, especially in industries such as steel—as demonstrated in the Means study— were responsible for either the downturn in aggregate economic activity or the slow recovery after mid-1938, or both (U.S. Temporary National Economic Committee 1939–40). Questions, however, were raised about the quality of the BLS wholesale price statistics that Means had used as the basis of his analysis. In 1939, Saul Nelson made a study showing that BLS was failing to capture various discounts and secret price concessions made by sellers (Stigler and Kindahl 1970). The basis for some further questions came from a study of steel prices conducted by BLS for the Office of Price Administration (OPA). Among other things, the OPA study, based on purchasers' prices, showed much more price cutting in 1939 and 1940 than was evident in the WPI (Stigler and Kindahl 1970, 17–18).

The first comprehensive critique of the WPI after World War II was the Stigler Report of 1961 (National Bureau of Economic Research 1961). The report cited "several types of evidence suggest[ing] very strongly that the price quotations obtained from manufacturers do not faithfully measure the movements of prices, quite aside from the usual problems of quality change" (p. 69). Part of the evidence had to do with the frequent reliance of the WPI on a single price report; another part was a comparison of the WPI with prices paid by government units, showing that WPI prices were higher and more rigid than average bid prices on government contracts. In their 1970 study based on prices supplied by buyers, Stigler and Kindahl found no evidence to suggest that price rigidity or "administration" of prices was a significant phenomenon (Stigler and Kindahl 1970, 9).

The 1970s also witnessed a number of government reports that pointed in the same direction, namely, that BLS was not reflecting actual transaction prices. The most prominent of these was the study by Ruggles (COWPS 1977); earlier, a presidential commission had criticized the WPI for not reflecting transactions prices (Report of the President's Commission 1971). It was late in the 1970s that BLS announced a major long-range overhaul of the PPI, which would move to probability sampling, increase coverage, greatly extend the range of transactions covered by the PPI, and put special emphasis on obtaining transaction prices.

Successive editions of the *BLS Handbook of Methods* demonstrate BLS's continuing interest in obtaining actual transactions prices. Thus, in 1976:

> The Bureau attempts to base the WPI on actual transaction prices. Companies are requested to report prices less all discounts, allowances, rebates, free deals, etc., so that the resulting net price is the actual selling price of the commodity for the specified basis of quotation. The Bureau periodically emphasizes to reporters the need to take into account all discounts and allowances. However, list or book prices are used if transaction prices are unobtainable. (U.S. Department of Labor 1976, 110)

This was essentially repeated in 1982, midway through the revision program, with the Bureau emphasizing in addition that "rebates and other forms of price concessions granted by producers to their distributors . . . are reflected as decreases in the PPI. . . . Conversely, terminations in rebate programs are considered price increases" (U.S. Department of Labor 1982, 44).

According to the Bureau, list prices were used for only about 20 percent of traditional PPIs (U.S. Department of Labor 1982, 44). I believe that the 20 percent figure was probably the lower end of a range whose higher end was not known. Support for this skepticism comes from Richard Ruggles, who, in his study for COWPS, took a one-in-fourteen sample of wholesale price observations as of March 1975, for which he was able to obtain the source of the price quotations (COWPS 1977, 120):

	N	%
List price	116	18
List price minus discounts	421	67
Average realized unit price	56	9
Unknown	36	6
Total	629	100

Ruggles noted that the forms filled out by price reporters "often show relatively few changes in discounts." He thought it reasonable to assume that the discounts that firms do report to the BLS were "the more regularized and standardized discounts which apply to all purchasers," for example, cash or trade discounts. He went on to say that, even with a fixed discount structure, over the business cycle firms could change prices by altering the classification of customers and thus their eligibility for discounts. He concluded that list prices adjusted for discounts "may not reflect the actual changes in transaction prices." He stated further, "There is of course no way of determining from the questionnaires whether the producers are reporting all of the discounts which they actually give to their customers" (COWPS 1977, I-18).

The 20 percent figure for list prices cited by BLS in 1982 is repeated in its 1988 *Handbook* (U.S. Department of Labor 1988, 126):

> The use of list prices in the industrial price program has been the exception, not the rule. Even before the conversion on the methodology of the Producers Price Index Revision (PPIR), a BLS survey showed that only about 20 percent of traditional commodity indexes were based on list prices. Inasmuch as the PPIR methodology is more systematic than the traditional methodology in concentrating on actual transaction prices, the use of list prices is even less frequent now.

In the *Handbook*'s latest revision, BLS takes note of the list price problem, promising to devote more time and resources to it, but refrains from discussing why firms may be unwilling to report transactions prices. Thus, in an April 1978 article, John Early states: "One of the continuing concerns of the Producer Price Program has been to obtain real transaction prices rather than list prices at which no sales occur. While the program has had substantial success in this effort the revision will expand and intensify it. It should be realized that in some industries the list price and the transaction price are the same" (Early 1978, 18).

But that is all. The following year, in an article reporting the results of a pilot survey testing the new PPI procedures, Early emphasized the need for good cooperation from business:

> One critical factor in both surveys is the cooperation received from American companies, because they are the only possible source for the required information. Most companies have been highly cooperative in both the present and revision programs. They generally realize the important role that accurate price statistics play in fiscal and monetary policy decisions, which in turn are major determinants of the Nation's economic health and the performance of individual companies. Many companies also use the data extensively in their own market and economic research activities, and more and more companies are using the data to escalate prices in long-term contracts for items they sell or buy.

He presented response rates for four pilot industries and noted that, in some industries, response was "low enough to suggest the need for special attention." He noted further that intensive reviews were "being conducted to determine both the causes and effects of high refusal rates in some industries" (Early 1979, 19).

What motivated me to write this paper, as I mentioned earlier, was the behavior of steel prices in the early 1980s. I had been interested to read in the *Wall Street Journal* of 23 September 1985 that discounting from list prices for steel mill shapes and forms was very severe because of weak demand (see

Russell 1985). In one sense, this was scarcely news because the domestic industry had experienced a steep decline in production and employment early in the decade and had experienced only a weak recovery as the overall economy expanded. It was around this time that one began to read about the "Rust Belt" and near-depression conditions in steel mill towns. The same 1985 *Wall Street Journal* article quoted a very large producer as saying that the actual selling price of a ton of sheet steel "equals the level of 5 years ago."

One would have thought that the BLS steel price index, reflecting a new sample and new procedures instituted in July 1982 under the PPI revision, would provide evidence of the substantial price reductions that had taken place. But, as of August 1985, the PPI for cold-rolled carbon sheets was 26.8 percent *above* its level of April 1980. In fact, the entire iron and steel index showed scarcely any response to the true demand conditions in the industry. The decline in the BLS iron and steel price index from the July 1981 business cycle peak to the November 1982 trough was 1 percent, or about average (median) for nine recessions from 1937 to 1982 (excluding the end of World War II). These issues are discussed in some detail in Betsock and Gerduk (chap. 8 in this volume).

Is it possible that the steel industry is not unique and that, despite the steps that BLS has taken to improve the quality of reporting, it is still not obtaining transactions prices from producers in several other industries? In his study for the Stigler Report, John A. Flueck compared BLS prices with prices bid on government contracts for a wide variety of commodities. He found that BLS series changed less frequently than the government series and that, in the short run, the BLS series changed by smaller magnitudes than did the government series. Flueck's data included such commodities as aluminum sheet and ingot, steel sheet and plate, brass bar, plywood, gummed tape, auto tubes, storage batteries, linoleum, plate glass, enamel, and several chemicals (Flueck 1961, 427). The Stigler and Kindahl study covered a fairly broad array of industrial products, concentrating on those typically viewed as having administered prices (Stigler and Kindahl 1970, 5).

9.2   Obtaining Transactions Prices

Long years of experience with a voluntary survey had demonstrated to BLS that obtaining actual prices was no simple matter. Very briefly, what is needed is a proper sample design, a willingness of sampled firms to participate in the survey on an ongoing basis, and a willingness of firms to submit the information that BLS desires.[2] This paper does not consider sampling problems as such, although its thrust is concerned with potential bias insofar as some "cooperating" firms do not report actual transactions prices while others do not

---

2. For recent descriptions of current methodology, see U.S. Department of Labor (1988, 125–43) and U.S. Department of Labor (1986).

participate at all. Obviously, it would be highly desirable if I could present information that evaluated the validity of the price quotations reported to BLS, but I have no such information except for what I have alluded to in the steel industry. What I do have is some information on response rates.

9.2.1   Response Rates

Response rate can be defined in many different ways. As used here, *response rate* refers to the willingness of firms to submit to the BLS or Census Bureau what are purported to be the desired statistics—relative to potential respondents. For purposes of comparison, the only meaningful response rate in a sample survey must be a rate that is based on a probability sample and that is now possible as a result of the improvements that BLS made in its revamped PPI.[3] This section compares response rates in some large-scale, probability-based surveys of business firms conducted by BLS and the Census Bureau. All are voluntary, and most are conducted monthly or quarterly.

The focus on business as distinct from households or governments is important because the PPI is directed at business. Large-scale surveys are preferable to those directed to a particular (say, four-digit) industry because the PPI covers primarily all detailed manufacturing and mining industries. Since the PPI is a monthly survey, comparisons should be made with other surveys conducted periodically within the year—monthly or quarterly. Finally, since the PPI is voluntary, it should not be compared with mandatory surveys, even though the Office of Management and Budget (OMB) concluded, on the basis of some broad findings, that response rates to voluntary and mandatory surveys do not seem to be different (Coffey 1987).

9.2.2   Producer Price Index

BLS collects its price data by means of two surveys: an "initiation" survey and a "repricing" survey (BLS terminology). The former is a one-time informational survey in which the field agent, if permitted by the firm, examines the company books and follows a sampling procedure to select the items to be priced, including the host of details that define each "price." The repricing survey is the monthly mail survey in which the firm reports prices for the monthly PPI. The Bureau draws a probability sample of establishments in a given four-digit industry from a comprehensive file of establishments reporting under the unemployment compensation program. By the time they are contacted, some firms are out of business, and others turn out to be engaged in an industry or activity different from their designated classification. Some

---

3. Before the 1975–85 revision, the response rate to the producer price survey was said to be very high—in the neighborhood of 95 percent. But that result was not based on a probability sample that made a proper accounting of cooperators and noncooperators. In seeking participants for its price survey, BLS made a practice of contacting firms until it encountered a cooperator; the large number of firms that refused BLS when first approached did not enter BLS's calculation of the response rate. Consequently, the prerevision response rates were of very limited value.

up-to-date results on response rates at initial contact are presented in table 9.1. These are based on what BLS refers to as Cycle B, which represents a resampling of every SIC being used for the PPI.[4] This particular cycle, which lasted several years, was completed in 1992 and covered all of manufacturing and mining and a few other industries.

At the time of the initial visit, the BLS agent explains the price collection program, its importance, and the confidentiality of individual reports.[5] After the agent has examined company records for the purpose of sampling transactions, the company is asked to supply from two to sixteen items—price quotations—ordinarily on a monthly basis. Within the past year or so, small firms were requested to remain in the program for five years; previously, there was no time limit. The largest firms, which are chosen "with certainty," are expected to remain in the sample continuously.

In table 9.1, productive firms (establishments) are properly classified firms still in business that supplied the agent with all items requested by the agent plus those firms supplying *some* of the items requested. Where the firm agreed to supply only some of the requested prices, it was treated as a partial cooperator.

At this stage, the response rate ranges from 83.5 percent (weighted by sales) to 82.3 percent (unweighted). The difference in favor of larger firms, however, is not very striking.

Table 9.2 provides data on "repricing" (pricing) for December 1989. The first 5 rows come from actual BLS tabulations made available to me. The data refer to price quotations and not firms.

Row 1 shows the number of price quotations for which respondents in the initiation survey said they would report. It is the equivalent of the number of potential cooperators as determined in the initiation survey times an average that falls between two and sixteen.

Row 2 represents items "permanently discontinued." It includes known business deaths, cases in which the respondent ceased selling the item permanently and for which a substitute could not be found, and firms who agreed to report but never did or who, in the past, reported at least once but for reasons of their own no longer submit reports. BLS employs a more or less fixed procedure for dropping quotations. If a quotation is missing with no apparent explanation for two months, the firm is contacted by phone. Another call is made at the end of six months. If there is still no answer at the end of nine months, the quotation is assigned to the "permanently discontinued" category, but each analyst makes his own decision about such cases.

Row 3 represents items for which prices were submitted but that BLS rejected for some reason.

4. Under the PPI revision, Cycle A ran from January 1979 to January 1986 for manufacturing and mining industries.
5. This is explained in U.S. Department of Labor (1988, 128).

Table 9.1   Producer Price Index Survey: Response at Initiation

| | | Establishments (%) | |
		Weighted	Unweighted
1. Productive		71	65
2. Refusals		14	14
3. Out of business		7	11
4. Out of scope		4	6
5. Misclassified		3	4
Response rate ([row 1]/[rows 1 + 2])		83.5	82.3

Source: Bureau of Labor Statistics, unpublished data. See the text.

Table 9.2   Producer Price Index: Response in Repricing, December 1989

1. Items potentially in PPI from initiation survey	90,591
2. Less "permanently discontinued"	21,154
3. Less "repriceable" items not used by BLS	1,622
4. Equals items potentially available for PPI	67,815
5. Actual number of items received for preliminary December 1989 PPI	48,452
6. Estimated late reports (3 percent of row 5)	1,454
7. Seasonal items and "off-cycle" items (9.5 percent of rows 3 plus 4)	6,596
8. Estimated items not being reported for repricing ([row 4] − [rows 5 + 6 + 7])	11,313

Estimated Refusal Rate:

$$[(.786)(\text{row } 2) + (.5)(\text{row } 8)]/[(\text{row } 1) - (.214)(\text{row } 2)] = .259$$

Response Rate = .741

Source: See the text.

Row 4 is row 1 less rows 2 and 3. It is the potential number of items that—if reported—would be used for the preliminary PPI that month.

Row 5 is the actual number of items used by BLS in the preliminary December 1989 index. It is considerably less than either row 4 or row 1, but important qualifications should be noted in rows 6 and 7.

Row 6 makes an allowance for late reports. This figure (3 percent of row 4) is the upper end of a "2–3 percent" suggested by Richard Pratt of the Statistical Methods Division, Office of Prices and Living Standards, BLS.

Row 7 is an allowance for seasonal items and those reporting for less than twelve months. At the time of the initiation survey, the cooperating firm informs the BLS field agent of seasonal patterns in which no prices may be reported in particular months or other patterns involving fewer than twelve monthly prices per year. A firm that sells an item every month of the year but is willing to supply data for only one month in each calendar quarter is treated as though it made sales in only four months of the year. The figures for the adjustment in row 7 come from BLS tabulations.

Row 8 is a residual, equal to row 4 less rows 5, 6, and 7. It consists of two main parts, a breakdown of which is not known by BLS. One part represents items with irregular monthly pricing. That is, at the time of the initiation survey, the firm informs BLS that it does not sell in every month of a year but that it cannot specify which months will be blank. BLS sends this firm a normal schedule that calls for twelve monthly reports, but, obviously, the absence of a report from such a firm is not necessarily a sign of noncooperation. The other part, however, represents firms that are dropping out without having informed BLS and that would in time (say, nine months) be assigned by BLS to the "permanently discontinued" group.

To get a nonresponse rate on repricing, it is necessary to combine appropriate components of rows 2 and 8 divided by an appropriate total.

For row 2, Richard Pratt has estimated that 78.6 percent represents refusals. This is what remains after estimating that business deaths are 5 percent of row 1, a figure based on the attrition experience of these establishments. For row 8, I arbitrarily decided that half this row represented refusals. The denominator reflects row 1 minus business deaths. This yields a nonresponse rate of .259 (22,283/86,064) or a response rate of .741. These are unweighted. An OMB response survey conducted in 1983–84 suggested that 2 percentage points should be added to the unweighted figures, which would yield a rate of .761. This times the .835 response at initiation yields a combined rate of .635 on a weighted basis. Note that this is seasonally adjusted after a fashion and says nothing about the validity of the price quotations submitted by the respondent.

9.2.3 International Price Program

The BLS international price program is somewhat similar to the PPI; a subsample of the quarterly sample is now being used for monthly prices. The quarterly survey employs a probability sample with five to six thousand importers and an equal number of exporters covering some thirty thousand products; about fifteen hundred firms are added to each program yearly. The program is now open ended, but BLS hopes to put the sampling on a four-year cycle. Response rates at initiation are similar to those of PPI: 79 percent for importers and 82 percent for exporters. The figures are about the same whether weighted or unweighted.

Table 9.3 shows a few figures on repricing (pricing) for the fourth quarter of 1989. The 5 percent slippage figure in row 7 reflects the fact that about 5 percent of those who appeared to agree to cooperate at the initiation survey in fact drop out and are not included in the mailing figure in row 1. The combined response rate of 67 percent for both exports and imports is possibly a little better than the rate for the PPI.

9.2.4 Employment Cost Index

The employment cost index is a quarterly survey based on a probability sample of private firms and government. In the private sector, more than four thousand establishments report wage and benefit costs per hour or other unit

Table 9.3   Export and Import Prices: Response Rates

	Exports	Imports
Response at initiation (recent experience)	.82	.79
Response on repricing, 4th quarter 1989		
1. Mailing	10,160	12,923
2. Less known business deaths	220	461
3. Equals potential prices available for index	9,940	12,462
4. Actual returns	8,600	11,070
5. (No transactions in 4th quarter)	980[a]	2,300[a]
6. Response at repricing ([row 4]/[row 3])	.865	.888
7. Adjusted for 5 percent slippage	.822	.844
8. Combined response ([row 7] × response at initiation)	.674	.667

Source: Bureau of Labor Statistics, unpublished data.
[a]Included in row 4.

of time. Once chosen, firms are requested to remain in the sample for four years, but, in the December 1987 survey of response rates referred to in table 9.4, the average age of the sample is two and a half years. The response rate is 69.7 percent for all manufacturing. These figures refer to the reporting of wages; about 95 percent of firms reporting wages will also report benefits. The response figures may be slightly higher because the refusal rate includes some late reporters. According to BLS, weighting would make little difference.

BLS conducts an annual occupational-employment survey. For 1986, the response rate that is comparable to the "good data" total in the employment cost survey is 79.5 percent for all manufacturing, with only small variations among the twenty two-digit manufacturing industries. The overall weighted figure is within 1 percent of the unweighted.

9.2.5 Census Surveys

From the Census Bureau, we have three voluntary surveys based on probability samples: retail sales, wholesale sales, and the value of private nonresidential construction put in place.[6] Although the trade examples refer to a single month, they are representative of recent experience in the opinion of Census Bureau specialists. Results appear in tables 9.5–9.7.

Table 9.8 summarizes the results of the response surveys just described. About all that I would venture to say at this stage is that the response rate for the PPI looks low relative to the Census sales surveys and somewhat low relative to the others. The Census Bureau's survey of wholesale trade is perhaps the closest to the PPI in terms of the kinds of companies covered; its response rate is much higher than that of the PPI. It is difficult to draw inferences about

6. The Census Bureau's Monthly Industry Survey, covering shipments, inventories, and orders received by manufacturers, is not a probability sample.

Table 9.4   **Employment Cost Survey: Response Rate, December 1987**

	All Private Industries		Manufacturing	
	N	%	N	%
Original sample of establishments	5,940		944	
Less out of business	746		135	
Less out of scope	318		41	
Less no job match	135		18	
Equals eligible establishments	4,741	100.0	750	100.0
Good data	3,417	72.1	523	69.7
Refusals	1,324	27.9	227	30.3

Source: Bureau of Labor Statistics, unpublished data.

Table 9.5   **Retail Sales: Response Rates, August 1989**

	No. of Firms	Estimated Sales Volume ($bil.)
1. Initial sample	12,197	146.4
2. Less out of business	877	0
3. Less out of scope	404	2.3
4. Equals potential respondents	10,916	144.1
	(100.0)	(100.0)
5. Less initial refusals	1,104	9.0
	(10.1)	(6.2)
6. Equals total mailed	9,812	135.1
	(89.9)	(93.8)
7. Less new refusals in August	37	[a]
	(0.3)	
8. Less failed to report	1,135	13.6
	(10.4)	(9.4)
9. Equals reports received	8,640	121.5
	(79.1)	(84.3)

Source: Bureau of the Census, unpublished data.
Note: Percentages are given in parentheses.
[a]Included in row 8.

any one survey from such a small sample of surveys. A major problem is that hard data on the response at repricing are not available; this information can come only from special BLS investigations.

The figure for the PPI in tables 9.2 and 9.8 includes some estimates on my part. An independent judgmental estimate of BLS specialists for the PPI puts the response rate in the "low sixties," a figure that is viewed by BLS as a low response.[7]

---

7. Thomas Tibbetts, assistant commissioner, Division of Industrial Prices, Bureau of Labor Statistics, conversation with author, 24 January 1990.

Table 9.6   **Wholesale Sales: Response Rates, August 1989**

	No. of Firms	Estimated Sales Volume ($bil.)
1. Initial sample	3,577	151.3
2. Less out of business	63	a
3. Less out of scope	176	7.3
4. Equals potential respondents	3,338	142.1
	(100.0)	(100.0)
5. Less initial refusals	320	13.2
	(9.6)	(9.3)
6. Equals total mailed	3,018	128.9
	(90.4)	(90.7)
7. Less new refusals in August	13	a
	(0.4)	
8. Less failed to report	248	10.6
	(7.4)	(7.5)
9. Equals reports received	2,757	118.3
	(82.6)	(83.2)

Source: Bureau of the Census, unpublished data.
Note: Percentages are given in parentheses.
aIncluded in row 8.

Table 9.7   **Private Nonresidential Construction Survey: Response Rates, 1988**

Month	% of Projects	% of Dollar Volume of Work Put in Place
1	41	50
2	53	65
6	60	73
12	60+	75–76

Source: Bureau of the Census, unpublished data.
Note: Similar results would obtain for Multifamily Residential Construction Survey according to the Census Bureau.

9.2.6   Factors Affecting Response Rates

What are the factors that affect response rates? I believe that three are important: the complexity of the survey (the "burden" problem); the nature of the data (proprietary issues) and who is asking for the information; and legal issues. I am not aware that legal issues, which may be a special aspect of proprietary problems, have ever been discussed in connection with government price surveys, although Stigler and Kindahl mention the problem in passing. It is taken up briefly here and more fully further on. I am assuming

Table 9.8   **Summary of Total Response Rates**

	Frequency	Date	Response Rate
BLS:			
Producer prices	Monthly	Late 1989	64 wtd.
International prices[a]	Quarterly	1989:4[b]	67–67
Employment cost	Quarterly	Dec. 1987	70
Occupational-employment	Annual	1986	80
Census:			
Retail sales	Monthly	Aug. 1989	84 wtd.
Wholesale sales	Monthly	Aug. 1989	83 wtd.
Private nonresidential construction	Monthly	1988 avg.	73 wtd.[c]

Source: See tables 9.1–9.7 and the text.
[a]These results refer to the quarterly sample, not to the smaller monthly sample.
[b]Repricing survey.
[c]After six months. Similar results are obtained for private *multifamily* construction.

that the relative effort by each government agency to collect the data is constant across surveys.

The burden of a survey is a common problem. In the fall of 1988, OMB conducted a small survey concerning the burden of the PPI repricing survey (Form BLS 473P). Most respondents said that it was an easy survey to answer, but there was a certain amount of complaining about government surveys generally. I assume that the general complaints are common to all surveys. Individual responses are available in the OMB Docket Library in docket 1220-0008.

Proprietary issues involve two closely related considerations: the nature of the data and who is asking for the information. Some proprietary data are more confidential than others. Because they can often be reasonably approximated by (literally) an outside observer, employment data would seem to be less confidential than, say, profits of a nonpublic corporation. A careful observer can probably make a reasonably good guess about annual sales volume of a trade establishment. Price data are of several different kinds. Some are available for the asking through price lists, while others may vary from customer to customer even when price lists are published by the seller; this latter type is highly confidential information.

The source of the data request is also important. Generally speaking, a government agency will do better than a private individual or institution in obtaining price information, although there are private price surveys, such as the survey of spot steel prices referred to in International Trade Commission (ITC) reports (U.S. International Trade Commission 1988, 39–40).

Stigler and Kindahl had poor success in enlisting cooperation from sellers in their survey of industrial prices: "Industrial companies are generally reticent to report selling prices other than list prices. . . . The reticence no doubt stemmed partly from reasons of commercial interest, despite our promise of complete confidentiality" (Stigler and Kindahl 1970, 23, 26).

Although businesses provide BLS with much proprietary information in the price surveys, no one—including the Bureau—really knows the extent to which even cooperating firms may be holding back information. The following, from a *Wall Street Journal* story (Carnevale 1989) is suggestive. AT&T complained to the Federal Communications Commission (FCC) that MCI gave discounts to several large customers for telecommunications services but failed to include this information in its filings with the FCC. MCI responded that it provides discount services under contract to big business customers but does not file these details with the FCC. In its complaint, AT&T maintained that it was illegal for MCI not to provide tariff information for services MCI offered to such firms as Merrill Lynch, Westin Hotels, United Airlines, the Pentagon, the University of Colorado at Boulder, and others. According to AT&T, the offer to Merrill Lynch was 8.5 percent below the lowest rate specified in MCI tariffs.

Legal issues must be of importance in response rates to government price surveys. Stigler and Kindahl stated that, in addition to reasons of commercial interest, "potential legal complications also discourag[e] the reporting of selling prices. The Robinson-Patman Act places a substantial burden on any seller to justify differences in price . . . and *it was often cited to us as a reason for noncooperation.* Buyers, on the other hand, had fewer legal or commercial doubts and cooperation was much greater" (1970, 23, 26; emphasis added). No doubt, the very poor response that Stigler and Kindahl elicited from *sellers* was due partly to the fact that they were acting as private individuals. BLS can offer firms more convincing assurances regarding confidentiality.

The Bureau has gone to considerable lengths over a long period of years to assure respondents to its surveys that any information supplied by the individual firm will be held in the strictest confidence and cannot be used against the firm by another agency of the government. U.S. courts have upheld the Bureau in resisting attempts of private individuals and firms to gain access to individual company data as well as attempts by agencies of the government for similar information. There can be little doubt that BLS enjoys an excellent reputation so far as confidentiality of data is concerned. The problem is whether this view of the Bureau is universally shared by all businesses. Surely, some of the firms who choose not to participate in the price survey at initiation and some of the cooperating firms that either fail to send in reports each month or send in partial reports must have a degree of skepticism regarding BLS assurances. Such firms hold back because they are fearful that the data that they supply may fall into the wrong hands.

This kind of concern should not be passed over lightly. In this regard, the experience of the Census Bureau in getting firms to report inventory statistics is instructive. The problem revolved around the use of the LIFO (last-in first-out) method of inventory accounting, a technique that has the effect of reducing book profits and profits taxes during periods of inflation. The material that follows is excerpted from a report on inventory statistics of which I was a joint author and concerns the so-called conformity requirement as stated in sections 472(c) and (e) of the 1954 tax code (Foss, Fromm, and Rottenberg 1981, 73–74):

> There are many aspects of income determination where firms may use one accounting method in reporting to Internal Revenue Service (IRS) for calculating its tax liability and another for financial reporting to shareholders, creditors, and others. For example, a firm may use accelerated methods of depreciation for tax purposes but straight-line methods for reports to stockholders. . . . However, if a firm has adopted LIFO, IRS bars use of a different valuation method for financial reporting to the public or to creditors. Failure to abide by this requirement may result in withdrawal of permission to use the LIFO method for determining tax liability. LIFO is apparently viewed as a [tax-reducing] privilege which IRS grants and may revoke. . . . The rationale of the IRS position is that a firm should not be permitted to report a low profit for tax purposes and a high profit to the public.

In the mid-1970s, the IRS conformity requirement was hindering the compilation of inventory statistics by the Census Bureau. The Census Bureau wanted firms that used the LIFO method to report their inventories on a non-LIFO valuation basis so that valuation methods across all firms could be more or less uniform. Despite the fact that reports to the Census Bureau are governed by title 13 of the U.S. Code, which states, among other things, that the information in such reports may be used for no purpose other than statistical and prohibits the disclosure of individual firm data under pain of criminal prosecution, some firms refused to cooperate with the Census Bureau *on advice of legal counsel* "because of concern that the IRS conformity requirement would be violated" (Foss et al. 1981, 74).

This impasse was resolved after the Census Bureau took steps to explain to the IRS how IRS regulations were adversely affecting response rates. Following a series of discussions, IRS issued a regulation permitting firms to report the information requested by the Census Bureau without fear of losing their LIFO privileges (see the appendix). The episode is interesting because it shows how sensitive firms can be regarding compliance with the law. To me, it demonstrates that mere assurance of confidentiality from BLS may not be sufficient for some firms to assuage the fear that, by reporting to the Bureau, they may be exposing themselves to enforcement action or private lawsuits.

I have been impressed by the experience of Stigler and Kindahl and was especially impressed in the late 1970s by what most persons would consider some innocuous data requests that the Census Bureau made regarding inventory valuation methods. Even though the Federal Trade Commission is enforcing Robinson-Patman far less vigorously than it was in the early post–World War II period, it remains the law of the land and cannot fail to be taken into account by all but the smallest businesses when asked by BLS to supply price data.

9.3   The Robinson-Patman Act

The Robinson-Patman Act is a federal statute directed against price discrimination. It was passed in 1936 as an amendment to certain provisions of the Clayton Act at a time of widespread concern over the future of small business. In particular, the sponsors of the legislation believed that large national chain stores, mail-order houses, and other large buyers were wresting price concessions from small suppliers that would lead, if unchecked, to the disappearance of small firms. The chief provision of the new law prohibited the charging of different prices for goods of the same quality where the effect would result in a "substantial lessening of competition." Such price discrimination is legal, however, if it can be proved that these price differences are based on cost differences, if the price differences were made to meet competition "in good faith," or if they were based on perishability or obsolescence of the product.

If Robinson-Patman were limited in its scope, it might be dismissed as one of many specialized obstacles to the working of competition in the U.S. economy. In fact, however, its scope is far reaching not simply because it applies to commodities sold in interstate commerce but also because price discrimination is a common economic phenomenon, one of the most prevalent forms of marketing practice (Varian 1989, 598). Price discrimination in economics involves charging different buyers different prices even though marginal costs are the same or charging the same price to different buyers where marginal costs are different. Economists have long known that it always pays to discriminate if you can do so. As Phlips (1987, 953) put it, "Compared with a uniform price, discriminating prices are not only closer to the highest price a particular customer will pay; they also make it possible to serve customers who would not be able to buy at the uniform price."

Although the professed intention of the sponsors of Robinson-Patman was the preservation of competition, the law in fact became a device to protect established, independent wholesalers and retailers (Adelman [1953] 1969). The administration of the law by the Federal Trade Commission was anticompetitive in its effects, at least through the 1970s. For much of its history, attempts at price cutting have been discouraged. For example, in concentrated markets, a seller might hesitate to make price cuts that would be met immediately by competitors. The same seller might cut prices, however, to one or more purchasers as a first step toward a more general price reduction. Or a new entrant might decide that the best way to gain a foothold in a new market was through price reduction. If, however, he is required to cut prices to purchasers in all markets, old and new, he may decide against the new venture. As the Stigler Report pointed out, the FTC never attempted to differentiate between the seller who wished to make a secret price cut and the monopsonist who extracted unjustified concessions from his suppliers to the detriment of his competitors (Report of the Task Force on Productivity and Competition [Stigler Report] 1969, 839).

In recent years, enforcement of the law as reflected in cases brought to court by the FTC has diminished greatly, averaging less than one per year in the 1980s, a substantial decline as compared to the experience of the 1950s and 1960s. The more recent FTC behavior undoubtedly reflects a response to the widespread criticism of the act as well as a changed attitude at the FTC and in the courts.[8] The FTC's main concern now appears to be anticompetitive practices. It seems to be looking at results in the marketplace rather than at the practices themselves. In the new view, practices that involve price differences may be overlooked if they bring about greater efficiency.[9] It would be a mistake, however, to assume that the act is now and has been in recent years a complete dead letter. Moreover, since the law continues to have the backing of small business, it still has powerful support in the Congress.

9.3.1 Robinson-Patman Today

Since the Federal Trade Commission's enforcement of Robinson-Patman has been minimal for more than a decade—although late in 1988 the FTC brought a case against book publishers for granting larger discounts to certain retail chains than to other retailers[10]—what can be said about Robinson-Patman today? Do businessmen take account of it in their pricing decisions? The fact is that little is known about compliance with this statute. On the basis of recent evaluations of Robinson-Patman and recent conversations with Robinson-Patman specialists—mainly but not exclusively lawyers—I have the impression that the law is very much alive but that businessmen have learned how to live with it in a diversity of ways.[11]

The deterrent effect of the law now comes primarily from private suits, which may involve treble damages in addition to the certainty of legal costs, both of which may be substantial. According to Earl Kintner, a former FTC chairman, and Joseph Bauer (Kintner and Bauer 1986, 607–8):

> The present vitality of the Robinson-Patman Act has been sustained by private litigants. And indeed, there are still literally dozens of reported private actions each year reflecting what must be hundreds of such claims (or counts in other actions) that are being filed. Knowledge of this potential for

---

8. For criticism in addition to the Stigler Report, see "Report of White House Task Force on Antitrust Policy" ([1968] 1969) and Justice Department (1977). For some of the very extensive literature, see American Bar Association (1980).

9. See, e.g., a 1982 statement by James C. Miller, former FTC chairman, in Kintner and Bauer (1986, 606–7, n. 108).

10. *Harper and Row, Publishers, Inc., et al.*, D.9217–9222 (complaints issued 20 December 1988).

11. For some fairly recent assessments, see "The Robinson-Patman Act" (1986).

litigation plays an important role in marketing decisions and preventive counseling. However, of late the likelihood of success in a private enforcement action has been diminished somewhat by restrictive, and even hostile, readings given the act by various court decisions.

In the past few years, there have been from twenty to thirty private lawsuits per year involving Robinson-Patman, although some of these have been countersuits in response to an initial suit.[12] But, if Robinson-Patman is dead, its death—or at least its moribund condition—has perhaps been exaggerated. In March 1990, a North Carolina jury in a federal court awarded Liggett and Myers Company a record treble damages judgment of $148.8 million against Brown and Williamson Tobacco Corporation for discriminatory pricing practices under Robinson-Patman.[13] In August 1990, a federal judge threw out this jury verdict, maintaining that the goal of the antitrust laws was "to promote consumer welfare, not to discourage aggressive price competition" (Green 1990). The plaintiffs are appealing. Although the judge's decision is in keeping with the newer thinking on the part of the courts and the Federal Trade Commission, the very large award and the still uncertain outcome of this case cannot help but reinforce the feeling among businessmen that Robinson-Patman is still very much alive.

Some specialists, asked about compliance suggest that it is necessary to differentiate between large and small firms. One defined a large firm as one that is large enough to have a general counsel or that sells according to a "sales policy." Large firms are very much aware of Robinson-Patman. Small firms either are not aware or tend to ignore it. One Robinson-Patman specialist told me recently, "When you talk to sales and marketing people about prices, price discrimination is always the $64,000 question."

Lawyers offer all kinds of advice to their clients for overcoming the restrictions against discrimination. In one view, the easiest defense against Robinson-Patman is "to make sure it does not apply to a [covered] transaction at all" (Scher 1986, 533). For example, since Robinson-Patman prohibits the sale of the *same* product to different buyers at different prices, a price concession may be made within the law if the specifications of the product are altered slightly (Scher 1986, 541–42; Whiting 1986, 713). Critics of Robinson-Patman have pointed out that the statute thus encourages an increase in product differentiation and "denies the economy the advantage of longer production runs" (Justice Department 1977, 176).

According to another attorney, the essence of "good" Robinson-Patman counseling is to find a "sophisticated" way by which a firm can cut prices without having the price concession show up in the price quotation. As an

12. Robert M. Klein, American Bar Association, telephone conversation with author, 17 January 1990.
13. *Liggett Group Inc. v. Brown & Williamson Tobacco Corp.*, DC MNC, No. C-84-617-D, 3/2/90, 58 ATRR345.

example, a manufacturer may devise an advertising campaign that would be of definite benefit to a particular customer or a particular class of customers. As a result of the concession, the seller's advertising costs would be higher and its net revenue lower, but the price itself would be unaffected.

9.3.2 How Robinson-Patman Might Affect Business Response

Against this background, what can be said about the business response to the PPI survey? The paragraphs that follow, which are necessarily speculative, attempt to delineate various kinds of responses. Since the incentive to discriminate is still strong, and since sanctions against discrimination are now mainly in the form of private suits, which have been increasingly difficult to win, I conclude that there is much noncompliance with Robinson-Patman today.[14] Some of the *noncompliance,* especially among large firms, leads such firms to omit the reporting of prices that are discriminatory by Robinson-Patman standards. Some of the noncompliance among the same firms leads them to report prices that are not true transactions prices, such as list prices. I have no doubt that there are many firms that comply with the law completely. Some conceivably make no attempts to get around the law because of respect for the law, because of the prospective costs of a lawsuit, or because the costs of changing commodity specifications, for example, are too high. These firms report prices that BLS can accept at face value.

Another group ignores the law completely. It is not likely to report to BLS at all. These firms should be found mainly among the refusals at initiation, although there are other reasons for refusals. My guess is that most firms would fall in between the group that ignores the law completely and the group that complies completely.

Sellers who discriminate by making specials deals with one or a few buyers are unlikely to report them to BLS. Although Stigler and Kindahl elicited much better cooperation in obtaining prices from buyers than from sellers, they found that even buyers who supplied data for their investigation were unwilling to report "extraordinarily favorable deals" (Stigler and Kindahl 1970, 27). The data on response rates in repricing in the PPI (see table 9.2 above) suggest that even cooperating firms often fail to report prices to BLS regularly. Special deals or discounts from list that firms prefer not to report to BLS could well be important reasons for missing reports. Furthermore, these are not likely to be the sorts of things that a business would report in response

14. Although the plaintiffs lost their appeal in the Circuit Court, their petition for certiorari was granted by the Supreme Court (see Barrett 1992). It remains to be seen how the Liggett and Myers case against Brown-Williamson will affect business behavior. The same question could be raised about the recent Texaco case. In June 1990, in a nine to zero decision, the Supreme Court found that Texaco had violated the Robinson-Patman Act by selling gasoline to two large distributors at discounts that it did not give to smaller retailers. The Justice Department supported Texaco in a brief filed with the Court (Greenhouse 1990). Conceivably, both these cases could lead to greater compliance by business, but they might also make businesses less willing to participate in voluntary surveys, especially price surveys.

to a follow-up telephone call from BLS asking why they failed to send in a particular price. Sellers who discriminate but who use a "sophisticated" method like the advertising example given above may well report but are not likely to report a correct transactions price to BLS.

9.4   What Can Be Done to Improve Reporting of Transaction Prices?

Now that BLS is using a probability sample and has a clearer idea of its response rate, perhaps it should reconsider the universal applicability of its policy of pricing commodities with highly detailed specifications. In its effort to obtain a pure price measure, BLS seems to be pursuing a policy that maximizes specificity. Response rate seems to be viewed as something independent. If my hypothesis is correct, the two are closely related, and there may be a trade-off between them. A system of somewhat less detailed specification might elicit a higher response rate and be optimal with respect to BLS's ultimate objective—obtaining information on the monthly behavior of prices in each industry. The PPI system, in which nonresponse is more than one-third, would seem to require a reconsideration of the entire approach.

For example, if BLS used somewhat broader commodity specifications at the individual firm level, this might permit the firm to combine customers more easily, and this in turn would make it easier for the firm to conceal special deals. The case for broader classifications is strengthened when one remembers that, under Robinson-Patman, a true price cut can be masked by an apparent change in specifications. Another method of combining could take the form of averaging over a period of time. At present, BLS seeks the shipments price on Tuesday of the week containing the 13th of the month. Perhaps if the prospective cooperator were given the option of reporting on a monthly or quarterly average basis, willingness to participate at initiation and steady participation in repricing would be improved.[15]

In this regard, it is encouraging to see that the steel industry may at long last be reporting transactions prices to BLS (Betsock and Gerduk, chap. 8 in this volume). Large steel companies that in the past would report only list prices for flat-rolled steel products now seem willing to report transactions prices. While expressing uncertainty about why the industry has changed its attitude about reporting, Betsock and Gerduk note that companies are reporting with a one-month lag *average* transactions prices applicable to well-defined commodities. They admit the possibility that a changing mix of customers may introduce distortions into the average prices being reported; this would give the appearance of price change where none existed. Unless that is demonstrably biased, it would seem to be a small price to pay—together with the one-month lag—for obtaining transactions prices in this particular industry.

15. According to Thomas Tibbetts of BLS, "a fair number" of respondents submit average monthly figures to BLS as a compromise offer.

Steel is not unique among American industries. From past studies (e.g., Flueck 1961) there is reason to believe that many other commodities suffer from the biases that were evident in flat-rolled steel. Now that BLS has introduced probability sampling, it could pay special attention to those industries where response rates give the appearance of being well below average. BLS might consider offering such industries the same arrangement that was worked out for flat-rolled steel. For this paper, I would have examined detailed industry response rates, but I was given access to response rates of only a limited number of detailed industries.

There is a large body of price data available from the General Services Administration and the Department of Defense covering items bought by the federal government. Researchers could make comparisons of the behavior of federal prices with comparable prices in the revised PPI in order to highlight problems. As indicated earlier, this was done on a large scale by Flueck for the Stigler Report; it was also carried out on a much smaller scale by Ziemer and Galbraith (1983, 164–73).

9.5 Concluding Remarks

BLS should pay close attention to laws and regulations that may affect the data that they are collecting because the kind of data that business is willing to submit is to some extent a function of business compliance with the law. Field agents need instruction in these matters. The solicitation of help from outside groups such as the American Bar Association should be undertaken with this in mind. Most important, BLS questions should be framed so as to maximize response of good-quality data. Improving the low response rate in the PPI survey may mean a greater BLS acceptance of averaging over time and/or greater acceptance of broader commodity specifications.

Appendix
Revenue Procedure 76-36

26 CFR 601.204: Changes in accounting periods and in methods of accounting. (Also Part I, Section 472; 1.472-1.)

Rev. Proc. 76-36

Sec. 1. Purpose

The purpose of this Revenue Procedure is to modify the provisions of Rev. Proc. 75-36, 1725-2 C.B. 565, relating to the furnishing of financial data to the Bureau of Census (Census) and the Bureau of Economic Analysis (BEA), which are agencies within and under the jurisdiction of the United States Department of Commerce.

Sec. 2. Scope

The scope of this Revenue Procedure is limited to those taxpayers who provide Census with information concerning inventory, for which the taxpayers employ the last-in, first-out (LIFO) inventory method, as described in section 472 of the Internal Revenue Code of 1954.

Sec. 3. Background

.01 Rev. Proc. 75-36 sets forth the procedure to be used by the Internal Revenue Service in the examination of Federal income tax returns involving the LIFO inventory requirements of section 472(c) of the Code for the taxable year in which the taxpayer elects or reelects to use the LIFO inventory method, or extends an existing LIFO election to cover all or a greater portion of its inventories, and Census or BEA requests that the taxpayer furnish certain financial information to the appropriate agency.

.02 Section 472(c)(2) of the Code and the regulation issued thereunder provide, in part, that once the LIFO method is elected, it must be used in all subsequent taxable years, unless the Secretary of the Treasury or the Secretary's delegate determines that the taxpayer has used some procedure other than the LIFO method for any such subsequent taxable year in order to ascertain the income, profit, or loss of such subsequent taxable year, for the purpose of a report or statement covering such taxable year to shareholders, partners, or other proprietors, or beneficiaries, or for credit purposes.

.03 Census collects data on inventories of manufacturing and wholesale firms in the economic census conducted every five years. Similar data are also collected in monthly and/or annual surveys for manufacturing, wholesale, and retail firms. These data are collected under the authority of title 13, United States Code, 1.3 U.S.C.A. section 9 (Supp. 1975) (title 13). Section 9 of title 13 states that the information collected may not be used "for any purpose other than the statistical purposes for which it is supplied" and further prohibits "any publication whereby the data furnished by any particular establishment or individual under this title can be identified." This section also does not permit "anyone other than the sworn officers and employees of the Department or bureau or agency thereof to examine the individual reports."

.04 Under the provisions of title 13, data collected in Census surveys are exempt from disclosures under the Freedom of Information Act. Data on individual firms may not be released because (1) they are "specifically exempted by statute," and (2) they are "commercial or financial information obtained from a person and privileged or confidential." (Section 552(h)(3) and (b)(4) of title 5, United States Code, 5 U.S.C.A. section 552 (Supp. 1975).)

.05 Census requires taxpayers to submit financial information in the year of the LIFO election, reelection, or extension, as well as in subsequent taxable years. Certain of the required information is not available on a LIFO basis (for example, inventory on a location basis) and some taxpayers have been reluctant to submit the required information because Rev. Proc. 75-36 is limited to the year of the LIFO election, reelection, or extension.

.06 The information to be furnished to Census will not be furnished by the taxpayer to any other persons nor will it be furnished to other government agencies unless otherwise authorized by the Service.

Sec. 4. Application

In the examination of returns, a taxpayer's LIFO election will not be terminated for Federal income tax purposes solely because the taxpayer has furnished financial information required by Census to Census on a non-LIFO basis, for the year of the LIFO election, reelection, or extension, as well as for subsequent taxable years. This Revenue Procedure applies to all financial information collected by Census under the authority of title 13, and exempted from disclosure under the Freedom of Information Act, under the authority of title 5, United States Code, 5 U.S.C.A. section 552 (Supp. 1975). . . .

Sec. 6. Effect on Other Documents

To the extent provided herein, Rev. Proc. 75-36 is modified.

Sec. 7. Inquiries

Inquiries in regard to this Revenue Procedure should refer to its number and be addressed to the Commissioner of Internal Revenue, Attention T:C:C, 1111 Constitution Avenue, N.W., Washington, D.C. 20224.

26 CFR 601.105: Examination of returns and claims for refund, credit or abatement, determinations of correct tax liability. (Also Part I, Section 167; 1.167(a)-11.)

Asset depreciation range system; aircraft and air transportation assets. Asset guideline classes, asset guideline depreciation periods and ranges, and annual asset guideline repair allowance percentages are set forth for aircraft and air transportation assets first placed in service after April 15, 1976; Rev. Proc. 72-10 modified.

References

Adelman, Morris. [1953] 1969. The consistency of the Robinson-Patman Act. *Journal of Reprints for Antitrust Law and Economics* 1:521–40.

American Bar Association. Antitrust Section. 1980. *The Robinson-Patman Act: Policy and law.* Monograph no. 4. Chicago.

Barrett, Paul M. 1992. High court to hear antitrust appeal on cigarette maker's pricing strategy. *Wall Street Journal,* 17 November 1992, 2.

Carlton, Dennis. 1986. The rigidity of prices. *American Economic Review* 76:637–58.

———. 1989. The theory and facts of how markets clear: Is industrial organization valuable for understanding macroeconomics? In *Handbook of industrial organization,* ed. R. Schmalensee and R. D. Willig. Amsterdam: North-Holland.

Carnevale, Mary Lu. 1989. AT&T accuses its rival MCI over discounts. *Wall Street Journal,* 8 September, A4.

Coffey, Jerry. 1987. Business response survey: Initial findings. Paper presented at the annual meeting of the American Economic Association.

Council on Wage and Price Stability (COWPS). 1977. *The wholesale price index: Review and evaluation.* Washington, D.C.

Early, John F. 1978. Improving the measurement of producer price change. *Monthly Labor Review* 101 (April): 7–15.

———. 1979. The producer price index revision: Overview and pilot survey results. *Monthly Labor Review* 102 (December): 11–19.

Flueck, John A. 1961. A study in validity: BLS wholesale price quotations. Staff Paper no. 9. In *The price statistics of the federal government: Review, appraisal and recommendations.* General Series no. 73. Washington, D.C.: National Bureau of Economic Research.

Foss, Murray, Gary Fromm, and Irving Rottenberg. 1981. *Measurement of business inventories.* Washington, D.C.: U.S. Bureau of the Census.

Gordon, Robert J. 1990. What is new-Keynesian economics? *Journal of Economic Literature* 28 (September): 1115–71.

Green, Wayne E. 1990. Judge sets aside $148.8 million verdict in Brown & Williamson cigarette case. *Wall Street Journal,* 28 August, A4.

Greenhouse, Linda. 1990. Texaco loses in high court on discounts. *New York Times,* 15 June, D4.

Justice Department. 1977. *Report on the Robinson-Patman Act.* Washington, D.C.

Kintner, Earl, and Joseph Bauer. 1986. The Robinson-Patman Act: A look backwards, a look forward. *Antitrust Bulletin* 31 (3): 571–609.

Means, Gardiner C. 1935. *Industrial prices and their relative inflexibility.* 74th Cong., 1st sess., S. Doc. 13.

National Bureau of Economic Research. 1961. *The price statistics of the federal government: Review, appraisal and recommendations.* General Series no. 73. Washington, D.C.

Okun, Arthur. 1981. *Prices and quantities: A macroeconomic analysis.* Washington, D.C.: Brookings.

Phlips, Louis. 1987. Price discrimination. In *The new Palgrave: A dictionary of economics.* New York: Stockton.

Report of the President's Commission. 1971. *Federal statistics,* vol. 1. Washington, D.C.: U.S. Government Printing Office.

Report of the Task Force on Productivity and Competition (Stigler Report). 1969. *Journal of Reprints for Antitrust Law and Economics* 1, pt. 1 (Winter): 829–81.

Report of the White House Task Force on Antitrust Policy. [1963] 1969. *Journal of Reprints for Antitrust Law and Economics* 1 (Winter): 633–826.

The Robinson-Patman Act: A symposium. 1986. *Antitrust Bulletin* 31 (3).

Scher, Irving. 1986. How sellers can live with the Robinson-Patman Act. *Business Lawyer* 41 (February): 533–54.

Stigler, George, and James Kindahl. 1970. *The behavior of industrial prices.* New York: Columbia University Press (for the National Bureau of Economic Research).

U.S. Department of Labor. Bureau of Labor Statistics. 1976. *BLS handbook of methods for surveys and studies.* Bulletin no. 1910. Washington, D.C.

————. 1982. *BLS handbook of methods for surveys and studies.* Bulletin no. 2134-1. Washington, D.C.

————. 1986. *Producer price measurement: Concepts and methods.* Washington, D.C.

————. 1988. *BLS handbook of methods for surveys and studies.* Bulletin no. 2285. Washington, D.C.

U.S. International Trade Commission. 1988. *Annual survey concerning competitive conditions in the steel industry.* Publication no. 2115. Washington, D.C.

U.S. Temporary National Economic Committee. 1939–40. *Iron and steel industry and investigation of concentration of economic power.* Washington, D.C.: U.S. Government Printing Office.

Varian, Hal R. 1989. Price discrimination. In *Handbook of industrial organization,* ed. R. Schmalensee and R. D. Willig. Amsterdam: North-Holland.

Whiting, Richard A. 1986. Robinson-Patman: May it rest in peace. *Antitrust Bulletin* 31 (3): 709–32.

Ziemer, Richard C., and Karl D. Galbraith. 1983. Deflation of defense purchases. In *U.S. national income and product accounts: Selected topics,* ed. Murray F. Foss. Studies in Income and Wealth, vol. 47. Chicago: University of Chicago Press (for the National Bureau of Economic Research).

Comment   Robert W. Crandall

Betsock and Gerduk deal with a rather common problem in the measurement of industrial prices: the use of list prices versus transactions prices. For many years the Bureau of Labor Statistics (BLS) had relied on list prices for steel industry prices in the producer price index (PPI). This may have been satisfactory if list prices moved with actual transactions prices, but in the 1980s changes in list prices clearly did not mirror changes in transactions prices. BLS discovered in 1982 and again in 1986 that transactions prices and list prices moved in opposite directions. As a result, BLS was forced to reexamine its approach to collecting price data in its 1990 resampling of the industry.

Betsock and Gerduk point out the difficulties in linking a new set of steel prices to the old price series when transactions data are not available for earlier years. They also discuss the effect of changes in industry structure on steel price reporting. The new, competitive minimills generally provide transactions prices for bar and rod products, but the older integrated firms sell in two quite different markets, in which prices may diverge. For sheet and plate products in particular, the large steel companies sell to large buyers under annual contracts. Month-to-month deviations in these contract prices are likely to be quite small. In addition, the larger mills also sell on the spot market, often through steel service centers. The mix of contract and spot sales is unfortunately changing, further complicating BLS's problem.

Robert W. Crandall is a senior fellow in the Economics Studies Program at the Brookings Institution.

The authors distinguish between actual price quotations at a point in time versus average monthly prices, suggesting that BLS has traditionally preferred the former for the PPI. Why this preference should exist is not clear to me. Nor is the problem of trying to obtain price data from different divisions or even from buyers seemingly an insuperable one. If the PPI steel series is to measure the movement in prices received by manufacturers, it would seem desirable to check price quotations with both buyers and sellers—a point made by Stigler and Kindahl (1970) two decades ago.

In their revised paper, Betsock and Gerduk tell us that BLS was finally able to persuade most of the large integrated producers to submit average transactions price data with a one-month lag. The authors seem somewhat surprised by these firms' change of heart. For decades, they had refused to supply transactions prices, preferring instead to give BLS unrealistic list prices. But, with the continuing growth of competition from minimills, reconstituted integrated companies, and imports, it now appears that the industry has essentially given up on the notion that it can prevent price cutting from announced list prices. The minimills are now invading even the sheet products and are poised to drive the integrated firms from the structural steel market. "Administered pricing" for steel has been relegated to the dustbin of history.

The authors are rather oblique in their discussion of the current steel price sampling methodology. It would be very helpful if they explained more precisely their current procedures, including the number of reporters, the number of contract price reports, the number of spot price reports, and their distribution by steel mill product.

Foss's paper takes up an important issue that is raised by Betsock and Gerduk: the reluctance of sellers to report transactions prices. He carefully reviews the response rate of firms to other government surveys and finds that the response rate to the PPI is somewhat lower than for all the other surveys in his study. He concludes from this that firms are more reluctant to report price data than any other type of economic information.

Foss's explanation for the low response rate to the PPI survey is that firms are afraid that such responses could be the basis for Robinson-Patman Act actions even though BLS assures businessmen that their individual responses will be protected from other agencies' inquiries. If this explanation were correct, one would expect to find that industries subject to the greatest probability of Robinson-Patman Act actions would have the lowest reporting rates. Moreover, one would also expect response rates to vary with the degree of Robinson-Patman enforcement over time. Given the recent inactivity of the Federal Trade Commission (FTC) in Robinson-Patman litigation, one would expect businesses to be less and less fearful of providing price data to the BLS. Foss reminds us, however, that private treble damage suits are still a threat in this area.

I believe that there are at least two other explanations for the low response rates to BLS price surveys. First, businesses in some concentrated industries may not want anyone to know when they depart from tacitly collusive list prices to expand their market share. Second, the fear of the possible imposition of price controls may inhibit firms from reporting actual transactions prices. If the tacit collusion theory is correct, response rates should vary across industries, with the most concentrated having the lowest response rates. If the price control theory is valid, response rates should fall after periods of price controls but rise again after long periods of relative price stability.

Interestingly, the steel industry has engaged in a variety of pricing practices that have been claimed to be overtly or tacitly collusive. The Judge Gary dinners, of course, are legend. In the 1930s and 1940s, the use of basing-point pricing by steel companies became quite controversial, and the FTC was eventually successful in attacking this pricing policy in the *Triangle Steel Conduit* case in 1948.

Foss's theory deserves to be tested against the evidence, but I am skeptical that the Robinson-Patman Act alone explains much of the variance in response rates. I would add a few more dimensions to the theory of firms' reluctance to comply with BLS requests.

Reference

Stigler, George, and James Kindahl. 1970. *The behavior of industrial prices*. New York: Columbia University Press (for the National Bureau of Economic Research).

V   Price Indexes for Defense

10   The Deflation of Military Aircraft

Richard C. Ziemer and Pamela A. Kelly

10.1   Introduction

The Bureau of Economic Analysis (BEA) entered into an agreement with the Department of Defense (DOD) in 1975 to develop a measure of defense purchases in constant prices and an official defense deflator. Prior to this effort, no official measures of price change for purchases of military-specific goods and services had been developed. Initial results of the study and the methodology were published in the report *Price Changes in Defense Purchases of the United States* (U.S. Department of Commerce 1979). Current- and constant-dollar estimates of defense purchases were incorporated into the national income and product accounts (NIPA) with the 1972 benchmark published in December 1980. Quarterly and annual series are available for the period 1972 to date and are published in the *Survey of Current Business*.

This paper may be considered a sequel to the general overview of the deflation of defense purchases found in an earlier work (Ziemer and Galbraith 1983). Although the paper focuses on aircraft, the techniques described apply to most other purchases of weapons systems by DOD. Defense purchases in constant dollars, other than weapons systems and compensation, are generally derived by deflation. Specification pricing, the same technique as employed by the Bureau of Labor Statistics (BLS), is used to develop price indexes from data on prices paid by DOD. These indexes are used to deflate current-dollar defense purchases. Categories of purchases for which price data are not available from DOD are deflated using proxy price indexes such as the producer price index (PPI). Constant-dollar purchases of military compensation are derived by extrapolating base year compensation by the number of active duty personnel by rank. Constant-dollar purchases of civilian compensation are de-

Richard C. Ziemer and Pamela A. Kelly are economists with the Bureau of Economic Analysis, U.S. Department of Commerce.

Copyright is not claimed for this paper.

rived by extrapolating base year compensation by the number of hours worked by employees by grade and step. A more detailed description of the methodology used in estimating the full range of national defense purchases may be found in U.S. Department of Commerce (1988).

The purpose of the paper is to describe in some detail the types of data that are available to BEA and the techniques used to transform these data into current- and constant-dollar defense purchases of aircraft. The paper is divided into three sections. The first section briefly reviews the general pricing techniques used in the development of prices for military equipment. The description focuses primarily on the way in which certain price-determining characteristics are treated and how this may differ from other price indexes such as the PPI and the consumer price index (CPI).

The second section, which contains the bulk of the paper, gives a detailed look at these techniques using a case study approach. We have devised price and quantity data for two hypothetical fighter aircraft. These data are used to portray many of the situations that we observe in the actual data. We hope that this detailed methodology will shed some light on what the published defense purchases series does and does not show.

The third section contains a brief summary of defense purchases of aircraft. These data illustrate the effect of these techniques on actual data.

10.1.1   Background

The goal of the defense price work was to develop measures of constant-dollar defense purchases within the framework of the NIPAs (U.S. Department of Commerce 1979, 21). This goal, coupled with the procedures used by DOD for purchasing weapons systems, dictated many of the procedures used in constructing the measures of price change. Following is a brief review of some of these procedures.

Defense purchases in the NIPAs are recorded on a delivery basis. This means that during the period that a given aircraft is being manufactured and DOD is making progress payments to the producer, BEA does not record a defense purchase. The progress payments appear as additions to business inventories. The purchase is recorded only when DOD takes delivery of the completed unit; at that time, there is also recorded a reduction in business inventories. The time lag between initiating production and the delivery of a completed unit can be as much as four years for some aircraft.

Most weapons systems are purchased by DOD as components of a system rather than as a single item. An aircraft, for example, usually has four major component contracts: engines, avionics (i.e., electronic devices for use in aviation), armament, and the airframe and assembly. In addition, there may be many smaller components that are purchased separately, such as tires and ejection seats. The engines, avionics, etc., appear as a defense purchase in the GNP when DOD accepts the item from the contractor, and at that time the price for these components will appear in the defense price index. These components are then furnished to the airframe and assembly contractor. When DOD accepts the completed aircraft, only the delivery of the airframe and assembly operation is recorded as a defense purchase in the GNP—the other components having been accepted earlier—and only then do the airframe and assembly price appear in the defense purchases price index.

Defense purchases of weapons systems in the NIPAs are derived primarily from data on quantities and prices of components delivered in each time period. The basic series are calculated as follows:

(1) $$C_t = P_{it} \times Q_{it},$$

(2) $$K_t = P_{ib} \times Q_{it},$$

(3) $$D_t = \frac{C_t}{K_t},$$

(4) $$I_t = \frac{P_{it} \times Q_{ib}}{P_{ib} \times Q_{ib}},$$

where C = deliveries in current dollars, D = implicit price deflator, P = price of item at delivery, t = time period of delivery, i = ith component $(i = 1, n)$, K = deliveries in constant dollars, I = fixed-weighted price index, Q = quantity of item delivered, and b = base period.

While price and quantity estimates are collected and processed for many series, there are some items for which data are not readily available. For these items, an alternative measure for the purchase is used. Data on disbursements for a class of weapons systems (e.g., Air Force combat aircraft) are available from DOD. These data are adjusted to exclude progress payments on items for which price and quantity data are processed. The remaining disbursements are assumed to be for items that are paid for at the time of delivery and represent current-dollar purchases of unpriced items. Constant-dollar purchases are the value of the unpriced items deflated by the price index for priced items. Total purchases of weapons systems are the sum of the priced and unpriced items.

10.1.2   Measurement of Quality Change

The technique used to construct the detailed price series is of critical importance in the development of any measure of quality (or price) change. A technique known as specification pricing is used to develop the price measures for defense purchases. This is the same technique that is used by BLS in the PPI and CPI. Specification pricing consists of defining the price-determining characteristics for a given item that is to be priced and pricing items with identical characteristics over time. Price-determining characteristics for defense purchases are the physical characteristics of an item that influence its price. In addition to the physical configuration (e.g., number of engines, number of seats, etc.), price-determining characteristics for an aircraft would include

(1) materials or design that affect the aircraft's length of service, need for or ease of repairs, weight, speed, or maneuverability; (2) mechanical features that affect overall operation, efficiency, or the ability of a component to perform its function; and (3) safety features such as ejection seats. Price-determining characteristics would not include features of style, appearance, comfort, convenience, or design solely to make the aircraft appear different. Nonphysical criteria that affect the purchase price, such as the number of units purchased on a given contract or the rate at which the aircraft are to be produced, are not included as part of the specification to be priced.

Items being purchased, however, do not usually maintain the same specifications for long periods of time. Products are continually being modified, which can result in changes to the price-determining characteristics. When a change occurs in the price-determining characteristics of an item being priced, the change is evaluated to determine if it is a quality change. For defense purchases, the criteria for quality change are (*a*) that there is a physical change to the item and (*b*) that the change enhances the ability of the item to perform its mission. Each weapons system is designed for a particular mission within the overall defense program. A wide variety of missions are performed by various aircraft, from the delivery of nuclear bombs by the B-52, to long-range reconnaissance by the SR-71. Each of these missions requires an aircraft with somewhat different characteristics. The Navy's F-14 fighter aircraft, for example, has as its mission to protect a fleet of ships from enemy aircraft. This requires that it be fast, be maneuverable, have sophisticated electronics for detecting enemy aircraft at great distances, and be able to destroy the enemy aircraft before they reach the fleet. The Air Force's A-10 attack aircraft, on the other hand, has as its mission to supply close air support of ground troops. This mission requires less speed than a fighter aircraft, but the A-10 must be able to fly close to the ground, have some protective armor, and be able to destroy enemy tanks. Each physical change to an aircraft is examined to determine if it improves that aircraft's ability to perform its mission. If it does, the cost of producing that physical change is taken as the value of the quality change, and the price is adjusted accordingly. Any other change in the price paid by DOD for that item is defined as a price change.

This procedure is known as the "performance/cost-of-production" method of adjusting for quality change. Changes in performance are not used to value the quality of an item; they are used only to determine whether there has been a quality change. The value of the quality change is determined by the cost of producing the change. The following example may help clarify this technique. Assume a fighter aircraft that flies at Mach 1 with a price of $1,000 in period T. In period $T + 1$, a physical change is made to the aircraft that allows it to fly at Mach 2. An increase in speed helps a fighter aircraft perform its mission. The price of the aircraft increases to $1,500, but the cost of making the change was $300. These data yield a quality change of $300 and a price change of $200. Therefore, there is a price increase of 20 percent and a quality increase of 30 percent even though the speed of the aircraft has doubled.

Methods of adjusting for quality change other than the performance/cost-of-production method have been proposed. An alternative method of adjusting for quality change was presented in Gordon (1990). In the case of commercial aircraft, Gordon adjusted prices of identical models by a quality factor based on changes in net revenue relative to changes in the prices of aircraft purchased. Gordon found that, in the period 1965–82, net revenue rose much faster than price because jet technology brought about declining real costs for fuel, maintenance, and crew per unit of output (Gordon 1990, chap. 4). (For a discussion of the concepts of quality adjustment, see Triplett [1983]).

The procedures described above may yield somewhat different measures of price change than price indexes such as the CPI and PPI (U.S. Department of Labor 1988). The primary cause of this is the treatment of certain price-influencing characteristics. Listed below are four characteristics that are treated as price changes in defense purchases but not in the calculation of the PPI or CPI:

- *Buy size:* Differences in price due to a difference in the number of units ordered on one contract.
- *Production rate:* Differences in price due to changes requested by DOD in the production rate, such as for stretch-outs due to budget constraints.
- *Learning curve:* Differences in price due to differences in position on the learning curve (see below).
- *Producer:* Differences in price due to different producers for the same item.

In addition, any changes to a weapons system that are for the remedy of defects are defined as *not* being quality changes. It is assumed that, when a weapons system enters into production, it fits together and works.

10.1.3 Splicing Price Series

A major problem is encountered in the development of any quantity or price series when a product disappears and is replaced by a new product. The new product will not match the specifications of the old product; therefore, the price of the new product may not be directly comparable to the price of the old product. The old and new price or quantity series must be spliced together to form a continuous measure over time. There exist several procedures that can be used to handle this problem.

The first procedure is called a direct link procedure. The price of the new product is linked to the level of the price index for the old product. This procedure assumes that the entire difference in price level between the old product and the new, at the time of the introduction of the new product, is due to a difference in quality.

The second procedure is called a direct comparison. The price of the new item is directly compared to the price of the old item. This method assumes that there is no difference in quality between the two items and that any difference in the price paid is a price change.

The third procedure, and the one used for most new weapons systems, is to treat the new product as a quality adjustment to the old product. This is done by evaluating the physical differences between the old and the new products to determine whether there has been a quality change. If it is determined that there are quality differences, the cost of producing those physical changes is defined as the value of the changes, and the price is adjusted accordingly. Any other change in the price paid by DOD for the new item is a price change. However, when this procedure is used for introducing a new weapons system, the price of the new system must also be adjusted for learning-curve effects.

The learning curve represents the reduction in labor hours required for producing successive units of a new weapons system of a given technology. The new system may be superior to the system it replaces. However, the price of early units of the new system will be overstated relative to the old system, which has already experienced significant learning. In keeping with the cost analysis community, BEA assumes that, by the hundredth unit of production of a new fighter aircraft, additional learning is relatively minor. The price of the hundredth unit of the new system is compared with the price of the old system at the link point to yield the best estimate of the actual resource cost difference between the two systems. BLS waits to introduce a new product into its price index until that product has established a market share—at which time most learning has already occurred. BEA treats the higher prices for the first ninety-nine units over the hundredth unit of the new system as price increases relative to the old system. Each of these units is included in the price index as it is delivered. A more detailed discussion of learning curves and the technique for introducing new models is contained in appendix A.

10.2 Case Study

The case study uses two hypothetical aircraft to illustrate many of the data sources and procedures used in the preparation of defense purchases in the NIPAs. The case study highlights military aircraft, but the procedures are typical for most military equipment purchases. The case study begins with price derivation and continues through index creation. In the process, quality adjustments, learning curves, and splicing techniques are examined.

A new fighter aircraft, the F456, replaces an older fighter aircraft, the F123. Both aircraft include the same general component systems, but the F456 incorporates quality improvements in all components except engines. For this example, the aircraft are produced simultaneously for two years. Table 10.1 shows the price and quantity information for the last four contracts of the older aircraft, the F123. Table 10.2 shows the entire contract history for the newer aircraft, the F456. An addendum containing information pertaining to quality

Table 10.1   **F123 Unit Prices by Contract ($thousands)**

Contract number	8	9	10	11
Contract quantity (units)	70	75	75	75
Delivery year	1975	1976	1977	1978
Contractor-furnished equipment (CFE)	2,205.8	2,463.6	2,741.0	2,876.2
Airframe	1,359.4	1,506.2	1,652.8	1,737.9
Flight controls	194.7	218.0	246.7	257.0
Penetration aids	10.1	11.8	12.8	13.5
Communications equipment	8.9	10.2	12.0	12.5
Radar equipment	273.3	305.9	353.8	372.4
Fire control equipment	111.8	127.1	140.9	147.5
Weapons and armament systems	247.6	284.5	322.0	335.4
Navigation equipment	97.9	113.5	133.4	140.3
Navigation equipment (CFE)	89.8	104.5	123.5	129.8
Navigation equipment (GFE)	8.1	9.0	10.0	10.5
Government-furnished equipment (GFE)	2,097.3	2,335.1	2,489.6	2,594.4
Engines (2 per aircraft)	1,459.7	1,601.0	1,640.6	1,705.4
Other GFE	637.6	734.1	848.9	888.9
Total	4,400.9	4,912.2	5,364.0	5,610.9

change between contracts appears at the bottom of table 10.2. Notes providing additional information about the F456 also appear at the bottom of table 10.2.

To facilitate the presentation of this case study, we have made some simplifying assumptions:

1. Typically, aircraft deliveries for a given contract year begin a year or more after the contract year. In addition, deliveries for that contract can extend over more than one year. In the case study, only one contract is delivered in a year for each aircraft system. For example, all fifty-five F456 aircraft in contract 5 are delivered in 1981; therefore, we will refer to contract 5 as the 1981 F456.

2. The estimates will be shown annually; however, BEA produces quarterly estimates in current and constant dollars for the national income and product accounts.

3. Typically, the component prices developed for the estimation of defense purchases evolve from different sources. To start, prices are derived from budget estimates that contain a minimum of detail. Later, detailed contractor cost reports become available as the contract goes into production. At the completion of the contract, a final contractor cost report shows the final costs. As shown, the F123 and F456 prices represent estimates based on final contractor cost information. The data used for quality adjustment come from engineering change orders, which are DOD-approved engineering changes in the design or production of the weapon system.

4. The F123 contract history includes information for contracts 8–11. We excluded a substantial portion of the history for this aircraft; however, this

Table 10.2   F456 Unit Prices by Contract ($thousands)

Contract number	1	2	3	4	5	6	7	8	9	10	11	12
Contract quantity (units)	10	30	40	40	55	55	55	60	60	60	60	65
Delivery year	1977	1978	1979	1980	1981	1982	1983	1984	1985	1986	1987	1988
Contractor-furnished equipment (CFE)	12,932.9	7,817.6	6,390.8	5,528.7	6,114.8	6,824.1	7,210.8	10,995.6	9,366.4	9,418.3	10,184.3	10,402.6
Airframe	8,321.5	4,895.0	3,965.3	3,407.7	3,696.3	4,057.5	4,306.9	5,733.2	5,204.6	5,507.5	5,775.2	5,889.0
Flight controls	652.4	567.3	521.2	494.3	687.0	682.3	725.2	764.3	815.1	840.4	873.2	897.8
Penetration aids	43.2	34.6	31.8	25.4	26.3	26.9	27.2	27.1	27.3	28.0	28.1	28.9
Communications equipment	86.8	44.5	35.6	23.1	23.6	25.1	28.0	29.6	30.1	31.4	33.7	38.0
Radar equipment	2,880.9	1,371.8	932.1	677.0	749.3	1,048.5	1,102.3	3,113.0	2,096.6	1,771.7	1,802.3	1,844.1
Fire control equipment	436.1	335.5	298.5	268.3	280.5	301.3	329.4	585.2	457.0	485.5	894.7	903.1
Weapons and armament systems	512.0	568.9	606.3	632.9	651.7	682.5	691.8	743.1	735.8	753.9	777.1	801.8
Navigation equipment	569.1	376.6	312.3	249.8	257.1	279.0	302.2	534.6	458.5	469.9	474.6	500.2
Navigation equipment (CFE)	523.8	349.2	289.9	230.4	2.1	2.2	2.8	10.8	3.2	3.3	3.7	3.9
Navigation equipment (GFE)	45.3	27.4	22.4	19.4	255.0	276.8	299.4	523.8	455.3	466.6	470.9	496.3
Government-furnished equipment (GFE)	3,675.0	3,554.8	3,723.3	3,835.2	4,949.0	5,103.9	5,690.7	6,793.6	6,900.3	8,004.1	7,694.8	8,172.0
Engines (2 per aircraft)	1,640.6	1,705.4	1,925.2	2,125.7	3,059.8	3,353.2	3,532.8	3,692.4	3,806.4	4,658.9	4,702.8	4,911.6
Other GFE	2,034.3	1,849.4	1,798.1	1,709.5	1,889.2	1,750.7	2,157.9	3,101.2	3,093.9	3,345.2	2,992.0	3,260.4
Total	17,176.9	11,749.0	10,426.4	9,613.6	11,320.9	12,207.0	13,203.8	18,323.7	16,725.2	17,892.3	18,353.6	19,074.9

Addendum: Quality issues: contract 3 = fire control software update, price declines; contract 5 = engine upgrade; contract 10 = engine upgrade; contract 5 = CFE navigation equipment to GFE; contract 6 = radar enhancement to offset advances in enemy missile technology; contract 6 = GFE mix of equipment changes, less quality; contract 7 = GFE mix of equipment changes, more quality; contract 8 = model B introduced; contract 9 = correction of minor deficiency in flight controls; contract 11 = GFE fire control to CFE.

Note: contract 1 = existing engine used for new aircraft; contract 3 = buy size for engines falls as older system disappears; contract 4 = bottom of learning curve (no learning for weapons systems); contract 9 = bottom of learning curve for new model except radar (10).

was done so as to highlight the F456 and to avoid duplication of examples. For the same reasons, we have made the unlikely assumption that no quality adjustments were needed for the F123.

Because of the nature of this case study, many of the complexities of the work to develop current- and constant-dollar defense purchases are obscured. The estimates are required long before good information becomes available. For example, learning curves must be determined with the first production contract, and the percentage changes in the level of quality for a product must be estimated before prices can be calculated.

10.2.1 Price Derivation

BEA uses many different data sources for price derivation, but the best source is the contractor cost report. An example of this type of report for the fifth F456 contract appears in figure 10.1. The report shows recurring and nonrecurring costs by element code, or system component, as of the date on the report. Estimates of these costs at the completion of the contract are also displayed. Additional sections provide information on the type or terms of the contract (sec. 5, Contract Type), the total value of the contract (sec. 6, Contract Price), and any cost-sharing arrangements that prove applicable (sec. 7, Contract Ceiling). Many editions of these reports exist for a single contract because of reporting requirements; however, the report where the "To Date" section equals the "At Completion" section, such as found in this example, is the final source of price information available to BEA.

The report indicates that the total of nonrecurring and recurring costs for the fifty-five F456 airframes (element code A1) is $246.8 million. When developing a time series for a chosen pricing component, BEA must attempt to maintain the composition of that item over time. As such, the costs described as nonrecurring, by definition, must be excluded from the price-estimating procedure. Given recurring costs of $181.4 million and a contract quantity of fifty-five airframes, the per-unit cost of the airframe is $3.299 million. To obtain the per-unit price, BEA multiplies the per-unit cost by a profit (or loss) factor that allocates a proportional value of total profit and general and administrative (G&A) costs to the individual components.

Generally, the profit factor equals the total contract price divided by the total manufacturing cost. For a firm-fixed-price contract as shown in the example, no adjustments need to be made to this formula. As a result, the profit factor for this contract is 1.120393, or 570,000/508,750. The estimated price for the airframe is $3.696 million, or $3.299 million × 1.120393. Cost-sharing agreements typical of many types of contracts complicate this procedure because of the additional elements of target and ceiling prices. Whatever the procedure, the final goal is to obtain the actual value of contractor profit given the negotiated terms of the contract.

The detail at which BEA derives prices often depends solely on the amount of data provided in the contractor reports. Most of the prices derived for the

COST DATA REPORT Dollars in 000's	1. Program Buy 5 - F456	2. [ ] RDT&E [ ] Procurement		3. Contractor ABC Aerospace, Inc.	4. Report as of 31 Dec 1982
5. Contract Type FFP	6. Contract Price 570000	7. Contract Ceiling N/A	REMARKS		

		To Date — Costs Incurred			At Completion		Costs Incurred	
Element Code	REPORTING ELEMENTS	Non-Recurring	Recurring	TOTAL	Units	Non-Recurring	Recurring	TOTAL
A	AIR VEHICLE - F456	65394	300277	365671	55	65394	300277	365671
A1	Airframe	65394	181453	246847	55	65394	181453	246847
A2	Flight Controls		33726	33726	55		33726	33726
A3	Penetration Aids		1291	1291	55		1291	1291
A4	Communication Equipment		1159	1159	55		1159	1159
A5	Radar		36783	36783	55		36783	36783
A6	Fire Control		13770	13770	55		13770	13770
A61	Software		6342	6342	55		6342	6342
A62	Other fire control		7428	7428	55		7428	7428
A7	Navigation Equipment		103	103	55		103	103
A71	System A		103	103	55		103	103
A72	System B		0	0	55		0	0
A8	Weapons Delivery		23994	23994	55		23994	23994
A9	Armament		7998	7998	55		7998	7998
B	SYSTEMS TEST & EVALUATION			11862				11862
C	SYSTEM PROJECT MANAGEMENT			59384				59384
C1	Engineering Management			23495				23495
C2	Support Project Management			27393				27393
C3	Other System Project Management			8496				8496
D	DATA			38579				38579
D1	Technical Publications			29391				29391
D2	Engineering Data			2345				2345
D3	Management Data			102				102
D5	Other			6741				6741
E	KITS			5902				5902
F	OTHER PROGRAM SUPPORT			27352				27352
	TOTAL MANUFACTURING COST			508750				508750
	General & Administrative			40000				40000
	TOTAL COST			548750				548750
	Profit			21250				21250
	TOTAL PRICE			570000				570000

Fig. 10.1 F456 cost report

F456 were calculated at the second level of element code detail (A1, A2), which is the lowest level of information shown for most elements. Although more detail exists for fire control and navigation equipment, inconsistencies between the reports for different contract years create difficulties.

For example, early contract years for the F456 display the cost information in the same format as shown in figure 10.1. Later years show fire control equipment without the added breakdown. If we had priced fire control equipment in two sections (software and other), then an adjustment would be needed when the detailed information is no longer available. We can avoid the need for an adjustment without losing much accuracy by pricing these components at a higher level of detail.

Another situation involves the weapons delivery and armament elements. Table 10.2 shows a price for the combination of these two components. The F456 reports (fig. 10.1) show them as separate items; however, the F123 reports exhibit them as a single element without additional detail. Because of this, we have chosen to combine the F456 elements to resemble the component classifications used for the F123 more closely. A more consistent time series for the weapons/armament component results. The prices displayed in table 10.2 represent the data included under the Air Vehicle element code.

As seen in tables 10.1 and 10.2, the navigation equipment components procured under both contractor-furnished equipment (CFE) and government-furnished equipment (GFE) are combined to make a single pricing series. In 1981, the majority of the CFE navigation equipment switched to GFE navigation equipment; however, the total composition of navigation equipment remains the same. Owing to the method by which BEA processes quality adjustments, switches between priced series can cause some calculation problems. To avoid these problems, we combine these two very similar series and process at the total navigation equipment level. A detailed discussion of price series switches appears later in this paper.

Problems arise when attempting to develop consistent price series for the remaining elements, such as project management or technical publications. No quantities are associated with these elements, thus making it difficult to develop per-unit prices. The contract quantity for the air vehicle could be used as a proxy quantity; however, the composition of these elements changes, so any series developed in this manner would be inconsistent over time. For example, both the 1981 and the 1982 F456 contracts have air vehicle quantities of fifty-five; however, more than fifty-five technical publications were bought in the 1982 contract. Using air vehicles as a proxy quantity in this case causes an apparent price increase for technical publications when in fact the price might be stable. Also, because the share of these items to the total value of the contract varies over time, we cannot allocate them over the Air Vehicle elements.

As mentioned earlier, current dollars equal the sum of the products of prices and quantities delivered in a given time period. Constant dollars equal the sum of the products of the quantities delivered in the given time period and the corresponding base prices. Any adjustments needed for differences in quality over time for a given product are made in the base price. As a result, constant dollars reflect purchases of a varying mix of consistent product series.

Although BEA maintains price and quantity estimates for a large number of defense purchases, insufficient data on prices, quantities, or both require us to use an alternative approach when developing current and constant dollars for some items. The unpriced items such as data and project management, as well as the costs classified as nonrecurring, must be included in current- and constant-dollar defense purchases. As mentioned earlier, data are available for disbursements by class of aircraft. Progress payments, however, are not available. The method by which estimated progress payments are removed from disbursements is referred to as the "ratio method."

The "ratio method" uses disbursements data from financial reports to approximate purchases, in any given time period, for those items not specifically priced. For example, an aircraft contract represents purchases of $1,000 over a five-year period. Of the $1,000, only $750 appears in the data base of priced items. The remaining $250 is spread over the five years of the program by assigning 25 percent of all disbursements to current dollars in the time period when the disbursement is made. If disbursements in the first year are $200, the current-dollar unpriced items are $50 ($200 × .25). To calculate purchases, the $50 is then added to any current dollars that result from deliveries of aircraft in that year. This procedure assures that all appropriate DOD expenditures appear as defense purchases. To obtain constant dollars, the current dollars for unpriced items are deflated using the priced items as a proxy. Constant-dollar purchases then equal the sum of constant dollars for priced and unpriced items.

10.2.2   Price Series Splicing

A common problem in developing current- and constant-dollar defense purchases occurs with the introduction of new products. The case study example illustrates this problem with the F123 that ends in 1978 and the F456 that begins in 1977. A common method used to deal with this problem is to treat the new product as a quality adjustment to the old product. An evaluation of the physical differences between the old and the new systems in this case shows that quality improved for all components except engines. (The previously upgraded engines for the F123 are used without modification for the first four contracts of the F456.)

The procedure to calculate the quality adjustment for the new product is similar to the method used to calculate the value of quality change for a model change in a single system. Prices at comparable levels of production efficiency for both systems are estimated in prices of a single time period. The technique for choosing a comparison time period varies with the circumstances of the product series.

In the case study example, both the F123 and the F456 were produced in 1977. We need to estimate the value of quality change in 1977 dollars, so it is logical to choose 1977 as the comparison time period. This eliminates the need to adjust the calculated value of quality change to dollars of another time period and, therefore, reduces the amount of the estimation error in the calculations.

Although prices already exist for the F456 in 1977 dollars, they reflect costs at the top of the learning curve and represent an inefficient level of production. If the actual 1977 F456 prices are used in the quality-adjustment calculations, the value of quality change between the two aircraft would be grossly overstated. To eliminate this problem, prices at the bottom of the learning curve for the new system are chosen—1980 F456—as the starting point for the estimation procedure. These prices represent the point where labor efficiency in the new system is comparable to that in the old system. Once the new 1977 prices for the 1980 F456 have been estimated by removing a value for price change between these two time periods, they can be directly compared with the prices for the F123. The difference between the adjusted F456 prices and the F123 prices equals the value of quality change for the new system in 1977 dollars.

For example, the price of the F123 airframe in 1977 (contract 10 in table 10.1) is 1,652.8. The price of the F456 airframe at the bottom of the learning curve is 3,407.7 (contract 4 in table 10.2). Estimating and removing price change between 1977 and 1980 gives a price for the F456 airframe in 1977 dollars. The value of the price change must be based on a relevant price series that reflects a pure price change. The BEA has a limited choice of proxies for this purpose. The price series for another aircraft can provide a good source of price change if production of the other aircraft remains steady in the relevant time period. If such a source is unavailable, then we have to use a general price index for aircraft or aircraft components to estimate price change. For the purposes of this case study, a historical DOD procurement index series was used to estimate price change between contracts. In this case, the value of price change between 1977 and 1980 for the airframe is 888.7, and the resulting price estimate for the airframe in 1977 dollars is 2,519.0. Taking the difference between the prices for the two systems gives a quality adjustment of 866.2 (2,519.0 − 1,652.8) in 1977 dollars.

Often, the time period chosen for the splice represents the time when the decision was made to proceed with the procurement of the new product. This is generally the case when the two products do not have an actual overlap time period. For example, the government decides to procure the F456 in 1976 and deliveries start in 1977. If we assume that the F123 was last delivered in 1975, then we would estimate the F123 in 1976 prices and compare it with the estimates for an efficiently produced F456 in 1976 prices. The resulting values of quality change must then be adjusted to reflect prices comparable to the first delivery prices of the F456.

As the table 10.2 notes to contract 4 mention, the 1980 F456 represents the bottom of the learning curve for all components except the weapons and armament systems, which have no apparent learning curve. Because there is no need to adjust the 1977 F456 price for weapons and armament systems in order to derive a comparable level of production efficiency with the F123, the two systems can be linked without adjustments. The price of the F456 weapons and armament systems is 512.0 in 1977, and the price for similar F123 systems is 322.0 in 1977. If we assume that the entire difference in price is due to quality improvement, then the value of the quality change is 190.0 (512.0 − 322.0). Table 10.3 displays the quality adjustments by component for the entire F456 program.

A splicing technique must also be used when data sources for a single system change to the extent that the component prices no longer represent the same items. For example, contractor data exist for a substantial portion of a program, but budget documents provide the only available information for current and future contracts. The contractor information details cost data by component. The budget documents provide a single price for the combination of airframe and all other contractor-furnished equipment. Obviously, the contractor-furnished airframe price and the budget document airframe price represent different levels of detail and cannot be used in the same price series without adjustments.

One way in which we can handle this situation is to make a quality adjustment to the existing series. For example, on the basis of the last available contractor information, the price of the airframe could be quality adjusted using the sum of the prices of the other components as the value of the quality improvement. This estimate could then be used with the price derived from the budget documents. This procedure may sound acceptable, but it has many problems in practical application. For example, the budget documents include not only the same components extracted from contractor reports but also an unspecified and variable mix of other items. An estimate could be developed to account for this problem; however, the value developed for the quality adjustment in such a case becomes very judgmental.

The preferred way in which to handle the problems associated with changing data sources is to develop an alternative price series composed strictly of budget data. This series would then be used to move the primary pricing components, which are derived from contractor reports, in the relevant time periods. For those time periods in which the contractor data are available, the budget data series remains inactive and does not influence the derivation of current- and constant-dollar defense purchases. This procedure holds an advantage because it requires no arbitrary decisions about the composition of the budget aggregation.

10.2.3   Quality Valuation

Once component prices have been established for the systems and the two weapons systems have been spliced, the next major step in constructing a

Table 10.3   Value of Quality Adjustments for the F456 ($thousands)

	1	2	3	4	5	6	7	8	9	10	11	12
Contract number	1	2	3	4	5	6	7	8	9	10	11	12
Contract quantity (units)	10	30	40	40	55	55	55	60	60	60	60	65
Delivery year	1977	1978	1979	1980	1981	1982	1983	1984	1985	1986	1987	1988
Contractor-furnished equipment (CFE)												
Airframe	866.2							530.2				
Flight controls	118.6							17.3	0.0			
Penetration aids	6.0											
Communications equipment	5.0											
Radar equipment	146.7					235.1		511.3				
Fire control equipment	57.4		0.0					97.6				
Weapons and armament systems	190.0										400.0	
Navigation equipment	51.2				0.0			127.5				
Navigation equipment (CFE)	46.9				−235.0			.2				
Navigation equipment (GFE)	4.4				235.0			127.3				
Government-furnished equipment (GFE)												
Engines (2 per aircraft)										640.1		
Other GFE					710.5	−300.0	319.0	736.1			−444.9	
Total	414.7											

current- and constant-dollar series is the valuation of quality change within a particular system. For simplicity, we assume that the quality for each of the components of the F123 remains the same for the four contracts shown. We can then concentrate on the quality adjustments needed for the F456.

The first quality issue listed in the addendum to table 10.2 appears in 1979 (contract 3) when the contractor updates the fire control software. In the F456 program, the fire control software update incorporates new processing technology that increases the speed of calculations. The important point in this case is that the price of the improved software is less than the price of the original software—335.5 in 1978 and 298.5 in 1979. Given the performance/ cost-of-production method of adjusting for quality change and the rule that the cost of producing the physical change is the value of the quality improvement, we would not make any adjustments for the software update (see sec. 10.1.2 above).

The next quality issue appears in 1981 (contract 5) when the government purchases upgraded engines. The new engines increase the performance of the aircraft and, therefore, qualify as a quality adjustment. The value of the quality change equals the difference in prices between 1980 and 1981 less an adjustment for price change. In the example, quality change is 710.5 (3,059.8 − 2,125.7 − 223.6), where 223.6 is the estimate of price change based on a relevant price indicator series. The engine upgrade shown in 1986 (contract 10) is processed in the same manner.

The 1981 contract also includes another type of quality adjustment. In the example, contractor-furnished equipment and government-furnished equipment both include purchases of navigation equipment. In this contract year, the majority of the navigation equipment formerly procured from the prime contractor switched from CFE to GFE. The price for this equipment in 1981 is 235; therefore, the value of quality change for CFE navigation equipment is −235, and the value of quality change for GFE navigation equipment is 235. As mentioned earlier, switches such as this can cause problems in later calculations. In this case study, these two subcomponents never influence the final results. All processing is done at the level of total navigation equipment, where the quality-adjustment effect is zero.

The next quality adjustment occurs in 1982 (contract 6) when the radar is improved to offset advances in enemy missile technology. This quality adjustment is similar to the engine upgrade mentioned before. In this case, the value of the quality change is 235.1 (1,048.5 − 749.3 − 64.1), where 64.1 is the estimate of price change between 1981 and 1982.

The contracts for 1982 and 1983 (contracts 6 and 7) show the effects of changes in the mix of equipment for other GFE. For simplicity in this case study, we assume that the other GFE component contains a consistent mix of equipment in most contracts. Typically, the other GFE components of an aircraft system can vary substantially from one contract to the next. In these two contracts, the number of repair kits purchased falls in 1982 and resumes in

1983. The value of the repair kits not purchased in 1982 is 300, so the value of the quality adjustment for this component is −300. In 1983, we assume that the price of repair kits has increased by the same amount as the remaining components within other GFE; therefore, the value of the repair kits purchased and, thus, the quality adjustment is 319.0.

A model change usually requires some additional considerations when calculating the value of quality adjustment. In many instances, the price series will exhibit learning-curve characteristics, and additional steps must be taken so as not to overstate the value of the quality adjustment.

In 1984 (contract 8), deliveries for the new B model of the F456 begin. The data show evidence of a learning curve for some components of the new model, including the airframe, radar equipment, fire control equipment, navigation equipment, and other GFE. Quality improves for flight controls, but no learning curve is evident. The remaining components (penetration aids, communications equipment, weapons, and engines) do not have significant quality changes. In the example, the bottom of the learning curve for the new model is reached in 1985 for all components except radar equipment. The bottom of the learning curve for the radar equipment appears in 1986.

To calculate the correct value of the quality adjustment, we estimate the price of the A model in 1984 prices. Then we estimate the price of the B model at the bottom of the learning curve (1985 for all items except radar) in 1984 prices. The difference between the estimated prices for the B model and the estimated prices for the A model equals the value of quality adjustment for the new model.

For example, we estimate the price of the airframe for the A model in 1984 dollars as 4,507.2 (4,306.9 × 1.0465), where 1.0465 is the factor used to adjust for price change between 1983 and 1984. As mentioned earlier, for the case study, the value or factor used to adjust for price change between two time periods comes from a DOD procurement price indicator series. The price of the B model in 1984 dollars, derived from prices at the bottom of the learning curve, is 5,037.4 (5,204.6/1.0332), where 1.0332 is the factor used to adjust for price change between 1984 and 1985. The value of the quality adjustment for the new model airframe equals the difference between 5,037.4 and 4,507.2, or 530.2. The same procedure is used for all components; however, for radar equipment, the factor accounts for price change between 1984 and 1986. Also, because flight controls do not have a learning curve, no adjustment was necessary. The calculation of the quality adjustment for this component is identical to that for the engine upgrades explained earlier.

The next quality issue appears in 1985 (contract 9). A minor problem was discovered in the flight controls for the new B model. An engineering change order was instituted to correct the production deficiency responsible for the flaw in the flight controls, and the cost of the correction is $7,000 per aircraft. Although such a case, by its very nature, indicates a quality improvement, BEA would not make any adjustment in the constant-dollar purchases series.

In other words, the cost of the correction of a deficiency on a production aircraft will appear as a price change. As mentioned earlier, it is assumed that, when a system starts into production, it fits together and works.

The last quality-adjustment issue mentioned in the notes to table 10.2 concerns a GFE-CFE switch in 1987 (contract 11). Some fire control equipment previously included in the other GFE component is now being purchased as CFE. This case shows the opposite of the situation explained earlier for navigation equipment, but, in this situation, the two pricing series remain separate. On the basis of contractor cost information, the price of the fire control equipment is 400.0. Thus, the value of quality improvement for CFE radar equipment is 400.

Previously, we alluded to calculation problems when making quality adjustments for switches between pricing series. Assuming no other quality adjustments, the net effect on the total quality for the aircraft after a price series switch should be zero. In order to achieve this result, the quality adjustment for one series must equal a value that will offset the constant-dollar implications of the quality adjustment in the other series. The technique by which this is done involves some concepts not yet discussed in this case study; therefore, at this time, we will say only that the value of the quality adjustment for other GFE is -444.9. Appendix B discusses the problems of switches and quality valuation in detail.

10.2.4 Quality Factors

To account for quality adjustment in constant-dollar defense purchases, BEA adjusts the base price of a series to reflect the change in quality. Each current price reflects a certain level of quality in the product series, so we derive a quality-adjusted base price for every current price. The technique by which this is done involves the derivation of quality factors and cumulative quality factors. Quality factors are a way of expressing the value of quality change as a percentage change. Cumulative quality factors allow us to compare levels of quality over a sequence of contracts. Each current or contract price in a price series has a quality factor and a cumulative quality factor.

For example, a product originally costs $500 and a quality improvement occurs that is valued at $50. Quality improves by 10 percent; therefore, the quality factor is 1.100. Subsequently, the price of the product rises to $700, and another quality adjustment occurs that is valued at $35. This new quality adjustment is a 5 percent improvement over the already improved product, and the quality factor is 1.050. The two values of quality improvement are not comparable, given the price changes, and cannot be added; however, using quality factors, the difference in the levels of quality between the first and the latest observations can be expressed as another percentage change. This cumulative quality factor for the newest version of the product equals the product of the quality factors, or 1.155 (1.100 × 1.050).

In general, the quality factor equals a quality-adjusted price divided by a non-quality-adjusted price. In practice, we use two variations of this equation to derive quality factors. The method used depends on the situation and the assumptions made about the price and quality values available for use in the equation. The two methods are shown below (U.S. Department of Commerce 1975, 65). Equation (5) shows method 1, the adjusted current price link method, and equation (6) shows method 2, the back link method:

$$(5) \qquad\qquad F_s = \frac{P_s}{P_s - V_s},$$

$$(6) \qquad\qquad F_s = \frac{P_{s-1} + V_s}{P_{s-1}}$$

where F = quality factor, V = value of quality change, P = price, and s = contract sequence.

Although the above equations can be expressed in notations indicating time, quality factors really represent changes in quality over a sequence of contracts or purchases. Often, this loosely corresponds to time; however, that is not always the case. Because contracts may overlap in a real time series, the boundaries of time with regard to quality are not clear. Also, a quality factor may represent the change in quality between two different systems in the same time period. In that case, s represents the new system and $s - 1$ represents the previous or older system. For example, to splice the F456 to the F123, we develop a quality adjustment in 1977 based on prices for each system in 1977.

The adjusted current price link method, which is the most commonly used technique, uses the current product price as the quality-adjusted price in the numerator. The denominator is an estimate of the non-quality-adjusted price, which is derived by subtracting the value of quality change from the current price. This equation generates a legitimate quality factor only when the price and quality values are expressed in terms of the same level of production efficiency.

The back link method uses product prices from the previous contract in the equation. The quality-adjusted price in the numerator is the price of the previous contract plus the value of the quality adjustment between the two contracts in question. The denominator is the price of the previous contract. The implications of this technique require that the price and quality values used in the equation are expressed in terms of the same price level as well as the same level of production efficiency.

For example, if P_{s-1} and Q_s are expressed in dollars of different time periods, then a quality adjustment based on the sum of these two values (P_{s-1} and V_s) ignores any price change evident between the two time periods represented by the contracts $s - 1$ and s. If P_{s-1} is \$100, P_s is \$200, and V_s is \$90, then, using the back link method, the resulting quality factor is 1.9, or

(100 + 90)/100. Prices between contract $s - 1$ and contract s increase 10 percent, so $s - 1$ and s dollars are not equivalent. But, by using the back link method to calculate the quality factor, an assumption of equivalence is made. As a result, the quality factor in this example would be overstated.

We generally use the back link method when the value of the quality change and the two prices are all expressed in comparable dollars but the levels of production efficiency differ. This is the case when splicing two price series or when changing models. The value of quality change incorporated in the new product is based on an estimate of an efficiently produced item in that time period. In other words, the price is adjusted for the learning curve before the quality calculation is done. During the procedure, a price for the older product is also generated for that time period if a price does not already exist. The back link method allows us to estimate a meaningful value in the numerator, namely, the price of the previous product if a quality adjustment had occurred. For example, the 1977 F123 airframe price of 1,652.8 plus the value of quality change of 866.2 for the 1977 F456 airframe is a realistic estimate of a quality-improved airframe in 1977 dollars.

On the other hand, in a case where the learning curve is a factor, the adjusted current price link method generates a meaningless denominator because the price and quality values represent different levels of production efficiency. For example, in 1977, the price of the F456 airframe is 8,321.5, and the value of the quality change is again 866.2. Using the adjusted current price link method, the quality factor is 1.116, or 8,321.5/(8,321.5 − 866.2). The quality factor is meaningless because the denominator has no economic meaning. The price of 8,321.5 is abnormally high because of the learning-curve considerations, but the quality change value of 866.2 already includes adjustments to remove the learning-curve effect. Therefore, using this method to calculate the quality factor understates the value of quality change. It should be noted that, if a price that had been adjusted for the learning curve were used in place of 8,321.5, then this equation would generate a legitimate quality factor equal to that generated by the back link method.

Given comparable prices and quality values, either the back link or the adjusted current price link technique can be used to obtain the correct quality factor. In practice, we find it easier to calculate quality factors by making a distinction between these two methods. In the case study, the back link method was used to calculate component quality factors in those time periods when prices are at the top of the learning curve—1977 and 1984. The adjusted current price link method was used in all other time periods.

For example, for the 1977 (contract 1) F456 airframe, the price is 8,321.5, and the value of quality change is 866.2. The price for the previous observation is 1,652.8, or the price of the F123 in 1977. Using the back link method, the quality factor is 1.5241, or (1,652.8 + 866.2)/1,652.8. In 1986, the quality factor for the engines using the adjusted current price link method is 1.1593, or 4,658.9/(4,658.9 − 640.1).

Once the quality factors have been calculated, cumulative quality factors for the product series must be derived. The cumulative quality factor is 1.000 for the first observation of a pricing component, and subsequent cumulative quality factors accumulate multiplicatively from this point. The choice of the base year has no relevance in the equation. As in equations (5) and (6), the cumulative quality factor is derived for each product series by contract sequence:

$$(7) \qquad M_s = M_{s-1} \times F_s,$$

where M = cumulative quality factor, F = component quality factor, and s = contract sequence.

In the case example, as mentioned earlier, we are assuming that quality is unchanged for the F123. As a result of this assumption, the quality factors for each of the F123 components for contracts 8–11 must equal 1.000. The cumulative quality factors for these contracts also equal 1.000.

Cumulative quality factors change when the new system is introduced. For the 1977 F456 airframe, the quality factor is 1.5241. When multiplied by the cumulative quality factor for the previous contract (1.000), the cumulative quality factor for the airframe in 1977 is also 1.5241. The next available airframe quality adjustment occurs in 1984 when the B model is introduced. The quality factor for the 1984 airframe is 1.1176, and, when multiplied by the cumulative quality factor for 1983, the cumulative quality factor for 1984 is 1.7034, or (1.5241×1.1176). In other words, the quality of the B model of the F456 is 70.3 percent greater than that of the F123.

Tables 10.4 and 10.5 show the component quality factors and cumulative quality factors for each contract.

10.2.5 Base Price Derivation

Cumulative quality factors allow us to calculate base prices for any base year with little difficulty. We do this by calculating what we call a *non-quality-adjusted base price* for each component series for the base year in question. The non-quality-adjusted base price equals the base period current dollars divided by the product of the base period quantity and base period cumulative quality factor. In other words, for a given base year, the non-quality-adjusted base price is the base price for the first observation of a component series.

$$(8) \qquad N = \frac{P_b}{M_b},$$

where N = non-quality-adjusted base price, M = cumulative quality factor, P = price, and b = base period.

This simple equation illustrates the procedure when only one contract is delivered in the base year. If different contract values exist in the base period, then each of the contract quantities must be multiplied by its respective price in the numerator and its cumulative quality factor in the denominator.

Table 10.4   F456 Quality Factors by Contract

Contract number	1	2	3	4	5	6	7	8	9	10	11	12
Contract quantity (units)	10	30	40	40	55	55	55	60	60	60	60	65
Delivery year	1977	1978	1979	1980	1981	1982	1983	1984	1985	1986	1987	1988
Contractor-furnished equipment (CFE)												
Airframe	1.5241	1.0000	1.0000	1.0000	1.0000	1.0000	1.0000	1.1176	1.0000	1.0000	1.0000	1.0000
Flight controls	1.4808	1.0000	1.0000	1.0000	1.0000	1.0000	1.0000	1.0232	1.0000	1.0000	1.0000	1.0000
Penetration aids	1.4681	1.0000	1.0000	1.0000	1.0000	1.0000	1.0000	1.0000	1.0000	1.0000	1.0000	1.0000
Communications equipment	1.4186	1.0000	1.0000	1.0000	1.0000	1.0000	1.0000	1.0000	1.0000	1.0000	1.0000	1.0000
Radar equipment	1.4148	1.0000	1.0000	1.0000	1.0000	1.2891	1.0000	1.4432	1.0000	1.0000	1.0000	1.0000
Fire control equipment	1.4073	1.0000	1.0000	1.0000	1.0000	1.0000	1.0000	1.2830	1.0000	1.0000	1.8085	1.0000
Weapons and armament systems	1.5899	1.0000	1.0000	1.0000	1.0000	1.0000	1.0000	1.0000	1.0000	1.0000	1.0000	1.0000
Navigation equipment	1.3838	1.0000	1.0000	1.0000	1.0000	1.0000	1.0000	1.4030	1.0000	1.0000	1.0000	1.0000
Navigation equipment (CFE)	1.3795	1.0000	1.0000	1.0000	0.0089	1.0000	1.0000	1.0636	1.0000	1.0000	1.0000	1.0000
Navigation equipment (GFE)	1.4368	1.0000	1.0000	1.0000	12.7500	1.0000	1.0000	1.4062	1.0000	1.0000	1.0000	1.0000
Government-furnished equipment (GFE)												
Engines (2 per aircraft)	1.0000	1.0000	1.0000	1.0000	1.3025	1.0000	1.0000	1.0000	1.0000	1.1593	1.0000	1.0000
Other GFE	1.4885	1.0000	1.0000	1.0000	1.0000	0.8537	1.1735	1.3260	1.0000	1.0000	0.8706	1.0000

Table 10.5   F456 Cumulative Quality Factors by Contract

Contract number	1	2	3	4	5	6	7	8	9	10	11	12
Contract quantity (units)	10	30	40	40	55	55	55	60	60	60	60	65
Delivery year	1977	1978	1979	1980	1981	1982	1983	1984	1985	1986	1987	1988
Contractor-furnished equipment (CFE)												
Airframe	1.5241	1.5241	1.5241	1.5241	1.5241	1.5241	1.5241	1.7034	1.7034	1.7034	1.7034	1.7034
Flight controls	1.4808	1.4808	1.4808	1.4808	1.4808	1.4808	1.4808	1.5151	1.5151	1.5151	1.5151	1.5151
Penetration aids	1.4681	1.4681	1.4681	1.4681	1.4681	1.4681	1.4681	1.4681	1.4681	1.4681	1.4681	1.4681
Communications equipment	1.4186	1.4186	1.4186	1.4186	1.4186	1.4186	1.4186	1.4186	1.4186	1.4186	1.4186	1.4186
Radar equipment	1.4148	1.4148	1.4148	1.4148	1.4148	1.8238	1.8238	2.6321	2.6321	2.6321	2.6321	2.6321
Fire control equipment	1.4073	1.4073	1.4073	1.4073	1.4073	1.4073	1.4073	1.8056	1.8056	1.8056	3.2655	3.2655
Weapons and armament systems	1.5899	1.5899	1.5899	1.5899	1.5899	1.5899	1.5899	1.5899	1.5899	1.5899	1.5899	1.5899
Navigation equipment	1.3838	1.3838	1.3838	1.3838	1.3838	1.3838	1.3838	1.9415	1.9415	1.9415	1.9415	1.9415
Navigation equipment (CFE)	1.3795	1.3795	1.3795	1.3795	0.0122	0.0122	0.0122	0.0130	0.0130	0.0130	0.0130	0.0130
Navigation equipment (GFE)	1.4368	1.4368	1.4368	1.4368	18.3197	18.3197	18.3197	25.7612	25.7612	25.7612	25.7612	25.7612
Government-furnished equipment (GFE)												
Engines (2 per aircraft)	1.0000	1.0000	1.0000	1.0000	1.3025	1.3025	1.3025	1.3025	1.3025	1.5099	1.5099	1.5099
Other GFE	1.4885	1.4885	1.4885	1.4885	1.4885	1.2708	1.4912	1.9773	1.9773	1.9773	1.7214	1.7214

Once the non-quality-adjusted base price has been derived, the base price for any individual contract within the component series can be calculated. The base price equals the non-quality-adjusted base price multiplied by the cumulative quality factor:

(9) $B_s = N \times M_s$,

where N = non-quality-adjusted base price, M = cumulative quality factor, B = base price, and s = contract sequence.

For example, the base year for consideration is 1975 = 100. The F123 engines have a price of 1,459.7, a quantity of 70, and a cumulative quality factor of 1.000 in the base year. Using equation 8, the non-quality-adjusted base price for engines is 1,459.7, or (1,459.7 × 70)/(70 × 1.000).

The cumulative quality factor for engines changes for the 1981 contract of the F456. Using equation (9), the base price for the 1981 engines is 1,901.2, or (1,459.7 × 1.3025).

Table 10.6 displays the 1975 = 100 base prices for each of the component contract values. Table 10.7 displays the resulting price indexes using the price, quantity, and base price information. Table 10.8 shows purchases in constant 1975 prices.

10.3 Conclusions

This case study has examined many issues and procedures common to the work done at the Bureau of Economic Analysis for the derivation of the constant-dollar defense purchases series for military equipment. Aircraft, which is the largest of the durable goods aggregations, accounted for 8.7 percent of defense purchases in 1982. Since 1982, the portion of defense purchases attributable to aircraft has fluctuated between 8.3 and 11.9 percent. Since the 1987 high of 11.9 percent of defense purchases, aircraft's share of the total has gradually declined to 10.5 percent in 1989. The aircraft series detailed in this case study is typical of most of the major equipment purchases included in defense current and constant dollars. Some additional observations might prove useful.

10.3.1 Highlights

The base year presented in the case study is 1975. During that time, the F123 is a mature program with efficient production quantities, and the F456 has not yet appeared. Base prices represent prices at efficient production levels. Consider another base year. In 1984, the deliveries of a new model F456 begin, and, as explained earlier, many of the components such as the airframe and radar equipment have learning curves. As a result, a time series using 1984 base prices would reflect inefficient production levels for many of the components. Given multiple aircraft series in a 1984 = 100 base, the case study aircraft will have a relatively higher importance solely because of the location of the base period in relation to this aircraft's learning curve.

Table 10.6 Base Prices, CY 1975 = 100 ($thousands)

	1	2	3	4	5	6	7	8	9	10	11	12	Non-Quality-Adjusted Base Price
Contract number	1	2	3	4	5	6	7	8	9	10	11	12	
Contract quantity (units)	10	30	40	40	55	55	55	60	60	60	60	65	
Delivery year	1977	1978	1979	1980	1981	1982	1983	1984	1985	1986	1987	1988	
Contractor-furnished equipment (CFE)	3,325.3	3,325.3	3,325.3	3,325.3	3,325.3	3,437.0	3,437.0	3,952.9	3,952.9	3,952.9	4,116.1	4,116.1	2,205.8
Airframe	2,071.9	2,071.9	2,071.9	2,071.9	2,071.9	2,071.9	2,071.9	2,315.6	2,315.6	2,315.6	2,315.6	2,315.6	1,359.4
Flight controls	288.3	288.3	288.3	288.3	288.3	288.3	288.3	295.0	295.0	295.0	295.0	295.0	194.7
Penetration aids	14.8	14.8	14.8	14.8	14.8	14.8	14.8	14.8	14.8	14.8	14.8	14.8	10.1
Communications equipment	12.6	12.6	12.6	12.6	12.6	12.6	12.6	12.6	12.6	12.6	12.6	12.6	8.9
Radar equipment	386.6	386.6	386.6	386.6	386.6	498.4	498.4	719.3	719.3	719.3	719.3	719.3	273.3
Fire control equipment	157.3	157.3	157.3	157.3	157.3	157.3	157.3	201.8	201.8	201.8	365.0	365.0	111.8
Weapons and armament systems	393.6	393.6	393.6	393.6	393.6	393.6	393.6	393.6	393.6	393.6	393.6	393.6	247.6
Navigation equipment	135.4	135.4	135.4	135.4	135.4	135.4	135.4	190.0	190.0	190.0	190.0	190.0	97.9
Navigation equipment (CFE)													
Navigation equipment (GFE)													
Government-furnished equipment (GFE)	2,408.8	2,408.8	2,408.8	2,408.8	2,850.3	2,711.5	2,852.0	3,162.0	3,162.0	3,464.8	3,301.6	3,301.6	2,097.3
Engines (2 per aircraft)	1,459.7	1,459.7	1,459.7	1,459.7	1,901.2	1,901.2	1,901.2	1,901.2	1,901.2	2,204.0	2,204.0	2,204.0	1,459.7
Other GFE	949.1	949.1	949.1	949.1	949.1	810.2	950.8	1,260.7	1,260.7	1,260.7	1,097.5	1,097.5	637.6
Total	5,869.5	5,869.5	5,869.5	5,869.5	6,311.0	6,283.9	6,424.5	7,304.8	7,304.8	7,607.6	7,607.6	7,607.6	4,400.9

Table 10.7   Implicit Price Deflators (CY 1975 = 100)

	\multicolumn{14}{Delivery Year}													
	1975	1976	1977	1978	1979	1980	1981	1982	1983	1984	1985	1986	1987	1988
Contractor-furnished equipment (CFE)	100.000	111.688	168.561	169.782	192.190	166.264	183.889	198.546	209.797	278.167	236.952	238.266	247.428	252.733
Airframe	100.000	110.797	168.882	168.908	191.387	164.476	178.405	195.837	207.872	247.592	224.763	237.843	249.402	254.318
Flight controls	100.000	111.939	143.126	156.078	180.753	171.419	238.258	236.619	251.514	259.050	276.268	284.835	295.960	304.281
Penetration aids	100.000	116.754	153.853	170.513	214.798	171.568	177.647	181.700	183.726	183.051	184.402	189.130	189.806	195.209
Communications equipment	100.000	114.296	222.983	216.984	282.126	182.721	187.176	198.823	221.897	234.577	238.539	248.842	267.069	301.146
Radar equipment	100.000	111.939	227.142	215.235	241.072	175.105	193.794	210.362	221.156	432.766	291.457	246.291	250.551	256.362
Fire control equipment	100.000	113.698	149.933	161.252	189.743	170.522	178.301	191.523	209.385	289.936	226.398	240.540	245.120	247.409
Weapons and armament systems	100.000	114.901	130.067	138.998	154.026	160.784	165.560	173.385	175.747	188.780	186.925	191.523	197.417	203.692
Navigation equipment	100.000	115.936	180.560	191.371	230.601	184.435	189.851	206.023	223.190	281.346	241.325	247.326	249.769	263.270
Navigation equipment (CFE)														
Navigation equipment (GFE)														
Government-furnished equipment (GFE)	100.000	111.340	123.199	131.216	154.571	159.215	173.629	188.235	199.533	214.854	218.227	231.014	233.064	247.520
Engines (2 per aircraft)	100.000	109.678	112.393	116.833	131.888	145.623	160.935	176.369	185.816	194.210	200.206	211.381	213.372	222.846
Other GFE	100.000	115.144	146.593	160.111	189.458	180.119	199.058	216.077	226.962	245.986	245.404	265.339	272.607	297.069
Total	100.000	111.617	147.665	152.777	177.637	163.790	179.383	194.258	205.523	250.844	228.961	235.189	241.253	250.734

Table 10.8 Constant Dollars (CY 1975 = 100)

	Delivery Year													
	1975	1976	1977	1978	1979	1980	1981	1982	1983	1984	1985	1986	1987	1988
Contractor-furnished equipment (CFE)	154,404	165,432	198,685	265,190	133,010	133,010	182,889	189,037	189,037	237,172	237,172	237,172	246,963	267,544
Airframe	95,158	101,955	122,674	164,111	82,875	82,875	113,953	113,953	113,953	138,936	138,936	138,936	138,936	150,514
Flight controls	13,631	14,605	17,488	23,255	11,534	11,534	15,859	15,859	15,859	17,702	17,702	17,702	17,702	19,178
Penetration aids	706	756	904	1,200	592	592	814	814	814	888	888	888	888	962
Communications equipment	623	667	793	1,046	505	505	694	694	694	757	757	757	757	820
Radar equipment	19,131	20,497	24,364	32,097	15,466	15,466	21,266	27,413	27,413	43,160	43,160	43,160	43,160	46,757
Fire control equipment	7,825	8,384	9,957	13,103	6,293	6,293	8,652	8,652	8,652	12,110	12,110	12,110	21,901	23,727
Weapons and armament systems	17,331	18,568	22,505	30,378	15,745	15,745	21,650	21,650	21,650	23,618	23,618	23,618	23,618	25,586
Navigation equipment	6,850	7,340	8,694	11,402	5,417	5,417	7,448	7,448	7,448	11,400	11,400	11,400	11,400	12,350
Navigation equipment (CFE)														
Navigation equipment (GFE)														
Government-furnished equipment (GFE)	146,812	157,299	181,387	229,563	96,352	96,352	156,767	149,131	156,861	189,717	189,717	207,885	198,094	214,602
Engines (2 per aircraft)	102,181	109,480	124,077	153,271	58,389	58,389	104,568	104,568	104,568	114,074	114,074	132,242	132,242	143,262
Other GFE	44,631	47,819	57,310	76,291	37,963	37,963	52,199	44,563	52,293	75,643	75,643	75,643	65,852	71,340
Total	308,066	330,071	388,765	506,155	234,779	234,779	347,104	345,616	353,346	438,290	438,290	456,458	456,458	494,496

In both 1985 and 1986, the actual number of F456 aircraft remains the same; however, purchases measured in constant dollars change because the engine was upgraded in 1986.

In the notes to table 10.2, the second item indicates that the buy size, or the contracted quantity, for the engines falls because of the discontinued production of the F123. This issue raises an important point that has not yet been addressed in the case study. Buy size does not affect the definition of a specification. When the engine quantities fall from 210 (105 aircraft × 2 engines each) in 1978 to 80 in 1979, the price for a set of engines increases from 1,705.4 to 1,925.2. This translates to a substantial increase in the implicit price deflator for engines.

The base price derivation and quality-adjustment methods described in the case study offer us considerable flexibility. BEA can easily calculate defense purchases on any base because much of the preliminary work done for the published series need not be repeated for another base. Given prices, quantities, and quality factors, the derivation of base prices for any year can be completely automated.

10.3.2   Actual Data

Table 10.9 displays the implicit price deflators (IPD) and fixed-weighted price indexes for new aircraft implicit in the published defense purchases series. Table 10.10 shows the price indexes for various aircraft from which the published fixed-weighted index was calculated.

The differences between the two published series in table 10.9 indicate the effects of quantity shifts. For example, in 1986, the fixed index declines 7.4 percent, while the IPD increases 4.5 percent. Much of the difference can be attributed to the B-1. The B-1 price declines because of the learning curve, so the fixed-weighted index falls. The B-1 quantities increase 800 percent between 1985 and 1986. The large shift in the relative importance of the B-1 causes the IPD to increase. In addition, higher deliveries of C-5 aircraft in 1986 also help increase the IPD; the C-5 has no effect on the fixed-weighted index because it was not delivered in the base year.

The price indexes shown in table 10.10 exhibit many of the qualities highlighted earlier in this paper. For example, learning curves can be seen for many of these systems. The B-1 has a short life in which the prices drop dramatically as the buy sizes increase. The TR-1 prices drop steadily for many years because of the relatively small quantities purchased in each contract. In 1988, the F-14 index rises dramatically owing to deliveries of a new model that is moving down a learning curve.

Generally, when a learning curve is evident, indexes start very high and drop to a level similar to the other systems in that time period. The B-1 starts above 300 and drops to almost 130 at the bottom of its learning curve. The exception to this is when a system is high on its learning curve in the base

Table 10.9   **Implicit Price Deflator and Fixed-Weighted Price Indexes for Defense Purchases (CY 1982 = 100)**

	Fixed	IPD	% Change Fixed	% Change IPD	Difference in Change, Fixed − IPD
1972	39.1	46.7			
1973	43.2	48.7	10.3	4.2	6.0
1974	46.4	54.1	7.5	11.2	−3.7
1975	52.5	55.7	13.1	2.9	10.1
1976	53.5	58.4	2.0	4.8	−2.7
1977	57.1	62.5	6.8	7.1	−0.4
1978	64.4	67.9	12.7	8.6	4.1
1979	75.1	73.2	16.6	7.9	8.8
1980	79.8	78.8	6.3	7.6	−1.3
1981	89.3	87.2	11.8	10.7	1.1
1982	100.0	100.0	12.0	14.6	−2.6
1983	110.8	108.6	10.8	8.6	2.2
1984	129.8	125.6	17.2	15.6	1.6
1985	131.3	117.8	1.1	−6.2	7.3
1986	121.6	123.1	−7.4	4.5	−11.9
1987	113.4	108.5	−6.7	−11.9	5.2
1988	110.5	99.9	−2.5	−7.9	5.4
1989	112.7	99.5	2.0	−0.4	2.4

year. By rule, the index in the base year must be 100; therefore, these systems usually have very low indexes; the TR-1 is an example.

Changes in buy size produce interesting results in the price indexes for individual systems. The stretch-out in the A-10 program best illustrates the effect of buy size on prices. The price index increases 34.8 percent in 1982, 48.2 percent in 1983, and 8.5 percent in 1984. Four contracts were delivered during that time period, during which quantities fell from 142 to 60 to 20 in each of the last two buys.

Table 10.10   System-Level Price Indexes for Military Aircraft (CY 1982 = 100)

	A-7	A-10	C-130	KC-10	E-3	TR-1	F-15	F-16	B-1	F-14	F-18	A-6	E-2	EA-6	P-3	CH-53	AH-1	C-12	UH-60
1972	19.5	31.2	26.5	16.4	40.1	16.9	45.6	34.8	0.0	57.3	0.0	36.2	59.5	49.1	43.5	30.2	29.3	23.5	19.6
1973	20.4	32.6	28.6	17.9	46.1	18.2	54.4	44.3	0.0	57.6	0.0	37.5	59.4	41.8	42.5	37.3	35.1	28.9	23.3
1974	23.8	38.6	32.3	20.7	47.0	19.8	64.0	56.8	0.0	51.4	0.0	41.3	56.2	41.4	41.5	37.1	36.9	30.7	25.1
1975	24.8	49.6	37.5	23.7	62.4	23.5	76.0	64.9	0.0	55.6	0.0	49.9	51.8	42.1	47.3	35.2	37.1	33.0	26.9
1976	27.8	80.3	38.5	24.8	62.4	23.5	61.2	50.4	0.0	58.4	0.0	55.9	59.9	52.5	57.2	47.6	47.2	39.8	35.2
1977	31.3	74.4	46.8	29.8	64.9	28.7	62.9	54.2	0.0	58.9	0.0	50.9	73.5	61.4	72.9	49.7	52.9	44.3	53.5
1978	43.7	69.6	49.8	31.8	64.3	28.7	64.4	77.8	0.0	64.1	0.0	57.1	70.0	60.7	70.4	57.2	49.3	53.4	67.1
1979	54.0	66.6	62.2	39.4	78.2	30.5	70.5	102.2	0.0	68.3	0.0	69.8	87.5	65.4	70.9	65.2	51.3	58.3	90.7
1980	55.9	67.0	80.7	51.0	95.6	37.6	77.7	87.7	0.0	74.2	75.1	78.6	92.4	75.4	87.2	79.1	59.0	77.4	77.7
1981	65.4	74.2	91.0	103.5	98.3	63.6	85.0	90.9	0.0	87.6	101.3	82.0	98.9	85.0	90.6	94.3	71.0	86.7	83.8
1982	100.0	100.0	100.0	100.0	100.0	100.0	100.0	100.0	0.0	100.0	100.0	100.0	100.0	100.0	100.0	100.0	100.0	100.0	100.0
1983	126.7	148.2	106.5	110.4	102.4	100.2	116.4	108.2	360.5	96.6	103.1	81.3	103.6	100.2	108.4	125.0	126.9	104.4	101.1
1984	118.5	160.8	118.2	114.1	102.3	87.1	121.5	126.0	331.7	99.3	111.0	98.1	104.3	97.3	117.7	120.6	168.4	104.4	98.7
1985	0.0	0.0	125.9	119.2	104.7	59.2	136.5	117.0	349.7	104.3	107.5	116.9	106.3	92.7	118.3	108.7	109.2	104.4	98.3
1986	0.0	0.0	122.6	116.5	98.8	54.0	146.6	116.4	190.8	106.1	118.2	147.1	115.7	86.0	120.4	116.5	103.0	104.4	100.8
1987	0.0	0.0	113.1	106.3	104.2	50.7	140.6	105.4	133.6	103.6	117.3	136.7	118.4	91.9	121.5	114.6	95.9	104.4	105.1
1988	0.0	0.0	120.0	114.4	123.5	51.7	144.1	100.8	131.9	161.7	114.8	151.9	115.7	101.6	121.3	111.2	93.5	105.4	110.2
1989	0.0	0.0	120.0	114.4	128.7	54.9	140.7	103.9	135.8	159.3	116.0	148.6	118.4	117.7	121.5	117.9	96.2	106.4	114.1

Appendix A
Learning Curves

Cost analysts have observed that, as more units of a complex item are produced, the labor hours required for producing successive units falls. This relation is called the organizational learning (or progress) curve. The earliest publication on a learning curve for aircraft was Wright (1936). Since that time, a considerable amount of research on this phenomenon has been undertaken by cost analysts and economists. A recent nonmathematical review of learning-curve research is contained in Argote and Epple (1990).

Most common forms of the learning curve are represented by a smoothly decreasing function for labor hours per unit of output as the number of units produced increases. The simple form of the curve is the "unit" or "Boeing" curve, in which the learning rate is defined as the percentage that labor hours decline as the quantities produced double. The following example depicts a learning rate of 10 percent:

Unit No.	Labor Hours
4	100
8	90
16	81
32	73

The labor hours saved per unit decrease by 10 percent as the number of units produced doubles. Learning curves are usually expressed in terms of the slope, which is 100 minus the learning rate. The example above represents a 90 percent learning curve.

The learning curve is important in deriving the appropriate price for splicing in a new weapons system. The splice price should represent the quality difference between the two systems at a comparable phase in the production cycle. Because of learning, prices of initial units of the new system will be overstated relative to the old weapons system where significant learning has already taken place. Splicing with the price for the first unit would result in the value of the resources saved in learning being treated as additional quality in the new system. The initial splice price would be very high, prices would drop after the splice period, and overall price change for the new system would be understated.

It is assumed that, by the hundredth unit of production of a new fighter aircraft, additional learning is relatively minor. Therefore, the price of the hundredth unit, expressed in dollars of the time period when the first production contract is signed, represents the best estimate of the actual resource cost difference between the two systems. Note that this estimate does not account for changed technologies between the two aircraft.

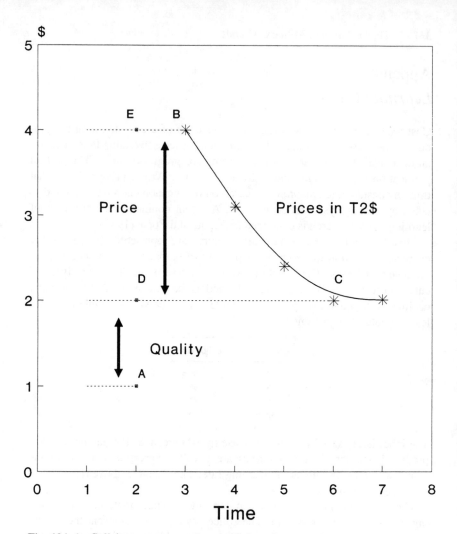

Fig. 10A.1   Splicing weapons systems with learning

Table 10A.1   **Alternative Splicing for Price Indexes**

Time Period	Price Per Unit			Price Indexes				
	F-I	F-II		F-I	F-II	Combined		
		$ of T	Actual			P1	P2	P3
Base = −1	2,000	3,200	3,200					
−1	2,000			100.0		100.0	100.0	100.0
0	2,500			125.0		125.0	125.0	125.0
1	3,000			150.0		150.0	150.0	150.0
2	3,000	8,500	9,000	150.0	281.3	230.8	150.0	450.0
3		6,500	8,000		250.0	250.0	133.3	400.0
4		5,000	7,000		218.8	218.8	116.7	350.0
5		4,000	7,500		234.4	234.4	125.0	375.0
6		3,500	8,000		250.0	250.0	133.3	400.0

Figure 10A.1 illustrates the procedure. Point A represents the price of the old system at time period 2, when the decision is made to purchase a new system. The curve BC represents the estimated resources needed to produce the new system in factor prices of time period 2. Point C is the hundredth unit of the new system. The difference in price of this unit, when compared to the old system, represents the difference in quality between the two systems $(D - A)$. The remaining difference in the expected price of the new system $(E - D)$ is recorded as a change in price.

A numerical example of how the learning curve is used to create an adjusted price and splice two series together may help clarify the procedure. Figure 10A.2 and table 10A.1 present data to splice the aircraft F-II to the aircraft F-I. In order to simplify the illustration, we have assumed that there are no quality changes to the aircraft during this period.

The initial production contract for the F-II was signed in time period 0, when the F-I was being delivered at a price of $2,500 ($A$ on fig. 10A.2). In dollars of time period 0, the F-II is expected to have a price of $8,500 ($B$) for the first lot purchased and drop to $3,500 ($C$) for the fifth lot. These prices are derived by estimating the unit resource requirements (labor, materials, etc.) and expressing them in terms of time period 0 dollars. These estimates represent the expected savings in resources due to learning. Adjusting these prices for expected price change yields the price to be paid.

The hundredth F-II will be delivered from the fourth lot at a price of $4,000 ($D$) in time period 0 dollars. When compared to the F-I price of $2,500 ($A$) in time period 0, this price yields a quality difference (or, more specifically, a resource cost difference) of $1,500 ($D' - A$). In short, one F-II is the equivalent of 1.6 F-Is in period 0 dollars. The F-I, however, has increased in price by 25 percent from the base period price of $2,000 ($E$). Therefore, the base price for the F-II must be adjusted to maintain the ratio of 1:1.6. This yields a F-II base price of $3,200 ($F$).

Using the derived base price for the F-II, a price index can be constructed for the spliced series (table 10A.1). The actual prices paid for the F-II are used to calculate the index; the quality link is carried in the new base price. The constant period 0 estimates are used only to estimate the resource-cost difference between the two systems. This procedure yields a high splice price for the F-II, thereby causing the price index to jump dramatically and then decline (index P1).

P2 shows the price index that would result if the same price data were used for the two aircraft, but the direct link procedure was used to splice the price series. This assumes that the entire difference in price between the two aircraft is due to a difference in quality. P3 shows the price index that would result if the direct comparison method were used to splice the two series. This method assumes that there is no difference in quality between the two aircraft.

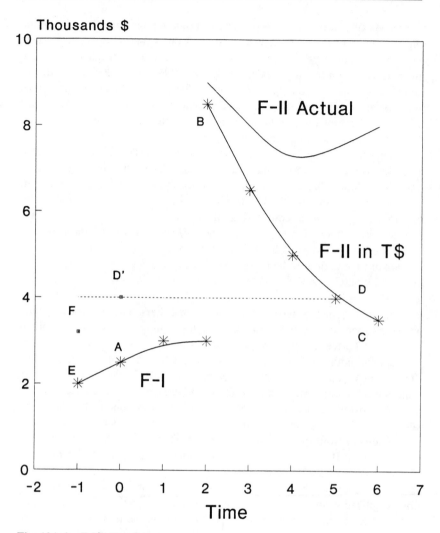

Fig. 10A.2   F-I/F-II splice

Appendix B
Analysis of Price Series Switches

Quality factors and the level of detail at which BEA derives prices lead to some problems for a few situations. Although the pricing series appear fairly detailed, they generally refer to a group of items. At times, BEA has sufficient information to subdivide these groups; however, details for many groups remain vague. A problem arises when an element of one pricing group shifts to another pricing group. In the case study, this situation can be observed in 1981 when some contractor-furnished (CFE) navigation equipment shifts to government-furnished (GFE) navigation equipment. Also, in 1987, some fire control equipment embedded in the other GFE series shifts to the CFE fire control series. Because the quality implied by the sum of these components remains the same, the sum of the base prices should also remain unchanged.

The way in which we derive quality factors implies that the percentage change in the price due to a quality adjustment translates to the same percentage change in the base price. But the relative importance of a product in the shift time period seldom equates to the same relative importance in constant prices. As a result, in most product shift cases, the quality factor technique produces a discrepancy between the changes in value of the two base prices in question.

For example, in 1987 some fire control equipment previously bought as GFE is now bought as CFE. Based on the contractor cost report, the value of this equipment equals 400. Using the adjusted current price link method, the quality factor for the CFE component is 1.8085, or $894.7/(894.7 - 400)$. Using the same technique and -400 as the value of the quality change for the GFE equipment, the quality factor is 0.8821, or $2,992/[2,992 - (-400)]$. On a $1975 = 100$ base, the effect on the CFE fire control base price is $+163.2$, and the effect on the other GFE base price is -148.7. The technique calculates a discrepancy in the base price in this example because prices have changed by different amounts in the two series. In other words, the relative importance of the two series has not remained constant.

When attempting to solve this problem, the detail contained in the price source documents often prohibits a simple solution. For example, the best way in which to solve the product switch problem is to group together over the life of the series those products that are involved in the switch. This, in fact, was done for the CFE-GFE switch of navigation equipment in 1981.

Unfortunately, switches usually involve nonspecific GFE data and more detailed CFE data such as the fire control equipment switch mentioned above. In the case study, the 1987 switch is valued at 400. This value most likely was obvious from the contractor price report. Assuming no quality adjustments due to a shift in contractor, we then estimate the current effect on the GFE series as being -400. In other words, no information was actually available about the price of the product when it was procured under GFE. In fact, it is only an assumption based on an odd GFE price change that the newly observed fire control product on the contractor cost report was once included under the GFE series. Therefore, it would be impossible to group the GFE fire control equipment with the CFE fire control equipment over the life of the aircraft.

The only way to solve the base price discrepancy problem in this case is to calculate a quality-adjustment value that will force the changes in the two base prices to offset. The calculation of the quality adjustment is explained best as a two-step procedure. First, the desired quality factor is derived by setting the base prices prior to the product switch equal to the base prices after the product switch. The quality valuation for one of the products must be available in order to solve the equation.

The following list defines the variables used in the subsequent equations:

a = first product;
b = second product;
M = cumulative quality factor before the switch;
F = quality factor for the switch;
N = non-quality-adjusted base price;
B = current price of product$_b$ in the base year;
R = product of any quality factors after the switch year up to and including the base year;
P = price of product$_b$ at the time of the switch; and
V = value of quality for product$_b$.

(B1)
$$M_a N_a + M_b N_b = M_a F_a N_a + M_b F_b N_b,$$

or, solving for F_b,

(B2)
$$F_b = \frac{M_a N_a + M_b N_b - M_a F_a N_a}{M_b N_b}.$$

F_a is known because the quality valuation for product$_a$ was determined beforehand. N_a is also known for the same reason. If the product switch happens after the base year, then N_b is known. If the product switch happens before the base year, then the following should be substituted for N_b in the above equation:

(B3)
$$N_b = \frac{B}{M_b F_b R_b}.$$

Solving for F_b, the equation becomes

(B4)
$$F_b = \frac{B}{M_a N_a F_a R_b + B - M_a N_a R_b}.$$

Then, for the second step, the quality factor equation is solved for the value of the quality change. In this case, the adjusted current price link equation is used:

(B5)
$$F_b = \frac{P}{P - V},$$

or, solving for V,

(B6)
$$V = \frac{-P + PF_b}{F_b}.$$

References

Argote, Linda, and Dennis Epple. 1990. Learning curves in manufacturing. *Science,* 23 February, 920–24.

Gordon, Robert J. 1990. *The measurement of durable goods prices.* Chicago: University of Chicago Press (for the National Bureau of Economic Research).

Triplett, Jack E. 1983. Concepts of quality in input and output price measures: A resolution of the user-value resource-cost debate. In *U.S. national income and product accounts: Selected topics,* ed. Murray F. Foss. Studies in Income and Wealth, vol. 47. Chicago: University of Chicago Press (for the National Bureau of Economic Research).

U.S. Department of Commerce. 1975. *Measuring price changes of military expenditures.* Washington, D.C.: U.S. Government Printing Office.

———. 1979. *Price changes of defense purchases of the United States.* Washington, D.C.: U.S. Government Printing Office.

———. 1988. *Government transactions.* Methodology Paper Series MP-5. Washington, D.C.: U.S. Government Printing Office.

U.S. Department of Labor. 1988. *BLS handbook of methods.* Bulletin no. 2285. Washington, D.C.: U.S. Government Printing Office.

Wright, T. P. 1936. Factors affecting the cost of airplanes. *Journal of Aeronautical Science* (February): 122–28.

Ziemer, Richard C., and Karl D. Galbraith. 1983. Deflation of defense purchases. In *U.S. national income and product accounts: Selected topics,* ed. Murray F. Foss. Studies in Income and Wealth, vol. 47. Chicago: University of Chicago Press (for the National Bureau of Economic Research).

Comment   Arthur J. Alexander

The goal of defense price estimates, according to Ziemer and Kelly, is to develop measures of constant-dollar defense purchases within the framework of the national income and product accounts. What is not stated is that constant-dollar purchases are proxies for physical items and quantities: a fundamental principle governing the conceptual basis for estimating constant-dollar purchases is that, if the number of identical items purchased in two periods does not change, then the index of constant-dollar purchases should not change. This principle provides the rationale for many of the assumptions and procedures described in the paper.

Defense deflators and price indexes for individual products, while useful for many purposes in their own right, are produced here as means to achieve the main goal. However, it is in the calculation of the price indexes that the central problem arises. This problem is the "performance/cost-of-production"

Arthur J. Alexander is president of the Japan Economic Institute (JEI) of America in Washington, D.C., a nonprofit research organization funded in part by the Japanese government.

Views expressed in this paper are the author's own and are not necessarily shared by JEI or its research sponsors.

method of quality adjustment. According to this method, products are examined to determine whether they have changed from one period to another; if a change is determined to be associated with an increase in quality, "the cost of producing that physical change is taken as the value of the quality change, and the price is adjusted accordingly" (Ziemer and Kelly, chap. 10 in this volume, p. 310). Product characteristics and performance are used only to determine if there has been a quality improvement; they are not used to evaluate the size of the improvement.

The use of cost as a measure of quality change ignores the possibility of improvements in technology and productivity and can severely overestimate price changes and underestimate output. Productivity in the design and production of military products can be substantial. Because of such productivity gains, newer and better products can actually be less costly to produce than older products. Under such conditions, the "performance/cost-of-production" method would measure no change in quality.

One example of an improved product costing less to produce was the F100 turbojet engine used in the F-16 and F-15 aircraft. More than eighty design changes were incorporated in this engine over the four-year period 1984–87, resulting in significant improvements in reliability and maintainability: maintenance manhours per flight hour were cut by 15 percent; unscheduled engine removals were reduced by 43 percent; support costs fell by one-third (Alexander 1988, 68). Yet the cost of these changes when introduced into production was actually negative—the engine was less costly to produce. Indeed, in six case studies of reliability improvement, there were no examples of cost increases. According to the Bureau of Economic Analysis (BEA) approach, these improvements in quality would not have been captured.

The reason that the F100 engine could be improved and quality increased with no increase in production cost was that the manufacturer, Pratt and Whitney, had become smarter over the years—smarter because of additional experience and because of the $120 million in design and test expenditures that the U.S. Air Force invested in these design changes. These payoffs to research and development (R&D) are biased downward by the BEA approach.

The problem faced by defense product price estimators is that price changes can arise from three sources: (1) changes in input factor costs; (2) changes in the productivity of producing goods of a given quality; and (3) changes in the quality of the good. These changes are illustrated in figure 10C.1, where the solid lines represent time period 1 input factor costs (W1) and the dashed lines are for period 2 factor costs (W2). The observed points are A and B; A is on the line showing the nominal cost-quality relation at period 1 values of factor costs and productivity levels. In period 2, the whole curve shifts downward because of productivity improvements. The distance C4–C1 represents the shift in productivity; inflation in factor costs is captured by C2–C1 or C5–C3 (these need not be the same); the cost of quality improvement is C5–C2 or C3–C1. Note that the BEA would measure the value of quality change as C4–

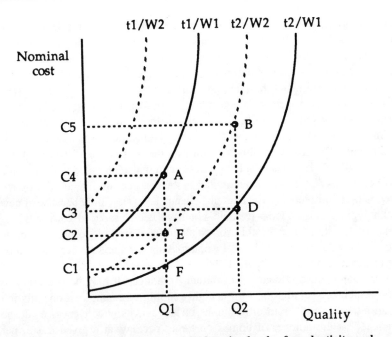

Fig. 10C.1 Cost-quality relations with changing levels of productivity and input factor costs

C3; if this value were negative because of strong productivity growth, it would record no quality change at all. The approach therefore generates the paradoxical outcome that, the larger the amount of productivity growth, the smaller the measured value of quality improvement. Price deflators are therefore too high and the estimated quality of output and calculated productivity growth too low.

Does this actually occur? In order to test the possibility of biased estimates, I calculated the productivity change implicit in the fixed-weighted price index for aircraft (Ziemer and Kelly, chap. 10 in this volume, table 10.9); productivity change was estimated by dividing an input factor cost index for aircraft by the fixed-weighted price index. From 1972 to 1982 (the years for which I happened to have a common set of data), input costs rose by 8.5 percent annually, while the aircraft price index (presumably, holding quality constant) increased at a 9.9 percent rate—implying that military aircraft production productivity actually fell by about 1.3 percent per year. Given the billions of R&D dollars devoted to military aircraft in each year's defense budget, this outcome is unlikely. Indeed, independent estimates of productivity for transport aircraft and jet engines showed annual productivity increases of 5.0 and 2.0 percent (Alexander and Mitchell 1985, 186, 190).

Unfortunately, dealing with the problem of measuring quality change is far more difficult than simply describing it. Hedonic price indexes are probably not feasible because of the sparse time series of most types of military equipment and because of the restricted market for defense equipment, where outliers may persist for longer periods than in more competitive markets. Some practitioners have used combat models to evaluate quality-quantity trade-offs for military aircraft, but these are applicable only to the gross characteristics of equipment. One technique that may be useful has been adopted in price surveys for the producer price index; this method requires manufacturers to estimate what it would have cost to produce the last-period model in the current period. The answer to this question is a measure of the distance C4–C2 in figure 10C.1. Equivalently, the producer could also be asked what it would have cost to produce the current model in the last period; this question, however, is more problematic since often a change is feasible only because of new technological knowledge—it could not have been produced earlier. These kinds of questions are feasible for small product improvements of a basic model. They become hypothetical when making comparisons across models, for example, from the F-4 to the F-16.

For nonincremental changes in military products, it may be necessary to look at their several missions. For a highly simplified example, if one mission of an attack aircraft is to drop bombs on targets, its effectiveness could be evaluated as the number of bombs on target per day, at a given range, per dollar of aircraft capital cost and support cost. Calculation of this measure would draw on such characteristics as payload, sensors, flight control systems, ordnance delivery computers, reliability, maintainability, and all the other design features and components that enable the aircraft to perform this mission. A weighted sum of all the missions would yield a quality index for the aircraft. Just setting out such a simplified approach to mission analysis gives a sense of the difficulty in implementing it, but it is the performance of the mission that ultimately lends value to the military equipment and to the notion of quality. Ultimately, analysts will ignore mission performance only at their peril.

Introducing the concept of mission in evaluating the quality of military products forces one to consider the existence of enemies. If an enemy develops a better air-defense system that reduces the effectiveness of an aircraft system, the quality of the aircraft declines; it becomes economically obsolete. If sold on secondhand markets, the price of the aircraft would fall to reflect its lower mission effectiveness. A similar effect would also be found for an antibiotic whose quality is measured as the lethality against a certain strain of bacteria; if a resistant strain evolved, the measured quality of the antibiotic would fall, as would its price.

It would be theoretically correct to show that military products have value only in performing specified missions and that we may be spending more but getting less because of enemy reaction. In a broader sense, the value of defense is a matter not only of constant-dollar purchases and productivity but also of the reactions of others. Correct and accurate measures of defense expenditures that properly account for such reactions may reveal surprising pictures of the value of defense.

References

Alexander, Arthur J. 1988. *The costs and benefits of reliability in military equipment.* P-7515. RAND, December.

Alexander, Arthur J., and Bridger M. Mitchell. 1985. Measuring technological change of heterogenous products. *Technological Forecasting and Social Change* 27 (2/3): 161–95.

VI BEA's Treatment of Computer Prices and Productivity Measurement

11 Panel Discussion: Implications of BEA's Treatment of Computer Prices and Productivity Measurement

Chair: Frank de Leeuw

Statements: Edward F. Denison   Charles R. Hulten
Zvi Griliches   Thomas K. Rymes

Comments: Arthur J. Alexander   René Durand
Edwin R. Dean   Michael Harper

The panel discussion considered implications of BEA's treatment of computer prices for productivity measurement. Following prepared statements, panelists were given the opportunity to comment on each other's statements. This was followed by comments by members of the audience (most of which appear here).

Discussion

Edward F. Denison

The computer price index of the Bureau of Economic Analysis (BEA) invites attention because it behaves so differently from prices in general. From 1973 to 1988, the implicit deflator for computers fell 91 percent, while that for nonresidential business GNP as a whole rose 138 percent. Based on this comparison, the real price of computers was 4 percent as high in 1988 as in 1973, and it fell more than 19 percent a year. The percentage decline continued to be nearly as large from 1982 to 1988, 18.3 percent a year, as it had been from 1973 to 1982, when it was 20.0 percent.

Use of this index has greatly affected many important economic magnitudes that are measured in constant prices. These include the growth rate and the composition of GNP, the growth rate and the composition of investment and the capital stock, and—of great interest to me—growth rates of productivity in the business sector, in durable goods manufacturing, and in the production of computers. Unit labor costs, often compared with those in other countries, are also much affected. If one starts with data for the rest of the economy and

Edward F. Denison was senior fellow emeritus at the Brookings Institution and former associate director for national accounts at the Bureau of Economic Analysis.

then adds computer production, one finds that inclusion of computers greatly improves the record of recent economic performance, both absolutely and in comparison with the past, in all these respects and also with respect to price stability. It has created an incipient recovery in productivity growth.

The sharp drop in the computer price index does not affect GNP in current prices. It does make the current-price series for economic depreciation grow more slowly and, in consequence, current price series for net national product, national income, and corporate profits on a national income basis grow more rapidly.

The special problem in deflating computers is that models change frequently and performance characteristics of successive models are very different. The problem is not confined to computers but is especially pronounced in their case. I take it to be obvious that the deflation of computers should follow rules applicable to other goods of their class.

My own particular interest is in analysis of the sources of past economic growth and alternative ways of changing the future growth rate (Denison 1989). One source of growth is saving, that is, the increase in the capital stock used in production. A second source is advances in technological, managerial, and organizational knowledge of how to produce at low cost. In two-way breakdowns of growth, the former is included in the contribution of total factor input and the latter in output per unit of input.

Such a division of growth is obtained, however, only if net saving or investment, including investment in computers, is measured by consumption forgone and capital is measured as the sum of past net saving.[1] In constant prices, this result is obtained by deflating investment by prices of consumer goods.[2] This procedure, of course, is not followed by BEA in compiling the national accounts but has gained increasing support, including mine. The need for a consumption forgone measure is my main point, but I shall leave it there.

BEA's procedure is to deflate components of investment by their own prices. The method of handling changes in products, both for capital goods and for consumer goods, is to equate the quantities of product or capital that different goods represent by their costs (or prices) at a common date. If one product costs twice as much as another, it is twice as much product. One effect of this procedure, as Tom Rymes taught me about twenty-five years ago, is that advances in knowledge that take the form of improvements in capital goods end up as contributions made to growth by capital and total factor input while all other advances in knowledge raise output per unit of input. This is inconvenient. But, until the computer price index was introduced, the

1. In any given year, consumption forgone (hence net investment) valued in constant prices equals the quantity of consumer goods that resources devoted to increasing the capital stock would have provided if devoted instead to production of consumer goods by the methods used in the base year.
2. This leaves open the question of deflating the smaller part of computer output that does not become business investment. Perhaps it should be deflated like other consumer goods—if only there were agreement on what that means in the case of computers.

amounts involved were not great. They could be approximated and, if one wished, transferred from capital to advances in knowledge so as to permit a clean division of growth sources.

The method of equating different products by their costs at a common date can be implemented by any of several techniques, the choice depending on available information and the nature of the problem. One method is to link price indexes for overlapping models in order to obtain a price series suitable for deflation. BEA has published, but not incorporated into the national accounts or kept up to date, a price index for computers that is based on this technique. It indicates a drop in the real price of computers that is sharp but much smaller than that indicated by the index that *is* used. The procedure differs from that usually applied when new products appear in that the price link is made as soon as the new model appears instead of at a later date. In general, new products tend to come in at prices above those at which they later settle. Unit costs are high until bugs are eliminated and volume expands. Buyers are those for whom the new model is especially useful. The linked model price index probably drops too much because of premature linking.

I believe that the linked index, updated and if possible adjusted for any bias arising from the date of linking, would implement the cost concept for handling new or altered products better than the index used now. This applies to measurement of both national product and capital stock.

Another theoretically possible method of equating different capital goods is by their relative abilities to contribute to production, as measured by their marginal products at a common date. Some of the acceptance of the computer price index probably stems from the belief that it is such a measure, although it is not and BEA does not make this claim.

The only characteristics of various computer models that are compared in compiling the index are output characteristics, such as memory capacity and speed, that indicate what can be done with the computer. None are requirements for other inputs. If one uses the BEA price index to deflate an index of the value of computers produced, one gets an index of the quantity of output that the computer and all other inputs that are used with computers can produce, not what the computer contributes. Enormous resources besides computers themselves go into producing the output ascribed to computers. They include labor, computer programs, phone services, building, and many other items, including the time of many people in this room. BEA's computer price index is the same whether use of a new model requires more labor and other resources as the old or less. For example, if a new model does twice as much as an old and uses half as much of, say, labor to do it, it will be counted as representing only twice as much capital as the old model, whereas an alternative new model that also does twice as much as the old but uses twice as much labor to do so will also be counted as twice as much capital as the old. Thus, output per unit of labor will be four times as high with the first new computer as with the second, but the two computers would be counted as the same amount of capital. I can think of no standard by which this is reasonable.

While BEA does not equate different models by marginal product because it takes no account of inputs, neither—in my view—does it equate them by cost. What it compares is not, as it should be, the cost of producing two models of computers but instead the cost of producing the output characteristics used in constructing the price index. This is the same as an attempt to equate capital goods by marginal product, which, as just stated, fails because it does not consider inputs.

For two main reasons I would find the increase in the constant price value of computers that results from use of the computer price index hard to accept or interpret even if in some sense it measured marginal products.

First, the demand for computers is a schedule, not a point. Users vary greatly in the value of the contributions that computers make to their output, and the value of various uses to which computers are put by a single user also varies greatly. With the real price of computers only 4 percent as high in 1988 as in 1973 and only 30 percent as high as it had been as recently as 1982, it is certain that computers were put to uses that would have been submarginal in earlier years. When computers are deflated by the BEA index, the quantities purchased and in use explode. If the index measured the cost of computer capability accurately, then I would have no problem with the quantity of computer services corresponding to the uses made of computers in 1973 or 1981. But the much bigger quantity purchased for less important uses is given an equally high unit value. In terms of ability to contribute to the nation's production, this causes 1988 output of computers to be overstated relative to earlier years.

Second, computers and peripheral equipment have many capabilities. Not all capabilities are used by any single owner, and some that are used may be unimportant to him. I surmise that, as computers became more versatile and owners more numerous, the average user cared about only a smaller and smaller proportion of the things a computer can do. If so, a quality adjustment based on a computer's features, as distinguished from features actually *used,* overstates the increase in computer input into production.

Jack Triplett has raised an interesting point that invites comment. Suppose that we are comparing output in two years. Everything produced in either year either is or could be produced in the later year, and a valuation can therefore be placed on it. Now we know that in current price, if certain assumptions are made about equilibrium and proportionality of factor cost and market price, both resource costs and prospective marginal products of various capital goods are proportional to prices and hence to each other. This means that, if the latest year is the base year, the weights for different goods are the same whether indexes are based on cost or on marginal product. If quantity indexes for each type of capital good are also the same, indexes for total investment and capital stock based on resource cost are the same as indexes based on marginal product. This is neat but less helpful than it seems.

First, the use of the most recent year does not solve the problem of comparing present models with those no longer being produced, to which a value in the most recent year must be imputed. Imputation by using estimates of the relative production costs of different models (comparable to the linked model method) and imputation by use of output price characteristics (comparable to the BEA computer price index method) will place different values on the discontinued models. Both are said to represent the cost method, so one must choose between them. And the marginal product method, if it could be implemented, would yield still a different value. As one works backward in time and these discontinued models enter the calculations, output in past years, valued in most-recent-year prices, will be different depending on the method adopted to impute the base year value. I should expect cost-based and marginal product–based series to differ substantially as one goes back in time. Second, there is, in any case, no reason to confine oneself to the use of the most recent year as the base year, especially when the choice of base year affects the outcome in important ways.

So much for the computer price index as such. My conclusion is that, despite the admirable care and ingenuity devoted to its construction, it is neither fish nor fowl. It conforms to no sensible criterion.

However, despite the fabulous growth in productivity in computer production that the index implies, the index would have had only a limited effect on business-sector productivity if it had not interacted with two other characteristics of the government's GNP and productivity measures. One is the use of fixed 1982 price weights to combine quantities of different products in constructing real GNP. Before 1982, computers are underweighted relative to the share of resources they used then. In 1973, the share of output of computers measured in current prices was seven times their weight in 1982 prices. In contrast, after 1982 computers are overweighted. By 1988, their weight was three and one-third times as big in constant as in current prices, and, by 1990, it must be four and a half times as big or more.

The other characteristic is the use of GNP instead of NNP to measure output when the Bureau of Labor Statistics (BLS) calculates productivity change. Because the computer has much more weight in GNP than in NNP, the computer price index has much more effect on it. Elsewhere, I have discussed the quantitative effect of interaction between both these measurement practices and the computer index on series for productivity in business and smaller segments of the economy, and, of course, they have an enormous effect on comparisons by industry or end product.

Zvi Griliches

I want to draw your attention to the paper that was circulated before the workshop by Jack Triplett (1991) because it deals in detail with some of the points that Edward Denison raised. Sometimes I have a feeling of déjà

Zvi Griliches is Paul M. Warburg Professor of Economics at Harvard University and program director of Productivity and Technical Change Studies at the National Bureau of Economic Research.

vu. Some of this, it seems to me, we have been arguing over for thirty years, and I thought it had gone away. But, apparently, old ideas just keep on reappearing.

I think that there are a number of real points that Edward Denison raises, and some I think are beside the point. One of the points that he raises is that the computer index is moving too much, is making too much of a difference, and is not really comparable to the rest of the system. He is right about this, but he is right, not because the computer index is wrong, but because the way it is used is wrong. It is used wrongly because its weight is kept constant. There is also the additional problem of measuring the growth in real value-added, which comes from the fact that the inputs into the computer industry have not been themselves deflated by the same kind of an index. This produces an extra big growth in value-added there relative to somewhere else. That would not matter so much in the total if these inputs were produced domestically, but, since many of these components are imported, we are attributing the growth in foreign productivity to domestic productivity.

It is also true that many other commodity prices are badly measured. This fact does not seem to me, however, to be a good argument for also measuring computers badly. Now, his constructive suggestion is to forget about measuring capital prices entirely and go over to the deflation of capital goods by consumer prices. This is one way of solving the problem, but it will not help if we want to know where, in what industry, the productivity growth is occurring. It is a reasonable approach for welfare measurement except that one does not really get away from the real problem. It assumes that we know how to measure consumer prices, but all the same issues are going to arise there just the same: in the measurement of services, in the measurement of the use of personal computers at home, in the measurement of automobiles and video-cassette recorders and other consumer equipment. There is no escape; there is no rest for the weary.

Then there is an assorted set of complaints about hedonic indexes per se, and that is where the déjà vu enters in. I really think that these complaints are fundamentally wrong and that Jack Triplett has basically said most of what there is to say. Hedonics are used, primarily, to do what supposedly the consumer price index (CPI) and producer price index (PPI) are trying to do, to figure out what should have been the price of this item last year if you had been able to collect it. How do you adjust for the fact that the chicory in the coffee mixture has changed? There is no conceptual difference between the amount of chicory in your coffee and measuring the size of the disk in your computer. When one looks at computers, their prices differ depending on what the disk capacity is, depending on the amount of memory, and depending on the clock speed. One can buy inputs that will, in fact, change these computers and bring them up to a different clock speed or to a different memory size.

Now, there is a technical issues as to whether the marginal price of memory or the marginal price of a disk should be computed from the add-on prices that one can also get in the market. But that is a detail, and I do not think that this is the substantive problem. Nor do I think that the use of input measures, the characteristics, instead of performance measures, which is what Rosanne Cole was beating me over the head with yesterday, is the real problem.[3] We did not use output measures in our PC price index but rather resource cost measures. If we had used the right measures of performance, we would have indeed gotten better estimates of how the computers really differ and a better estimate of the price index. This is the issue of how one is to get a good hedonic estimate, but that is a question of implementation, not of substance.

In any case, now we do have in the computer area the evidence on matched models. They do not decline by 30 percent per year; they decline by about 20 percent per year. Well, Ed Denison says that this is still too much because the early price declines are somehow not representative. But, as Erwin Diewert would say, that is again an index number problem. It is not a substantive problem. The right way to compute such indexes is to weight these changes, weight them and change the weights as one goes along. If the price declines are occurring during a period when very few of these models are being bought, then they will have very little weight in the total. And that is all there is to it. There is no special mystery about that.

The objections that are being made against adjusting for differences in quality or capacity could have just as well been applied to all other goods in the producer or consumer price indexes. The same objection could be made to pricing automobiles and considering whether better upholstery matters. Some people, after all, do not care about upholstery. However, others do care, and consequently, there is a market price for upholstery.

One of the issues that floats around is really the issue of whether there is an equilibrium. Another issue is the question (one that most of the index number literature rides roughshod over), Is there a representative consumer? One is aggregating over many different consumers with different tastes and constructing just one number. There will be some people who will gain more from a particular change, and there will be some people who will gain less, and we are, somehow, skating over it. There are some answers to this problem. One can turn to expenditure functions and assume that the marginal utility of income is the same for everyone. But that is just another way of begging the question. Or one can say, Well, I am dealing with only one commodity at a time, and this is not a big problem in this case. But such responses are ultimately not very convincing.

There is, in fact, a real problem here. But my reading of it is that, by and large, it leads to a serious understatement of the gains from new technology. The simplest way of thinking about it is what happens if BLS or BEA were to

---

3. This refers to Rosanne Cole's comments about the use of the clock rate (logic cycles per second) as a characteristic of microcomputers in the paper on microcomputer prices by Ernst R. Berndt and Zvi Griliches (chap. 2 in this volume).

use a hedonic index, and there are only two or three models available in a particular period when the new machine has just begun to appear in the market. Let us say that all these models are on the line in some quality dimension, that we have agreed that this quality dimension is real and that people actually want it, and that it affects both costs and consumer value. But there are only three models, and they are all relatively small in size. There are people out there, however, who would like to buy a bigger package, a PC with more memory, with more power. But it is not available in this period. Now, next period it becomes available, and, lo and behold, its price is actually right on the earlier estimated price-quality line.

In this case, what the hedonic method will do is to say that the price has not declined. But the new package was not available last year because the true shadow price of that package was higher than may be indicated by its position on the estimated line, both because, in fact, it is not that simple to do the engineering to get it out there at roughly proportional cost and because the market was not there to produce it in large enough quantities, the economies of scale were not there yet that would allow such entry. As long as there is discreteness, the hedonic price indexes will underestimate the gains from either extending the spectrum of models or filling it in.

There is also a debit. The debit is that, to the extent that models go out, the hedonic index procedure will underestimate the loss to somebody of these models disappearing. Thus, if there is a decline in the demand for 4K RAMs and they are no longer produced, there will be a loss to somebody. Now what happens, in fact, is that things like 4K RAMs become a specialty item and that the few people who actually want them can still get them, but only at much higher prices. There is then a subset of models whose prices are actually rising, even though positive technological change is occurring throughout. It may be possible to capture some of that with appropriate weighting of the various components.

While there are real problems of measurement, my feeling is that, for most new goods, if we do not use suitable chain indexes and adjust for quality change, we will be underestimating the improvements in quality that are occurring. But, as far as long-run comparisons are concerned, I do not think that they are really possible. They are not really possible in Ed's framework, nor is it really possible to get good estimates in the framework that I prefer.

We have now, approximately, three times the per capita income of what our grandparents had, perhaps even more. Are we three times as happy as they were? Are we that much wealthier? I do not think that this is a question that can really be answered. One can easily think of things that go in the other direction that have been lost. In different ways, this is related to the fact that what these indexes measure is just a subset of outputs, a subset of consumer consumption. Much of what consumers get or do not get does not go through the market. It is in the environment, in our interrelationships among ourselves. There are externalities, both positive and negative, and they are just not being measured by our statistical system. But we should not use the fact that we cannot measure everything right to prevent us from trying to do what we can do slightly better.

Charles R. Hulten

One of the most important consequences of the BEA computer adjustment is, for me, the insights that it provides into the lingering controversy between Edward Denison, on the one hand, and Dale Jorgenson and Zvi Griliches, on the other. This debate had seemed to me to be about the appropriate methodology of growth analysis. But, in light of Denison's recent book (Denison 1989), it now appears that it is really about the underlying goals of productivity analysis.

Total factor productivity (TFP) is conventionally defined as the ratio of output to total factor input, measured in terms of the resource cost. In the neoclassical interpretation of Solow-Jorgenson-Griliches, the appropriate resource cost associated with capital is the sum of past investment adjusted for physical depreciation and retirement. The resulting TFP ratio is then interpreted as the shift in the aggregate production function for a given level of capital and labor. In this "Hicksian" framework, the Denison-Jorgenson-Griliches debate seemed to be about the most appropriate definitions of output and capital for measuring the magnitude of the shift.

However, Denison's endorsement of the Rymes approach to productivity analysis sheds new light on the old debate. In the Rymes view, technological change is seen as reducing the quantity of resources needed to reproduce the existing stock of capital. Thus, the conventional perpetual inventory estimate of capital overstates the actual amount of saving (consumption forgone) implied by the stock. Or, put differently, the conventional measure includes a component that is more appropriately classified as technical change.

The appropriate concept of TFP, in this alternative paradigm of capital, would exclude this technological component of capital from the denominator of the TFP ratio. The resulting concept of "TFP" is a ratio of output to the resources needed to sustain the level of output, and, as such, it incorporates part of what had previously been assigned to capital (in the old TFP concept). As a consequence, a source of growth analysis based on the alternative "TFP" concept would assign a larger role to productivity change and a smaller role to capital formation.

It would thus seem that the core of the Denison-Jorgenson-Griliches debate is, in the final analysis, a debate over whether "TFP" is a better measure of productivity change than the neoclassical TFP. But, before addressing this

Charles R. Hulten is professor of economics at the University of Maryland and a research associate of the National Bureau of Economic Research.

issue, it is useful to consider the question of how one might measure the alternative "TFP." The answer to this question sheds surprising light on the issue of which concept is the more appropriate measure of productivity change.

T. K. Rymes proposes to measure "TFP" using a Harrodian measure of technology in which "TFP" is equal to the conventional TFP divided by labor's share of income. This amounts, conceptually, to defining "TFP" as the Harrod rate of technical change, H. The Harrodian H is, itself, defined as the rate at which the production function shifts, measured along a constant capital-output ratio (instead of along a constant capital-labor ratio, as with Hicksian TFP). In terms of figure 11.1, Hicksian TFP is associated with the shift in the function $f(K/L, t)$ between the points a and b, whereas H is associated with the shift measured between a and c.

Furthermore, since the growth rate of output, $\dot{Q}$, is the same under either concept of productivity, the use of "TFP," cum $\dot{H}$, implies that capital must also be modified by subtracting $\dot{H}$ from the growth rate of the conventional (commodity) measure, $\dot{K}$. In other words,

$$\dot{Q} = (1 - \pi)\dot{L} + \pi \dot{K} + \text{TFP} = (1 - \pi)\dot{L} + \pi(\dot{K} - \dot{H}) + \dot{H},$$

where $\dot{L}$ is the growth rate of labor, and π is capital's income share. The resulting Rymesian concept of capital, $\dot{K} - \dot{H}$, strips commodity capital of the

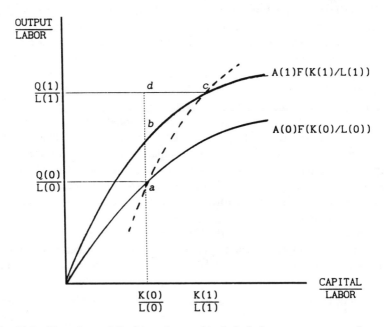

Fig. 11.1   **Two views of the importance of technical change as a source of economic growth**

technological component and thus corresponds to the notion of capital measured in terms of the resources needed to reproduce it.

I have offered an alternative solution to the problem of measuring "TFP" (Hulten 1975). I proposed a measure of the *consequences* of technical change for the growth rate of output. This differs from the "amount" of technical change when some inputs, like capital, are a produced means of production and therefore change as a result of the shift in technology. This "capital endogenous" measure of the effect of technology, $\dot{Z}$, was shown to be related to both the Hicksian and the Harrodian parameters of technical change:

$$\dot{Z} = \dot{H} + \frac{\pi}{(1 - \pi)} \dot{B} = \left[1 + \frac{\pi}{(1 - \pi)} \sigma\right] \dot{A} + \pi\sigma\dot{R},$$

where $\dot{H}$ is the rate of Harrodian technical change, as before, $\dot{B}$ is the bias, and $\dot{A}$ and $\dot{R}$ are the corresponding Hicksian parameters. When technical progress is Harrod neutral, $\dot{B} = 0$ and $\dot{Z} = H$, implying that the $\dot{Z}$ defined above is equivalent to the Rymesian solution to measuring "TFP."[4]

The $\dot{Z}$ function defined above has a straightforward interpretation in terms figure 11.1. Suppose that the economy is in a steady state at point a with a static level of technology. Suppose, further, that a once-over shift occurs that makes capital and labor more productive. The output per worker will immediately jump to b, and this additional income will go, in part, to increasing the size of the capital stock. This generates still more income, and thus more saving, etc., until the diminishing marginal returns to capital bring the economy to rest at, say, point c. The $\dot{Z}$ measure of technical change can be interpreted as the rate of growth of output between the points a and c—that is, as the *total change* in output due to the shift in the technology—and this is larger than the initial change from a to b.

This leaves the following question. There are two ways of looking at technical change: the Jorgenson-Griliches-Solow conception of TFP, which is based on the Hicksian classification of growth and the perpetual inventory concept of capital, and the Harrod-Rymes approach, associated with the Harrodian classification of technical change and the Rymesian concept of capital, K/H. Which of these alternative paradigms is correct?

These alternatives seem fundamentally incompatible, and, indeed, there are heavy overtones of the Cambridge Controversies in capital theory. It is thus surprising that the correct answer is that *both* approaches are correct. Correct, that is, for different questions. The Jorgenson-Griliches approach is correct for answering the structural question of how much the production function has shifted relative to a given capital-labor ratio. In this approach, the total change in output per worker (a to c in fig. 11.1) is decomposed into two elements: the Hicksian shift in technology (a to b) and the change in output associated with capital formation (b to c).

On the other hand, our discussion of the $\dot{Z}$ function indicates that the entire

---

4. Note that TFP $= \dot{A} = (1 - \pi) \dot{H}$.

change (*a* to *c*) was the result of the shift in technology. The $\dot{Z}$ approach, or, more generally, the "TFP" approach, is appropriate for answering the question, How much more output growth is there because of technical change? or, How important is technical change as a source of output growth? This leads to the conclusion that it is *not* appropriate to use the Hicksian approach to conclude that technical change explains *ab/ad* percent of the growth rate of output.

To summarize, the questions, How much? and, How important? are separate issues that require different pieces of information to answer correctly. The advocacy of either the (*A, K*) view of the world or the (*H, K/H*) view as a *joint* answer to both questions is thus wrong. Moreover, since knowledge of (*A/K*) leads directly to knowledge of (*H, K/H*) because $\dot{A} = (1 - \pi)\dot{H}$, it should be clear that these supposedly contradictory paradigms are really different aspects of the same problem.

This leads us back to the Denison-Jorgenson-Griliches debate. Denison's endorsement of the Rymes paradigm can now be interpreted as a desire to measure the consequences of productivity change on output growth. The objective of Jorgenson and Griliches, on the other hand, was to measure the amount of technical change, and what was really a difference in goals became an unresolvable debate of methods.

Thomas K. Rymes

I agree with much—very much—of what Charles Hulten has said. If I have been guilty, in previous discussions, of claiming to be a source of truth, I can only apologize. My only defense is the usual one of seeking academic product differentiation.

I would like to reiterate how much I am indebted to Lawrence Read. He found a way of making operational Harrod's conception, which I shall be using, of technical progress.

Modern advanced economic systems are characterized by very large flows of outputs, only a small part of which is final consumption. I shall assume— just for purposes of exposition—that the flow of consumption output is homogeneous. The rest appear as additions to capital stocks and intermediate outputs. The economic system has very large flows of inputs. There are assumed, for simplicity, to be two kinds of primary inputs, inputs not produced, that is, by the economic system: (1) the flow of working, labor, and (2) the flow of waiting, the willingness of individuals to postpone present consumption to carry, maintain, and augment the stock of capital. The remaining inputs constitute the capital and intermediate inputs and are simultaneously part of the flow of outputs. I shall concentrate on the distinction between the primary and the produced inputs.

I shall compare two price indexes for capital goods such as computers. One

Thomas K. Rymes is professor of economics at Carleton University.

is the BEA index, the other an index that is not adjusted, or not as fully adjusted, for quality change as is the BEA index. I will use the supposed difference between the BEA index and one not adjusted for quality change to get at just how the quality-adjusted price indexes affect total factor productivity, both at the aggregate and at the industry level. This is what I was invited to do. Even while I believe that the BEA indexes are perfectly meaningful, I wonder along with Edward Denison and others exactly how we should be using them.

Let me go to the equations. Let c and dk be the growth rates of the output of the consumption and capital goods industries; l, k, w, and r the growth rates of labor input, capital input, wage rates, and rate of return, with subscripts c or k indicating the consumption and capital goods industries; p_c and p_k the growth rates of the price of consumption goods and the price of capital goods; SL and SK the share of labor and capital inputs, with subscripts c or k indicating the industry; and t and h two different conceptual rates of total factor productivity called Solow and Harrod residuals, with subscripts c or k indicating the industry. Using Divisia indexes, the traditional measure of total factor productivity advance, or Solow residual, in the consumer good industry is

$$c - \{SL_c l_c + SK_c k_c\} = t_c = \{SL_c w_c + SK_c(r_c + p_c)\} - p_c.$$

If p_k is said to be overstated and is replaced by a p_k^* such that $p_k^* < p_k$ and $k_c^* > k_c$, then the revised Solow residual is

$$c - \{SL_c l_c + SK_c k_c^*\} = t_c^* = \{SL_c w_c + SK_c(r_c + p_c^*)\} - p_c.$$

It follows that $t_c^* < t_c$ or the Solow residual will be reduced.

In the computer-producing or producer goods industry, however, the Solow residual would be

$$dk - \{SL_k l_k + SK_k k_k\} = t_k = \{SL_k w_k + SK_k(r_k + p_k)\} - p_k,$$

and, when the "quality adjustments" are made,

$$dk^* - \{SL_k l_k + SK_k k_k^*\} = t_k^* = \{SL_k w_k + SK_k(r_k + p_k^*)\} - p_k^*,$$

and, even though the "quality-adjustment" appears for both produced outputs and inputs, the Solow residual for the producer goods industry would be increased.

You are familiar with these Solow residuals. The rate of growth of the output of the consumption good less the competitive shares (equal to partial elasticity weights) times rates of growth of the labor input and the capital stock in the production of consumption equals the Solow residual in that industry. And so on.

In the full elaboration of the work that Alexandra Cas and I do on this case (Cas and Rymes 1991), the k's, as vectors, represent the flows of the services of capital goods of many kinds, the net services of capital goods that earn net returns to capital, capital consumption allowances, and the whole flow of intermediate inputs as well.

The Solow residual can be expressed in terms of the rate of change in input prices minus the rate of change of output prices. Let us focus on the computer-producing industry. (It is understood that there are many capital goods industries.) Suppose that the residuals had been derived with price indexes that are not adjusted for changes in quality and that now they are derived with price indexes adjusted for quality. Because adjusted price indexes fall much more dramatically, the output of the computer good industry rises much more dramatically, and the stock of capital or the flow of computer goods services in the production of consumption goods rises much more rapidly.

What happens to the Solow residuals? The rate of growth of the stock of capital in the production of the consumption goods is increased. The rate of change in the price of the capital goods in the production of consumer goods is decreased. If you increase the rate of growth of the capital in the production of the consumption goods and decrease the rate of growth of one of the prices of an input in the production of consumption goods, the result must be that the rate of technical progress, or the Solow residual, for the production of consumption goods must fall. As illustrated in the equations, $t_c^* < t_c$.

In the computer-producing industry, the use of the quality-adjusted price indexes increases the rate of growth of the output of the industry. If the computer good industry happens to be using some of its own output (the computer good industry certainly uses computers in the production of computers), a component of the capital input will also be rising more rapidly. Nevertheless, since the output of the industry is larger, the net result is that the Solow residual for the computer good industry is increased. What we have done is to redistribute increases in total factor productivity away from the production of the consumption good to the computer industry or to capital goods industries in general.

Now, as we have heard in this conference, the sharp fall in the quality-adjusted price index for computers is really a function of the sharp fall in the quality-adjusted price of semiconductors. So I disaggregate and make the qualitative adjustment for the semiconductors in the production of computers. The rate of growth of the capital input in computers will be raised, and one of the prices of an input into the production of computer goods will also be lowered. The result is that productivity advance, originally shown as taking place in the production of computers, is shifted over to the semiconductor industry.

However, in pursuing this further, the sharp fall in the quality-adjusted price index for semiconductors basically reflects a sharp fall in the quality-adjusted price index for chips, so I go back to the chip-producing industry and run the same drill. Indeed, as Ellen Dulberger suggests, I should make the quality adjustment for the ceramic inputs being used in the production of the chip industry, and that shoves some of the productivity advance back into the non-metallic minerals industry.

You see the basic thrust of my argument. If I say that there is a difference between the unadjusted and the quality-adjusted price indexes for capital goods and the quality-adjusted price indexes always run below the unadjusted indexes, all I end up doing is trying to backtrack through the set of industries that are interrelated, trying to find out where the productivity advance actually occurs. That is the basic idea behind the work of Zvi Griliches and others because they are really interested in the problem of where in this interrelated system of industries the productivity advance does occur.

One final note on this sort of chain that I ran through. You obviously have a fair amount of trouble with traditional measures of total factor productivity if it turns out that the nonmetallic industry uses a substantial amount of computers in its operations. However, such interdependence is not insurmountable because we have, with advances in national accounting, input-output systems to handle the interdependence.

If there is a difference between the BEA and the non-quality-adjusted price indexes for produced outputs and inputs, we really do have a very severe problem in allocating traditional measures of total factor productivity among industries.

The conception of Roy Harrod, made operational by Lawrence Read, is that the primary inputs in the economic system are working, labor, and waiting, the postponement of present consumption, which is embodied in and appears as stocks of capital goods. You have to study advances in the productivity of those inputs in an economy characterized by technical interdependence. You can get measures by industry of rates of technological advance, total factor productivity, or Harrod residuals, which are not the same as the traditional measures advocated by Zvi Griliches and, I believe, Erwin Diewert.

Here are the alternative measures. In the computer-producing or producer goods industry, the Harrod residual would be

$$dk - \{SL_k l_k + SK_k(k_k - h_k)\} = h_k = \{SL_k w_k + SK_k(r_k + p_k + h_k)\} - p_k.$$

Again, if p_k is said to be overstated and is replaced by a p_k^* such that

$$p_k - p_k^* = dk^* - dk = k_k^* - k_k,$$

the revised Harrod residual would be

$$dk^* - \{SL_k l_k + SK_k(k_k^* - h_k^*)\} = h_k^* = \{SL_k w_k + SK_k(r_k + p_k^* + h_k^*)\} - p_k^*.$$

The Harrod residuals for the producer goods industries would be raised, but not to the same extent as the Solow residuals.

The Harrod residuals in the consumer good industry would be

$$c - \{SL_c l_c + SK_c(k_c - h_k)\} = h_c = \{SL_c w_c + SK_c(r_c + p_k + h_k)\} - p_c.$$

The revised Harrod residuals for the consumption good industry would be

$$c - SL_c l_c + SK_c(k_c^*(k_c^* - h_k^*)\} = h_c^*$$
$$= \{SL_c w_c + SK_c(r_c + p_k^* + h_k^*)\} - p_c.$$

Since $k_c^* - k_c = p_k - p_k^* = h_k^* - h_k$, it follows that the Harrod residual for the consumption good industry would be essentially unchanged.

In the Harrod representation of total factor productivity, with factors being the nonproduced primary factors of production, when one talks about the rate of capital growth in the production of consumption goods, one must take into account the fact that those capital goods, themselves, are being produced with ever-increasing efficiency. The "deflator" here is h_k, the rate of technical progress or total factor productivity in the production of the capital goods.

By adjusting the rate of growth of capital in the consumption good industry for the rate of technical progress in the production of such capital goods, I obtain the rate of growth of primary inputs involved in the production of the capital goods so that h_c, the Harrod residual, in the production of consumption goods, gives the measure of the rate of technical progress in the production of consumption goods in terms of the working and waiting directly and indirectly involved throughout the economic system in the production of consumption goods. One does the same thing with respect to production of capital goods.

As the Divisia equations illustrate, the revised price indexes would result in the gross output of the computer good industry being increased, which by itself would result in the Harrod residuals being increased. The increased flow of semiconductor inputs, because of the revision in their price indexes to take account of their qualitative improvement, which would reduce the Solow residuals, would be offset by the fact that the Harrod measures would adjust for the productivity advance in the semiconductor industry, in the chip industry, in the ceramics industry, and so forth. The Harrod residuals would measure the productivity improvement of the primary inputs of working and waiting, directly and indirectly involved in the production of computers, taking account of the complete interdependence of technology in modern economies.

That is really the basic point of my presentation. I was asked to take into account the effects that the introduction of the BEA computer price index would have on the measurement of total factor productivity. The traditional measures or Solow residuals are arbitrarily changed as one tries desperately to trace the qualitative improvements in produced inputs through all the industries of the economy. I have tried to demonstrate very simply that the Harrod residuals are very largely invariant to this because they always take into account the interdependence of modern economic systems in measuring productivity advance.

Comments by Panelists

Denison: Let me first correct one misunderstanding by Zvi Griliches. When I was speaking of the effect of using gross rather than net output, I was talking about depreciation.

Griliches: I know, but I was talking about different things.

Denison: Yes, intraindustry sales, and that is why I agree with what you said about industry data. I've written about that elsewhere, but today time restricted me to the totals.

Now as to the point about different capital being appropriate for different uses and users. Forget computers for a minute, and let me go back to the 1920s, when I was growing up in Chicago. The truck had replaced the horse and wagon in almost everything, but there were two exceptions. One was milk delivery. The horse went from house to house, and the milkman ran out to the back door and looked to see whether you wanted your usual two quarts of milk or had left a note saying that you wanted a quart of cream instead or only one quart of milk. Then he ran back for the correct order. The horse was much more efficient than the truck in that sort of stop-and-go activity. The other activity was ice delivery. As the iceman came by, he looked in your window, where you had placed a four-sided card. If you wanted ice, the side of the card showing twenty-five, fifty, seventy-five, or one hundred pounds was placed on top to indicate the amount. The horse had to stop at the house of each customer while the iceman looked at the card, cut the ice to the desired thickness, brought it inside, and put it into your refrigerator. The horse was smarter than the truck, which required more direction, and worked out much more satisfactorily.

Now what I'm trying to illustrate is that what's good for one use isn't good for another, as I said earlier. For these uses, the horse was still better than the truck. Horses continued in use until the electric refrigerator replaced ice and purchase of milk at the chain store became so much cheaper than home delivery that the latter ceased. Where one really sees quality improvement is not in the price, except by chance, but in quantities. The quantity of trucks increased, and the quantity of horses and wagons went down, and that's how you knew there was a quality improvement and that technical progress was occurring. And you might never have known it from any change in prices. If the truck had come in and its price had then stayed flat forever and the price of the horse and wagon had also stayed flat, you would know it only from changes in relative quantities; you would not know from prices that there had been any technical progress. And that's one of the things that makes quality adjustment difficult if one is trying to use marginal products to equate things.

The other complication has to do with the time of linking because, if you're trying to equate products by relative cost, you want, I think, to compare costs at a time when the new product is in quantity production like the old. You do not want to compare costs when production of the new product is at the beginning of the learning curve because it is so much more expensive than an established product and it is being used by only a very few people for very specialized uses.

Now, the last point really doesn't prove anything, but, nevertheless, it is remarkable that the period of very slow productivity growth and the period of the spread of the computer happen to be the same. One suggested explanation is that the input into computer use has been expanding and everyone's been spending his time learning how to use computers and so on but that the output hasn't happened yet. Another explanation has been that everyone is busy using the computer to help him compete with somebody else. He may be taking someone else's business away as a result, but, when he and his competition are combined, nothing has happened. Well, these explanations may be correct, or it just may be that we're overestimating how much the computer is contributing to efficiency, but there is certainly a bit of a mystery there.

Griliches: I think that the part of Edward Denison's concern about the unrepresentativeness and the timing of the introduction of new products into the price index would be taken care of by proper weighting; new products with low sales would get very little weight. This is no different from the current treatment of Cadillac purchases: they have little effect on the final index since their sales are rather low, relative to the car market as a whole.

I mostly agree with T. K. Rymes except that my conclusion is different. I am interested in the structural equation. He is interested in the reduced form. I am interested in knowing where the productivity change occurred because I am interested in understanding it and, possibly, also in affecting it. I would like to be able to connect the productivity numbers to R&D expenditures in industry and the particular scientific advances responsible for the productivity advances. Unless I know where the productivity change is coming from, I will have no way of affecting it. But, if all I can observe is some homogenized piece of manna falling down, then I am left without any useful explanation. It is true, however, as both Charles Hulten and T. K. Rymes emphasize, that some of the productivity growth would not occur without additional investment and that some of this investment is induced by technological change. A complete causal analysis would, in fact, account for it. But productivity accounting should be viewed as a tool for, an input into, such an analysis; it is not a substitute for it.

I am not sure that I see the relevance of Edward Denison's horse and tractor example except that it illustrates how difficult index construction can be. In fact, as old commodities decline in importance, they may find a particular niche in which they are still superior, and their prices would actually go up while quantities are declining. Again, appropriate weighting would take care of most of this problem. I think that Ed was saying, implicitly, that the quantities are important. I agree. They help us interpret what is happening to prices. The question of validating a particular interpretation of observed price changes, using quantity data, is also implicit in the Norsworthy and Jang paper (chap. 4 in this volume). In their framework, the hedonic price index is being validated by putting it into the demand functions for inputs and the supply functions for outputs and asking whether that kind of a respecification of the demand structure explains the facts better.

Hulten: A lot of the debate over the total factor productivity concept is, in my view, obscured by the use of terms that mean different things to different people. I would therefore like to make two proposals about the terminology of productivity analysis. First, I'd like to propose that the term *total factor productivity* be reserved for the shift in the production function measured at the prevailing capital-labor ratio (i.e., for the partial derivative of the production function with respect to time, holding capital and labor constant). As I noted in my preceding remarks, TFP, defined this way, is a measure of the extent to which technical change has improved the productivity of a given dose of inputs.

This implies that proponents of the Rymes-Harrod view of capital and technology must find a term for the *total factor productivity* to describe their effects. But, in exchange for this concession, the neoclassical school should acknowledge that TFP is *not* a valid measure of the importance of technical change as a source of economic growth. Capital is an endogenous variable in the set of equations determining the dynamic behavior of the economic system, and a shift in the production function (i.e., *total factor productivity* in the neoclassical sense) will cause capital stock to expand. Equivalently, one can think of technical change as making capital less costly to produce, so that a given rate of saving will generate a larger capital stock. Either way, the total increase in output that results from a shift in the production function exceeds the size of the total factor productivity residual.

As I noted previously, it is precisely the question of "importance" that motivates the concepts of capital and technology advocated in the various articles and books by T. K. Rymes and in my work also (see esp. Hulten 1979). The consequence of technical change is not the same thing as the amount of technical change, and the distinction should be clearly labeled. So my second proposal is that the neoclassical camp drop the term *importance of TFP as a source of growth* in describing the results of their growth analyses.

Rymes: I want to make three points. First, Charles Hulten really has a Fisherian concept, which is shared with René Durand at Statistics Canada (see Hulten 1975). It's a question of the timing of entrance of the improved capital goods into the stock of capital; it is not Harrod's concept.

Second, I want to disabuse Zvi Griliches of one thing. Harrod residuals are not, repeat not, only for steady states. And there is no infinite regress involved in Harrod residuals. Maybe I'm giving Harrod too much credit, but his axioms on economic growth are not locked into steady states or infinite regresses.

But let me come back to the point that Zvi Griliches makes. He says, "What I want to know is where it occurred, in what industry did the productivity advance occur?" And I share that view. The calculations that I presented show different rates of productivity advance by industry in the Harrodian sense. What I claim is that the Harrod residuals provide a more useful picture in terms of, say, a much better prediction of the behavior of relative prices than do the traditional measures of where technical progress occurs.

We can aggregate the Harrod residuals to get measures for the aggregate economy. The weights that are attached to each industry's residual are its weights in the final output of the economy by industry. So Edward Denison's end use approach is being met as well.

Finally, we still need to consider the fact that, in a world in which technical progress takes the form of constant changes in the characteristics of produced inputs used in the economy, characteristics price indexes for such inputs will always be falling relatively to the price index for consumption goods. This will be the case even if the consumption goods price index is adjusted for characteristics changes as well. In other words, constant price net capital formation will always be shown as rising relatively to the output of consumption goods, and the price indexes of capital formation will always be falling relatively to the price indexes of consumption goods.

I'm not sure that the governor of the Bank of Canada, John Crowe, if confronted with the facts that the prices of consumption goods were flat and the prices of new capital goods, or net capital formation, were declining, would conclude that price stability would require that price indexes of consumption goods be allowed to rise. I share the basic point expressed, I think, by Edward Denison and Charles Hulten that the end thing that we should be focusing on is the flow of consumption in the economy because that is what maximizes welfare.

The BEA (and new BLS) computer price indexes are "correct." Should they be used to "deflate" gross fixed capital formation? A case can be made for the deflation of gross fixed capital formation with consumption good price indexes. I have also suggested that the use of the BEA indexes for the calculation of total factor productivity at the industry level is all right, provided those estimates are Harrod rather than Solow residuals.

Comments from the Floor

Arthur J. Alexander: As somebody who's been working in product characteristics space for about twenty years, I'm a little less sanguine about it now than
I used to be. We haven't taken sufficient account of the question of whether
the mapping from characteristics space into utility or production or profitabil-
ity space is really happening in our statistical estimates. Is this transformation
or mapping really there? We don't look at final user's utility because it's very
hard to get at; instead, we go on to the analysis of characteristics because it's
a lot easier to deal with, rather than looking at how productive is that computer
in one use or another use, or how good is a VCR or a stereo system, or how
much does it contribute to utility—and making quality adjustments that way.

We have taken the easier step of finding the characteristics that seem to do
the job as an intermediate product as a proxy for utility; we've accepted that
proxy and worked with it, but we haven't verified that, in fact, the transformation and the mapping are doing the job that we want them to do. There's
accumulating evidence that they may not be doing the job, that true measures
of quality or performance or productivity are moving somewhat differently
than measures based on characteristics. We have to take some time now to do
some more work to see whether, in fact, the use of characteristics is appropriate and whether the transformations and the mappings that we are assuming
are there are really there and really doing the job that we want them to do.

Edwin R. Dean: Edward Denison's book dealt almost as much with the BLS
productivity program as it did with the BEA computer deflator, and the present discussion seems to have dealt with both. It might be a good idea to relate
Ed's ideas to the BLS productivity program.

First of all, just for your information, where do things stand? Both in its
labor productivity series and in its multifactor productivity series, BLS is currently using output measures based on BEA NIPA data, after adjustments.

For the capital part of its denominator in the multifactor productivity series,
BLS begins its rather complex calculations of capital services by using the
BEA capital investment series. Of course, like the output series, since December 1985, these investment series have reflected computer investment calculated by BEA with the deflator currently being discussed.

So we have continued to use these BEA measures. We are not necessarily

Arthur J. Alexander is president of the Japan Economics Institute of America, Washington,
D.C.
    Edwin R. Dean is associate commissioner of the Office of Productivity and Technology of the
Bureau of Labor Statistics.

pleased with every detail of the BEA computations, but we are certainly in accord with the general approach that underlies the BEA computer deflator.

The intellectual antecedents for our multifactor model are numerous. Four of them have been before you in person this afternoon. Certainly, Edward Denison's work has been one of our main intellectual antecedents. Charles Hulten, Erwin Diewert, Zvi Griliches, and others, including Dale Jorgenson, have also been important in this work.[5] But on the questions of the overall model and of capital inputs, our general approach has been closer to that of Erwin Diewert and Zvi Griliches than it has been to Edward Denison. And it would be redundant for me to try to repeat some of the things that Erwin Diewert and Zvi Griliches have said in explaining their views.

I think one point is worthy of some emphasis as far as our general approach is concerned. Zvi Griliches made a distinction between a structural equation approach and the reduced-form approach, as he would characterize T. K. Rymes's general model. We are very interested in issues of substitution between inputs, and you do not do a good job of capturing the prices that producers pay attention to in adjusting their input mix if you adjust the actual market prices paid by producers for productivity change, as T. K. Rymes would have us do. So, since one of our purposes is to be able to shed light on policy questions related to substitution among inputs, we are strongly attracted, in addition to the reasons that Erwin Diewert and Zvi Griliches outlined before, to an approach that takes into account quality adjustments, but we do not want to adjust these prices further for productivity changes. To adjust input prices for productivity change, as T. K. Rymes does, is to break the link between input prices paid by producers and the input prices used in productivity measurement.

That doesn't mean that we're entirely happy with BEA's use of base-period weighting in computing output. It doesn't mean that we're entirely happy with the kinds of input prices that have gone into the BEA computer model, but we are in accord with BEA's general approach to the computer price index.

René Durand: I would like to make two comments. The first relates to T. K. Rymes's presentation. In his model, as in our dynamic model, the capital stock does not appear as a primary input in the productivity equation. Capital is replaced by what Rymes calls the stock of waiting. Waiting is measured in homogeneous forgone consumption units of some base year and is not affected by quality changes just like hours worked measured in sacrificed hours of leisure. However, in Rymes's model, capital goods still appear as an output of the productive system, and, in that respect, the quality adjustment of the capital stock remains an issue.

In our dynamic framework, capital goods are neither primary inputs nor

5. W. Erwin Diewert participated in the panel discussion but did not submit his statement for publication.

René Durand is assistant director of the Input-Output Division of Statistics Canada.

outputs of the productive process. Output is given by the infinite flow of present and future consumption over an infinite time horizon, and capital as an input is replaced by the stock of waiting, although our measure of waiting, derived dynamically, differs from Rymes's measure of waiting. Consequently, the issue of the quality adjustment of the capital stock deflator as such vanishes.

Over a limited time horizon, optimal growth is characterized by the "maximum" consumption path subject to some side condition for the capital stock at the terminal date. That capital stock represents the discounted value of future consumption and constitutes a pure stock of wealth. Consequently, and following Denison, we believe that the capital stock must be deflated by a final consumption deflator. Of course, the quality adjustment of the price deflator of consumption goods remains an issue, but that problem is of much less acuity than the quality adjustment of the capital goods deflator given the importance of computers in the capital stock and the rapid evolution of computers.

The second comment bears on Charles Hulten's reconciliation of T. K. Rymes's productivity model with the Jorgenson-Griliches model. This reconciliation sheds much light on the two alternative models and on how they are linked, and it is certainly welcome. However, I oppose Hulten's suggestion that we call Rymes's residual something other than multifactor productivity growth. On Hulten's figure 11.1, indeed, Rymes's production gain is decomposed into a shift in the production function (associated with the neoclassical productivity gain) and a move along that production function as productivity growth affects the growth of the capital stock. However, Hulten uses capital as an input rather than the stock of waiting. Were he to use the stock of waiting instead, then the production gain would be attributed entirely to a shift in the production function as both values of the capital stock in period 1 and 2 correspond to the same value in the stock of waiting. Therefore, with waiting instead of capital as an input, the whole production gain results from a pure shift in the production function, and I do not see why this shift would not be called technical progress.

Michael Harper: First of all, I don't think that it's useful to analyze the advance of computers in the context of a steady-state growth model or even in terms of a single shift in a steady-state model. I think that it's a dynamic process and involves ongoing change.

Second, if there is an innovation that improves a capital good, at what point does productivity change occur? Does it occur when the invention is made? Does it occur when the capital good is made, or does it occur when the consumption is actually realized? I think it occurs when the invention is made in the sense that the production possibility set is expanded at that point, but we

---

Michael Harper is chief of the Division of Productivity Research of the Bureau of Labor Statistics.

can't measure it yet because we can't really observe it. We can first observe it in a market when investors reveal their evaluation by purchasing capital goods. So I think that that's the reason we at BLS prefer the approach of Erwin Diewert and Zvi Griliches and haven't switched to the other approach.

Rymes: I want to respond to Edwin Dean. I do not agree with the idea that our measures don't answer your questions. I will address this as tightly as I can. You want to know what the determinants are of changing relative prices. You want to know this because maximizing firms choose input combinations on that basis. The goods that fall relatively in price are the ones that they switch over to in their choice of technique.

It is my claim that you want Harrod residuals. Take two industries as an example. You want measures for the two industries, of the rate of technical change, taking account of all the direct and indirect effects through the whole economic system, that will predict—that will be associated with—the change in relative prices that's taking place. My claim, as I thought the use of the computers and semiconductors examples illustrated very clearly, is that the Harrod residuals do this. The traditional residuals simply do not. The price of computers is falling very rapidly, quality adjusted. The price of semiconductors is falling slightly less rapidly, quality adjusted. What the traditional measures of factor productivity will do when you make the adjustment for such change is to show the productivity advance in computers reduced and the productivity advance in semiconductors increased. The movement in the traditional measures of the rates of productivity advance at the industry level that you get does not answer your question. When you, Edward Denison, or I am interested in the basic microeconomics of the movement of, or the prediction of, the relative prices of produced inputs in the economic system and substitution among the inputs, the Harrod residuals give us a clue as to what's going on. As far as I can see, the traditional measures do not. The puzzle is why you still prefer the traditional measures.

References

Cas, Alexandra, and Thomas K. Rymes. 1991. *On concepts and measures of multifactor productivity in Canada.* New York: Cambridge University Press.
Denison, Edward F. 1989. *Estimates of productivity change by industry.* Washington, D.C.: Brookings.
Hulten, Charles. 1975. Technical change and the reproducibility of capital. *American Economic Review* 65 (December): 956–65.
———. 1979. On the importance of productivity change. *American Economic Review* 69 (March): 126–36.
Triplett, Jack E. 1991. Two views on computer prices and productivity. Discussion Paper no. 45. Washington, D.C.: Bureau of Economic Analysis, U.S. Department of Commerce, July (rev.).

Contributors

Arthur J. Alexander
Japan Economic Institute
1000 Connecticut Avenue, N.W., Suite 211
Washington, D.C. 20036

Ernst R. Berndt
National Bureau of Economic Research
1050 Massachusetts Avenue
Cambridge, MA 02138

Thomas Betsock
Division of Industrial Prices and Price Indexes
Bureau of Labor Statistics
Postal Square Building, Rm. 3840
2 Massachusetts Avenue, N.E.
Washington, D.C. 20212

Rosanne Cole
530 East 72nd Street
New York, NY 10021

Robert W. Crandall
The Brookings Institution
1775 Massachusetts Avenue, N.W.
Washington, D.C. 20036

Edwin R. Dean
U.S. Department of Labor
Office of Productivity and Technology, Rm. 2150
2 Massachusetts Avenue, N.E.
Washington, D.C. 20212

Edward F. Denison
The Brookings Institution
1775 Massachusetts Avenue, N.W.
Washington, D.C. 20036

Ellen R. Dulberger
IBM Corporation
Program Manager, Economics
Mail Drop #209
Old Orchard Road
Armonk, NY 10504

René Durand
Input-Output Division
Statistics Canada
23rd Floor, R. H. Coats Building
Tunney's Pasture
Ottawa, Ontario K1A 0T6
CANADA

Kenneth Flamm
The Brookings Institution
1775 Massachusetts Avenue, N.W.
Washington, D.C. 20036

Murray F. Foss
American Enterprise Institute
1150 17th Street, N.W.
Washington, D.C. 20036

375

Irwin B. Gerduk
Division of Industrial Prices and Price
  Indexes
Bureau of Labor Statistics
Postal Square Building, Rm. 3840
2 Massachusetts Avenue, N.E.
Washington, D.C. 20212

Zvi Griliches
National Bureau of Economic Research
1050 Massachusetts Avenue
Cambridge, MA 02138

Michael Harper
Department of Productivity and Tech-
  nology, Rm. 2140
Bureau of Labor Statistics
2 Massachusetts Avenue, N.E.
Washington, D.C. 20212

Charles R. Hulten
Department of Economics
University of Maryland
College Park, MD 20742

Show-Ling Jang
Department of Economics
National Taiwan University
21, Hsu-Chow Road
Taipei, TAIWAN 10020

Pamela A. Kelly
Bureau of Economic Analysis
BE-57
U.S. Department of Commerce
1401 K Street, N.W.
Washington, D.C. 20230

Paul R. Liegey, Jr.
U.S. Department of Labor
Bureau of Labor Statistics, Rm. 3260
2 Massachusetts Avenue, N.E.
Washington, D.C. 20212

Marilyn E. Manser
Office of Research and Evaluation, Rm.
  4915
U.S. Bureau of Labor Statistics
2 Massachusetts Avenue, N.E.
Washington, D.C. 20212

John R. Norsworthy
Department of Economics and Manage-
  ment
Rensselaer Polytechnic Institute
Troy, N.Y. 12180

Stephen D. Oliner
Board of Governors of the Federal Re-
  serve System
Division of Research and Statistics
Washington, D.C. 20551

Joel Popkin
Joel Popkin & Company
1101 Vermont Avenue, N.W.
#201
Washington, D.C. 20005

Marshall Reinsdorf
Office of Economic Research
Bureau of Labor Statistics
2 Massachusetts Avenue, N.E.
Washington, D.C. 20212

Thomas K. Rymes
Department of Economics
Carleton University
Ottawa, Ontario K1S 5B6
CANADA

Jack E. Triplett
Chief Economist, BE-3
Bureau of Economic Analysis
U.S. Department of Commerce
1401 K Street, N.W.
Washington, D.C. 20230

Allan H. Young
Bureau of Economic Analysis
U.S. Department of Commerce
1401 K Street, N.W.
Tower Building, Room 705
Washington, D.C. 20230

Richard C. Ziemer
Bureau of Economic Analysis
BE-57
U.S. Department of Commerce
1401 K Street, N.W.
Washington, D.C. 20230

Author Index

Subject Index

AAGRs (average annual growth rates), 65–66, 89

Age: of computer models, 1; effect in microcomputer market, 77; in hedonic equation, 6; in secondhand computer market, 21; of technology to estimate obsolescence, 97–98. *See also* Depreciation; Model age; Retirements, computer; Vintage

Age concept: as component of best-technology computers, 33; effect on computer price, 42; to estimate depreciation, 97–98; to estimate price change, 21, 57; in estimating computer retirement, 38; in mainframe depreciation rates, 43–47; measure in computer pricing model, 22; price change related to, 36. *See also* Obsolescence

Aircraft: component contracts for military, 308–9; learning curve for, 337–39; price-determining characteristics, 309–10, 312–30; price indexes for commercial and military, 13–14

ASM (Annual Survey of Manufactures), 135–38

ASP estimates. *See* Average selling price (ASP)

Average price (AP) series, BLS, 241–48

Average prices: in Dataquest data, 114; in PPI steel industry price indexes, 269

Average selling price (ASP), 165–66

Backwardation, normal: to estimate spot market price, 189; of forward prices, 172,

182; theory of, 171. *See also* Forward prices; Futures prices; Spot price

Base price: calculation of, 330; for defense component contract values, 331t; derivation of, 327, 330–31; factors influencing, 339–41

Bayes-Leamer factor asymptotic approximation, 75, 77nn13,14, 78n15, 83n19

Benchmark measures (for microcomputer performance), 95–97

Best-practice technology models, 2, 23–26, 30–36, 56–57. *See also* Nonbest technology models

Bias: in BEA data, 57–58; in BLS price indexes, 164; with commodity substitution, 232–34; in consumer price measures, 11; in CPI, 210, 227–31; in CPI retail outlet substitution, 231–50, 256; in DRAM market forward prices, 181; in intermediate good price measurement, 2; in measured total factor productivity, 132; in new chip introductions, 201–2; potential in transaction price reporting, 281–82; in steel industry price indexes, 261

Billing price (in chip contract), 165, 182–88

Book prices: average, 165–66, 182; levels for sheet steel, 270–71; for PPI steel price indexes, 264–65, 266, 268, 270

Capital goods: comparison of two price indexes for, 362–66; equating, 352–53; hedonic price deflation for, 133–35

HC
106.3
C714
vol.57

345207

DATE DUE

MADELEINE CLARK WALLACE
LIBRARY
WHEATON COLLEGE
NORTON, MA 02766
(508) 285-7722

DEMCO